Magnus Carlsen:
60 Memorable Games

Andrew Soltis

First published in the United Kingdom in 2020 by B.T. Batsford
An imprint of B.T. Batsford Holdings Ltd
43 Great Ormond Street
London
WC1N 3HZ

ISBN: 9781849946506

A CIP catalogue record for this book is available from the
British Library.

25 24
10 9 8 7 6 5 4 3

Reproduction by Rival Colour, UK
Printed and bound by CPI Books, Chatham, UK

This book can be ordered direct from the publisher at
www.batsfordbooks.com, or try your local bookshop

Contents

Introduction:
What Made Magnus

As 2020 began Magnus Carlsen celebrated ten straight years as the world's highest rated player. He held three world championship titles, in blitz, rapid and "classical" chess, an unprecedented achievement. Within days of the new year he broke the record for playing more than 107 straight games without a loss.

The term "super-tournament" has no precise meaning. But it has come to mean a round robin with classical time controls, in which each player is an elite grandmaster. In recent years the Sinquefield Cup, Norway Chess, Wijk aan Zee and the Gashimov Memorial have become synonymous with super-tournament.

Bobby Fischer never won a super-tournament. Garry Kasparov won outright or tied for first place in 35 super-tournaments in his nearly-30-year career. His fans said this was further evidence that he was the greatest player in chess history.

But Magnus Carlsen won some 40 super-tournaments, plus another 14 "super" speed tournaments before he was 30.

"What makes Carlsen different?" is a good question. But a better one is: How did he make himself different?

The simplest answer is that he played an extraordinary amount of chess and did it long before he was a master. One on-line database, Chessgames.com, contains 1,000 games he played before he was 17.

In contrast, Kasparov played his 1,000[th] game when he was 27 – and had already been world champion for five years, according to the same source.

Of course, large numbers of games, even of a famous player, are typically missing from databases, especially in their early years. But the 1,000[th] game of Fabiano Caruana preserved by Chessgames.com came after he had been competing in tournaments for 16 years. Carlsen did it in half that time.

Playing a lot doesn't necessarily teach. What did Carlsen learn from so much chess?

Playability

Perhaps the most important is the ability to judge which positions *are easier to play than others.*

Carlsen – Vasily Ivanchuk
Sao Paolo 2011
Nimzo-Indian,
Three Knights Variation (E21)

1 d4 ♘f6 2 c4 e6 3 ♘c3 ♗b4
4 ♘f3 b6 5 ♕c2 ♗b7 6 a3 ♗xc3+
7 ♕xc3 ♘e4 8 ♕c2 f5 9 g3 ♘f6
10 ♗h3 0-0 11 0-0 a5 12 ♖d1
♕e8 13 d5 ♘a6 14 ♗f4 exd5
15 ♗xf5 dxc4 16 ♘g5! ♕h5
17 ♖xd7! ♔h8 18 ♖e7? ♘d5
19 ♗g4 ♕g6 20 ♘f7+ ♔g8
21 ♗f5 ♕xf5 22 ♕xf5 ♘xe7
23 ♘h6+ gxh6 24 ♕g4+ ♘g6
25 ♗xh6

Carlsen missed opportunities to put the game away earlier (18 ♖ad1! ♘xd7 19 ♖xd7, for example).

His comment here is revealing: "White certainly has the easier game."

That is, it is easier to find good moves for White than it is for Black. And it is easier for Black to err than for White.

This was borne out by the rest of the game: 25...♖f7 26 ♖d1 ♖e8 27 h4! ♘c5 28 h5 ♗c8 29 ♕xc4 ♘e5 30 ♕h4 ♘c6? (30...♘e6!) 31 ♖d5! ♘e6 32 ♕c4 ♘cd8? 33 ♕g4+ ♘g7 34 ♕xc8 **Resigns**.

Now you might say: "So what? Carlsen wasn't trying to evaluate the position in the diagram. He was just stating a personal opinion."

Oh, but he was evaluating the position. He was judging it in terms of *playability*. That is not a precise concept. There is no metric to quantify it and computers cannot appreciate it. But in real-life situations, playability is as valid as more familiar ways of evaluating a position, such as piece mobility or pawn structure.

Over and over in Carlsen's notes to his games he said the move he chose was the one that lead to an "easier" position, the "more pleasant" game, a "more comfortable" one. Playability was a crucial factor for him in deciding whether to take an irrevocable step, such as sacrificing a pawn or the Exchange.

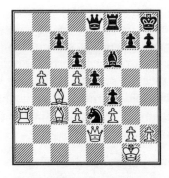

Karjakin – Carlsen
World Championship match,
3ʳᵈ playoff game, New York 2016

White has just played 30 ♖a3. Computers recommend 30...♕d8, 30...♕b8, 30...♕c8 and 30...♗h4. But they can't find a significant advantage after any of these moves.

Carlsen chose **30...e4**. It forced a trade of bishops, allowed him to maintain his knight on e3 and opened the dominating square e5 to his queen.

Some engines say his winning chances declined, slightly or to a large degree, after **31 dxe4 ♗xc3 32 ♖xc3 ♕e5**.

But grandmasters around the world who followed the game on-line smiled when they saw 30...e4!. They knew that it was exactly the kind of move you should play in such a position. Regardless of what machines say, Black's winning chances were soaring. The position was simply much easier for him to play.

They were right, as Game 47 shows. If there is any single Magnus move that saved the world championship title he first earned in 2013, it was 30...e4!.

Universality

What else did his early tournament experience teach Carlsen? An answer is remarkable versatility.

Every great player has *his* kind of positions, the ones he knows best from past experience. But every great player, and this includes world champions, has other positions that he does not know as well and consequently plays less well.

Very early in his career Carlsen amassed an extraordinary amount of experience in virtually every opening, every pawn structure and every endgame.

Versatility is not just a feature of his play, according to Vishy Anand. It is his main strength. Magnus is "capable of being many different players," Anand told the *New Yorker* magazine. "He can be tactical. He can be positional."

In another interview Anand was asked to compare Carlsen with an earlier paragon of versatility, Anatoly Karpov. Anand knew them both. He had played nearly

100 games with Karpov and well over 100 with Carlsen. "I think Carlsen's much more universal," Anand said. "There haven't been many such players at all, perhaps Spassky in his best years."

Like almost every 1 e4 player, Carlsen learned how to play the Ruy Lopez. But he also played the Ponziani Opening, the Bishop's Opening and the Vienna Gambit as well as the exotics such as 1 e4 e5 2 ♘f3 ♘c6 3 d3, the Four Knights Game with 4 a3, the King's Gambit Accepted with 3 ♘c3 and even 1 e4 e5 2 ♕h5 (in rapids and blitz).

As Black he defended the Ruy Lopez, as do most of the world-class players of the last half century. But he also adopted the Philidor's Defense and brought 1 e4 e5 2 ♘f3 ♘c6 3 ♗b5 ♗b4!? out of mothballs. He used oddities against top-notch opponents, such as meeting Vladimir Kramnik's 1 e4 e5 2 ♘f3 ♘c6 3 ♗c4 ♘f6 4 d3 with 4...♕e7 5 ♘c3 ♘a5. In the 2019 Norway Chess (blitz) tournament he defeated Caruana with 1 e4 g6 2 d4 ♘f6 3 e5 ♘h5.

Of course, there have always been strong grandmasters who varied their openings. But Carlsen weaponized his versatility. It was a huge asset when playing rivals who spent enormous amounts of time preparing to play him.

Most elite grandmasters are obsessed with openings. Hikaru Nakamura spends about 80 percent of his study time preparing his first moves for future opponents. He spends another 10 percent reviewing his games and the final 10 percent on endgames, he said on Reddit.com in 2014.

But preparing for Magnus is almost impossible. Since he and Nakamura first met over the board in 2006, Carlsen defended against his 1 d4 with the King's Indian, Nimzo-Indian, Grünfeld, Bogo-Indian and Queen's Indian Defenses and the Slav and various other versions of the Queen's Gambit Declined.

He "seems to feel at home in all" kinds of positions, Jan Timman said. "He is not hampered by the prejudices that used to be part and parcel of classical chess," Timman added. One of Carlsen's seconds, Jon Ludwig Hammer, joked that a regular opening for Magnus means one he has played more than twice in a row.

Against lesser mortals, Carlsen's opening versatility can be devastating. In the final days of 2019, he won this game.

Carlsen – Bartosz Socko
World Blitz Championship,
Moscow 2019
*Queen's Indian Defense,
Fianchetto Variation (E15)*

1 d4 ♘f6 2 c4 e6 3 ♘f3 b6 4 g3 ♗b7 5 ♗g2 c5 6 d5

This quasi-gambit dates back at least to Fritz Sämisch in the 1920s.

6...exd5 7 cxd5!?

But Sämisch played 7 ♘h4 and that is still the standard move.

7...♗xd5 8 ♘c3 ♗xf3

Bartosz Socko – and his wife, IGM Monika Socko – were among the world's experts at defending the Black position after 6...exd5. He didn't show it.

9 ♗xf3 ♘c6 10 ♗f4 ♗e7 11 0-0 0-0 12 e3 ♘e8 13 h4!

For his pawn, Magnus has kingside prospects (♕c2/♘g5) and potential pressure on the center (♕a4/♖ad1).

The rest was inexactly played – well, it was a blitz tournament. But Black was clearly uncomfortable, even in an opening he knew well.

13...h6 14 h5 ♘c7 15 ♕a4 ♘e6 16 ♖ad1 ♖c8 17 ♘d5 ♘xf4 18 gxf4 ♖e8 19 ♔g2! ♗f8 20 ♖g1 ♘e7?? (Black remains worse

after the computer-recommended 20...♘b4 21 ♘xb4 and 20...b5 21 ♕xb5 ♖b8 21 ♕e2) **21 ♘f6+! gxf6 22 ♖xd7 b5 23 ♕xa7 ♖a8 24 ♖xd8 Resigns**.

Carlsen plays so well in so many different openings that the choice of the first moves seems irrelevant to him. When his game with Kramnik began at Wijk aan Zee 2010, he closed his eyes and remained motionless for nearly two minutes. He was trying to choose between 1 e4 and 1 d4. Kramnik joked afterward that he wondered if he should wake him up.

Before a game two years later at Wijk aan Zee, Carlsen asked his father to pick a letter from "a" to "h." He chose "f." So Carlsen played 1 ♘f3 that day and defeated Vugar Gashimov.

Memory

There are other attributes that made Carlsen exceptional. For example, he developed a remarkable memory very early. By age five he reputedly could recite the populations of all 422 Norwegian municipalities.

Chess memory is a more specific brand. Carlsen's memory of middlegame themes and not just opening variations was noticeable in his first master-level results.

Carlsen – Adnan Orujov, Peniscola 2002, began **1 e4 e5 2 ♘f3 ♘c6 3 d4 exd4 4 ♘xd4 ♘f6 5 ♘xc6 bxc6 6 e5 ♕e7 7 ♕e2 ♘d5 8 c4 ♗a6 9 b3 0-0-0 10 g3 ♖e8 11 ♗b2 f6 12 ♗g2 fxe5 13 0-0.**

These moves look odd, if not bizarre. But the little previous experience that there was had shown that White stands well if he carries off the maneuver ♕d2-a5.

The game confirmed this: **13...g6 14 ♕d2! ♘b6 15 ♕a5 ♔b7 16 ♗a3 ♕f6 17 ♗xf8 ♖hxf8 18 ♘c3 ♕e7 19 ♘a4!.**

The threat is 20 ♘c5+. Black would be lost after 19...♘xa4 20 bxa4 followed by ♖ab1+

(20...♗xc4 21 ♖ab1+ ♔a8 22 ♕xc7 ♖b8 23 ♗xc6+ or 22...♗a6 23 ♖fd1).

Carlsen would be the first to admit that his rivals prepare their openings better than he does. They often win short games while he is playing 70+ moves. This was an exception:

19...d6 20 ♗xc6+! ♔xc6 21 ♕xa6 e4 22 c5 dxc5 23 ♘xc5 ♔xc5 24 ♖fd1 ♕e5

25 b4+ ♔xb4 26 ♖ab1+ ♔c3 27 ♖b3+ ♔c2 28 ♕e2 mate.

Gata Kamsky ridiculed the role that openings played in the games of today's elite players. "All they have to do is simply memorize those preparations, get to the board and just show the preparation," he said in *New In Chess* in 2011 "There is no chess skill involved in that! It's just all memory, and that's it."

This is not Carlsen. He does not sit down and memorize dozens of inexplicable moves that a computer tells him to play. Rather, he has a sponge-like memory that picks up and retains striking *ideas* from games he has seen. This became noticeable after the game **Carlsen – Sipke Ernst** from the C group of Wijk aan Zee 2004:

1 e4 c6 2 d4 d5 3 ♘c3 dxe4
4 ♘xe4 ♗f5 5 ♘g3 ♗g6 6 h4 h6
7 ♘f3 ♘d7 8 h5 ♗h7 9 ♗d3
♗xd3 10 ♕xd3 e6 11 ♗f4 ♘gf6
12 0-0-0 ♗e7 13 ♘e4 ♕a5
14 ♔b1 0-0 15 ♘xf6+ ♘xf6
16 ♘e5 ♖ad8 17 ♕e2 c5

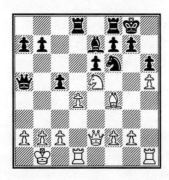

Magnus won in stunning style:
18 ♘g6 fxg6? 19 ♕xe6+ ♔h8
20 hxg6! ♘g8 21 ♗xh6 gxh6
22 ♖xh6+ ♘xh6 23 ♕xe7 ♘f7
24 gxf7 ♔g7 25 ♖d3 ♖d6
26 ♖g3+ ♖g6 27 ♕e5+ ♔xf7
28 ♕f5+ ♖f6 29 ♕d7 mate!

How much of this was "prep"—that is, what Carlsen had studied just before this game?

The answer he gave Lubosh Kavalek after the game was that he didn't even know his opponent played the Caro-Kann: "Ernst left my preparation at move one!" Carlsen said.

When the opening unfolded he remembered that 17 ♕e2 was "book." But it took him 25 minutes to figure out why.

And that's how he remembered that 18 ♘g6 had been played before. The first new move was 24 gxf7!, improving over 24 ♕f6+, which had led to a draw in a previous game.

Other Factors

Another Carlsen strength that came from playing so much is psychological: *He learned how to deal with losing.*

Many Soviet-era players grew up believing that two draws were better than a win and a loss. A loss was a psychological blow that cannot be repaired quickly. "When you beat your opponent in a chess game, you destroy his ego," as Kasparov said "For a time you make him lose confidence in himself as a person." The agony of defeat far outweighs the thrill of victory, Soviet juniors were taught. After losing, a player needed to recover, perhaps by making a quick draw.

Carlsen's rivals can be plagued by memories of defeat. Nakamura recalled his spectacular collapse against Carlsen at Zürich 2014. Computers said he had an advantage of greater than +6.00 for several moves and it grew to double digits. Then he lost. "I had nightmares about the Carlsen game for four days afterwards," he said.

Carlsen has had bad periods. In the middle of his record non-losing streak in 2019-20, he suffered a meltdown in speed and blitz tournaments. "When things start to go wrong, it is easy to doubt oneself. I tried to play more aggressively rather than trying to play safer, but it doesn't really seem to work out any more," he said. "I am constantly doubting myself."

But Magnus manages to recover from defeat more easily than his rivals. Tigran Petrosian used to say that he was more upset when his Spartak team lost at football than when he lost at chess. Carlsen is similar: "I get more upset at other things than chess," he told Dylan Loeb McClain. "I always get upset when I lost at Monopoly."

After he lost a game in his first high-profile tournament, Wijk aan Zee 2004, he won his next three games. He moved on to the Aeroflot Open and lost in the first round. Then he beat grandmasters in the next three games, beginning with this:

Carlsen – Sergey Dolmatov
Aeroflot Festival, Moscow 2004
Réti Opening (A04)

1 ♘f3 f5 2 d3 d6 3 e4 e5 4 ♘c3 ♘c6 5 exf5! ♗xf5 6 d4 ♘xd4

7 ♘xd4 exd4 8 ♕xd4 ♘f6? 9 ♗c4 c6 10 ♗g5 b5 11 ♗b3 ♗e7? 12 0-0-0 ♕d7 13 ♖he1 ♔d8

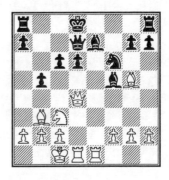

14 ♖xe7! ♕xe7 15 ♕f4 ♗d7 16 ♘e4 d5 17 ♘xf6 h6 18 ♗h4 g5 19 ♕d4 Resigns.

What else made Magnus? His speed chess experience gave him a better clock sense than anyone, perhaps anyone ever. When he and his opponent have only seconds left he has a superior feeling of which moves to play and how quickly to play them.

This is evidenced in two ways. First, he has been able to dominate the increasingly popular tie-breaking playoffs. He was "Mister Tie Break" as the Russian magazine *64* called him on its cover in January 2016. Between 2007 and 2019 he hadn't lost such a major playoff.

Another valuable quality he acquired as a pre-teen is knowing how to swindle. He often outplayed opponents in bad and even lost positions. By the time he was 30 he had swindled more opponents than Mikhail Tal in his entire career.

Loek van Wely – Carlsen
Wijk aan Zee 2016
Grünfeld Defense (D83)

1 d4 ♘f6 2 c4 g6 3 ♘c3 d5
4 ♗f4 ♗g7 5 e3 0-0 6 ♖c1 ♗e6
7 cxd5 ♘xd5 8 ♘xd5 ♗xd5
9 ♗xc7 ♕d7 10 ♗g3 ♗xa2
11 ♘e2 ♗d5 12 ♘c3 ♗c6 13 h4
♖d8 14 ♕b3 ♕f5 15 h5 e6
16 hxg6 hxg6 17 ♕d1 ♘d7
18 ♗d3 ♕a5 19 ♔f1 ♘f6 20 ♗e5
♖ac8 21 ♕d2 ♘g4 22 ♗xg7
♔xg7 23 f3 ♕g5?? 24 fxg4 ♖xd4
25 ♔e1 ♕e5 26 ♘e2 ♖xg4 27 e4

His piece sacrifice at move 23 was unsound and now he knew. He could try 27...♖h8 28 ♖xh8 ♔xh8 and grovel in a lost endgame after 29 g3 and 30 ♕c3.

But White was severely short of time. Magnus gambled on **27...♖xg2** and allowed **28 ♕h6+ ♔f6**.

Fans who watched the game on-line were told by computers that

29 ♕h4+ g5 30 ♕h3! would trap the g2-rook and win.

But White played a natural defensive move, **29 ♖c3?**.

After **29...♖d8! 30 ♕h3 ♕g5 31 ♖f1+ ♔g7 32 ♕f3 ♖d7 33 ♖f2** his advantage had evaporated.

A good swindler knows to retain material until there is a good reason to swap (not 33...♖xf2).

Carlsen's **33...♖g4** immediately induced a collapse, **34 ♘f4 ♕h4 35 ♗e2? ♖g1+ 36 ♗f1 ♔g8 37 ♘e2?** (37 ♘g2!) **♖xf1+! 38 ♔xf1 ♖d1+ 39 ♔g2 ♗xe4 White resigns**.

Engines pointed out that 36...e5! was better and that 36...♔g8? threatened nothing. But his moves had the proper, jarring effect.

Stamina

All great players have an intense will to win. "Not winning a tournament is not an option for me..." Carlsen said in 2011.

But many of his rivals have the same desire. What helps make Magnus different is he combines this with the stamina that allows him to play and play. This makes him reminiscent of another great player.

Bobby Fischer – Bent Larsen
Zürich 1959
White to play

Bobby Fischer was often criticized in his teenage years for playing out "obviously drawn" endgames. These were not "book" positions but ones with, for example, equal pawns, all on the kingside, like this.

Mikhail Tal ridiculed Fischer. It was naïve to think experienced grandmasters could be defeated in a position like this, just by prolonging the game, he said. "What's the matter?" Tal wrote in the tournament book about this position. " 'Why is the game not drawn here,' the reader might rightfully ask." Fischer played another 42 moves before accepting a draw.

Kasparov described Carlsen as essentially a positional player – "more Karpovian...with Fischer-like intensity." But Carlsen is Fischer on steroids.

Nigel Short – Carlsen
London 2009
White to move

Even Fischer might have accepted a draw. Instead, the game went **69 ♕b5+ ♕d5 70 ♔xa4 ♕xb5+ 71 ♔xb5 draw**. "It's always nice to end with bare kings," Carlsen said. He also played his last-round game at Wijk aan Zee 2020 until he and Wesley So had just their kings left.

Whether intentional or not, both Fischer and Carlsen followed a premise of the Soviet School: If you keep tension in the position long enough, opponents get nervous and err. This was basic to the thinking of Soviet players when they played abroad. "Western players can play ten good moves. But if the position continues to be unclear they may make one silly move and lose," as Alexander Khaliman put it.

In addition, if you keep trying to win, opponents may consider a position so hopelessly drawish that they will make needless concessions. A case in point was Carlsen's game with Nakamura at the 2018 Sinquefield Cup. Their rivalry had become legendary – and lopsidcd. They had played nearly 120 games by that time and Carlsen had won over and over.

Carlsen – Hikaru Nakamura
Sinquefield Cup 2018
Black to move

Carlsen had failed to make inroads for more than 20 moves with queens and rooks on the board. With just rooks on, Nakamura can defend easily, for example, with 62...♚g6 63 g5 ♚h5!.

There are even stalemate tricks such as 62...♖c7 63 g5+ ♚h5! 64 gxf6 ♖f7 65 fxg7 ♖xg7+ 66 ♚h3 ♖g3+!.

But Nakamura chose **62...g5?**,

granting Carlsen a protected passed h-pawn. Play went **63 h5 ♚g7 64 ♚f2 ♖b7 65 ♖a3 ♚h6 66 ♚e3**.

Magnus had made progress but the game should still be drawn as 66...♖d7 67 ♖d3 ♖b7 68 ♚d2 a5 shows (69 ♚c3 a4 70 ♚c4 ♚g7 71 ♖a3 ♖d7! and ...♖d4+ or ...♖d3).

Nakamura made another concession, **66...a5??**. He believed he had an impregnable fortress after **67 ♖xa5 ♖b3+ 68 ♚f2 ♖b2+ 69 ♚g3 ♚g7 70 ♖a7+ ♚g8 71 ♖a1 ♚g7 72 ♖f1 ♖a2 73 ♖f2 ♖a3**.

But Carlsen has famously said he does not believe in fortresses. First, he freed his king, **74 ♖d2 ♖a7 75 ♚f2 ♚f7 76 ♚e2 ♖b7 77 ♖d3**.

Then he sent it on a march on a great circle route: **77...♖a7 78 ♚d2 ♚e6 79 ♚c3 ♚e7 80 ♚c4 ♖c7+ 81 ♚b5 ♖c1 82 ♖b3 ♚f7 83 ♚b6 ♖c2 84 ♚b7 ♖c1 85 ♚b8 ♚g8 86 ♖b6 ♚g7 87 ♖b7+ ♚g8**.

Finally he broke the c-file barrier at the cost of a pawn,

88 ♖c7! ♖b1+ 89 ♔c8 ♖b3 90 ♔d7! ♖xf3 91 ♔e6 ♖f4 92 h6!.

Nakamura resigned after 92...♔h8 93 ♖b7 ♔g8 94 ♖g7+ ♔h8 95 ♔f7 ♖xe4 96 ♔g6 ♖a4 97 ♖h7+ because he was losing all of his pawns, 97...♔g8 98 ♖e7 ♖a8 99 ♔xf6 and ♔xg5, for example.

Carlsen routinely wins endgame positions that were rated equal by computers. In fact, he has won more positions that were roughly even at move 60 than anyone in history. Again, his experience can help explain it. By 2020 he had played more than 550 games that went beyond move 60, according to databases. Garry Kasparov played fewer than 250 such games in his entire career.

Magnus Myths

His spectacular rise caused Carlsen-watchers to come up with theories to explain him. Early in his career, older GMs said he was simply a cheapo artist. He was a master of the ICC whose lack of depth would be exposed when he faced his elders. "He's an unusually weak player," Viktor Korchnoi said. All he does is prompt his opponents to make mistakes: "He knows what will cause them to err!" Korchnoi said. He did not consider that a skill.

Korchnoi eventually changed his opinion. So did Khalifman, a strong grandmaster who won a FIDE knockout world championship in 1999. Khalifman was struck by the lineup of players in the top section of Wijk aan Zee 2007. Thirteen of the 14 players had "schooling," he said. They followed the proven precepts of the Mikhail Botvinnik method: Study your own games and detect weaknesses. Read the classics of chess literature, like Aron Nimzovich's *My System*. Study comes before playing.

The 14th player in the tournament was Magnus. Every day during the tournament Carlsen played dozens of speed games on the Internet. That was bound to show up as superficiality in his moves, said Khalifman. But after examining his "classical" games, Khalifman admitted he was wrong. "Carlsen didn't read Nimzovich and doesn't need to," he said in the August 2008 issue of *64* magazine. "To hell with Nimzovich."

Quite a different criticism came from other GMs. They said

Carlsen is "a child of the computer era." He was a Fritz clone, programmed by constant study with engines to play the way they do.

This is the greatest Magnus myth. He didn't even use a database during the first years he took chess seriously. His first coaches were amazed at what he called his "computer incompetence."

"Honestly, when I was about 11-12 I didn't even know what ChessBase was," he told an interviewer from Chesspro.ru. "Back then I simply put a board in front of me, took the books I was studying at the time and looked at everything on that. And the first time I needed a computer for chess was when I started to play on the internet."

Intuition

It is remarkably difficult to explain how Carlsen chooses the moves he does. Often it seems more whim than algorithm.

Carlsen – Michael Adams
World Cup 2007
Nimzo-Indian Defense,
Classical Variation (E36)

1 d4 ♘f6 2 c4 e6 3 ♘c3 ♗b4 4 ♕c2 d5 5 a3 ♗xc3+ 6 ♕xc3 dxc4 7 ♕xc4 b6 8 ♗f4 ♗a6 9 ♕xc7 ♕xc7 10 ♗xc7 0-0 11 ♘f3 ♖c8 12 ♗f4 ♘bd7

13 ♘d2 ♖c2 14 ♖b1 ♖ac8

He explained what happened next by saying, "I simply couldn't resist the urge to put my knight on a1." Play went **15 ♘b3 ♗c4 16 ♘a1** He went on to win in 77 moves.

Among those who appreciated how un-computer-like Carlsen was is the American grandmaster Sam Shankland: "I saw some statistic that of the top ten players in the world he matches the top choice of the computer the least of all of them." That is, Carlsen's rivals are more likely to play the candidate move that machines regard as best.

But computers have also shown us that the difference between the objectively "best" move and the second-best and even the third-best is often slight. What impressed Shankland is that of the same top-ten players, Carlsen is the one most likely to select one of the computer's three top choices. "Magnus might not play the best move any more often than anyone else," Shankland said. "But he always plays a good move ...because his natural feel is so great."

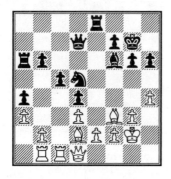

Carlsen – Sergey Karjakin
Wijk aan Zee 2013
White to move

Computers look at moves like 29 ♕c2 with the possibility of going to c4.

Carlsen chose **29 ♕h1!** with the idea of maximizing his strength on light squares after **30 ♔g1!**.

Computers said his idea only made matters worse. Yet White's position slowly improved and, after a trade of queens following a prepared ♕h3, Carlsen slowly ground down his opponent in 92 moves.

Another myth is that Carlsen is a calculating machine. Yes, he can visualize positions five, ten or more moves into the future. But so can Caruana, Nakamura, Wesley So, Alexander Grischuk, Levon Aronian and several others. One of his prime advantages over them is superior ability to evaluate the end-positions of their mutual calculations. His opponents choose forcing moves in order to reach a position they consider satisfactory for them. But the position is not nearly as good as they thought, as several games in this book can show.

"Play Magnus"

That is the name of the popular software that allows you to play a game with a computerized Carlsen. The different levels are based on his skill and playing style at different ages.

When you take on Magnus-at-5, he asks you, "Can you beat me while I'm busy reading geography books?" His father tried to get him interested in chess at that age but he was more into memorizing the capitals, populations and flags of the world's countries. His strong suit was curiosity, not obvious intelligence.

"Despite some of the pre-conceptions about me I wouldn't say I have a freakishly high IQ. I am just someone who is naturally curious. I like to stretch myself," he recalled to the British newspaper *The Daily Telegraph*.

"I was doing jigsaw puzzles before I was two. A year later I started memorizing the names of motor cars. Then it was onto geography. By the time I was five or six, I was studying maps," he said.

His father Henrik Carlsen, an information technology consultant, is a chess player of about 2100 strength. He tried to interest Carlsen again at age 6, without success. Magnus-at-6 would rather dress up as Pirate Captain Sabertooth than play chess.

At 7 he had moved on to pretending to be Harry Potter. But he felt a bit of sibling rivalry when he saw his father and sister Ellen play chess. "I was lucky," Carlsen later told Shortlist.com. "I was brainwashed by my parents into believing video games were bad for me. So, because the weather was sufficiently bad and I was sufficiently bored, I started playing my father chess at eight."

He didn't beat Ellen, a year older than him, until he was eight and a half and couldn't defeat his father even at blitz until he was nine. Henrik Carlsen recalled: "I asked him if he wanted to play in the Norwegian under-11 championship the next summer. He agreed and almost every day he studied chess two or three hours." By then he was reading his father's chess books, such as Bent Larsen's *Find the Plan* and Eduard Gufeld's *The Complete Dragon*. He developed the ability to study without a board and pieces. He read books, looked at the diagrams and visualized the moves as he went from page to page. He played in his first tournament at the age of eight

years and seven months. He soon had a trainer, Torbjorn Ringdal Hansen. But he appears to be more self-taught than any world-class player in memory. "For as long as I can remember, I have liked to learn things for myself by trial and error, rather than have them drummed into my head by someone else," Magnus said.

At the end of his life, Vasily Smyslov asked listeners to guess what he considered his greatest achievement. Was it beating Mikhail Botvinnik in a world championship match? Or was it winning two Candidates tournaments? No, he said, it was winning a junior tournament with an 11-0 score. And his most memorable game was one he won when he had been playing for only a few months.

Carlsen's experience was similar. A year after his introduction to tournament chess, he won the Norwegian under-11 championship with a score of ten wins and two draws. He called it "the single most important tournament win for me... That was a big deal for me." After a year of taking chess seriously his rating rose 1,000 points, to about 1900 (Hikaru Nakamura's first posted rating was 684 in January 1995, when he was seven years and two months old. By July 1996 it was 1500).

Henrik Carlsen gave up his job and began to work as a consultant in 2001 to have more flexibility in his work hours. Norway's best player, Simen Agdestein, took over as Magnus' trainer. Carlsen found himself playing regularly on the ICC, about 7,000 games from 2001 to 2004, according to Agdestein.

When Magnus was 12 the Carlsens, including his three sisters and his mother Sigrun Carlsen, a chemical engineer, packed into the family's 1994 Hyundai and took off to travel about Europe. He played 150 tournament games and tied for first in the world under-12 championship. He was awarded the international master title in August 2003.

When he only tied for ninth in the world under-14 championship it seemed like a minor setback. But he was the only international master in the tournament, which included Ian Nepomniachtchi and Maxim Vachier-Lagrave. Within six months he had his first grandmaster norm. He was on his way.

1
Magnus' Morphy

By the time Carlsen was world champion he had forgotten the way he once played. He discovered this when he tested the app "Play Magnus."

When Carlsen played against the 12-year-old clone of himself, he concluded the app designers got it wrong. "Magnus 12 is only going for king attacks and he has no technique," he said. "It's all tactics. That's not right. That's not how I played at that stage."

But then Carlsen took another look at games he played when he was 12. That was a shock. "I realized it was right," he said of the app. At 12 he was tactics-focused, just like "Magnus 12."

This game has his most impressive finish from his early years. He could have played much better, by shifting between queenside pressure and kingside threats. But then we would have never seen his sparkling queen sacrifice.

Carlsen – Hans Harestad
Copenhagen 2003
Ruy Lopez,
Tchigorin Defense (C98)

1	e4	e5
2	♘f3	♘c6
3	♗b5	a6
4	♗a4	♘f6
5	0-0	b5
6	♗b3	♗e7
7	♖e1	d6
8	c3	0-0
9	h3	♘a5
10	♗c2	c5
11	d4	♕c7
12	♘bd2	♘c6

13 d5!

The knight would be offside after 13...♘a5 14 b3.

13	...	♘d8

14 a4!

Unlike computer-oriented juniors, the young Carlsen read books. And like generations before him he was taught in textbooks how 14...b4? was punished by 15 ♘c4! in a José Capablanca game, 15...a5 16 ♘fxe5 ♗a6 (16...dxe5 17 d6) 17 ♗b3 dxe5 18 d6 ♗xd6 19 ♕xd6!.

14 ... ♖a7

Black's rooks were not connected so 15 axb5 was a threat (15...axb5?? 16 ♖xa8).

Control of the open a-file is enough for a small White plus after 14...♖b8 15 axb5 axb5 16 b4.

15 ♘f1

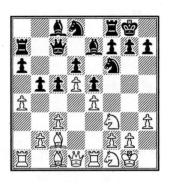

But now we can see why 14...♖a7? was a mistake.

If the d8-knight moves to b7, White can isolate the a-pawn, e.g. 15...♗d7 16 ♗e3 ♘b7 17 axb5 ♗xb5.

That pawn will be a middlegame target after, say, 18 b3 and 19 c4.

Another problem is that on a7 the rook makes a plan of ♗e3 and b2-b4 more desirable, since ...c4?? or ...cxb4?? would hang the rook.

15 ... g6

16 ♗h6! ♖e8

17 ♘g3

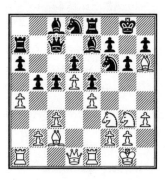

White's options include doubling rooks on the a-file after ♖a2.

That's a problem for many mature players – too many good plans.

For example, 17...♕b8 would protect the a7-rook so that he can continue ...♘b7 and meet axb5 with ...axb5.

But White can ignore the queenside and shoot at the king, with 18 ♘h2 and 19 f4!.

Also good is the more aggressive 18 ♕d2 and 19 ♘f5! (19...gxf5?? 20 ♕g5+ and mates).

17 ... ♘d7

18 ♘h2 f6!

This move frees a square for the d8-knight (19 f4? ♘f7).

But it should have given Magnus a reason to consider h3-h4-h5!.

19 ♗e3 ♘b6

20 axb5 axb5

21 ♗d3

This demonstrates Carlsen's inexperience. After 21 ♖xa7 ♕xa7 22 h4 he would have stood better on both wings.

But after 21 ♗d3 his queen can be misplaced after 21...♖xa1 22 ♕xa1 ♗d7 and ...♘f7.

21 ... ♗d7

22 ♕d2 ♘f7

23 ♖xa7 ♕xa7

24 ♕e2?

Magnus has delayed h3-h4-h5 so long that Black can make queenside threats. Here 24...c4! 25 ♗c2 ♖a8 is at least equal for Black. Black should play ...c4 on one of the ensuing moves.

24 ... ♕a6

25 ♘g4 ♔g7

26 ♗c1 ♘a4

It is frustrating to search for an attack that isn't there – 27 ♕e3 and 28 ♘h6 wouldn't threaten anything.

Also 27 ♘e3 c4 28 ♗c2 ♘c5 and now 29 ♘ef5+? gxf5 – isn't close to being a sound sacrifice.

27 ♗c2 ♖a8

28 ♕e3 c4

29 ♖f1 ♘c5?

Black's position is solid enough and 29...♕a7 or 29...♗xg4 30 hxg4 ♗d8! and ...♗b6 would give him good winning chances.

30 ♘h6 ♘g5

Carlsen prepared 31 ♘xf7 ♔xf7 32 f4! with a strong attack.

Black could have defended better with 30...♘xh6 31 ♕xh6+ ♔g8 and ...♗f8.

31 f4! exf4

At first glance, 31...♔xh6 32 fxg5+ fxg5 looks harmless (33 h4 ♔g7).

But 33 ♖f7! is deadly – 33...♖e8 34 ♖xe7 ♖xe7 35 ♕xg5+.

After 33...♗d8 Carlsen could choose between two wins, 34 h4 and 34 ♕f2!, which threatens 35 ♘f5+ gxf5 36 ♕h4+ and mates.

32 ♕xf4

Black intended 32...♔xh6 but now appreciated 33 h4!.

There is no forced win after 33...♖f8! 34 hxg5+ fxg5.

But the absence of the Black queen from the kingside defense means White has the better chances after 35 ♕h4+ ♔g7 36 ♗xg5.

32 ...   ♗xh3?

33 ♕h4!

The trap was transparent (33 gxh3?? ♘xh3+). Magnus is winning now.

33 ...   ♗d7

34 e5!

It is hard to criticize such a nice combination but he could have won without pyrotechnics.

For example, 34 ♗e3! and 35 ♗d4! creates a threat of ♕xg5 that is surprisingly hard to meet.

Also good is reversing the move order of Magnus' combination,

34 ♘h5+! and then 34...gxh5 35 e5!, with the game's finish after 35...dxe5.

Or 34...♔xh6 35 ♘xf6+ ♔g7 36 ♗xg5.

34 ...   dxe5

35 ♘h5+! gxh5

The mundane finish is 35...♔h8 36 ♗xg5 fxg5 37 ♕g3 and ♕xe5+ (or 37...♗d6 38 ♕xg5).

Carlsen could have announced mate in three moves.

36 ♕xg5+! fxg5

37 ♖f7+   ♔xh6

38 ♖xh7 mate!

This is the closest we have to a "Morphy finish" by the young Carlsen.

The next time he would finish a game with a truly sparkling queen sacrifice, he got a lot more attention. It was the final game of the 2016 world championship match.

2
Total Board

Carlsen at 12 was not always as one-sided as that game indicates. Early on, he developed a good sense of how to conduct operations on the entire board. After his pressure on the enemy center leads to a static situation in this game, he turns to the queenside. Then he switches to a decisive kingside plan.

Yuri Zimmerman – Carlsen
Schwarzacher Open 2003
Grünfeld Defense (D84)

1	d4	♘f6
2	c4	g6
3	♘c3	d5
4	cxd5	♘xd5

Now 5 e4 ♘xc3 6 bxc3 has been played gazillions of times. Black gets more pressure on the d4-pawn with 5...♘b6?! but it isn't enough to equalize after 6 ♗e3.

5	♗d2

This was a trendy move at the time. White wants to retake with the bishop on c3 after ...♘xc3.

5	...	♗g7
6	e4	♘b6

Carlsen does not oblige him. He will enjoy an extra tempo compared with the 5 e4 ♘b6?! 6 ♗e3 variation but his knight is somewhat misplaced on b6.

Who benefits from these finesses? White, very slightly.

7	♗e3	0-0
8	♗b5

This is a sophisticated idea. White offers Black another extra tempo, after 8 ♗b5 c6 9 ♗e2.

But the tempo is ...c6, which prevents him from playing ...♘c6.

Black needs pressure on the d4-pawn in the Grünfeld, as 8 ♘f3 ♗g4! followed by ...♘c6 shows.

8	...	♗e6

Carlsen opts for a trade of bishops rather than 8...♘c6 9 ♘ge2.

His move fits in with the Hypermodern thinking of Ernst

27

Grünfeld's defense – to lure White's center pawns one square further and then exploit them.

Black would stand well now after 9 d5? ♗d7 – or even 9...♗c8 – followed by 10...c6!.

9   ♘f3

The tempo-losing battle could continue with 9...♗g4!? 10 ♗e2 ♗xf3! 13 ♗xf3 c5. Black has spent another move on his bishop. But after ...♘c4 he would have a fine game.

9   ...   ♗c4

This could be tested by 10 ♗xc4 ♘xc4 11 ♕b3 but the Grünfeld-style 11...♘xe3 12 fxe3 c5 13 ♕xb7 ♘d7 should suffice (14 0-0 ♗h6).

10   b3   ♗xb5

11   ♘xb5   ♕d7

12   ♘c3   ♘c6

13   ♕d2

Time is on White's side. If he can castle and develop his rooks,

his advantage in space promises a serious advantage.

Carlsen needs to pressure his center before then. But 13...e5? 14 d5 and ♗c5 isn't the right way.

13   ...   ♖ad8

14   ♖d1   f5!

This is. Now 15 exf5 ♖xf5 16 0-0 ♘d5 and later ...e5 dooms White's formerly impressive pawn center.

15   e5

It looked risky to weaken e6 with ...f5. But 15 0-0 fxe4 16 ♘xe4 ♕g4! would keep White from exploiting it.

After 17 ♘g3 e5 Black would have equalized.

15   ...   ♘d5

16   ♘xd5   ♕xd5

17   0-0   ♕b5

Carlsen's best plan is to double rooks on the d-file and tie White to the defense of his d4-pawn.

He is also watching for an opportunity to win it with ...f4.

18	&h6	&d5
19	&xg7?	&xg7
20	&c3	h6!

The trade of bishops seemed logical. It rendered ...f4 harmless and might have made the Black kingside vulnerable.

But now endgames (after ...&b4xc3) would favor Black because the d4-pawn is a chronic target.

A broad pawn center decreases in value as wood is exchanged, as Bobby Fischer reminded us.

21	&d2	&fd8
22	&fd1	&b4
23	&e3	e6

Carlsen is ready for a reorganization such as ...&5d7 and ...&e7-d5.

White can prevent that with 24 &c1 &5d7 25 &dc2 &b6 26 &c4.

He might be worse after 26...&e7 and ...&d5.

But how would Black make progress after that?

Another plan is 25...&e7 and ...&b4-d5, with the added idea of ...g5-g4.

White has an interesting sacrifice, 26 &xc6!? bxc6 27 h4 and &xc6. Then Black is better but his rooks are strangely ineffective.

| 24 | h4? | &e7! |
| 25 | &f4 | &h8 |

His rooks would play very well after 25...&a5! and 26...&b4. But Carlsen wants to open a second front and he can do it with ...g5.

| 26 | &g3 | &f7 |
| 27 | &f4 | &e8 |

Carlsen's idea is ...&d7-c8 and ...&g7/...&g8. This makes it safe enough for a winning ...g5!.

| 28 | &c2 | &b4 |
| 29 | &c4 | &d7 |

Not the dangerous 29...♘xa2? 30 ♕d2 b5 31 ♕xa2 bxc4 32 bxc4. By retreating to d7 Carlsen made his rook available for kingside reinforcement at h7 or g7 after ...g5.

30	♕d2	♘d5

| 31 | b4 | |

| 31 | ... | g5! |

Strategic thinking is over. It is tactics time. Now 32 g3 f4! 33 g4 gxh4 and ...♖g8 is lost.

32	hxg5	hxg5

| 33 | ♕xg5 | |

Plugging the h-file with the knight, 33 ♘xg5 f4 34 ♘h3, is doomed by 34...♕h4 and ...♖g7.

For example, 35 ♕d3 ♖g7 36 ♔f1 ♕g4.

Instead, White can set a trap with 34 ♘f3 ♕h7 35 ♔f1 ♖g7 36 ♕c2.

Then 36...♕h1+ 37 ♔e2 ♕xg2 38 ♖g1! turns the tables.

But this is foiled by 36...♘e3+! 37 fxe3 ♕h1+ 38 ♔e2 ♖xg2+.

33	...	♕h7

| 34 | ♔f1 | ♖g7 |

| 35 | ♕c1 | |

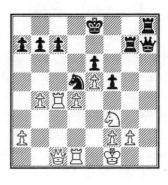

| 35 | ... | ♖xg2! |

This is not the only way to win – 35...f4! also does it, as in the last note.

But this is faster (36 ♔xg2? ♕h3+ mates).

| 36 | ♔e2 | ♕g7 |

White would love to sacrifice on c7 and eliminate that powerful knight.

But even 36...♕h5 37 ♖xc7 ♕g4! 38 ♖c8+ ♔f7 wins.

For example, 39 ♖xh8 ♕e4+ 40 ♔f1 ♕xf3 (41 ♕d2 ♘f4).

37	♖g1	♖h3!

| 38 | ♖xg2 | ♕xg2 |

| 39 | ♘e1 | ♕e4+ |

| 40 | ♔d2 | ♘f4 |

| 41 | ♕d1 | ♖d3+ |

| 42 | ♘xd3 | ♕xd3+ |

White resigns

3
Closing Gaps

Young players typically develop their skills unevenly. They may play the opening well but handle endgames horribly. They can calculate forcing variations but can't tell when an uneventful position is dead even or a White advantage to the tune of +0.50.

There were still major gaps in Carlsen's skill set in 2003. But he was closing some of them. He was beginning to win games in which he demonstrated both combinational talent and powers of evaluating simple positions. Here is a remarkable sacrifice which is essentially a forcing way to trade queens into a winning endgame.

Carlsen – Christian Laqua
Schwarzacher Open 2003
Catalan Opening,
Closed Variation (A46)

1	d4	♘f6
2	♘f3	e6
3	g3	d5
4	♗g2	♗e7
5	0-0	0-0
6	c4	c6

The closed variation of the Catalan is far less popular than the open one (6...dxc4). It defers tactics until the early middlegame.

7   b3

The next five moves could be played in different orders, with little difference.

There is no better place for Black's queenside pieces than ...♗b7, ...♘bd7 and ...♖c8. White's queen works best on c2 and his rook does well on d1.

7	...	b6
8	♕c2	♗b7
9	♘c3	♘bd7
10	♗b2	♕c7
11	♖ad1	♖ac8
12	e4	

This is the first move of the game that could be called forcing. Black should not allow the space-gaining 13 e5!.

12	...	♘xe4
13	♘xe4	dxe4
14	♕xe4	

The pawn structure grants White more space. Black lacks support for changing it with ...e5. He aims instead for ...c5.

Back in the 1970s, 14...c5 was the common continuation – until 15 d5! was found to be strong.

For example, after 15...♘f6 16 ♕c2 exd5 17 ♗e5! Black must misplace his queen or allow 17...♗d6 18 ♗xf6 gxf6 19 cxd5 and ♘h4-f5.

If the queen goes to c6, d7 or d8 White can assure himself an advantage with 18 ♘g5!, which threatens mate on h7 after ♗xf6.

Eventually defenders improved Black's chances with 15...♗f6, instead of 15...♘f6.

Then White would be worse after 16 ♗xf6? ♘xf6.

But the ♗e5 idea of the previous variation was so good that White found he could get a nice game with 16 ♗c1! and ♗f4.

14	...	♖fd8
15	♖fe1	c5

Another version of that maneuver is 15...♗f6 16 ♗c1!, again with a slight edge.

16	d5	♗f6
17	♗c1!	

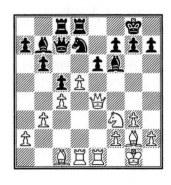

The idea is not just ♗f4 but also ♘g5.

This is very similar to the position that could have arisen after 14...c5 15 d5 ♗f6 16 ♗c1.

In this version each side has added one move – ♖fe1 for White and ...♖fd8 for Black. Which player benefits more?

Black has additional pressure on d5, such as 17...exd5 18 cxd5 b5 and ...♘b6.

However, on d8, the rook would be attacked after 19 ♘g5! ♗xg5? 20 ♗xg5.

Then 20...♖e8? 21 ♕xe8+ and 20...f6? 21 d6 are clearly bad.

Less obvious is 20...♖f8 21 ♕f5!, which threatens 22 d6.

The alternatives to 19...♗xg5 aren't pleasant either. Black loses after 19...g6? 20 d6!.

For example, 20...♗xe4 21 dxc7.

Also 20...♕c6 21 ♘xf7! so that 21...♔xf7? 22 ♕e6+ and ♗xc6.

Or 21...♕xe4 22 ♗xe4 ♔xf7 23 ♗xb7.

17   ...   ♕b8

Now 18 ♕g4 exd5 19 ♘g5 is good.

18   ♘g5!

It is tempting to play 18 ♗f4 ♕a8 first and then 19 ♘g5 ♗xg5 20 ♗xg5 ♖e8 21 dxe6! ♗xe4 22 ♗xe4.

Since 22...♕b8?? 23 exd7 is lost, Black would play 22...♖xe6 23 ♗xa8 ♖xe1+ 24 ♖xe1 ♖xa8.

There are two differences between 18 ♘g5! and 18 ♗f4 ♕a8 19 ♘g5, as we'll see.

18   ...   ♗xg5

19   ♗xg5   ♖e8

20   ♗f4   ♕a8

One of those differences is that in this move order, 20...e5 was possible.

But for positional reasons (the passed d5-pawn, the dead b7-bishop) White stands very well.

There is also a tactical trick, 21 ♗h6! with a threat of ♕g4.

For example, 21...♘f6 22 ♕f5 ♕d6 23 ♕g5 and 21...♘f8 22 ♗d2 and ♗c3 is close to lost.

In other words, this move order gives Black an option (20...e5) that was better than what happened in the game – but still bad for him.

Now comes a series of forcing moves beginning with a queen sacrifice. It does not win material but reaches a very favorable rook endgame.

21   dxe6!   ♗xe4

22   ♗xe4   ♖xe6

Black would be a pawn down after 22...♕xe4 23 ♖xe4 ♘f6 24 exf7+ or a piece down after 23...fxe6? 24 ♖xd7.

23	&xa8	&xe1+
24	&xe1	&xa8
25	&e7	

Let's scroll back to the note to 18 ♘g5.

If Carlsen had begun with 18 ♗f4 ♕a8 and played the same queen sacrifice, his bishop would now be on g5, not f4.

That would substantially help Black because of 25...♘f8! and 26...♘e6.

With his rook on the seventh rank, White would have a big advantage but not yet a winning one.

25	...	♘f8

But what about 25...♘f6 ? If the bishop were on g5, that would have been met strongly by 26 ♗xf6! gxf6 27 ♖b7.

Instead, the pawn-winning plan Magnus executes in the game would have led to 26 ♖b7 ♘e4 27 ♗b8 ♘c3.

However, he would still be winning because he can make slow progress with ♔g2-f3, while Black's pieces are passive.

For example, 26 ♔g2 ♔f8 27 ♖c7 ♔e8 28 ♗e5 and ♗xf6 (28...♔d8? 29 ♖xf7).

And did you see the trap in the last variation?

After 27 ♖b7 ♔e8 28 ♗e5 Black could play 28...♘d7 because 29 ♗xg7? ♔d8 and 30...♔c8 will trap the rook.

26	♖b7!	♘e6
27	♗b8!	♘d8
28	♖e7	

The threat of ♖e8 mate gains time to win the a7-pawn. Black finds a forcing way to make it a rook ending.

28	...	♘e6
29	♗xa7	♔f8!

Now 30 ♖d7? allows him to force a draw, 30...♔e8 31 ♖b7 ♘d8! (32 ♖c7 ♘e6 33 ♖b7 ♘d8).

30	♖b7!	♘d8
31	♖b8	♖xa7
32	♖xd8+	♚e7
33	♖d2	♚e6

When one player has an extra queenside pawn in a rook ending and each side has three kingside pawns, the outcome often depends on who can attack the kingside pawns.

Black could pose more problems with 33...g5, which discourages White's plan of h2-h4 and g2-g3.

After 34 ♚g2 f5 35 ♚f3 ♖a3 he would also stop a2-a4 and tie White's rook to the defense of the a2-pawn.

That shouldn't be enough to draw but White would need to figure out another way to win, perhaps after 36 h4 h6 37 h5 or 37 hxg5 hxg5 38 g4.

34	♚g2	h5
35	h4	g6

Both players safeguarded their kingside. Only the pawns at f2 and f7 are not protected by a fellow pawn.

But Carlsen's rook is much more active than Black's and he can win with routine moves, such as a2-a4, ♚f3 and ♖d5.

Therefore Black has to generate counterplay. Better practical chances were to be offered by 35...f6 36 ♚f3 g5 and 37 ♚e4 gxh4 38 gxh4 ♖g7 (39 f3 ♖g1).

36	♚f3	♚e5
37	a4!	♖c7
38	♖d5+	♚e6
39	♚f4	

The king is headed to g5.

Black can stop that with 39...f6 but then the g6-pawn will be vulnerable after 40 ♖d8.

Black soon runs out of moves, e.g. 40...♚e7 41 ♖g8 ♚f7 42 ♖b8 ♖c6 43 ♖b7+ ♚e6 44 ♖g7 or 43...♚f8 44 ♚e4.

Similar is 40...♖c6 41 ♔e4 ♖c7 42 ♖e8+ ♔f7 43 ♖b8 ♖c6 44 ♔d5 ♖e6 45 ♖b7+.

39	...	♖c8
40	♔g5	♖a8

41 f4!

This threatens 42 ♖e5+ ♔d6 43 ♔f6.

There was a good alternative plan of 41 f3 and 42 g4 so that 42...hxg4 43 fxg4 and 44 h5 creates a passed pawn.

For example, 41...♖c8 42 g4 ♖h8 43 ♖d1 should win but progress is slower after 43...♔e7 44 ♖e1+ ♔f8.

41	...	f6+
42	♔h6	

This is a mature move. White would still win after 42 ♔xg6 ♖g8+! 43 ♔xh5 ♖xg3 after 44 f5+ but allows Black's rook to get into the game.

But a good technician does not give his opponent even a glimmer of counterplay.

42	...	♖c8
43	♔g7!	

But now 43...♖a7+ 44 ♔xg6 would make it much easier because there is no ...♖g8+.

43	...	♖a8
44	a5!	

This deflects the rook or wins after 44...bxa5 45 ♖xc5.

This is much easier to calculate than 44 ♖d3 ♔f5 45 ♖d6.

44	...	♖xa5
45	♔xg6	♖a3
46	f5+	♔e7
47	♖d3	b5
48	cxb5	c4
49	♖e3+	♔f8?
50	b6!	**Resigns**

Also lost was 49...♔d7 50 ♖e4! in view of 50...cxb3 51 ♖b4 or 50...♖xb3 51 ♖xc4 ♖xb5 52 ♔xf6.

4
Bees of Opps

One of the hardest lessons for aspiring players was one that Magnus learned early: How to handle bishops of opposite color. "Bees of opps" tend to veto general rules and principles. It is easier to win some middlegames with them and nearly impossible to win some endgames with them.

Carlsen – Andre Diamant
Halkidiki 2003
Sicilian Defense, Accelerated Fianchetto (B37)

1	e4	c5
2	♘f3	♘c6
3	d4	cxd4
4	♘xd4	g6
5	c4	

Like Bobby Fischer, Carlsen favors opening moves that maximize his piece play, rather than ones that enhance his pawn structure. But like the young Fischer, he experimented with this Maróczy Bind structure, rather than 5 ♘c3 ♗g7 6.♗e3 and ♕d2.

5	...	♘f6
6	♘c3	d6
7	♘c2	

If you are not familiar with Maróczy Bind positions, this move looks odd. The idea is that after 7 ♗e2, Black can free his game a bit with a trade of knights, 7...♘xd4 8 ♕xd4 ♗g7, that misplaces White's queen.

White would prefer the other natural bishop move, 7 ♗e3. But that runs into problems after 7...♘g4! (8 ♗g5? ♕b6!).

7	...	♗g7
8	♗e2	0-0
9	0-0	

Chances seem evenly balanced. But there is a subtle difference. White would steadily improve his position if he is allowed to play ♗e3, ♖c1, ♕d2 and ♖fd1 and perhaps b2-b3.

Black would run out of useful moves long before White. What that means is he needs counterplay.

9	...	♘d7

There is no precise definition of "counterplay." But it is generally

37

understood as distracting an opponent from his intentions.

The Maróczy Bind structure is a powerful weapon because it stifles the natural Black counterplay of a Sicilian Defense, along the c-file and from ...b5-b4.

Lacking that, his best resource is attacking the e4-pawn, with ...♞c5 and its threat of ...♝xc3/...♞xe4 or with ...f5.

10   ♗d2   ♞c5

11   b4!

There had been little prior experience with this offer of a pawn. White might be able to attack along the a1-h8 diagonal after 11...♝xc3 12 ♝xc3 ♞xe4 13 ♝b2. He would also have compensation by pushing Black's minor pieces back, e.g. 13...♝d7? 14 b5 ♞e5 15 f3 ♞f6 16 f4.

11   ...   ♞e6

12   ♖c1   ♞ed4

Black found another way to trade minor pieces. He threatens 13...♞xc2 followed by 14...♞xb4.

13   ♞xd4   ♞xd4

14   ♗e3   ♞xe2+

15   ♛xe2

Piece trades diminish the benefits of a favorable pawn structure. But they don't entirely eliminate them here. White still has the better plans, such as f2-f4-f5 on the kingside or ♖fd1 and c4-c5 in the center.

15   ...   a5?

A fundamental strategic error based on the belief Black has time to rule out c4-c5. His inferiority would be kept to a minimum after 15...b6 and ...♝b7.

16   b5!

This concedes pawn control of c5 but it cannot be safely occupied. It was more important to deny Black's a8-rook a middlegame future, after 16 a3 axb4 17 axb4 ♝e6 and ...♖a3.

16 ... ♗xc3

Dragon players hate to trade this bishop, especially for a knight. But the exchange does two things that make sense.

First, it eliminates the piece that best exploits the newly-created hole at b6. Black avoided 16...♗e6 17 ♘a4! followed by ♘b6 and f2-f4-f5.

Trying to blockade the queenside with 16...b6 fails because the b-pawn could be hammered by 17 ♘a4 ♖b8 18 f3 and ♕f2.

17 ♖xc3

The other thing that ...♗xc3 did is create bishops of opposite color. This makes a draw more likely if the game reaches an endgame. But a loss is more probable in a middlegame, particularly if the kingside or center is opened further.

For example, 17...♗e6 18 f4! would prepare to overwhelm the king position with f4-f5.

Then 18...f5? makes matters worse after, for instance, 19 exf5 ♗xf5 20 g4 ♗d7 21 f5.

A quick win would follow 21...gxf5 22 gxf5 ♗xf5? 23 ♖xf5 ♖xf5 24 ♕g4+. and wins.

17 ... f6

Black's 15th and 16th moves would have worked well if he had

time to play both ...b6 and ...f6. But he doesn't. If he had started with 17...b6, White's kingside attack would roll on with 18 f4 f6 19 f5.

18 c5! dxc5

Else 19 ♖d1 and cxd6/...exd6 creates a doomed Black d-pawn.

19 ♖d1 ♕e8

The queen would look more active on e6, after 19...♕b6 and 20 ♗xc5 ♕e6.

But after 20 ♖xc5! ♕e6 21 f3 White could steadily improve his position with ♖c7, b5-b6 and ♕b5.

Instead, Black leaves e6 free for his bishop and retains the possibility of ...e5/...♖f7.

20 ♗h6

Carlsen is going for a middlegame kill rather than queenside penetration. Both are effective. It is hard to imagine

Black surviving 20 ♖xc5 e5 21 ♖c7 ♖f7 22 ♖xf7 and 22...♕xf7? 23 ♖d8+ or 22...♔xf7 23 ♖c1 and ♖c7+.

20 ... ♖f7

21 ♕c4

This rules out ...♗e6. Simpler was 21 e5 with a threat of 22 e6.

A key point in these scenarios is that ♗h6/...♖f7 made Black chronically vulnerable on the last rank. For instance, 21 e5 ♗e6 22 ♖xc5 ♖c8? looks natural. But it loses to 23 ♖xc8 ♕xc8 24 ♕d2! and ♕d8+.

21 ... e5?

The final error. Black might have resisted for many moves after 21...♗d7 22 a4 ♕c8, although defense would be difficult after 23 ♕xc5.

22 ♖d6!

The best chance for a knockout is to exploit the d8 square.

Magnus' simple threat is 23 ♖cd3 and ♖d8.

Note how Black's bishop plays no defensive role. That is common in middlegames with "bees of opps."

22 ... ♗d7

23 a4

This kills queenside counterplay and is more efficient than 23 b6 ♖c8 24 ♖xf6 ♗b5.

23 ... ♖c8

Black could have gotten his king off the pinning diagonal with 23...♔h8. But White would have a rich choice of winning plans, such as 24 ♖cd3 ♖d8 25 ♕xc5 and 26 ♕d5.

24 ♖cd3

The correct score of this game has been in doubt for years and some Magnus fans have wondered if Black really allowed 24 ♖xf6.

One explanation is the potential swindle: 24 ♖xf6 ♖d8 25 ♖cf3?? seems to overpower the pinned f7-rook.

But a move of Black's bishop – to g4, e6 or even ...♗xb5! – would have threatened ...♖d1+ and saved the day.

24 ... ♔h8

Black would have another last-rank trick after 25 ♕d5 ♖d8 26 ♕xc5 because 26...♖c8 27 ♕d5 g5 sets up ...♖c1+.

White could calculate all that and see how a luft move (28 h3, 28 g3 and even 28 h4) would win.

25   h3

This rules out all last-rank tactics and sends Black a message: "Try to find a good move."

25   ...   ♖c7

The safest way to win now is 26 ♖d1, so that ...c4 never attacks the rook. Then 27 ♕d5 would crash through.

26   b6!

But it was hard to pass up a flashy finish, such as 25...♖c6 26 ♖xc6 ♗xc6 27 ♖d8! and mates (27...♕xd8 28 ♕xf7).

26   ...   ♖c8

27   ♕xf7!   ♕xf7

28   ♖xd7   ♕g8

29   ♖c7

This threatens 30 ♗g7+. Also winning is 29 ♖xb7 and ♖dd7.

29   ...   ♕e6

30   ♖dd7   ♖xc7

31   ♖d8+!   resigns

This shows how the infamous opposite-colored bishops can provide a lasting initiative: They cannot be traded directly and they cannot defend the squares that the rival bishop can attack. Based on what he learned in games like this, Magnus became perhaps the greatest Bees-of-Opps middlegame player in history.

5
Moscow

When 2004 began, Magnus had made a strong impression in big-time chess locations, such as Stockholm, Copenhagen, Budva, Gausdal and Budapest. But when you can do it in Moscow, it is something else.

At the 3rd Aeroflot Festival he was dazzling. All nine of his opponents were grandmasters and he scored five wins and a draw against them. One of his victims was Sergey Dolmatov, who was later the chief trainer of the Russian national team.

"It was at the very start of the tournament, and I was sitting with some boy," he recalled. He had not heard of Carlsen and did not expect much of a 13-year-old. But, he said, "I have to say Magnus didn't leave me any chances." The same could be said of Carlsen's next-to-last round opponent.

Carlsen – Hannes Stefansson
Aeroflot Festival, Moscow 2004
Nimzo-Indian Defense,
Three Knights Variation (E21)

1	d4	♘f6
2	c4	e6
3	♘c3	♗b4
4	♘f3	

When Magnus found himself on the White side of a Nimzo-Indian, he had usually chosen 4 e3. But in 2003 he began experimenting with 4 ♘f3 and then 4...b6 5 ♗g5 and 4...0-0 5 ♕d3.

The knight move is flexible and may transpose into Queen's Indian Defense positions (4...b6 5 ♗g5 ♗b7 6 e3) or the Queen's Gambit Declined's Ragozin Variation (4...d5).

4	...	c5
5	g3	

Or into the old main line of the 4 e3 Nimzo-Indian, after 5 e3 0-0 6 ♗d3 d5.

5	...	♘e4
6	♕d3	

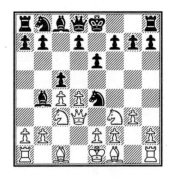

The variation beginning with 5 g3 was virtually non-existent until the 1980s.

Then, for many years, the main line was 6...cxd4 7 ♘xd4 ♛a5.

There was published analysis of 8 ♘b3 ♘xc3 9 ♗d2 extending past move 15.

6 ... ♛a5

This steers White into slightly calmer and largely unknown waters.

7 ♛xe4!

Carlsen avoids the tepid 7 ♗d2 ♘xd2, when Black is at least equal following 8 ♘xd2 cxd4 9 ♛xd4 0-0 or 8 ♛xd2 0-0.

7 ... ♗xc3+

8 ♗d2 ♗xd2+

9 ♘xd2 0-0

Black finds it harder to develop his queenside after 9...cxd4 10 ♛xd4 0-0 because of 11 ♛d6! or 11 ♗g2 ♘c6 12 ♛d6!.

10 ♗g2 d6

11 dxc5

White wants to get out of the pin on the d2-knight and this is better than 11 ♛e3 cxd4 12 ♛xd4 ♘c6! (13 ♛xd6 ♖d8).

11 ... dxc5

12 ♛e3 ♖d8

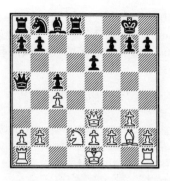

White's knight is pinned (13 0-0?? ♛xd2). That factor appears to win time for an equalizing ...♘c6-d4.

For instance, 13 a3 ♘c6 14 ♖d1 ♘d4 15 0-0 ♛c7 allows Black to play ...e5 and develop his bishop.

He would have a decent middlegame after 16 ♘b3 e5 or 16 b4 e5 17 bxc5 ♗g4.

13 ♖d1!

This gambit move may have been a rare young-Magnus innovation.

Black was a former world under-16 champion. He must have been disappointed to see what 13...♛xa2 looked like.

The simplest lines are:

(a) 14 ♛xc5 ♛xb2 15 0-0 with good compensation for a pawn. Black's first rank is exposed to tactics after 15...♘a6? 16 ♘e4!.

(b) 14 ♛c3, which prepares to trap the queen with 0-0/♖a1.

White would get his pawn back favorably after 14...♘c6 15 ♗xc6 bxc6 16 0-0 and ♘b3 or ♖a1, for example.

13   ...   ♕c7

But perhaps worst of all from Black's point of view is that Carlsen could offer a second pawn, 13...♕xa2 14 0-0.

That increases the tactical dangers on Black's first rank, as 14...♘a6? 15 ♘b3!, 14...♘c6 15 ♘b3 and 14...♕a5 15 ♘b3 show.

The critical continuation (after 13...♕xa2 14 0-0) is 14...♕xb2 15 ♘b3 ♕f6.

White can get both of his pawns back after 16 ♘xc5 ♘c6 17 ♗xc6 bxc6 18 ♕f3 ♕e7 (18...♕xf3?? 19 ♖xd8 mate) 19 ♕xc6 ♖b8.

14   0-0

Black underestimated the pressure Carlsen gets for free.

14   ...   ♗d7

Black has to figure out how to complete development. Clearly 14...♘c6 15 ♕xc5 and 14...b6?? won't do.

If he tries 14...♘a6 and 15...♗d7, White has the same 15 ♕f4! shot as in the game.

Then 15...♕xf4? 16 gxf4 ♖b8 17 ♘e4 is highly uncomfortable.

Better is 15...e5. White could transpose into the game with 16 ♕e3 ♗d7.

But he might do better with 16 ♕f3 since 16...♗d7 loses to 17 ♕xb7.

If Black pins the d2-knight with 16...♕d6, White can unpin it by 17 ♕h5! with the idea of ♗d5 and ♘e4.

For example, 17...♕e7 18 ♘f3 f6 19 ♖xd8+ ♕xd8 20 ♘h4 and 21 ♗d5+! or 21 ♗e4 g6 22 ♘xg6!.

15   ♕f4!   e5

Black would be verging on a "matter of technique" loss after 15...♕xf4? 16 gxf4 ♗c6 17 ♘b3!.

Then 17...♘a6 18 ♗xc6 bxc6 19 ♘a5! wins a pawn.

For example, 19...♖dc8 20 ♖d6 But 20 ♖d7 and 21 ♖fd1 is even better because Black's pieces don't play.

16   ♕e3

White spent two tempi (♕f4-e3) to provoke ...e5. Appreciating why this is worthwhile – and in this case, more than worthwhile – is difficult even for strong masters.

While Carlsen was in Moscow the veteran trainer Yuri Razuvaev tried to gauge his strengths. Along with Alexander Nikitin, former trainer of Garry Kasparov, he showed Magnus positions for hours and asked him to choose the best moves. In one way, they were unimpressed.

"We immediately said: He is an ordinary tactician," Razuvaev recalled in 2010.

But, he added, Carlsen more than made up for it with his uncanny ability to evaluate quiet positions.

"Magnus had positional talent on the level of Petrosian or Karpov," Razuvaev said.

16 ...   ♘a6

17 ♘e4

This knight yearns for d5. It could also get there via 17 ♘b1 ♗c6 18 ♘c3, which some computers prefer.

The biggest difference between that and the text is that 17 ♘e4 ♘b4? 18 ♕xc5 is not possible.

But 17 ♘b1 ♘b4 18 ♘c3 ♗e6 would allow Black to dream of ...♘c2-d4 or ...♖d4.

White would have all the winning chances after 19 b3 a6 (to stop 20 ♘b5). But no winning plan stands out.

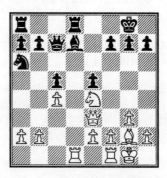

17 ...   ♗c6

Now 18 ♘xc5 ♗xg2 19 ♘xa6 ♕xc4 gives Black chances he doesn't deserve.

18 ♘c3!

One square, d5, makes the difference after 18...♗xg2 19 ♔xg2 and ♘d5.

White would still need a strong plan after, say, 19...♕c6+ 20 f3 f6 21 ♘d5.

But his ownership of the d-file counts a lot, as 21...♖d7 22 ♖d2

45

♘b4? 23 ♖fd1 ♘xd5 24 ♖xd5 or 23...♘xa2? 24 ♘xf6+ shows.

| 18 | ... | ♖d4 |

The elegant simplicity of his play led several Russian observers to call him "a young Smyslov."

But Vasily Smyslov said Carlsen was "a young Tal."

The rest of the game shows that Carlsen was no "ordinary tactician."

| 19 | ♘b5! | ♗xb5 |
| 20 | cxb5 | |

Black may have counted on the tactic 20...♕d7 since 21 bxa6 ♖xd1 22 axb7 ♖xf1+ doesn't work (23 ♔xf1?? ♕d1 mate).

Instead, 21 ♖xd4 exd4 would allow Carlsen to calculate his way to 22 ♕e4 ♕xb5 23 ♕xb7 ♖b8 24 ♕xa7.

Then Black's pieces seem more active than White's but tactics can turn against him because of the awkward knight – 24...♕xe2 25 b4 cxb4? 26 ♖c1! and ♗f1.

More likely – and more Magnus-like – is 22 ♕b3 or 22 ♕d3, with a "matter of technique" win after 22...♘c7 23 ♗xb7 ♖b8 24 ♗c6.

| 20 | ... | ♘b4? |
| 21 | ♕b3! | a5 |

The trapped knight is lost.

It might have been saved tactically by 21...♕b6 and 22 a3 ♘c6 (23 bxc6?? ♕xb3).

But White has so many positional plusses that he can win instead with 22 e3! and 22...♖xd1 23 ♖xd1 ♖f8 24 ♕c4 or 22...♖dd8 23 a3 ♘c6 24 ♗d5!.

| 22 | ♖xd4 | cxd4 |
| 23 | a3 | ♕c2 |

Also 23...♘c2 24 ♖c1 ♖c8 25 ♗e4.

| 24 | ♕xc2 | ♘xc2 |
| 25 | ♗xb7 | Resigns |

In view of 25...♖b8 26 ♗e4.

The veteran Russian chess official Yevgeny Bebchuk summed up the impression Carlsen made in Moscow. Bebchuk had seen a young Boris Spassky, a young Mikhail Tal, a young Anatoly Karpov and a young Garry Kasparov. "I can assert that there has never been anyone in history who played like this at 13," he said.

6
Precision Defense

Tigran Petrosian did not like to calculate when he did not have to. When he had Black he often tried to liquidate danger by trading pieces and offering a draw.

In contrast, Viktor Korchnoi loved to calculate. But it wasn't until he was in his 20s that he was able to defeat grandmasters with Black by counterattack and precise defense.

Of course, there were few GMs in those days and fewer opportunities to beat them. Nevertheless, Carlsen was beating strong players, including grandmasters with Black, before he was 15. Among his victims in 2004-5 were Maxime Vachier-Lagrave, Joel Lautier, Nick de Firmian and Ivan Cheparinov. Here's another:

Rune Djurhuus – Carlsen
Norwegian Championship 2005
Bishop's Opening (C28)

1	e4	e5
2	♗c4	♘f6
3	d3	♘c6
4	♘c3	♗b4
5	♘f3	

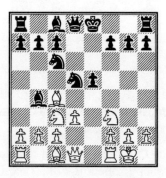

This is a trappy alternative to 5 ♘e2 d5 6 exd5 ♘xd5. It was revived by Bent Larsen in the 1960s although he rarely got an advantage after 5...d6.

5	...	d5
6	exd5	♘xd5
7	0-0	

The first trap is 7...♘xc3 8 bxc3 ♗xc3. Then 9 ♘g5! offers White a strong attack.

The game could become a miniature (9...♗xa1? 10 ♗xf7+ ♔e7 11 ♗a3+ ♔f6 12 ♕f3+! ♔xg5? 13 h4+ and mate next).

Or it could lead to continuing White pressure, 9...♕e7 10 ♖b1 ♘d8 11 ♘e4.

7   ...   ♗xc3

8   bxc3   0-0

There was no reason to be tested by 8...♘xc3 9 ♕e1 ♘d5 10 ♗a3!.

9   ♗d2

Carlsen's grandmaster opponent had had some success after 9...♗g4 10 h3 ♗h5 with 11 ♖e1 ♖e8 12 ♖b1.

9   ...   ♚h8

Old-style gambits exploited greed, such as grabbing a c3-pawn after 7...♘xc3 earlier.

But there are modern versions of trappy openings that exploit natural, solid-looking moves.

For example, 9...♗e6 looks like safe development. But it gives White the tactical chances he seeks after 10 ♘g5 ♗f5 11 ♕f3 ♘de7 12 ♖ae1.

Carlsen's move is designed to prepare ...f6 and ...♗e6. The immediate 9...f6 10 ♖e1 ♗e6? 11 d4 is dangerous.

10   ♘g5   f6

Not 10...h6? 11 ♕h5, when there is nothing better than the embarrassing 11...♚g8.

11   ♕f3   ♘ce7

12   ♘e4   b6

White can claim some progress. He discouraged ...♘a5 and has a lead in development.

But time is on Black's side. If allowed to play ...♗b7 and ...♘g6 he would be poised to deliver a powerful ...♘df4! and ...f5.

This means White has to find tactics or a way to open lines favorably.

There are tactics in lines such as 13 ♖fe1 ♗b7 14 ♖ab1 ♘g6? 15 ♘c5! (15...bxc5 16 ♖xb7).

But that trick disappears after 14...♖b8. Only a computer would like White's chances after 15 ♕h3 ♘g6 16 g3, for example.

13   d4!

An exchange of pawns on d4 helps White. He can try to force it with 14 ♖ad1 because then 15 dxe5 fxe5 16 ♕g3 sets up a nasty pin on the d-file.

13 ... ♗b7!

This seems risky because it weakens e6. For example, 14 ♖ad1 f5? 15 ♘g5 threatens 16 ♘e6.

Then 15...e4 16 ♕h3 or 15...♕d6? 16 dxe5 ♕xe5 17 ♖fe1.

But 14...♘g6!, instead of 14...f5?, sets up 15...♘df4!.

Chances would be roughly equal after 15 ♖fe1 ♕d7 16 ♕g3.

14 dxe5

Slower is 14 ♗d3 with the idea of ♕h5 and a mate threat on h7 or going for ♘g3-f5.

The chief drawback is 14...f5 and then 15 ♘g5 e4 16 ♕h3 h6.

But 17 c4! ♗c8! 18 cxd5 exd3 19 c4, with even chances.

Djurhuus opted for 14 dxe5 after seeing how well 14...fxe5 15 ♕h5 could turn out.

For example, 15...♗f5? 16 ♘g5 ♕g8 17 ♗d3 is excellent for him and 15...♘g6 16 ♖ae1 is roughly even.

14 ... ♘g6!

But he misjudged this reply. Carlsen wants to retake on e5 with his knight.

He would win a piece after 15 exf6? ♘xf6.

15 ♕e2?

His skill in bishops-of-opposite-color endgames would have become relevant after, say, 15 ♖fe1 ♘xe5 16 ♕e2 ♘xc4 17 ♕xc4 ♕d7 and ...♕c6.

White would have been happier to play 15 ♕h3 ♘xe5 16 ♗d3 ♘xd3 17 cxd3 or 15...♘df4 16 ♗xf4 ♘xf4 17 ♕g4, which is fairly even.

But Carlsen may have preferred 15...♕e8! because it makes 16...♘df4 more of a threat.

15 ... f5!

This wins material, since 16 ♘g5? ♘df4! is resignable.

49

16	♗g5	♕e8

And so is 17 ♘g3 ♘df4 18 ♗xf4 ♘xf4 19 ♕d2 ♕c6!.

17	♗xd5	♗xd5
18	♘d2	h6!

Less forceful but also winning is 18...f4 because the bishop is trapped and will be lost after 19...h6.

19   c4

When he chose 18...h6 Carlsen must have calculated 19 ♗e3 f4 20 ♗d4 c5.

Then 21 f3 cxd4 22 cxd4 would keep the game going a bit longer.

But by driving the bishop from the kingside, he made 20...f3! and ...♘f4 a faster win.

For example, 21 gxf3? ♘f4 is followed by mate or win of the queen.

19	...	♗b7
20	♕h5	♗xg2!

Also winning is 20...♔g8. It threatens 21...hxg5 and contains the same knight fork, 21 ♗e3 ♗xg2 22 ♔xg2? ♘f4+.

21	♖fe1	♗b7
22	e6!	

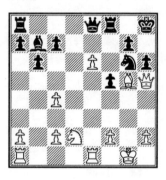

By now Carlsen was already an accomplished swindler. One of his first Black victories over a GM occurred when he overcame a +2.00 disadvantage and defeated Merab Gagunashvili at Wijk aan Zee 2004.

Here he has to avoid becoming the swindlee. That could happen after the natural 22...♘f4 23 ♕xe8 ♘h3+ 24 ♔f1 ♖axe8 – and then 25 ♗d8! (25...♖xd8 26 e7).

Better is 24...♖fxe8, although 25 ♗h4 g5 26 ♖e3 saves the trapped bishop (26...♘f4 27 ♗g3).

22	...	f4!
23	h4	♖f5

Now 24 f3 ♘e5 25 ♕xe8+ ♖xe8 26 ♗xf4 avoids a big material loss.

But 26...♞xf3+ 27 ♞xf3 ♜xf4 is hopeless (28 ♞d2 ♜xh4).

24	♛g4	♛c6
25	f3	♞e5!

Magnus has had several ways to win since move 19 but chose the most forceful.

26	♛xf5	♞xf3+
27	♔f2	

The rest of the game seems closer than it really is. White can resign here.

White has to give up at least a rook to avoid mate after 27 ♞xf3 ♛xf3.

27	...	♞xd2
28	♛d5	hxg5
29	♜ad1	♞xc4
30	♛xc6	♝xc6
31	hxg5	

Or 31 e7 ♜e8 32 hxg5 ♞e3.

31...♞e3 32 ♜d3 ♜e8 33 ♜g1 ♜xe6 34 ♜d8+ ♜e8 35 ♜xe8+ ♝xe8 36 ♔f3 ♞xc2 37 ♔xf4 ♞d4 38 ♜h1+ ♔g8 39 ♔e5 c5 40 ♜f1 ♝g6 41 a4 ♞c6+ 42 ♔d6 ♞b4 43 ♔e7 c4 44 ♜f8+ ♔h7 45 ♜c8 c3 (based on 46 ♜xc3 ♞d5+) **46 ♔f8 ♞d5 47 ♜a8 ♞c7 48 ♜c8 ♞e6+ 49 ♔e7 ♞c5 White resigns**

Here comes the c-pawn (50 ♜f8 c2 51 ♜f1 ♞b3).

7
Miniature

Carlsen's emerging style made it much more likely he would play long games than short ones.

In 2005, he had 23 tournament games that lasted 60 moves or more, according to databases.

But he had only five decisive games of 25 moves or less.

He was embarrassed in one of them, **Pelletier – Carlsen**, Biel 2005 – **1 d4 ♘f6 2 c4 e6 3 ♘c3 ♗b4 4 ♕c2 d5 5 cxd5 c5!? 6 dxc5 ♘xd5? 7 ♗d2 ♗xc5 8 ♘xd5 ♕xd5 9 e4 ♕d4 10 0-0-0 ♘d7 11 ♗b5 0-0?? 12 ♗c3 ♕xf2 13 ♕xf2 ♗xf2 14 ♗xd7 ♗e3+ 15 ♔c2 ♖b8** and he **resigned.**

But he won the other four short games and this is the most impressive.

Carlsen – Predrag Nikolić
Wijk aan Zee 2005
French Defense,
Tarrasch Variation (C08)

1	e4	e6
2	d4	d5
3	♘d2	c5

Predrag Nikolić had been close to the world's elite in the 1990s and he outrated Magnus by more than 100 points when this was played. This was one of his favorite openings.

4	exd5	exd5
5	♘gf3	c4

David Bronstein demonstrated that if the pawn structure is not immediately challenged, Black stands well, e.g. 6 ♗e2?! ♗d6 7 0-0 ♘f6 8 ♖e1 0-0.

6	b3

6	...	cxb3

White's knight is temporarily entombed on b1 after 6...c3 7 ♘b1 ♗b4 8 a3 ♕a5. Computers go to computer lengths to prove that 9 ♗b5+ favors White.

But even simple developing moves like 9 &d3 will force Black to eventually disengage on the queenside.

7   axb3

In the 1990s, 7 &b5+ &d7 8 ♕e2+ was considered a positional refutation of 5...c4. That judgment was proven overoptimistic by Nikolić himself in games that went 8...♕e7 9 &xd7+ ♘xd7.

7   ...   &b4

This bishop move was a favorite of Viktor Korchnoi and sometimes scares players into stopping ...&c3 with 8 &b2. That's not a bad move but White can do better.

8   ♘e5

Korchnoi had shown that 8 &b5+ &d7 9 &xd7+ ♘xd7 10 0-0 ♘e7 (not 10...♘gf6 11 ♖e1+) 11 c4 0-0 is relatively harmless.

Carlsen's move is based on 8...&c3? being refuted by 9 ♕f3!, which threatens mate on f7 as well as ♕xc3.

8   ...   ♘e7

9   &d3

There is little in 9 &b5+ ♘bc6.

9   ...   ♘bc6

10   0-0

After the natural 10...0-0 11 ♘gf3 White would stand better following 11...&f5 12 ♘xc6 bxc6 13 &xf5 ♘xf5 14 ♕d3.

The same goes for 11...♘xe5 12 ♘xe5 &f5 (Not 12...&c3? because of 13 &xh7+ ♔xh7 14 ♕d3+.) 13 &xf5.

10   ...   &c3?

11   ♖a4

Book moves are over. We are plowing new ground.

Carlsen would have more than enough compensation for a pawn after 11...♘xe5 12 dxe5 &xe5? 13 ♕h5.

For instance, 13...&d6? 14 &b2. Or 13...&f6 14 ♖e1 h6 (14...g6?

15 ♕f3) 15 ♖f4! with the intent of ♖xf6 if Black castles.

Better, but far from equal, is 12...h6 or 12...♗d7 (13 ♖h4).

11	...	♗xd4
12	♘xc6	♘xc6
13	♗a3	♗e6
14	♘f3	

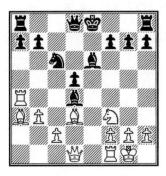

Play has been more or less forced since 11...♗xd4. It is time for Black to carefully evaluate his king's safety.

After 14...♗f6 15 ♖e1 ♗e7 he can castle.

But that's not safe enough after 16 ♕a1 0-0 17 ♗b2.

A neat continuation is 17...g6 18 ♗h8!, threatening ♕g7 mate.

Black would be lost after 18...f6 19 ♘g5! ♗d7 20 ♖h4! ♔xh8 21 ♖xh7+ ♔g8 22 ♗xg6.

Instead, 17...♗f6 18 ♗xf6 ♕xf6 averts disaster. But 19 ♕xf6 gxf6 20 ♖h4 would be a grim endgame to defend.

14 ... ♗b6?

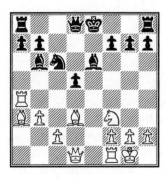

15 ♕a1!

The strength of this move goes well beyond the prospect of ♕xg7.

It enables White to increase pressure after 15...♕d7 with 16 ♖e1 0-0-0 17 ♗b2! ♖he8 18 ♘e5.

Then on 18...♘xe5 19 ♗xe5 f6 20 ♗g3 ♕c6 both 21 ♗xh7 and the Exchange sacrifice 21 ♖xa7 ♗xa7 22 ♕xa7 would hand White a big advantage.

Are we being too generous to him? Why not 17...f6, which stops both ♗xg7 and ♘e5 ?

The answer is: Black's king needs two minor pieces to defend it and 18 ♗d4! eliminates at least one of them.

White wins, for instance, after the sequence 18...♗xd4 19 ♘xd4 ♘xd4 20 ♕xd4 a6 21 ♗xa6! bxa6 22 ♖xa6.

15 ... ♕c7

16   b4!

White holds a major advantage after 16 ♕xg7 0-0-0 17 ♖e1 and a lesser one after 16 ♗b2 d4.

Carlsen is going for a knockout with b4-b5, which will be more powerful after 17 ♖e1.

16   ...   f6

Black would love to play 16...0-0 17 b5 ♘e7 18 ♘g5 ♗f5 so that 19 ♗xe7? ♕xe7 20 ♗xf5 ♕xg5.

Or 19 ♗xf5 ♘xf5 20 ♗xf8 ♖xf8 when he has weathered the storm at a minor material expense.

However, 18 ♖e1! makes ♘g5 as well as ♗b2 much stronger. Black cannot play ...f6 without losing the e6-bishop.

He would be losing after 18...♗c5 19 ♗b2, for example.

Also 18...♖fe8 19 ♗b2 ♗f5 20 ♖xe7 and ♗xf5.

But let's put Emanuel Lasker in Black's chair and ask him to defend. He might have tried 18...♖fe8 19 ♗b2 ♘f5!.

The reason is 20 g4 d4 and 21 gxf5? ♗d5! gives Black a compensating attack.

White gets back on track with 21 ♖xe6! and 22 gxf5.

17   ♖e1!

17   ...   ♔f7?

Lasker would have preferred 17...♘e5! 18 ♘xe5 fxe5.

Then 19 ♖xe5 0-0! again turns the tables because 20 ♖xe6 ♗xf2+ 21 ♔h1 ♕d7! forks the rooks.

But 19 b5! is much better.

White would hold the high cards after 19...♕f7 20 ♖xe5 0-0-0 21 ♔h1 ♖he8. But there's a lot of game left to play.

There is also 19...e4 which forces 20 ♗xe4! dxe4 21 ♖axe4 0-0-0 22 ♖xe6.

Then 22...♖d2 may be defensible (23 ♖e8+ ♖xe8 24 ♖xe8+ ♖d8 25 ♖xd8+ ♕xd8 26 ♕e1 ♕f6).

The computer suggestion of 23 ♖xb6 axb6 24 ♗c1 may be stronger.

18   b5   ♘a5

Black might last to move 25 after 18...♘d8 – but not much further, 19 ♘d4 g6 20 ♕c1! intending ♕h6.

19   ♕d1!

This may be the hardest move in the game for Carlsen to find.

He threatens 20 ♘g5+ but also the sparkling 20 ♖xe6! ♔xe6 21 ♗f5+!.

That would mate after 22 ♕xd5+.

A hidden point is that White would win a piece after 19...♕d7 20 ♗b4! ♘c4 21 ♗xc4 dxc4 22 ♕xd7+ and ♖e7+.

19   ...   ♖ae8

20   ♘g5+!   fxg5

21   ♕f3+   ♔g8

22   ♖xe6   Resigns

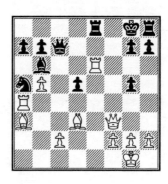

It really is lost: 22...♖xe6 23 ♕f8 mate or 22...♕f7 (and 22...♕d7) 23 ♗f5 and 24 ♖xe8+ ♕xe8 25 ♕xd5+.

8
More Strings

When Carlsen's great predecessors were young they had obvious strengths that provided many, if not most, of their points. Mikhail Tal, for example, won virtually all of his games at Zürich 1959 with sacrifices. There were similar tournaments that the pre-champion Anatoly Karpov won with positional play and pre-champ Garry Kasparov won with tactics.

Magnus used more strings on his violin. In a Gausdal tournament in 2005, he began some endgames with advantages and some with disadvantages. He won both. He outplayed opponents positionally and with mating combinations, as in:

Carlsen – Oystein Hole: 1 d4 d5 2 c4 c6 3 ♘c3 dxc4 4 e4 b5 5 a4 b4 6 ♘a2 ♘f6 7 e5 ♘d5 8 ♗xc4 e6 9 ♘f3 ♗e7 10 ♗d2 a5 11 ♘c1 ♗b7 12 ♘b3 ♘d7 13 0-0 ♖c8 14 ♖c1 0-0 15 ♕e2 c5 16 ♗b5 cxd4 17 ♖xc8 ♗xc8 18 ♘fxd4 ♘b8 19 ♕g4 ♔h8 20 ♖e1 ♕b6 21 ♗d3 ♗a6 22 ♗b1 ♘c6

23 ♗h6! ♖g8 24 ♗xh7! ♔xh7 25 ♗e3! ♖c8 26 ♘xe6! fxe6 27 ♕h3+ ♔g8 28 ♕xe6+ ♔f8 29 ♗xb6 ♘xb6 30 ♘xa5 ♖c7 31 ♘xc6! ♗c8 32 ♕b3 Resigns.

But his most exceptional game from the tournament was this:

Stellan Brynell – Carlsen
Gausdal Bygger'n Masters 2005
*Queen's Gambit Declined,
Semi-Slav Defense (D47)*

1	d4	d5
2	c4	c6
3	♘c3	♘f6
4	e3	e6

Carlsen also developed an early fondness for ...a6 and had played 4...a6 5 ♘f3 b5, with 6 b3 ♗g4 to follow.

5	♘f3	♘bd7
6	♗d3	dxc4
7	♗xc4	b5

He also had some experience in a super-sharp version of the Meran Variation, 8 ♗d3 ♗b7 9 e4 b4 with 10 ♘a4 c5 11 0-0 h6!?.

It scores much higher in tournament play than computers feel it deserves.

8	♗e2	♗b7

9	0-0

With the bishop on e2, 9 e4 b4 either costs White the e4-pawn or gets him into the crazy morass of 10 e5 bxc3 11 exf6 cxb2 12 fxg7 bxa1(♕) 13 gxh8(♕).

9	...	♗e7
10	e4	b4
11	e5!	bxc3
12	exf6	

But now 12...cxb2? 13 fxe7 bxa1(♕) 14 exd8(♕)+ ♖xd8 15 ♕b3! and 16 ♗b2.

12	...	♗xf6

He needs a quick ...c5. But 12...♘xf6 13 bxc3 c5 is a bit problematic after 14 ♕a4+.

13	bxc3	c5!

Now both 14 ♖b1 ♗e4 and 14 ♗a3 ♕a5 are excellent for Black.

14	dxc5	0-0

This move preserves tension longer than 14...♘xc5 15 ♗b5+ ♔f8 16 ♕xd8+ ♖xd8 (17 ♗a3 ♖c8).

White cannot keep the extra pawn at c5 or prove an advantage in any case.

15 &a3 &e7

16 ♕d4 ♕c7

If White wanted a quick draw, 17 c6 &xa3 18 cxb7 ♕xb7 was not the way to go because his c3-pawn remains weak (19 ♖fd1 ♖fd8 20 ♖ab1 ♕c7).

17 ♖ab1

This stops 17...♘xc5 in view of 18 &xc5 &xc5 19 ♖xb7 and 18...&xf3 19 &xe7.

17 ... &c6

18 ♕e3!

White, a grandmaster, is still looking for a tiny edge, such as 18...♖ab8 19 ♘d4! ♘xc5 20 ♘xc6 ♕xc6 21 ♖b4.

18 ... &xf3!

This leads to bishops of opposite color. But for once it is a good way of retaining winning chances and keeping losing chances low.

Instead, 18...&a4 would have been good enough for equality and could lead to a draw by repetition of moves (19 ♕e4 &c6 20 ♕e3 &a4).

19 &xf3 ♖ab8

Now 20 ♖bd1 prevents 20...&xc5?? 21 ♖xd7.

It also allows White to answer 20...♘xc5 with 21 ♖d4 followed by ♖c4 or ♖fd1.

Those wild and crazy computers point out (after 20...♘xc5 21 ♖d4) how 21...♘b3 could end up with a perpetual check, 22 ♖g4 &xa3 23 ♖xg7+ ♔xg7 24 ♕g5+.

20 c6 &xa3

21 cxd7 ♕xd7

22 c4

His c-pawn is no longer a weakness and many amateurs would come to the mistaken conclusion that White has the better chances.

He would have – if he could push his passed pawn, 22...&e7? 23 c5 ♖fc8? 24 c6!.

| 22 | ... | ♛e7 |
| 23 | ♖b5 | ♖xb5 |

Uniting White's queenside pawns was neither necessary nor harmful. They are easily blocked.

24	cxb5	♖d8
25	♖d1	♖xd1+
26	♗xd1	♛d6
27	♗f3	♗c5

| 28 | ♕e2 |

White seems lulled into thinking he will be shaking hands shortly.

That might have been the case after 28 ♕c3!. After 28...♕d4 29 ♕xd4 ♗xd4 a dead draw could come about in various ways, such as 30 ♔f1 ♔f8 31 ♔e2 ♔e7 32 ♗c6 ♔d6 33 f3 ♔c5 34 ♔d3.

Carlsen must keep queens on the board to have realistic winning chances.

28	...	♕d4!
29	g3	g6
30	♔g2	♔g7
31	♗c6	♗b6

Why doesn't White have the superior winning chances? After all, he has the famous "queenside pawn majority."

Yes, but there are two factors that matter much more. One is the difference in bishops.

White's bishop has no offensive power. While queens are on the board it can only defend.

Black's bishop, on the other hand, ties White's queen to the defense of f2.

That's not enough to give Black an edge. But it is enough to keep the game going.

| 32 | ♕f3 | f5! |

This is the second factor that favors Black. Carlsen has a *kingside* pawn majority.

They cannot create a useful passed pawn, as a queenside majority might.

But they can become a powerful offensive weapon if ...e5-e4 and ...f4-f3+ drives the White queen from the defense of f2.

A secondary plan is ...g5-g4 and ...h5-h4-h3+.

Note that if White offers a trade of queens, even by 33 ♕f4 ♕xf4 34 gxf4, Black could refuse, 33...♕b2!, for example.

33 ♕e2 e5

34 ♗b7 e4

35 ♗c6

White is still treading water. He does not have to worry about ...♕d3 at some point because a passed Black d-pawn is easily blockaded.

For example, 35...♕d3 36 ♕xd3 exd3 37 f4 ♔f6 38 ♗d5 followed by 39 ♗c4 d2 40 ♗b3 and ♔f3-e2.

35 ... ♔f6

36 ♗b7 ♔e5

37 ♗c6 g5

White's best bid for active defense was to play a2-a4 and ♕a2 at some point, to distract Black with a4-a5.

White may have looked at 38 a4 ♕xa4 39 ♕d2 and concluded 39...♕d4 40 ♕xd4+ ♔xd4 is a lost endgame.

But inserting 39 h4! gxh4 before 40 ♕d2! is a different story.

Then White threatens ♕d5+! in addition to ♕f4+.

He would hold after 40...♕d4 41 ♕f4+. For instance 41...♔e6 42 ♕h6+ ♔f6 43 ♗d7+! ♔e5 44 ♕f4+ and ♗xf5.

38 ♗b7

If White had appreciated Black's next move he might have tried 38 h3 h5 39 a4.

Then 39...♕xa4 40 ♕xh5 sentences his king to perpetual check.

Another point concerns 39...h4 40 gxh4 f4.

The threat of 41...f3+ looks fatal. But this is only a draw because of 41 ♕xe4+! ♕xe4+ 42 ♗xe4 ♔xe4 43 hxg5 ♔f5 44 h4.

However, there was a winning try, after 38 h3 h5 39 a4, in 39...g4.

For example, 40 hxg4 hxg4 41 ♕c2 e3.

White might have to go for 41 ♕a2 so that 41...e3? 43 ♕f7! opens the perpetual check door.

38 ... g4!

39 ♗c6 h5

Now 40 h3 gxh3+ (or 40 h4 gxh3+) turns out to be a losable bishop endgame because Black can create connected passed pawns.

For example, 41 ♔xh3 ♕xf2 42 ♕xf2 ♗xf2 and then 43 ♗e8 h4!.

Black wins after 44 ♔xh4 f4 or 44 gxh4 f4 45 h5 f3 46 h6? ♔f4 47 h7 ♗d4.

40 ♗e8?

The losing move. The drawing power of "bees of opps" is shown by 40 ♕c2! so that 40...h4 41 gxh4 f4 42 h3! liquidates pawns.

There is no win after 42...f3+ 43 ♔g3 e3 44 fxe3 ♕xe3 45 hxg4.

Or 42...g3 43 ♕xe4+! ♕xe4+ 44 ♗xe4 ♔xe4 45 fxg3.

40 ... h4!

41 ♕e1

White could resign after 41 gxh4 f4, e.g. 42 ♕c2 ♕a1 and ...f3+.

41 ... h3+

42 ♔g1 ♕b2

43 ♗c6 ♕xa2

The a2-pawn seemed irrelevant but there are scenarios in which the a7-pawn wins the game, as we'll see.

44 ♗b7 ♕b2

45 ♗c6 ♗d4

White has no good queen moves because 46 ♕f1 ♕c3 would threaten 47...a5 (48 bxa6 ♕xc6).

Also lost is 47 ♗b7 ♕f3 48 ♗c8 e3 and 48 ♗c6 f4 49 gxf4+ ♔d6 and ...g3).

46 ♗e8

To make Black work harder he needed to keep the bishop on the long diagonal.

Why? So that ...e3/fxe3 does not allow ...♕g2 mate.

46 ...   e3!

47 ♔f1

Or 47 ♗c6 e2 and a winning trade of queens (...♕a1).

47 ...   ♔f6

Black threatens 48...♗c3 now that the reply ♕xe3 is not check. For example, 48 ♗c6 ♗c3! 49 ♕e2 ♕c1+ and mates, or 49 ♕xe3 ♕b1+ 50 ♔e2 ♕c2+ 51 ♔f1 ♕d1+ and mates.

48	♕e2	♕c1+
49	♕e1	♕xe1+
50	♔xe1	exf2+
51	♔f1	f4
52	gxf4	♔f5
53	♗f7	♔xf4

White resigns

Among the winning plans is ...♔g5-h4 followed by ...♗e5xh2. White will play ♔xf2 but then ...g3-g2 must win.

9
Equanimity

It was inevitable when he began a steady diet of facing grandmasters that Carlsen would be surprised by his opponents' opening preparation. What mattered then was not so much the strength of the new move. After all, it was not likely to be a forced win.

Rather, it was how he reacted to the surprise. Even when Bobby Fischer was a world championship challenger, a popular Soviet view was that he reacted badly. He got nervous, anxious and tactically sloppy. (There is ample evidence to argue that this is true – and ample evidence that it is false.)

In the following game, Carlsen responds to a TN at the tenth move with equanimity. He realized he was going to lose the Exchange no matter what he did. He chose the way that made finding the best moves easier for him than for his opponent.

Baadur Jobava – Carlsen
Skanderborg 2005
Queen's Indian Defense (E12)

1	c4	♘f6
2	d4	e6
3	♘f3	b6
4	♗g5	h6
5	♗h4	♗e7
6	♘c3	c5

This is a rare variation which can be boring and balanced, after 7 e3 ♗b7.

Or it can be exciting and unbalanced after 7 e4.

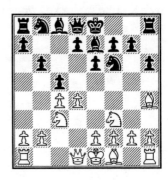

7 e4

The positionally desirable 7 d5 runs into 7...♘xd5! and 8 ♘xd5 ♗xh4 9 ♘xh4 exd5 10 ♕xd5 ♘c6.

Then Black's active pieces offset his backward d-pawn (11 g3 0-0 and ...♖e8).

7	...	cxd4
8	♘xd4	d6
9	♘db5!	

Black played 8...d6 to avoid 9 e5 but this renews the threat – 10 e5! dxe5 11 ♗xf6 gxf6 12 ♕f3 costs at least a piece.

9	...	a6

10 e5!

Jobava is improving on a game he lost, to Vasily Ivanchuk, that went 10 ♗xf6 ♗xf6!? 11 ♘xd6+ ♔e7 12 ♘xc8+ ♕xc8 and gave Black compensation for a pawn.

10	...	dxe5

Carlsen didn't like 10...axb5 11 exf6 gxf6 12 ♘xb5.

11 ♗xf6

White needed to insert this move because 11 ♕f3? allows 11...e4! and turns out badly after 12 ♘xe4 axb5! 13 ♘xf6+ gxf6! 14 ♕xa8 ♗b4+.

11	...	♗xf6

After 11...gxf6 12 ♕f3! there is no support for 12...e4 White wins material after 12...axb5 13 ♕xa8.

12	♕f3	axb5
13	♕xa8	

Jobava's opening preparation led him to expect an advantage after 13...♘d7 14 ♘xb5 0-0 15 0-0-0!.

13	...	b4!

This makes it more of a fight.

When computers begin to look at the position they see a White advantage after 14 ♕xb8 bxc3 15 bxc3 e4 16 ♖c1 ♗d7. But:

(a) The endgame, 17 ♕xd8+ ♔xd8 and ...♔c7/...♖a8, is balanced,

(b) 17 ♕b7 ♗a4 threatens 18...♗xc3+ (19 ♖xc3 ♕d1 mate), and

(c) 17 ♕a7 e3 18 fxe3 ♗c6 is the kind of position in which most humans would prefer Black.

14 ♘e4

Carlsen was more afraid of 14 ♕a4+ ♗d7 15 ♕xb4. But he underestimated 15...♗e7 followed by planting a knight on d4.

14 ...   ♗d7

15 ♘xf6+ gxf6

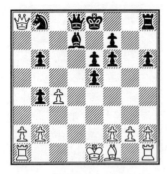

Carlsen wins this game because of evaluation, not calculation. He understood, much better than his opponent, the compensation he would have in an endgame.

He expected 16 0-0-0 ♘c6 17 ♕xd8+ ♔xd8 and eventually ...♘d4.

A good alternative is 16...♕c7 17 ♕f3 (otherwise 17...♗c6!) ♔e7.

16 c5?

Computers like 16 a3 and they find a White advantage after 16...bxa3 17 ♕xa3 or 17 b4 and 17...b3 18 ♖d1. That may have been his last chance for the upper hand.

16 ...   bxc5

17 ♕a7

Jobava will either regain his pawn or subject Carlsen to lasting pressure (17...0-0 18 ♖d1! ♕c8 19 ♗e2 followed by doubling rooks on the d-file).

17 ...   ♘c6

18 ♕xc5 ♘d4

19 0-0-0

This seems natural but Carlsen considered three moves, 19 ♖c1, 19 ♖d1 and 19 ♗d3, superior to this.

He would have plenty of resources in any case, as 19 ♗d3 ♖g8! 20 0-0-0 b3! shows.

The same goes for 19 ♖c1 b3! and 19 ♖d1 ♕a8!.

19 ...   ♕e7!

20 ♕xe7+ ♔xe7

Carlsen will have full compensation for the Exchange after ...♗c6, ...♖g8 and ...f5.

A careful way of meeting that is 21 ♖d2 ♗c6 22 f3. But most of the tactical opportunities lie with Black.

For example, 22...♖d8 23 ♗d3 f5 24 ♖e1 stops ...e4 but allows 24...♗xf3! 25 gxf3? ♘xf3 when the Black pawns are stronger than the bishop following 26 ♖ed1 ♘xd2.

21	♔b1?	♗c6
22	f3	

Jobava has no way to easily protect g2 and develop his kingside pieces. He offered a draw. Carlsen refused.

| 22 | ... | ♖g8! |

He could have played 22...♘xf3 because again his pawns count more than the bishop after 23 gxf3 ♗xf3 24 ♗d3 ♗xh1 25 ♖xh1 f5.

But when refusing a draw, the best reply on the board is usually to build pressure, not simplify.

| 23 | ♖c1 | |

Black wins after 23 ♖d2? ♘xf3 24 gxf3 ♗xf3.

23	...	f5
24	♖c4	♖b8
25	b3	f4
26	♔b2	f5!

There is no good defense to ...e4 once it is prepared by ...♗d5 and ...♔d6.

27	h4	♔d6
28	h5	♗d5
29	♖c1	e4

30	fxe4	fxe4
31	♖h4	

| 31 | ... | ♔e5 |

This is much better than 31...e5? 32 ♖g4 when White has counterplay with ♖g6+ or ♖g7.

32	♖g4	e3
33	♖g6	♗e4
34	♖xh6	♖g8

Yes, 34...e2 35 ♗xe2 ♘xe2 would have won a piece. Then 36 ♖c5+ ♔d4? 37 ♖xe6 ♔xc5? 38 ♖xe4 makes it a game again. But 36...♔d6! would have been easy.

35	♖c5+	♔d6
36	♖c4	♔d5
37	♔c1	e2
38	♖xd4+	♔xd4
39	♗xe2	♖xg2
40	♗d1	♖xa2

White resigns

It is mate after 41 ♖xe6 ♔c3!.

10
Textbook

Carlsen's crush of Alexander Beliavsky, formerly a world-class GM, was the early sensation of his third Wijk aan Zee invitational. But the game was virtually over by move 18 and required few moves that a mere master could not find:

1 e4 e5 2 ♘f3 ♘c6 3 ♗b5 a6 4 ♗a4 ♘f6 5 0-0 b5 6 ♗b3 ♗b7 7 d3 ♗c5 8 ♘c3 d6 9 a4 ♘a5 10 ♗a2 b4 11 ♘e2 ♗c8 12 c3 bxc3 13 bxc3 ♗b6 14 ♘g3 ♗e6 15 d4 ♗xa2 16 ♖xa2 0-0

17 ♗g5! exd4? 18 ♘h5! dxc3 19 ♘h4! ♔h8 20 ♘f5 Resigns (in view of 21 ♘fxg7 and ♗xf6).

More impressive was the game he played two rounds later. If the Beliavsky miniature could have come from an openings manual, the following would fit in nicely in an endgame textbook.

Carlsen – Giovanni Vescovi
Wijk aan Zee 2006
Sicilian Defense,
Taimanov Variation (B46)

1	e4	c5
2	♘f3	e6
3	d4	cxd4
4	♘xd4	♘c6
5	♘c3	a6
6	♘xc6	

Carlsen explained this move by saying it was "time to change" from 6 ♗e3. He had gotten good positions with 6 ♗e3 after 6...♘ge7 but less so following 6...♘f6.

| 6 | ... | bxc6 |

68

7	♗d3	d5
8	0-0	♘f6
9	♖e1	

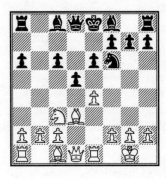

White usually intends e4-e5. Black can avoid that by 9...dxe4? 10 ♘xe4 ♘xe4 11 ♗xe4 ♕xd1 12 ♖xd1 at the expense of potentially weak pawns at a6 and c6.

9	...	♗e7

This makes ♕g4 stronger and that is why 9...♗b7 10 e5 ♘d7 is often preferred.

10	e5	♘d7
11	♕g4	

A more positional struggle arises after 11 ♘a4 and 12 c4 and then, for example, 11...c5 12 c4 d4 13 ♕g4.

11	...	g6

In previous games Black tried 11...♔f8 or even 11...♗f8 without much success.

The pawn move is more aggressive and encourages

complications such as 12 ♗h6 ♖b8 13 b3 ♖b4.

12	♘a4

Black's long-term difficulties are illustrated by 12...0-0? 13 ♗h6 ♖e8 14 c4 and then 14...♕c7 15 ♕g3 ♗b7.

Then he has nearly completed his development. But he lacks a plan, whereas White has a strong one. He can play h2-h4-h5 followed by hxg6 and, if allowed, a bishop sacrifice on g6.

Again Black can avoid immediate problems by liquidating, 15...dxc4 16 ♗xc4 ♘b6 17 ♘xb6 ♕xb6 18 b3 a5 and ...a4 or ...♗a6.

But then he has added a problem c-pawn to the mix and would be slightly worse after 19 h4 ♗a6 20 ♖ac1.

12	...	♕a5

Black does better keeping his king in the center, even after 12...h5.

Then 13 ♕g3 seems to make ♗xg6 a valid sacrifice.

But that allows an attack on the knight and rook with 13...♕a5!.

13	♗h6	♕b4!
14	♕xb4	♗xb4

69

15 c3

Vescovi thought for some time before choosing a retreat for his bishop.

If 15...♗e7, White can threaten to dominate the c-file with 16 c4.

That is dangerous for Black because he cannot easily connect rooks with ...♔e7 as in the game.

He would be worse, for example, after 16...♘c5 17 ♘xc5 ♗xc5 18 ♖ac1.

Or after 16...♗b7 17 ♖ac1 ♖c8 18 cxd5 exd5 19 ♗e2 and ♗g4 – and much worse after 18...cxd5?? 19 ♖xc8+ ♗xc8 20 ♖c1.

15 ... ♗f8

In principle, a trade of Black's better bishop should help White. The other option was 15...♗a5.

Carlsen had planned to meet it with 16 b4 ♗c7 17 f4 but knew that 17...a5! is the principled response.

He felt 18 b5 ♘b6 19 ♘xb6 ♗xb6+ 20 ♔f1 was good for him.

That would be hard to prove after 20...♗d7 21 ♖ab1 ♖b8.

For example, 22 c4 dxc4 23 ♗xc4 cxb5 24 ♗xb5 ♗xb5 25 ♖xb5 ♔d7!.

16 ♗xf8 ♖xf8

17 c4 ♔e7

Carlsen will control the c-file for a while but a timely ...a5 would eliminate the potential target at a6.

18 cxd5 cxd5

19 ♖ac1 ♖a7

There was no threat of 20 ♖c7 because of 20...♔d8 (21 ♖ec1? ♘xe5).

Therefore Black could have played the more useful 19...♖b8 or 19...a5/...♗a6.

20 b4!

Vescovi may have wrongly expected 20 f4. It's a useful move but not vigorous enough to prove a serious advantage after 20...a5.

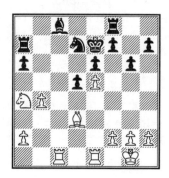

20 ... ♗b7

Here is a recurring phenomenon in Carlsen games. Neither of Black's last two moves deserves a question mark. But together they can share one.

The reason is that once Magnus has achieved two key pawn moves, b2-b4 and f2-f4, Black's chances for counterplay plummet.

He could have tried 20...h6 so that 21 f4 g5 gets his pawns off light squares and allows better defensive chances after 22 f5 ♔d8 and ...♖c7.

Black would be back in the game after 22 g3 ♗b7 23 ♔f2? f6!.

Better is 23 ♖c7 ♔d8 24 ♖ec1 with a winning threat of 25 b5!.

White would be close to winning after 24...gxf4 25 gxf4 ♖g8+ 26 ♔f2 ♖g4 27 ♔f3.

21 f4!   ♖c8

The time for ...a5 is past because White will push to b5 and hold a powerful passed b-pawn.

22 ♖xc8   ♗xc8

23 ♖c1   ♔d8

It cost Black a tempo to get rooks off the board and to keep a rook off c7.

That sounds cheap because he has time to offer another rook swap with ...♖c7.

24 ♔f2

But White can add to his long-term advantages by playing ♔e3-d4.

For instance, 24...g5 25 g3 h6 26 ♔e3.

His superiority becomes manifest after 26...♖c7 27 ♖xc7 ♔xc7 28 ♔d4 or 28 ♗e2 (and ♗h5).

24   ...   ♘b8

Carlsen was more concerned with 24...f6!.

He intended 25 exf6 ♘xf6 26 ♔e3 ♘g4+ 27 ♔d4.

He would win after 27...♘xh2? 28 ♘b6 ♗b7 29 ♖h1.

Or after 28...♗d7 29 ♘xd7 ♔xd7 30 ♖h1 and 29...♖xd7 30 ♗xa6.

But 27...♖f7 (instead of 27...♘xh2?) gets messy after 28 g3 g5.

25 ♘c5   ♖c7

26 ♖c2   ♘d7

71

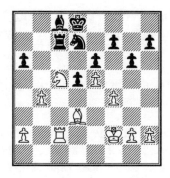

Carlsen is reaching positions that require visualization more than calculation. There is a difference.

After 27 ♔e3 ♘xc5 28 ♖xc5 ♖xc5 29 bxc5 he could not calculate much further with certainty.

But he could visualize that the c5-pawn keeps his king from penetrating beyond d4. That means a likely dead end.

Analysis confirms that even after a trade of bishops, such as 29...♔c7 30 ♔d4 a5 31 ♗b5 ♗d7 32 ♗xd7 ♔xd7, it is a dead draw.

27 ♘b3!

But what about 27 ♘xd7 ? The c5-square would be vacant after 27...♖xc2+ 28 ♗xc2 ♗xd7 29 ♔e3.

Black is close to a forced loss following 29...♔c7 30 ♔d4 ♗e8? 31 ♔c5.

But to play 27 ♘xd7 with confidence Carlsen might have to visualize correctly the position after 30...♔b6! 31 a4 h5.

Is that a win? Yes, after 32 a5+ ♔b5 33 ♔c3 and ♔b3/♗d3+.

But that is hard to prove when your clock is ticking.

27 ...   ♖xc2+

28 ♗xc2   ♘b8

The pragmatic endgame player knows that White's knight will be better than Black's for some time – and that there will almost certainly be a later opportunity to swap knights and get the same kind of position as in the 27 ♘xd7! analysis.

29 ♘d4

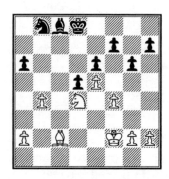

It is also possible to visualize, rather than calculate move by move, that Black would make matters worse by trying for ...f6.

Then White can allow ...fxe5/fxe5 and look for an opportunity to raid the kingside with the advance ♔f4-g5.

29 ...   ♗d7

30 g4!

72

Now 30...♘c6 31 ♘xc6+ ♗xc6 32 ♔e3 ♔c7 33 ♔d4 ♔b6 34 a4 is similar to the position that could have arisen after 27 ♘xd7!.

White's winning chances have improved because of g2-g4.

For example, after 34...a5 35 b5 ♗d7? White cannot force ♔c5. But he can win on the kingside with 36 h4!.

His plan is to advance the pawn to h6 and crash through with f4-f5.

For example, 36...♗c8 37 h5 ♗d7 38 h6 and now 38...♗c8 39 f5 threatens 40 fxg6 fxg6 41 ♗xg6! hxg6 42 h7.

No better is 38...♗e8 39 f5 because Black is in zugzwang (39...♔b7 40 ♔c5 ♔c7 41 b6+ and ♔d6).

30	...	h6
31	♔e3	♔c7
32	a4	♔b6
33	a5+	♔b7

Black's king is now confined to a few squares because of the vulnerability of the a6-pawn.

34	♗d3	♗a4
35	♗e2	♘d7
36	h4!	

This is near-zugzwang: Every Black move but one dooms him to a quick loss.

For example, 36...♔c7? 37 ♗xa6 or 36...♘f8 37 f5.

The one move that is not immediately fatal is 36...♔a7!.

But Carlsen would win with 37 h5! gxh5 38 gxh5 and then 38...♔b7 39 f5!.

He has enough pawns left after 39...♘xe5 40 fxe6 fxe6 41 ♘xe6 and ♘c5+ or ♔d4.

It is easier after 38...♘b8 39 f5 exf5 40 ♘xf5 and ♘xh6.

Or 39...♗d7 40 fxe6 fxe6 41 ♗g4.

36	...	♘b8
37	f5	gxf5
38	gxf5	♗d7
39	♗h5!	**Resigns**

How many difficult decisions did Carlsen have to make? At least eight. That is double the number in the Beliavsky crush and that is why it is a greater achievement.

73

11
Coffeehouse Carlsen

Magnus and his trainer Simen Agdestein remained close in rating until 2006. They had tied with one another in their national championship the previous year, when Agdestein won a rapid playoff.

They tied for the Norwegian title again in 2006 and drew the first two games of a playoff. Then they played two rapid games. This was the first of those and it shows Magnus at his freewheeling, coffeehouse best.

Simen Agdestein – Carlsen
Norwegian Championship
playoff, Oslo 2006
English Opening,
Four Knights Variation (A28)

1	c4	♘f6
2	♘c3	e5
3	♘f3	♘c6
4	e3	♗b4
5	♘d5	♗e7

This is reminiscent of 1 c4 e5 2 ♘c3 ♗b4 3 ♘d5 ♗e7!?, which had gained respectability more than a decade previously.

In this version, Black's lead in development would offset White's two bishops after 6 ♘xe7 ♕xe7 and ...d5.

6	**a3**	**e4!**

This is more daring than it seems. It is a virtual gambit because the e4-pawn is soon untenable.

7	♘g1	0-0
8	♕c2	♖e8
9	♘e2	

The game has transposed into a rare position that had arisen previously from a different move order, 5...e4 6 ♘g1 0-0 7 a3 ♗e7 8 ♕c2 ♖e8 9 ♘e2.

White has an unstoppable plan to win the e4-pawn with ♘g3 or ♘ec3.

In a previous game, 9...♘xd5 10 cxd5 ♘e5 was played. Black has some, but not enough compensation after 11 ♕xe4! ♗f6 12 ♕c2.

It is possible Carlsen knew all this. But databases indicate this was the first time he faced 4 e3 in a serious game.

9 ... ♘e5!

He would not have to give up a pawn after 10 ♘ec3? ♘xd5 and 11...f5.

10 ♘xf6+?

After this, Magnus can play ...d5 as an additional gambit – a sound one.

More testing is 10 ♘g3! because 10...♘xd5 11 cxd5 f5? is not available (12 ♘xf5).

Instead, 11...♘d3+! 12 ♗xd3 exd3 13 ♕xd3 and then 13...a5 and ...b6/...♗a6 was available.

In such a position the better tactician will usually prevail. For example, 14 0-0 b6 15 ♕c2 ♗a6 16 ♖d1 c6! 17 dxc6 ♖c8 and ...♖xc6.

10 ... ♗xf6

11 ♘c3

This is much better than 11 ♕xe4 d5!.

Then 12 ♕xd5? ♘d3+ is bad and 12 cxd5 ♗g4 sets the table for ...♘f3+.

Safest is 13 ♕c2. But White would find it hard to castle without giving back the second extra pawn after 13...♕xd5 14 ♘c3 ♕d7.

11 ... d5!

This looks like Coffeehouse Carlsen. But otherwise the e-pawn was lost with little to show for it.

12 cxd5

He would have plenty to show for it after 12 ♘xd5 ♗h4! followed by ...c6 or ...♕g5.

For instance, 13 b3 c6 14 ♘f4 ♗g5 or 13 ♗e2 ♗g4 14 ♗xg4 ♘d3+.

12 ... ♗f5

13 ♘xe4

This is extremely risky but otherwise Magnus could swap down into a bishops-of-opposite-color middlegame in which White is woefully weak on light squares.

For example, 13 ♗e2 ♘d3+ 14 ♗xd3 exd3 15 ♕b3 ♗xc3!.

Then 16 bxc3 ♕g5 so that 17 0-0? ♗h3 or 17 ♗b2 ♗e4 18 c4? ♕g4.

No better is 16 dxc3 ♕g5 17 ♗d2 ♕xg2.

13 ... ♗h4!

14 ♕a4

If this game had gone 14 ♗e2 ♕xd5 15 d3, would Carlsen have settled for the favorable endgame of 15...♖ad8 16 0-0 ♘xd3 17 ♗xd3 ♕xd3 18 ♕xd3 ?

Or would he have gone for the kill with 15...c5 and ...c4 ?

Both are strong. But the latter is more like Magnus, at least at age 16.

14 ... ♕xd5

15 ♘c3 ♕d8

16 d4

Agdestein abandoned hopes of kingside castling some time ago.

Staying in the center a few moves more – with 16 ♗e2 ♘d3+ 17 ♗xd3 ♗xd3 or

16 g3 ♘f3+ (17 ♔e2? ♘d4+ or 17 ♔d1 ♗f6) – was hardly palatable.

16 ... ♘d3+

17 ♗xd3 ♗xd3

18 ♗d2

White hurries towards 0-0-0. He would not last long after 18 g3 ♗f6 (threat of ...♗xd4) 19 ♘e2? ♕d5.

18 ... b5!

19 ♕b3

It is legal to castle after 19 ♘xb5 ♕d5 20 ♘c3 ♕xg2.

But 21 0-0-0 ♗xf2 is lost.

Also good would be 19...♕g5! 20 ♘moves ♖xe3+!.

19 ... ♕xd4?

The only real mistake Carlsen made in the game was allowing White to escape into a bad endgame with 20 ♕d5!.

He could have averted that with 19...♗c4! and 20...♕xd4.

20 0-0-0 ♕c5

21 g3 ♗c4!

22	♕c2	♗f6

23	♔b1

The two bishops eventually make themselves felt after 23 ♘b1 ♕h5 24 ♗c3 ♗e2 25 ♖de1 ♗f3 26 ♖hg1 ♗e4, for example.

23	...	a5

24	f3	♖ad8

The threat of ...♗d3 or ...b4 wins quickly. For example, 25 ♗c1 b4 26 ♘e4 ♗a2+! and ...♕xc2.

25	♔a1	b4

26	♘e4	♖xe4!

27	♕xe4	♗d3

This allows 28 ♗xb4!. Then Black needs 28...♕c2 29 ♖d2 ♕xd2 to win. Simpler was 27...bxa3!.

28	♖c1	♕xc1+

29	♗xc1	♗xe4

30	fxe4	bxa3

White is doomed to a lost pawn endgame after 31 ♔a2 axb2 32 ♗xb2 ♖d2 33 ♖b1. Worse is 31 ♔b1 axb2 32 ♗xb2 ♖b8.

31	h4	h5

32	♖f1	♗e5

33	♖g1	f6

White resigns

The final playoff game was even more one-sided: After **1 e4 e5 2 ♘f3 ♘c6 3 ♗b5 g6 4 c3 a6 5 ♗a4 d6 6 d4 ♗d7 7 dxe5** Agdestein played **7...b5??** and was lost after **8 ♗b3 dxe5 9 ♕d5! ♕f6 10 ♘xe5! ♘xe5 11 ♕xa8+**. This made Carlsen his country's champion.

12
Payoff

The training and homework Magnus underwent in these years paid dividends more than a decade later. Daniil Dubov, a young grandmaster who served as one of his seconds in the world championship match of 2018, said Carlsen studied much harder in those early days. "He told me he worked fanatically until 15 or 16, which is why he can afford to take it easy now," Dubov said.

What he learned in his prime study time began to show up when he seemed to win games without effort:

Carlsen – John Nunn
Youth vs. Experience match,
Amsterdam 2006
*Sicilian Defense,
Najdorf Variation (B90)*

1	e4	c5
2	♘f3	d6
3	d4	♘f6
4	♘c3	cxd4
5	♘xd4	a6
6	♗e3	

This was his early favorite way of dealing with the Najdorf. But

he had also studied – and played – 6 g3, 6 ♗g5, 6 ♗e2, 6 h3 and even 6 ♗d3.

6	...	e5
7	♘f3	

Whether the knight goes to f3 or to b3 it may have an ultimate goal of reaching d5.

Two months earlier at the Turin Olympiad, Carlsen's game with Julio Granda Zúñiga varied with 7 ♘b3 ♗e7 8 ♗e2 0-0 9 0-0 ♘bd7 10 a4 b6 11 f3 ♗b7 12 ♖f2 ♕c7 13 ♗f1 ♖fb8 and now 14 ♘c1! ♘c5 15 ♖d2 ♘e6 16 ♘1a2!.

The idea is ♘b4-d5 Black defended well with 16...♘d4 because 17 ♗xd4 exd4 18 ♖xd4 d5! and ...♗c5 is good for him.

But after 17 ♘b4 ♖d8 18 ♔h1 a5 19 ♘d3 ♘e6 20 ♘f2 he was only slightly worse when he blundered, 20...♘d7? 21 ♘b5 ♕b8 22 ♘xd6 resigns.

7	...	♗e7

8	♗c4

A major reason why some players prefer 7 ♘f3 is that White can control d5 with a bishop this way and retreat it to b3 when attacked.

8	...	0-0
9	0-0	♗e6

10	♗b3

A generation or two before, doubling pawns with ♗xe6 was considered a positional error in this and similar (i.e. Ruy Lopez and Giuoco Piano) positions. Then White loses his chance to occupy d5 or f5 with knights and has few prospects of attacking the e6-pawn.

That way of thinking has changed. Some masters have tried 10 ♗xe6 fxe6 11 ♘a4 and been rewarded by 11...♘bd7? 12 ♘g5! and ♘xe6.

But 11...♘g4 has proven an adequate response.

10	...	♘c6

11	♕e2

One of the lessons Carlsen was learning about this pawn structure is illustrated by a game he played against Vishy Anand a year later,

After 11 ♗g5 ♘d7 12 ♗xe7 ♕xe7 13 ♘d5 ♕d8 his knight looks great.

But he is approaching a strategic dead end, a point when he can't improve his position.

An ironic point about such positions is that White cannot attack the weakest Black pawn, at d6, because his knight is in the way.

11	...	♘a5
12	♖fd1	♘xb3
13	cxb3!?	

Carlsen's studying shows. This relatively new idea enables him to use the c-file and it frees c2 for a knight maneuver.

After the routine 13 axb3 ♕c7! and ...♖fc8 the c-pawn is a potential target for Black.

13 ... ♛e8

Carlsen threatened 14 ♘xe5 dxe5?? 15 ♖xd8 so Black's queen should move.

If 13...♛c7? 14 ♖ac1 the queen is misplaced.

Simplest is 13...♛a5 so that 14 ♗g5 and 15 ♗xf6 ♗xf6 16 ♖xd6? ♗xb3!.

On a5 the queen also prevents the knight maneuver to b4 that occurs in the game. But chances remain balanced after 13...♛e8.

14 ♘e1

A standard *priyome*, or positional plan, is ♗g5 followed by ♗xf6.

But with his queen on e8 Black can meet 14 ♗g5 with 14...♘h5. A bishop trade would allow him to later play ...♘f4.

14 ... h6

Three months later Sergey Karjakin chose 14...♘g4 against Magnus and obtained two bishops against two knights, 15 ♘c2 f5 16 f3 ♘xe3 17 ♘xe3.

He secured a balanced endgame after 17...fxe4 18 ♘xe4 ♖d8 19 ♘d5 ♛f7 20 ♛d3 ♗xd5 21 ♛xd5 ♛xd5 22 ♖xd5 ♚f7 23 ♖ad1 ♚e6.

When Carlsen pushed b3-b4-b5 too quickly, Karjakin seized the c-file and eventually won.

15 ♘c2 ♛d7

16 ♘b4 ♖fc8

17 f3

Carlsen can carry out a standard plan now with 17 ♘bd5 ♘xd5 18 ♘xd5. But 18...♗d8 is a solid position.

White cannot force matters with 19 ♗b6? ♗xd5 because 20 ♗xd8 ♗xb3 drops a pawn.

And 19 ♘b6 ♗xb6 20 ♗xb6 ♛b5! creates tactical problems for his queenside pawns (21 ♛xb5 axb5 22 ♖xd6? ♖xa2! 23 ♖xa2 ♖c1+).

17 ... ♗d8!

18 ♖d3

Now his plan is ♖ad1 and ♖xd6.

Black would not be lost if he had to defend the d6-pawn with ...♞e8 but his position is very passive.

18 ... a5

The other active defense was 18...♝a5 so that 19 ♞bd5 ♞xd5 20 ♞xd5 ♝d8, again with a kind of strategic dead end for White.

19 ♞bd5 ♞xd5

20 ♞xd5 a4

Undoubling the b-pawns makes more endgames losable. Sounder is 20...b5.

21 bxa4 ♖xa4

Nevertheless, Black's position remains solid. He would have greater chances for counterplay on the c-file after 21...♛xa4 and ...♖c6.

For example, 22 b3 ♛a3 23 ♛d1 ♝xd5 24 ♖xd5 ♖c6 and ...♖ac8.

22 b3 ♖a6

23 ♖ad1

Ossip Bernstein, a world-class player a century ago, made an ironic observation:

When a defender loses a weak pawn his position may seem to improve.

That could be true here if Black played 23...♚h8 and the game continued 24 ♞b4 ♖aa8 25 ♖xd6 and then 25...♛e7.

Then White has to find a way to meet 26...♝c7 – and 26 ♛b5? ♖a5 27 ♛e2 ♝c7 is not the answer.

His pieces would also remain uncoordinated after 26 ♝b6 ♝xb6+ 27 ♖xb6 ♖d8! and a draw is likely.

23 ... ♖a5?

It was Black's turn to move and that proved to be a psychological liability.

Active moves like 23...♖ca8 and 23...♖ac6 make 24 ♞b4! stronger.

A good alternative is 20...f5 with a threat of 21...fxe4 22 fxe4 ♝g4.

After 21 exf5 ♝xf5 22 ♖3d2 Black can play 23...♖ac6 safely because of 24 ♞b4 ♖c1.

24 ♞b6! ♝xb6

81

25 &xb6 &a6

26 &xd6 &e7

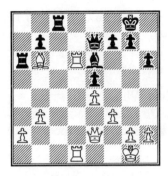

Once again Carlsen has a good bishops-of-opposite-color middlegame.

He would only be able to make slow progress after 27 &d8+ &xd8 28 &xd8 &c5+ 29 &f1!.

And it can turn out quite badly after 29 &h1 &a3 30 &d2 &xb3! (31 axb3? &c1+ 32 &d1 &a1! and wins). Carlsen finds a better way.

27 &b2! &g5

28 a4 h5

29 a5 h4

30 b4

With his b-pawn safe White is ready for 31 &d8+ &xd8 32 &xd8+ &h7 33 &d2! &xd2 34 &xd2 &a8 (otherwise 35 &d8!).

He can reach a technical rook-endgame win after 35 &c7 f6 36 &d6 &c8 (36...&c4 37 &b6) 37 &xe6 &xc7.

30 ... &aa8

31 &d2!

Now 31...&f6 32 &d8! drops a pawn.

On 31...&g6 White can forget about kingside counterplay with 32 h3 and then carry out a plan to push a passed b-pawn:

He could play b4-b5, &e3 and &b1 followed by a5-a6. When Black responds ...bxa6, White continues b5-b6-b7.

31 ... &xd2

32 &1xd2 &c4

33 &c5 &c8

34 &b6!

If Carlsen wins the b7-pawn, he could finish off with routine moves.

34 ... &c7

35 &f2 &h7?

Black's best chance for survival lies in tactical mistakes by White. There were better chances of that after 35...&c1.

For example, 36 &d6 &d7 37 &e2? &c4 38 &e1 &c2+.

36	&d6	&d7
37	&e3	f6
38	&xe5!	fxe5
39	&xe6	&xd2
40	&xd2	&xb4

41 &xe5!

Black's next-to-last hope was 41 &b6? &a4! with real drawing chances after 42 &xb7 &xa5 and ...&a2+.

| 41 | ... | &b2+ |

The last hope was 42 &e3? &xg2 43 &b5 &xh2 44 &xb7 h3

with technical difficulties to overcome. Or 43 &h5+ &g8 44 &xh4 &g5.

42	&c3!	&xg2
43	&h5+	&g6
44	&xh4	&a2
45	&b4	**Resigns**

"When was the first time that you thought you might become the best chess player in the world?" Carlsen was asked by *Esquire* magazine.

"When I was 16 or 17," he replied. "At that point, it was about taking the step from being a participant in the best tournaments in the world to being one of the guys who could win them, who could be pressing in games rather than defending."

"I felt the best players were not much better than me, and I had the chance to surpass them all."

13
Going Pro

When the ranks of 180 of the world's grandmasters in 1983 were analyzed by the 'Paris Express,' just 50 were identified as professional players. Another 25 were chess journalists. The rest had a variety of day jobs.

Chess professionalism changed radically in the next two decades and by 2007 Magnus was virtually a pro. He played 200 games and made a $250,000 profit after expenses that year, his family said.

But he still lacked some of the qualities of a professional. He could play whole sections of a game brilliantly, only to make a costly slip that undid his work.

A glaring example was his game with **Lajos Portisch** (Black) from Gausdal 2007. It began with a new gambit: **1 d4 d5 2 c4 e6 3 ♘f3 ♘f6 4 g3 dxc4 5 ♗g2 ♘bd7 6 0-0 ♖b8 7 ♕c2 b5 8 b3! cxb3 9 axb3 a6 10 ♘e5! ♘xe5 11 dxe5 ♘d5 12 ♖d1 ♕e7** (12...♕d7! 13 e4? ♘b4) **13 ♘c3 ♕c5**. Instead of 14 ♗xd5! exd5 15 ♗e3, Carlsen went for **14 ♖xd5 exd5 15 b4! ♕xb4?** (15...♕d4! 16 ♗e3 ♕xe5 17 ♗f4).

Carlsen could have won a dazzling miniature – against one of the greatest players of all time – with 16 ♘xd5!.

The main lines are 16...♕c5 17 ♘xc7+ ♔d8 18 ♕d3+ ♔xc7 (18...♗d7 19 ♘xa6) 19 ♗e3 and ♖c1(+) – and 16...♕c4 17 ♘xc7+ ♔d8 18 ♕d1+! ♔xc7 19 ♗d5!.

Instead, he chose **16 ♗a3?** and had to win the game all over again.

Carlsen – Vasily Ivanchuk
Morelia-Linares 2007
Grünfeld Defense,
Exchange Variation (D87)

1	d4	♘f6
2	c4	g6
3	♘c3	d5
4	cxd5	

12   ♖c1

Magnus regularly met the Grünfeld with this one variation, the Exchange. That is unusual for him because of his opening versatility. Against the King's Indian Defense he varied his choice of weapon, from the Classical Variation to the Averbakh, from the Sämisch to the Fianchetto and Gligorić.

4	...	♘xd5
5	e4	♘xc3
6	bxc3	♗g7
7	♗c4	c5
8	♘e2	♘c6
9	♗e3	0-0
10	0-0	♘a5

When he was Black in a Grünfeld, Carlsen played the more popular 10...♗g4 11 f3 ♘a5 as well as the rare 10...♗d7.

11   ♗d3   b6

White can grab a pawn with 12 dxc5 bxc5 13 ♗xc5.

But experience has shown that Black gets excellent compensation from 13...♕c7 14 ♗d4 e5 15 ♗e3 ♗e6 or 14 ♗b4 ♘c6 (15 ♗a3 ♕a5). Pawn sacrifices like that are common in the Grünfeld.

12   ...   cxd4

As White, Carlsen faced 12...e6 and played 13 e5 three years before in the Norwegian championship. He got little after 13...♗b7 14 ♘f4?! ♘c6 15 ♗e4 and accepted a rare-for-Magnus early draw.

13   cxd4   e6

Now if he proceeds routinely, 14 ♕d2 ♗b7 15 f3, Black should be OK after 15...♕d7 and ...♖ac8/...♖fd8.

14   ♕d2   ♗b7

You might expect 15 ♗h6 and ♗xg7. There's nothing wrong with that.

But after 15...♕e7 16 ♗xg7 ♔xg7 the position can quickly lose vitality.

All four rooks can be swapped after 17 ♖c3 ♖ac8 18 ♖fc1 ♖xc3 19 ♖xc3 ♖c8.

More adventurous is 17 ♕f4 ♖ac8 18 h4.

But tournament testing had shown that 18...♘c6 20 h5 ♖fd8 offers Black enough counterplay.

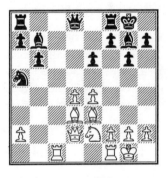

When this position became topical in the 1970s, masters intuitively understood that White will have several candidate moves that could be played now or at move 16, 17 or 18.

The candidates are ♗g5 or ♗h6 and the pawn pushes e4-e5 and h2-h4-h5.

But the proper move order was elusive. No sequence seemed to promise White anything solid.

15   h4

This move is possible because Black cannot play 15...♕xh4? due to 16 ♗g5 ♕g4 17 f3 ♕h5 18 ♘g3.

If Black halts the pawn with 15...h5, then 16 ♗g5! ♕d7 17 ♗h6 makes his king more vulnerable after a trade of bishops and ♕g5/♘f4.

15   ...   ♕e7

While Grünfeld-bashers were wrestling with White's move order, Grünfeld-defenders tried to determine the proper place for Black's queen in this and subsequent positions.

On d7 it would continue to exert some pressure on the d4-pawn in coordination with ...♘c6.

For example, 15...♕d7 16 ♗h6 ♗xh6 17 ♕xh6 ♘c6.

But before this game, it was thought that the queen was better on e7 because after ♗h6xg7 Black can secure some dark square control with ...e5 or ...♕f6.

16   h5

An obvious move. Yet 16 ♗g5 was common, until 16...f6! proved effective (17 ♗h6 ♖ad8 18 ♗xg7 ♕xg7 and 17 ♗f4 ♖ac8).

16   ...   ♖fc8

17 e5!

This was the first new move of the game. The alternatives, 17 h6 ♗f8, 17 ♗g5 ♛d7 and 17 ♗h6 ♘c6 18 ♗xg7 ♔xg7 had not turned up an advantage.

In retrospect, it is surprising that such a natural idea as 17 e5 went undiscovered previously.

White has a strong plan of ♗g5-f6 followed by ♛f4, with potential mating threats of ♗xg7 followed by h5-h6+ and ♛f6.

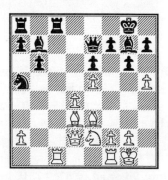

17 ... ♖xc1

Annotators concluded that Black's queen is misplaced and he should continue 17...♛d7.

Then 18 ♗g5 ♘c6 19 ♗f6? hangs the d-pawn, 19...♘xd4.

Better is 19 ♗b5 But it is not clear what White has after 19...♛d5 20 ♗c4 ♛d7 21 ♖fd1 (21 ♗f6? ♘xe5!) ♘a5.

18 ♖xc1 ♖c8

Once again 18...♛d7 and 19 ♗g5 ♘c6 would threaten the d4-pawn.

The queen seems well placed on d7 because it can retake on c8 after a rook swap, e.g. 19 ♗h6 ♖c8 20 ♖xc8+ ♛xc8.

But having the queen on the only open file isn't consequential because it can't penetrate to a key square.

White would keep the initiative with 21 ♗xg7 and then 22 ♘c3/ 23 ♘b5 or 22 h6+ ♔g8 23 ♛g5.

19 ♖xc8+ ♗xc8

20 ♗g5!

But the reverse is true: White's queen can penetrate on the c-file after 20...♛a3 21 ♛c2! ♗b7 22 ♛c7 (22...♛xd3? 23 ♛d8+ ♗f8 24 ♗h6).

Then 22...♛f8 23 ♗d8 stops 23...♛c8! and leaves Black passive following 23...♛e8 24 f3.

There is nothing conclusive then. But there are ways for Black to go wrong, such as 24...♛c6? 25 ♛e7 ♗f8 26 ♛g5 with a threat of hxg6 followed by ♘f4 and a winning sacrifice on g6.

| 20 | ... | ♕c7 |

Once again 20...♕d7 was the major alternative. Carlsen would continue his basic plan, 21 ♗f6 and ♕f4/♗xg7.

For example, 21...♘c6 22 ♕f4 ♗xf6? 23 exf6 ♕d8 24 hxg6 hxg6 25 ♕g5 (25...♘xd4 26 ♘f4 and a winning sacrifice on g6).

Better is 22...♗f8 23 hxg6 hxg6 24 ♕g5 ♘b4.

Then 25 ♗xg6 fxg6 26 ♕xg6+ ♗g7 27 ♘f4 gets into lengthy variations that leave White with good winning chances in a ♕+minor piece endgame.

21 ♗f6!

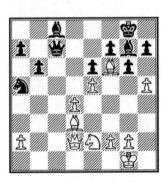

| 21 | ... | ♘c6 |

One point of 20...♕c7 is that now 22 ♕f4? ♗xf6! 23 exf6? ♕xf4 24 ♘xf4 ♘xd4 turns the game around.

There is, however, a problem with the queen being on c7 as Carlsen's 23rd move shows.

22 ♕g5

The threat is 23 ♗xg7 ♔xg7 24 h6+ and ♕f6.

| 22 | ... | h6 |

Magnus would win after 23 ♕h4 g5? 24 ♗e4! and be close to a win after 23...♘b4 24 ♗xg7 ♔xg7 25 ♕f6+ and 26 ♗e4.

23 ♕c1!

But this pinning move is more effective: 23...gxh5 is met by 24 ♗xg7 ♔xg7 25 ♘g3 and ♘xh5+.

| 23 | ... | g5 |

Now 24 ♗e4 ♗d7 25 d5 exd5 26 ♗xd5 is similar to what happens in the game.

But White's advantage disappears after 24...♗xf6 27 exf6 ♗d7 and ...♕d6.

24 ♗b5

Carlsen chooses to pick off the pinned knight rather than win with 24 ♗xg7 ♔xg7 25 f4 gxf4 26 ♕xf4 ♕e7 27 ♕e4 and ♕h7+.

24	...	♗d7
25	d5!	exd5
26	♘d4	♗xf6

27	exf6	♕d6

Black can lengthen the game with 27...♕e5 but 28 ♗xc6 ♕xd4 29 ♗xd7 ♕xf6 30 g4 is lost. Or 28 ♘xc6 ♕xf6 29 ♘xa7.

28	♗xc6	♕xf6
29	♗xd7	♕xd4
30	g3	♕c5

31	♕xc5	

This may be slower than 31 ♕e3 but simpler. The connected passed pawns are instructively blockaded.

31	...	bxc5
32	♗c6!	d4
33	♗b5!	♔f8
34	f4	gxf4
35	gxf4	**Resigns**

Carlsen's 34th move prevented Ivanchuk's king from reaching e5. His own king is heading for e4.

A plausible finish would arrive soon after 35...♔e7 36 ♔f2 ♔d6 37 ♗c4 f6 38 ♔f3 and wins.

14
The 10th GM

"Nine out of ten grandmasters," Bobby Fischer used to say, would play __this__ move, citing a natural, principle-based move. But Fischer played __that__ move, a surprising one, and won with it.

Carlsen turns that slightly upside down in this game.

Carlsen – Levon Aronian
Candidates match, Elista 2007
English Opening,
Symmetrical Variation (A30)

1	♘f3	♘f6
2	c4	b6
3	g3	c5
4	♗g2	♗b7
5	0-0	e6
6	♘c3	♗e7

It's been known since the 1930s that 7 d4 cxd4 8 ♘xd4 leads to 8...♗xg2 9 ♔xg2 ♕c8!. After White defends his c-pawn, Black can equalize with 10...♘c6.

If White plays 7 d3 and 8 e4, he will need to protect the e4-pawn in order to push d3-d4 safely.

7	♖e1	

Therefore this is the best way to seek the Maróczy Bind pawn structure, 7...d6 8 e4 followed by 9 d4 cxd4 10 ♘xd4.

7	...	d5

This move was Carlsen's choice when he had Black in this position. Earlier this year he quickly equalized after Veselin Topalov played 8 d4 dxc4 9 dxc5 ♗xc5.

8	cxd5	

The jury is out on the question of the best recapture now.

On 8...exd5 Black's center will come under pressure after 9 d4 0-0 10 ♗f4 ♘a6 11 dxc5 whether he accepts an isolated pawn, 11...♘xc5 12 ♖c1, or hanging pawns 11...bxc5 13 ♘e5.

8	...	♘xd5

Black would be content with a tiny endgame disadvantage after, say, 9 ♘xd5 ♕xd5! 10 d4 cxd4 11 ♕xd4.

The same goes for 9 e4 ♘b4 10 d4 cxd4 11 ♘xd4 ♘8c6 and a trade of queens.

9 d4!? ♘xc3

There is a little finesse in 9...cxd4 10 ♕a4+!?. Then 10...♕d7 11 ♕xd7+ ♘xd7 12 ♘xd4 is slightly better for White.

10 bxc3

10 ... ♗e4

This stops Carlsen's intended 11 e4.

The position would have offered him good winning chances after 10...0-0 11 e4 cxd4 12 cxd4 ♘c6 13 ♗b2 – and more than that after 11...♘c6 12 d5!.

This underlines one of White's resources after 11 bxc3. Until Black is fully developed there are tactical chances for Carlsen to favorably push one of his center pawns.

11 ♘e5 ♗xg2

12 ♔xg2 0-0

13 e4

This prompts Aronian to make his first difficult choice.

Clearly 13...♘c6?? is impossible and 13...♘d7 14 ♘c6 ♕e8 15 ♗f4 is unpleasant.

Pressuring d4 with 13...♗f6 is not promising after 14 ♘g4! ♗e7 15 d5!.

13 ... ♕c8

He prepares ...♘c6 or ...♘d7. But 13...cxd4 14 cxd4 ♗b4 might have worked better (15 ♖e3 f6 16 ♘f3 ♘c6).

14 ♕g4!

Carlsen threatens 15 ♗h6 ♗f6 16 ♘c4! and 17 e5.

After 16...♕c6 pins the e-pawn he has a surprisingly strong 17 ♔g1!.

Then 17...cxd4? 18 e5! wins.

Black should play 17...e5! and hope for 18 dxe5 ♗xe5 19 ♘xe5 ♕xh6.

But 18 d5! means a protected passed pawn and a lasting positional edge for White.

14 ... ♗f6?!

An echo of the last note is 14...♘c6 15 ♘xc6 ♕xc6 16 ♗h6 ♗f6.

Then 17 e5 would win – if it were legal. But again White has a strong 17 ♔g1!.

For example, 17...♔h8 18 e5 gxh6 19 exf6 ♖g8 20 ♕f4.

Or 18...♗xe5 19 ♖xe5 gxh6 20 ♖ae1.

15 ♘f3!

Threatening 16 e5 ♗e7 17 ♗h6.

15 ... ♔h8

"Nine out of ten masters," you might say, "would play 16 ♗f4."

16 h4!

But this way of targeting h7 is better:

After 16...♘d7 17 e5 ♗e7 18 ♕e4 White looks for ♘g5 and then ...♗xg5/hxg5 followed by ♖h1.

16 ... ♘c6

Now 17 e5 ♗e7 18 ♕e4 cxd4 19 cxd4 ♕d7! and ...♕d5.

17 ♗g5!

This move would have been ineffective after 16...♘d7 because ♗xf6 can be met by ...♘xf6.

But now 18 ♗xf6 gxf6 is a real weakening.

17 ... cxd4

Black cannot afford 17...♗xg5 18 hxg5! because 19 ♖h1 and ♕h5 is powerfully threatened.

He could avoid immediate collapse with 18...f5 19 exf5 ♖xf5.

But 20 ♕e4 targets the e6-pawn and sets up ♖h1 and g5-g6.

18 ♗xf6 gxf6

Nine out of ten amateurs would play 19 cxd4. But nine out of ten GMs would consider 19 ♕f4.

They would calculate 19 ♕f4 dxc3 20 ♕xf6+ ♔g8 and see that 21 ♘g5 ♕b7 22 ♕h6 f6 23 ♘xe6 ♖f7 is not decisive.

But they would notice that after 21 ♖ac1 White would regain his pawn and his heavy pieces would become dominating.

GMs wouldn't stop there. They would notice that 19...♔g7 is a temporary reprieve because of 20 h5!.

To stop 21 h6+ Black would reply 20...h6. Then 21 cxd4 is an improved version of 19 cxd4.

That leaves 19...♕d8 20 cxd4. White would have an extra pawn and a big edge after 20...♘xd4 21 ♖ed1 e5 22 ♘xe5!.

19   cxd4!?

Carlsen's choice seems obvious because d4-d5 is still on tap.

After 19...♕d8 20 ♖ad1 ♖c8 21 d5!, for example, his advantage is as great as in the 19 ♕f4 positions we considered (21...♘e5 22 ♕f4 ♘xf3 23 ♕xf3).

19   ...   e5

This is the reason many grandmasters would prefer 19 ♕f4.

White cannot easily avoid an endgame. But as we'll see, it is a much better endgame than they – and many a computer – appreciate at first.

20   ♕xc8   ♖axc8

21   d5

The main Magnus plan is h4-h5 followed by ♘h4-f5.

After 21...♘b4 22 ♖e2 ♖c4 23 ♖d1 h5 he could make slow progress with 24 ♘e1 and f2-f3, ♔f2.

21   ...   ♘a5

Aronian opts for a maneuver of his knight to d6, where it will blockade the d-pawn, negate ♘h4-f5 and force White to protect the e4-pawn.

22   h5!   ♘c4

23   ♘h4   ♘d6

One might say with greater confidence: Nine out of ten

experienced players would play 24 ♖ac1 – once they saw that 24...♖xc1? 25 ♖xc1 ♞xe4 26 ♖c7 is more than worth a pawn.

If Black prevents h5-h6 with 24...h6 White can continue 25 ♔f3 with the idea of 26 ♖c6 (26...♖xc6? 27 dxc6 ♖c8 28 ♖c1 and ♞f5).

Therefore 24...♔g8! 25 ♔f3 ♖fd8 26 h6 ♔f8 could transpose into the note to 24...♖c3.

24 h6

This creates two ways of winning: a last-rank mate and the creation of a passed h6-pawn if White gets to play ♖xh7.

24 ... ♖c3?

Black makes the most of the c-file. But the passive 24...♔g8! and 25 ♖ac1 ♖fd8 26 ♔f3 ♔f8 poses more of a problem.

White cannot make obvious progress because 27 ♔g4 ♔e7? 28 ♞f5+ is foiled by 27...♖xc1 28 ♖xc1 ♞xe4 and then 29 ♖c7 ♖xd5 or 29 ♞f5 ♞c5.

25 ♖ac1

Carlsen calculated 25...♞xe4 26 ♖xc3 ♞xc3 and saw that 27 d6! is good for him.

For example, 27...♖d8 28 ♞f5 ♞xa2? 29 ♖a1 and ♖xa7.

Or 27...♞a4 28 f4! exf4? 29 d7! and 30 ♖e8. This is why last-rank mates are important.

25 ... ♖fc8

26 ♖xc3 ♖xc3

Now 27 g4 ♔g8 28 ♞f5 ♞xf5 29 gxf5 would make sense if White could quickly play ♖g1(+) and ♖g7. But he can't.

27 ♞f5!

Carlsen would also have preferred to do this with his king on g4 so that ...♞xf5/♔xf5! was possible. But, again, he can't.

27 ... ♞xf5

28 exf5

Nevertheless, the knight trade is powerful. Black will lose if the now-unblockaded d-pawn gets to advance, supported by ♖d1.

But he is also doomed if White gets control of the c-file, such as 28...&d3? 29 &c1 and &c8 mate.

28 ... &g8!

29 &e4!

As noted earlier, the h6-pawn can become a winner, for example &g4+-g7 and &xh7.

29 ... &f8

30 &g4

30 ... &c7

The active defense is 30...&d3 31 &g7 &xd5.

Then 32 &xh7 threatens to queen after 33 &h8+ and 34 h7.

It forces 32...&g8 33 &g7+ &h8 (because 33...&f8 34 &g4 is resignable).

After 33...&h8 34 &xf7 White captures next on a7 or f6.

For example, 34...&a5 35 &xf6 &xa2 36 g4 and g4-g5-g6.

Or 34...&d6 35 &xa7 with ideas such as &f3-g4-h5-g6 and mate after &a8+.

31 &g7 b5

This stage is a good illustration of the power of the "absolute seventh rank."

32 &xh7 &g8

33 &g7+ &h8

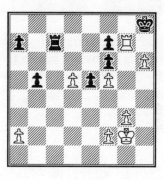

Black is so helpless that 34 &f3 b4 35 g4 a5 36 g5! fxg5 37 &e4 also wins.

But it is unnecessarily close, 37...a4 38 d6 &b7 39 &xg5! b3 40 axb3 axb3 41 &g1 b2 42 &b1.

34 d6 &d7

35 &f3 b4

36 &e4

Black cannot permit &d5-c6.

36 ... &xd6

37 &xf7

Among the winning scenarios is 37...a5 38 &a7 &d4+ 39 &f3 &d5 40 &g4 followed by &h5-g6 and &a8+.

37 ... &a6!

38	...	♚g8
39	h7+	♚h8
40	g5!	fxg5
41	f6	**Resigns**

The main threat is ♚f5-♚g6 and ♖f8 mate.

Good defenders give their opponents plausible ways to go wrong. The win would have been endangered by 38 ♚d5? ♖xa2 ♖xf6 b3.

38 g4!

The difference is that 38...♖xa2 39 ♖xf6 b3 allows 40 ♖f8+ ♚h7 41 g5! b2 42 ♖f7+ and ♖b7 followed by g5-g6 or ♚xe5.

This win tied the score after three games of this Candidates match. Aronian took a one-point lead twice more but each time Carlsen won the next game. But when he lost a rapid playoff game he found himself in a must-win position and lost. No one knew at the time how rare it would be for Magnus to lose a tiebreaker.

15
Magnus Fear

Carlsen's opponents were developing a healthy respect for his skill. But in some cases it became an exaggerated fear of his winning technique. Players resigned well before they should.

A striking illustration came later in his career. At Wijk aan Zee 2020, he had slowly improved his position against **Nikita Vitiugov**:

He had just moved his queen from f3 and threatened 30 ♘xh6+. He would win after 29...♔h7? 30 ♗xe6 and 31 ♗xg5.

But Black had two good moves, 29...♘d4 and 29...c4. Instead, he chose **29...f6?** and Magnus shot back **30 ♗d5!**.

Then came a surprise: **Black resigned**. Carlsen's pressure is great and victory was likely after 30...♕h7 31 ♕f3 followed by ♔g2 and ♖h1. But it wasn't inevitable.

"I think he was just fed up," Carlsen said.

Carlsen had legions of fans who followed his moves in real time by watching on-line coverage of his games. Sometimes the action they were watching ended suddenly without explanation.

Here's another example.

**Shakhriyar Mamedyarov –
Carlsen**
Wijk aan Zee 2008
*Sicilian Defense,
Closed Variation (B30)*

1	e4	c5
2	♘f3	♘c6
3	♘c3	g6

Carlsen's last move is a good choice since he was comfortable in the Dragon Variation and, in this move order, the Maróczy Bind (c2-c4) is not possible because the c-pawn is blocked.

4	g3	♗g7
5	♗g2	d6
6	0-0	

As Closed Sicilian Defenses go, this is a harmless version because f2-f4 is delayed.

Black usually gets a nice game with simple moves, 6...♘f6 7 d3 0-0 and ...♖b8/...b5-b4. Carlsen chooses a more unbalancing approach.

6	...	♗g4
7	h3	♗xf3

This secures Black control of d4 for the foreseeable future. If White later plays c2-c3 he creates a target for ...b5-b4.

8	♕xf3	♘f6
9	d3	0-0
10	♕d1	

This seems like the kind of position Carlsen would be more comfortable with if he were sitting on the other side of the board:

White has the two bishops and straightforward plans such as ♘e2/c2-c3/d3-d4.

10	...	♘d7

He has ways of conjuring up counterplay, such as 11 ♘e2 e6 12 c3 ♖c8 13 ♗e3 b5 and ...b4.

The knight on d7 is looking to come into play at c5, e.g. 14 d4 b4 15 dxc5 ♘xc5.

11	f4	c4!?

Now 12 ♗e3 cxd3 13 cxd3 ♗d4 is solid (14 ♗xd4 ♘xd4 15 ♕a4 e5) because Black's d4-knight is no worse than White's g2-bishop.

Much more double-edged is 13 ♕xd3 and then 13...♖c8 and ...♘a5-c4 or 14...♘b4.

12 dxc4 ♘a5

White's position will appear so promising – so Karpovian – after the next few moves that 12...♗xc3 13 bxc3 ♖c8 seems preferable.

Then Black would regain his pawn (...♘a5xc4). If White is going to prove that his two bishops matter he would have to attack, with f4-f5. That is risky – for both sides.

13 ♘d5! ♘xc4

14 c3 ♘db6

15 ♕e2

Carlsen will have to deal with the annoying d5-knight. The obvious way is 15...♘xd5 16 exd5 and then 16...♖c8 17 f5 ♘e5.

But that offers White more kingside pressure with ♗g5/♖f2/♖af1.

15 ... ♖c8

16 ♔h2 e6

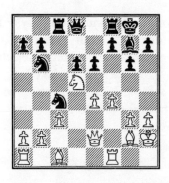

This is the other way of neutralizing the d5-knight.

Now 17 ♘e3 ♘xe3 18 ♗xe3 ♘c4 19 ♗f2 enables White to seek a superior pawn structure with ♖ad1 and b2-b3, then c3-c4!.

Black can thwart that with 17...d5 and get counterplay after 18 e5 f6 or 18 exd5 exd5 and ...♖e8.

17 ♘b4

On b4, the knight looks out of place. But so does the one at b6.

If nothing much happens in the next few moves, White could play ♖b1 or ♕f3 and improve his pawn structure with b2-b3 and eventually c3-c4!.

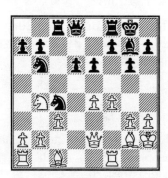

17 ... ♘a4!

Some computers say Carlsen has been playing second-best moves since the opening ended. But he is finding tactics.

He threatens 18...♘axb2! 19 ♗xb2 ♘xb2 20 ♕xb2 ♗xc3.

Then on 21 ♕b3 ♗xa1 22 ♖xa1 ♕b6 he has the superior chances.

18 f5!

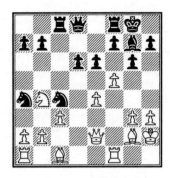

Mamedyarov's counter-idea is 18...♘axb2 19 ♗xb2 ♘xb2 20 fxe6!.

Then 20...♗xc3? loses to 21 ♘d5! followed by 22 e7 or 22 ♘xc3.

Also, 20...fxe6? 21 ♖xf8+ ♕xf8 22 ♖f1 ♕-moves 23 ♕xb2.

The best for Black after 20 fxe6! is 20...♘a4 and 21 ♖xf7 ♘xc3! with rough equality.

18   ...   ♖e8

19   fxe6

Both players must have considered 19 f6 ♗xf6 20 ♕f2 and possibly 20...♗e5 21 ♕xf7+ ♔h8.

Evaluating that position depends on what happens after 22 ♘d3.

Black cannot allow 22...♗g7 23 b3! or 22...♖f8 23 ♕xf8+ ♕xf8 24 ♖xf8+ ♖xf8 25 b3!.

Therefore 22...♘c5 23 ♘xe5 ♘xe5 24 ♕f2 ♖f8 and 23 ♘xc5 dxc5 24 ♕xb7 ♕d6 are critical. White may be better but it is hard to prove.

19   ...   fxe6

20   ♘d3   ♕b6

21   h4!

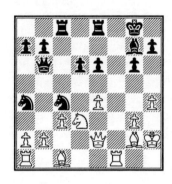

Mamedyarov has a new threat, 22 ♗h3 followed by 23 ♘f4 and a capture on e6.

21   ...   ♕a6

Carlsen can meet it with 22...♘cxb2!.

For example, 22 ♗h3 ♘cxb2! 23 ♗xb2 ♘xb2 24 ♕xb2 ♕xd3 or 24 ♘xb2?? ♕xe2.

22   ♖f2   ♘e5

23   ♘f4

Since Magnus outplays his opponent from here on, Mamedyarov should regret rejecting 23 ♘xe5 ♕xe2 24 ♖xe2 ♗xe5 25 ♗f4 or 25 ♗h6. Then it would be hard for him to lose.

23   ...   ♘c5

24   ♕xa6

Now 24...♘xa6 25 ♗h3 ♘c5 26 ♗e3! is nice because 26...♘xe4

27 ♖e2 will be followed favorably by ♗xa7 or ♗xe6+.

24 ... bxa6!

Magnus threatens ...♘g4+. Now 25 ♗h3 ♘ed3 is fairly balanced (26 ♖e2 ♖b8).

25 ♖e2

His knights maintain the balance after 25 ♔h3 ♘ed3.

25 ... h6

26 ♔h1 a5

27 ♗e3 a4!

It is remarkable how often in mutual time pressure Carlsen held a more "playable" position. He has more ways to improve his position than White does.

28 ♖d1 ♖c6

29 ♗d4

White could defend against 29...♖b6 with 30 ♗xe5 ♗xe5 31 ♘xg6 ♗xg3 32 e5.

29 ... g5!

This was available since move 25. Now 30 hxg5 hxg5 31 ♘h3 g4 32 ♘f4 ♖b6 and ...♖eb8 is progress for Black.

30 ♘h3 g4

31 ♘f4 ♖b6

32 ♘h5

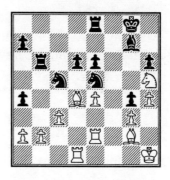

32 ... ♗h8!

This retreat wasn't necessary but it was a good practical decision:

It was hard to tell whether 32...♖eb8 33 ♘xg7 ♔xg7 34 ♗xe5+ dxe5 35 ♖dd2 was winnable.

Black's best winning chances might then lie in a well-timed ...a3 and, after b2-b3, in a ...♘xb3/axb3/...♖xb3 sacrifice.

33 ♖ed2 ♖eb8

White would have counterchances after 33...♘c4 34 ♖f2 ♖xb2 35 ♘f6+ ♗xf6 36 ♖xf6.

34 ♗xc5?

If Mamedyarov realized how bad things were getting he would have tried 34 ♗g1 ♘f7 35 e5! and then 35...♗xe5 36 ♗xc5 dxc5 37 ♖d7 and ♗e4.

34 ... dxc5

Now 35 ♘f4 ♗f6 stops ♖d8+.

The liquidating 36 b3 axb3 37 axb3 ♖xb3 38 ♘xe6 ♖xc3 is probably lost.

35 ♖d8+ ♔f7

36 ♖xb8 ♖xb8

37 ♖d2 ♘c4?

More accurate is 37...♔e7 so there is no ♖d7+. Black would be winning after 38 ♘f4 ♘c4 39 ♖f2 ♗e5.

38 ♖d7+! ♔e8

39 ♖xa7 ♗e5

40 ♖xa4 ♘e3

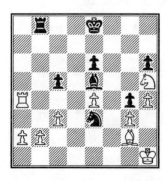

After studying the position, **White resigned**. And the chess world – or the part watching the game on-line – asked, "Why?"

The answer is that a strong ...♖d8! and ...♖d1+/...♖d2 cannot be stopped. White eventually loses his bishop but the variations are complex.

For example, 41 b3 ♖d8 42 ♔g1 ♖d2 43 ♗h1! (not 43 ♗f1 ♖d1) ♘d1 44 ♖a7 ♘xc3 45 ♘g7+ ♗xg7 46 ♖xg7 ♘e2+ 47 ♔f2 ♘d4+.

But fans felt cheated. Even after 48 ♔e3 ♖h2 and 48 ♔g1 ♖d1+ 49 ♔g2! (49 ♔h2? ♘f3+) h5! the position was worth playing out.

Black has other winning attempts, such as 43...♗xc3. But Magnus' army of fans didn't get to see what he had in mind.

16
Carlsen Luck

This was the year that his rivals began to complain about Carlsen's luck. "I don't think this is good for Magnus, such fantastic luck," Veselin Topalov said after he lost to him at Wijk aan Zee 2008 "You know he should have lost three games [in the tournament]. But he won all three."

In one of them, against Loek van Wely, Carlsen had a resignable position and only nine seconds to play 11 moves. He not only made the time control but his opponent resigned just before he was getting mated.

What many of his opponents did not appreciate is that players make their own luck, good and bad. Topalov did it disastrously when he lost to Carlsen for the first time, at Morelia-Linares 2007: He resigned in a drawable position.

There is no luck in the following game, just one grandmaster outplaying another.

Veselin Topalov – Carlsen
Morelia-Linares 2008
Alekhine's Defense,
Larsen Variation (B04)

1	e4	♘f6
2	e5	♘d5
3	d4	d6
4	♘f3	dxe5
5	♘xe5	

Black allows White to plant a knight in the center with the expectation that he can trade it off quickly.

He cannot challenge it safely with 5...♘d7 because 6 ♘xf7!

♔xf7 7 ♕h5+ is too risky (7...♔e6 8 c4).

| 5 | ... | c6 |

This makes 6...♘d7 possible. Carlsen had some experience facing 6 ♗c4 ♘d7 7 ♘xd7 ♗xd7 8 ♕f3 e6.

103

This looks like an inferior French Defense. But after 9 0-0 ♕f6 10 ♕xf6 ♘xf6 11 ♘d2 c5! it was a good Rubinstein Variation of the French, enough for equality.

6   ♗d3   ♘d7

A trade of knights eases Black's game so much that 7 ♘f3! has performed best in master games.

7   ♘xd7   ♗xd7

8   0-0   g6

9   ♘d2   ♗g7

10   ♘f3

Black's future depends on whether he can (a) find a better square for his d7-bishop and (b) liberate his game with a center pawn push.

If White discourages ...c5, he may allow a stronger ...e5 For example, 10 c3 0-0 11 ♖e1 ♕c7 12 ♘e4 ♖fe8 and ...e5!.

10   ...   0-0

11   ♖e1

An earlier game saw the remarkable 11 ♕d2. White wanted to play 12 c4! before Black could support ...♘b4 or ...♘f4.

However, 11...♗g4 12 ♘e5 ♗e6 is fine for Black because of the tactic 13 c4 ♘b4! 14 ♕xb4 ♕xd4, regaining the piece.

11   ...   ♗g4

12   c3

12   ...   c5!

This equalizes. But to play it Carlsen had to calculate 13 dxc5! ♘xc3!.

Then 14 ♕c2? ♗xf3 15 gxf3 ♘d5 or 15 bxc3 ♗c6 is good for Black.

The real test is 14 bxc3 ♗xc3 15 ♗h6 ♗xe1 – and not because of 16 ♗xf8 ♔xf8 17 ♕xe1 ♕xd3.

White has a tricky alternative in 16 ♕xe1 ♕xd3 17 ♘e5.

The point is that 17...♕e2 18 ♕c3! sets up 19 ♖e1 as well as eyeing a mate on g7.

For example, 18...♖fd8 19 h3! ♖d1+ 20 ♔h2! ♖xa1 21 ♘xg4 f6 22 ♕xa1 is a small edge for White.

But 17...♕d4! is the antidote. White would be worse after 18 ♘xg4 ♕xg4 19 ♗xf8 ♔xf8.

He can reach equality with 18 c6! – 18...bxc6 19 ♘xc6 ♕d6 20 ♘xe7+ ♔h8 21 ♗xf8 ♔xf8 – but no more than that.

Did Magnus see all that when he played 12...c5? Almost certainly not.

He probably sampled the possibilities after 13 dxc5 ♘xc3 14 bxc3 ♗xc3 and determined there was no way for White to gain a serious advantage by force.

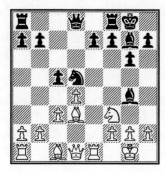

13 ♗e4?

When Topalov said Carlsen's "fantastic luck" was not good for him he meant that it would prompt him to have unrealistic expectations in future games.

But Topalov seems to have his own unrealistic expectations for the next four moves. He might have tried 13 h3 ♗xf3 14 ♕xf3 because of 14...cxd4 15 cxd4 ♗xd4 16 ♗h6.

Then 16...♖e8? 17 ♗b5 costs material.

Black would be forced into 16...♗g7 17 ♗xg7 ♔xg7. Then 18 ♗c4 (or 18 ♗e4) e6 19 ♖ad1 and ♗xd5 is roughly equal.

However, Black can improve with 15...e6! when the onus would be on White to maintain the balance.

13 ... cxd4

14 cxd4 e6!

Topalov should have realized he was in trouble. He can't defend his d4-pawn easily in the face of 15...♕b6 and 16...♗xf3.

Protecting it with 15 ♗e3 is problematic after 15...f5 or 15...♘xe3 16 fxe3 f5 17 ♗xb7 ♖b8.

And having rejected 13 h3 earlier he was reluctant to see what happens after 15 h3 ♗xf3 16 ♕xf3 ♖c8.

15 ♕b3

Topalov wants to indirectly swap his weak d4-pawn for the b7-pawn.

An alternative is 15 ♕a4 so that 15...♕b6 16 ♘e5.

But 15...♘b6 16 ♕b3 ♗xf3 17 ♗xf3 ♗xd4 18 ♗xb7? ♖b8 turns out badly.

So does 18 ♗h6? ♗xf2+ 19 ♔xf2 ♕h4+.

Also unpleasant is the endgame, (15 ♕a4 ♘b6) 16 ♕b4 ♗xf3 17 ♗xf3 ♕xd4 18 ♕xd4 ♗xd4, because of the weakness of the b2-pawn after 19 ♗xb7 ♖ab8 (20 ♗a6 ♘a4 and 20 ♗f3 ♘c4).

15 ...   ♗xf3

16 ♗xf3   ♗xd4

Now 17 ♕xb7 is bound to lose the b2-pawn after 17...♕a5 and ...♖ab8.

White could be lost as early as 18 ♗h6? ♖ab8 19 ♕c6 ♖fc8 20 ♕d6 ♖d8 and ...♖xb2.

17 ♗xd5   ♕xd5

18 ♕xd5   exd5

19 ♖d1   ♗g7

Annotators disagreed over whether White has better chances of drawing than of losing.

A quick glance indicates drawing is easy: 20 ♖xd5 and then 20...♖fd8 21 ♖xd8+ ♖xd8 22 ♗e3 ♗xb2 23 ♖b1 ♗f6 24 ♗xa7.

But 23...b6! exploits the last rank (24 ♖xb2?? ♖d1 mate) and

creates a losable ending (24 ♔f1 ♗a3).

20 ♔f1

To draw, White needs to activate both his a1-rook and king and also find the best square for his bishop.

Easy to say. But how to start? One method is 20 ♗e3 ♖fd8 21 ♖d2.

The forcing 21...d4 22 ♖ad1 ♖d7 23 ♗xd4 and 23...♖ad8 24 ♗c3 ♖xd2 25 ♖xd2 ♖xd2 26 ♗xd2 ♗xb2 is a losable bishop endgame.

White does better with rooks on the board so 20 ♗f4 ♖fd8 21 ♖ac1 makes sense. Then 21...♖d7 22 b3 followed by ♖d3 and ♔f1. Or 21...d4 22 ♖c7 b5 23 ♖b7.

20 ...   ♖fd8

21 ♗g5

This gains time for ♖d2. But the consistent 21 ♔e2 ♖d7 22 ♔d3 would reach a better version of what happens in the game.

For example, 22...♖c8 23 ♖b1 ♖c4 24 ♗e3 ♖a4 25 a3.

21 ...   ♖d7

22 ♖d2   h6

23 ♗e3

This hints at a trade of bishops, 23...b6 24 ♖ad1 ♖ad8 25 ♗d4.

Then 25...♔f8 26 ♖c1 ♗xd4 27 ♖xd4 ♔e7 is an endgame that

can go either way, draw or White loss.

23 ... d4!

24 🖳d3

The presence of bishops would cost White after 24 🖳c1? 🖳ad8 25 🖴f4 g5! 26 🖴g3 f5!.

Then the White king will not reach d3 and the passed d-pawn becomes a tactical danger (27 f3 d3 28 🖳c4? 🖴xb2! 29 🖳xb2? d2).

24 ... 🖳c8!

25 🖴d2?

If there is a single point where Topalov lost the game, this was it.

After 25 🖳c1 🖳dd8 26 🖳cd1 🖳c2 three similar rook endgames could come about:

One is 27 🖴xd4 🖴xd4 28 🖳xd4 🖳xd4 29 🖳xd4 🖳xb2 30 a4.

The second is 27 🖳3d2 🖳dc8 28 🖴xd4 🖴xd4 29 🖳xd4 🖳xb2 30 🖳4d2 🖳cc2 31 🖳xc2 🖳xc2 32 🖳d7! 🖳xa2 33 🖳xb7.

The third varies from the second with 30...🖳xd2 31 🖳xd2 b5 and

...🖳c3 or ...🖳c4, when Black is getting closer to a win than to a draw.

This hardly exhausts the possibilities because Black can retain his bishop. For example, 25 🖳c1 🖳xc1+ (rather than 25...🖳dd8) 26 🖴xc1 f5 and ...🖱f7-e6 also offers excellent winning chances.

25 ... 🖳c2

26 🖳b1 🖳e7!

This is a much better position for Black than in some of the earlier scenarios because of three factors:

One of White's rooks is passive, his king cannot quickly blockade the d-pawn with 🖱e2-d3 and Black has a rook on the seventh rank.

Among Carlsen's winning plans now is ...f5 and ...🖱f7-e6-d5-c4!.

27 a4 f5

28 b3

28 ... 🖳ec7!

107

Now 29 ♔e2 ♖a2 30 ♔d1 sets a trap: 30...♖cc2 31 ♖c1 ♖xc1+ 32 ♔xc1 ♖a1+ 33 ♔c2 and, if Black is not alert, 34 ♗c1! and ♔b2.

Instead, Black should be able to win on the kingside, beginning with 33...♖f1.

29	♗e1	♔f7
30	♖d2	♖c1

Releasing the blockade, 31 ♖d1 ♖xb1 32 ♖xb1 ♖c2!, is doomed, 33 ♗b4 ♗f6 and ...♔e6-d5.

31	♖xc1	♖xc1
32	♔e2	♖b1
33	♖d3	♔e6

Carlsen doesn't yet have a way for his king to penetrate the defense. But he can squeeze slowly, 34 ♗d2 g5 35 ♗e1 ♖b2+ 36 ♗d2 ♔d5 followed by 37...♗e5 38 g3 ♗c7 and 39...♗a5, for example.

34	h4	♔d5
35	♗d2	♔e4

36	♖g3	f4!

So that 37 ♖xg6? d3 is mate. Or 37 f3+ ♔f5 38 ♖g4 ♗e5 and ...♖xb3.

37	♖d3

37	...	♗e5

Care is required. The plan of ...g5-g4 works better after f2-f3+ has been provoked. Black would need a new idea after 37...g5 38 hxg5 hxg5 39 g4.

38	f3+	♔d5
39	♗e1	♗d6
40	♗d2	g5
41	hxg5	hxg5
42	♗e1	g4!

This would create a winning g-pawn after ...g3!.

For example, 43 ♗d2 g3! (threat of ...♖g1) 44 ♗e1 ♖b2+ 45 ♔f1 ♔e5 is zugzwang.

Black wins with 46 ♗a5 ♖b1+ 47 ♗e1 ♗b4 or 47 ♔e2 ♖g1.

43 fxg4 ♔e4

44 g5 and resigns

Before 44...♖xe1+ 45 ♔xe1 ♔xd3.

A similar finish would have been 44 ♖f3 d3+ 45 ♖xd3 ♖xe1+ or 45 ♔f2 ♗c5+ 46 ♔f1 d2.

Fabiano Caruana was victimized by more than a few shifts in fortune during games with Magnus. But in 2016 he told Chess24.com:

"Carlsen often saves bad positions or wins drawish positions because he keeps playing and trying to push and make the most of the result. From the outside it might look like luck, but it's really more the result of hard work."

As Carlsen tweeted in 2020, 'Luck is no coincidence.'

17
Upper Class

By now Carlsen was a member of the grandmaster elite. But he recognized there was a more exclusive club. Vladimir Kramnik and Vishy Anand were the world's best players and he was not yet in their class, he said. As for the GMs just below them, "I still don't think that I am better than players like Leko and Ivanchuk," he added.

Carlsen was surprised when he and Levon Aronian tied for first prize at Wijk aan Zee 2008 ahead of all four of them. "I don't know what happened," he said.

He was more experienced than when he was a year or two before. "But that shouldn't make the difference between struggling to make 50 percent and trying to win the tournament."

Vladimir Kramnik – Carlsen
Wijk aan Zee 2008
English Opening,
Symmetrical Variation (A30)

1	♘f3	♘f6
2	c4	e6
3	♘c3	c5

In six previous games as Black against Kramnik, Magnus had managed only three draws.

Their rapid game at the 2007 Melody Amber tournament went 3...d5 4 d4 dxc4 5 e4 ♗b4 6 ♗g5 b5 7 a4 c6 8 e5 h6 9 exf6 hxg5 10 fxg7 ♖g8 11 g3 ♗b7 12 ♗g2 c5 13 0-0 g4 14 axb5! gxf3? 15 ♗xf3 ♗xf3 16 ♕xf3 ♘d7 17 dxc5 ♗xc3 18 bxc3 ♘xc5 19 ♖fd1 ♕c8 20 ♖d6 ♕b7 21 ♕h5 ♖c8 22 ♖c6 ♘d3 23 ♖xc8+ ♕xc8 24 ♖xa7 resigns.

4	g3	b6
5	♗g2	♗b7
6	0-0	♗e7
7	d4	

This is the major alternative to 7 ♖e1 of Game 14.

7	...	cxd4
8	♕xd4	d6

The queen capture tempts inexperienced players to gain a tempo with 8...♘c6 but they soon appreciate that White is better after 9 ♕f4 and ♖d1.

9	♖d1	a6

Black anticipates ♘b5xd6. The d6-pawn is in no immediate danger now in view of 10 b3 ♘bd7 11 ♗a3 ♘c5.

110

10 ♘g5

What Carlsen remembered at this point is that 10 ♘g5 was "a fairly old" move and no longer regarded as dangerous to Black. But that was about all he remembered.

10 ... ♗xg2

11 ♔xg2 ♘c6

He did know that this knight usually serves better on d7 than on c6 but he had doubts about 11...♘bd7 12 ♘ge4.

12 ♕f4

White's thinking is straightforward. The only weak point in Black's armor is the d6-pawn and Kramnik can attack it with his queen, a rook, a knight on e4 and potentially a bishop on a3.

12 ... 0-0

13 ♘ce4

13 ... ♘e8!

Not 13...♘xe4? 14 ♕xe4, when the threat of ♕xh7 mate leads to 14...♗xg5 15 ♗xg5.

A pawn is falling after 15...♕xg5 16 ♕xc6 and Black would have a difficult defense after 15...♕c7 16 ♖ac1.

14 b3 ♖a7

15 ♗b2

Note that a8 has been freed for Black's queen. If White had gone after the d6-pawn with 15 ♗a3 Black might have tried 15...♕a8 because then 16 ♘xd6? e5 loses material.

15 ... ♖d7

Carlsen admitted that the ...♖a7-d7 maneuver wasn't necessary. "But I thought there was no better square for the rook anyway," he said.

16 ♖ac1

16 ... ♘c7!

This is an original approach. More common in similar positions is ...♕a8 and then ...b5.

Carlsen rejected that because he didn't know what it would accomplish. The White c4-pawn would not be easily attacked after ...b5xc4/bxc4.

Instead, he protected e6 so he can push White pieces back with ...f5 and even ...g5. He threatens to win a knight with 17...f5.

17	♘f3	f5
18	♘c3	

18	...	g5!

This looks overly aggressive. But the routine 18...♗f6 would allow White to reorganize his forces favorably with 19 ♕d2! and 20 ♘a4.

19	♕d2	g4
20	♘e1	

Another retreat, but 20 ♘d4 ♗g5! is bad for him (21 ♘xc6? ♗xd2 22 ♘xd8 ♗xc1 or 21 e3 ♘e5 and ...♕a8+).

20	...	♗g5
21	e3	♖ff7

This is a remarkably mature move. After making so much progress since 17...f5 it is tempting to continue with 21...♕a8 and 22 ♔g1 ♕b7.

But that's where it stops. The position is in balance after, say, 23 ♘e2 and ♘f4.

Why did Carlsen over-protect the d7-rook? Because Kramnik was preparing 22 ♘a4 and, if 22...♘e8, then 23 c5 bxc5 24 ♘xc5 with advantage.

22	♔g1	♘e8
23	♘e2	♘f6
24	♘f4	♕e8
25	♕c3	♖g7

The position is still fairly even. Carlsen was playing slowly and had 17 minutes left to reach move 40.

26	b4!	♘e4
27	♕b3	♖ge7
28	♕a4	

Computers want White to play f2-f3, now or earlier, and 28 f3 gxf3 29 ♘xf3 ♗h6 is certainly better than going after the a6-pawn as Kramnik does now.

28	...	♘e5
29	♕xa6?	♖a7!

Kramnik took on a6 because he mistakenly thought 30 ♕xb6 was playable.

Now he saw 30...♖eb7! 31 ♕d4 ♗f6 would win material.

| 30 | ♕b5 | |

He offered a draw.

30	...	♕xb5
31	cxb5	♖xa2

Carlsen rejected the offer. His only concern is that his b6-pawn will be vulnerable after, for example, 32 ♘fd3 ♘xd3 33 ♘xd3 and ♖c6

But 33...♔f7 34 ♖c6 ♖b7 35 ♖dc1 e5! shows how Black can improve slowly.

He would be winning after 36 ♖c7+ ♖xc7 37 ♖xc7+ ♔e6! 38 ♖xh7? ♘d2 and ...e4.

32	♖c8+	♔f7
33	♘fd3	♗f6
34	♘xe5+	dxe5

There was nothing wrong with 33...♘xd3 or here 34...♗xe5.

But Carlsen apparently decided he had greater winning chances with more material on the board.

35	♖c2	♖ea7
36	♔g2	♘g5!

The positional clincher will be ...e4!. That cannot be delayed for long (37 ♖dd2 ♖2a4 38 ♖c4 e4! or 38 ♗c3 e4!).

37	♖d6	e4!
38	♗xf6	♔xf6

Zugzwang looms: 39 ♖d1 ♘f3! 40 ♖xa2 ♖xa2 41 ♖b1 ♔e5.

39	♔f1	♖a1
40	♔e2	

| 40 | ... | ♖b1 |

This wins but Carlsen (and other annotators) did not mention

40...♘f3!, which might have forced resignation.

For example, 41 ♘xf3 gxf3+ 42 ♔d2 ♖7a3! and 43...♖f1. Or 41 ♘g2 ♖g1 42 ♘f4 ♖e1 mate.

41	♖d1	♖xb4
42	♘g2	♖xb5
43	♘f4	♖c5
44	♖b2	b5
45	♔f1	♖ac7

There are other ways to win, such as 45...♘f3 46 ♔g2 e5.

46	♖bb1	♖b7
47	♖b4	♖c4
48	♖b2	b4
49	♖db1	♘f3

50	♔g2	♖d7!

Another mating pattern arises (51 ♖xb4 ♖xb4 52 ♖xb4 ♖d1!).

51	h3	e5
52	♘e2	♖d2!
53	hxg4	fxg4
54	♖xd2	♘xd2
55	♖b2	♘f3
56	♔f1	b3!
57	♔g2	♖c2

White resigns

"I almost couldn't believe it," Carlsen said after beating a former world champion with Black. He didn't defeat Vishy Anand with Black in a "classical" game until their world championship match.

18
Evaluation Gap

As Magnus faced more and more world-class opponents he encountered opponents who were at least as good at calculation as him – and sometimes superior. They might consider longer variations and more candidate moves. But they often fell short of his evaluation skills.

In the following game, Alexander Grischuk found some elegant tactics when he chose his 21st and 22nd moves. What he failed to appreciate was a simple response that dragged him into a poor endgame.

Carlsen – Alexander Grischuk
Linares 2009
Sicilian Defense,
Scheveningen Variation (B84]

1	e4	c5
2	♘f3	d6
3	d4	cxd4
4	♘xd4	♘f6
5	♘c3	a6
6	♗e2	e6
7	0-0	♗e7
8	a4	♘c6

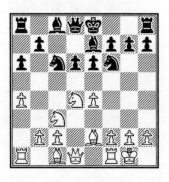

This position can come about in an amazing number of reasonable move orders. Along the way Black rejected sharper play with, for example, 7...b5, and White now passes up opportunities for a quick ♕e1-g3.

9	♗e3	0-0
10	f4	♕c7
11	♔h1	

But now we've reached a subtle stage. Black has not committed his c8-bishop yet and that's intentional.

After 11...♗d7 it occupies the best retreat square for his f6-knight – which it may need after g2-g4-g5 by White.

Moreover, Black can't fianchetto it directly because of 11...b6

115

12 ♘xc6 ♕xc6 13 e5! with ♗f3 to come.

11 ... ♖e8

This was once considered a somewhat "mysterious rook move" because the e-file is blocked.

12 ♗f3 ♗f8

But now the rook may turn out to be well-placed after ...♘xd4 followed by ...e5. For example, 13 g4 ♘xd4 14 ♗xd4 e5! 15 ♗e3 exf4 16 ♗xf4 ♗e6 gives him well-coordinated pieces.

13 ♕d2

Carlsen had learned how to play the waiting game, too.

If he had chosen 13 ♘b3 and prepared the space-gaining 14 a5, play might go 13...b6 14 g4 ♗b7 15 g5 ♘d7 with approximate equality.

But after 13 ♕d2 Black must avoid 13...b6 because of 14 ♘xc6 ♕xc6 15 e5.

If, instead 13...♗d7, then 14 ♘b3 b6 15 g4! favors White because d7 is occupied. The book continuation is 15...♗c8! 16 g5 ♘d7 17 ♕f2 or 17 ♗g2 and ♖f3-h3, with attacking chances.

13 ... ♖b8

This is the best "pass" for Black. White would have a comfortable edge after 13...♘a5 14 b3!.

It can grow after 14...♗d7 15 ♘de2 ♖ac8 16 ♖ad1.

Then 16...b5 17 e5! (17...dxe5 18 fxe5 ♕xe5? 19 ♗d4 wins a piece).

14 ♕f2 e5

15 fxe5

The positional treatment is 15 ♘de2 so that after ...exf4/♘xf4 he can retake on d5 with the c3-knight after ♘fd5.

Carlsen has another idea, playing ♘d5 and retaking with the e4-pawn.

15 ... dxe5

16 ♘b3

This threatens to misplace Grischuk's queen with 17 ♗b6.

White could meet 16...b6? with 17 ♗g5! followed by ♗xf6 and ♘d5.

16 ... ♘b4

Back at move 12 Grischuk could have met 12 ♗d3 with ...♘b4 and ...♘xd3.

Now ...♘b4 has a different purpose, to deter Carlsen from carrying out his ♘d5 plan (17 ♘d5? ♘bxd5 18 exd5 e4!).

But on b4 the knight surrenders the option of ...♘d4.

For example, 16...♗e6 17 ♗b6 ♕c8 18 a5 would allow a good pawn offer, 18...♗xb3 19 cxb3 ♘d4!.

Grischuk would have had excellent dark-square compensation after 20 ♗xd4 exd4 21 ♕xd4 ♕c7 and ...♗d6-e5.

17 ♗a7 ♖a8

18 ♗b6 ♕e7

The queen is not badly placed on e7 and could also end up there after 18...♕c6 19 ♘a5 ♕e6 20 ♗e2 and then 20...♕e7 21 ♗c4 ♗e6.

19 ♖ad1 ♗e6

An easier road to equality is 19...♗g4!.

Then 20 ♘d5 ♘bxd5 21 exd5 ♗xf3 22 ♕xf3 e4! makes Black's e-pawn as much of an asset as White's d6-pawn.

20 ♘d5! ♗xd5

21 exd5

Carlsen's threat of 22 d6! ♕d7 23 ♘c5 creates the first crisis of the game.

21 ... e4!

Black would have been in bad shape after 21...♕d6? 22 ♗c5 ♕d7 23 ♗xf8/♘c5. And he would be lost after 21...♘d7? 22 d6 ♕e6 23 ♘c5! (23...♘xc5 24 ♗xc5 ♘c6 25 ♗d5).

22 d6 ♕e6?

Grischuk was concerned about 22...♕e5 23 d7.

He must have looked at 23...♘xd7 24 ♖xd7 exf3 25 ♕xf3.

Then 25...f6 26 ♘d4! would be problematic.

So is 25...♖e7 26 ♖xb7 ♖xb7 27 ♕xb7 ♕e8 after 28 ♗g1! ♖b8 29 ♕c7 ♖c8 30 ♖e1!.

Instead of all this, he calculated an intricate forcing line that runs eight more moves.

117

23 ♘c5 ♕f5

It begins 24 d7 ♘xd7 25 ♘xd7 exf3.

Then 26 ♘xf8 ♖xf8 27 ♗c5 can be met by 27...fxg2+ 28 ♔xg2 ♕g6+ 29 ♔h1 ♖fd8! (30 ♗xb4 ♕e4+).

24 ♗e2!

Grischuk had seen this much shorter variation and realized he must trade queens (24...♕g5? 25 d7 is lost). He did not appreciate how bad this endgame is.

24 ... ♕xf2

25 ♖xf2

Black's e-pawn would be over-extended after 25...e3? 26 ♖f5! and he cannot play 26...♘bd5 27 ♖fxd5.

He would be lost after 26...♘e4 27 ♘xe4 ♖xe4 28 d7 ♘c6 29 d8(♕) or 29 ♖f3.

25 ... ♘bd5

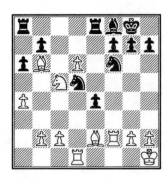

Carlsen has three promising moves and can play them in different orders.

The obvious ones are the d-pawn push and a4-a5, which protects the b6-bishop.

The direct 26 d7 ♖eb8! and then 27 a5? fails tactically because of 27...♘xb6 28 axb6 ♗xc5.

The third candidate, perhaps surprisingly, is ♖xf6.

At first (26 d7 ♖eb8) 27 ♖xf6 looks good in view of 27...♗xc5 28 ♖xd5.

However, after 27...♘xf6 we get a simplified endgame in which White has the two bishops and a queenside pawn majority, 28 ♘xe4 ♘xe4 29 d8(♕) ♖xd8 30 ♖xd8 ♖xd8 31 ♗xd8.

That's an advantage for White but a small one (31...♗c5 32 ♗f3 f5!).

26 a5?

It was Magnus' turn to miscalculate.

The best order was 26 ♖xf6! ♘xf6 27 a5! ♖eb8.

Then Black has no way to improve his position but White can make progress by pushing his queenside pawns (c2-c4 and b2-b4-b5) before regaining the Exchange with ♗c7.

26 ... ♘xb6

27 axb6 ♖ab8?

This was the final slip and it is fatal. Best was 27...♖ec8! 28 b4 ♖c6.

Then 29 d7 leads to 29...♗xc5 30 d8(♕)+ ♖xd8 31 ♖xd8+ ♗f8 and a tactical shot, 32 ♗xa6!.

Black would lose after 32...bxa6? 33 b7. But he should be able to draw after 32...♖xb6!.

28 ♖xf6!

Grischuk counted on 28 b4? ♖ed8!, when he would seize the advantage.

For example, 29 ♖xf6 gxf6 30 ♘xe4 f5.

Or 29 d7 ♗xc5 30 ♖xf6 gxf6 31 bxc5 ♖a8.

28 ... gxf6

29 ♘d7

Carlsen will regain the Exchange and be able to launch his queenside pawns.

29 ... f5

30 c4!

After 30...♔g7 31 ♘xb8 ♖xb8 32 c5 ♔f6 the fastest win is 33 ♗xa6!.

That works as in the game: 33...bxa6 34 c6 or 33...♔e6 34 ♗xb7! ♖xb7 35 c6 ♖xb6 36 d7 ♗e7 37 c7.

30	...	a5
31	c5	♗g7
32	♘xb8	♖xb8

Spoilsport computers recommend an easy win after 33 b3. Humans cannot resist:

33	♗a6!	♗f6

Or 33...bxa6 34 c6 and 35 c7 and a pawn queens.

34	♗xb7	♖xb7
35	c6	♖xb6
36	♖c1	♗xb2
37	d7	**Resigns**

19
Blindminded

Magnus still had problems with the world champion. In classical games against Vishy Anand, he scored only one win while suffering seven losses, amid several draws, before 2009. As usual, he fared better in speed games. But his most impressive early win from Anand came in the annual combination of speed and blindfold chess known as the Melody Amber tournament. Carlsen scored a respectable 6-5 in the 2009 version's speed section. But he was even better, 7-4, in the blind games.

Viswanathan Anand – Carlsen
Melody Amber Tournament
(blindfold), Nice 2009
*Sicilian Defense,
Rossolimo Variation (B30)*

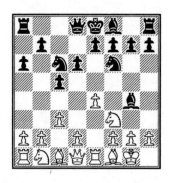

1	e4	c5
2	♘f3	♘c6
3	♗b5	d6

This is often arrived at via 1 e4 c5 2 ♘f3 d6 3 ♗b5+ ♘c6, which is more ambitious than 3...♗d7 4 ♗xd7+.

4	0-0	♗d7
5	♖e1	♘f6
6	c3	a6
7	♗f1	

Now either 7...g6? 8 d4 or 7...e5 8 d4 favors White.

| 7 | ... | ♗g4 |

As in Game 15, Carlsen signals that he is willing to play ...♗xf3.

The bishop move does not prevent 8 d4 because 8...cxd4 9 cxd4 ♗xf3? 10 gxf3 is quite nice for White after 10...e5 11 d5 ♘d4 12 ♗e3.

Instead, 9...e5 10 d5 ♘d4 11 ♗e3 and now 11...♘xf3+ 12 gxf3 ♗d7 is considered equal.

8	d3	e6
9	♘bd2	♗e7
10	h3	♗h5

There was less reason for 10...♗xf3 once White can retake

120

with the knight, 11 ♘xf3, and play 12 d4.

11 g4

If White does not try to exploit the h5-bishop he has few middlegame plans of promise.

For instance, after 11 a3 0-0 12 b4 Black would get a fine game with 12...b5 and ...♘d7/...♗f6.

11 ... ♗g6

12 ♘h4

Anand prepares f2-f4. He should not fear 12...♘xg4 13 ♘xg6 ♘xf2 because Black gets only two pawns for his knight and a vanishing attack after 14 ♔xf2 hxg6 15 ♔g1.

12 ... ♘d7

13 ♘g2

White's king would be slightly insecure after 13 ♘xg6 hxg6 14 f4 ♗h4 (15 ♖e3 ♕c7 16 ♘f3 ♗g3).

13 ... h5!

This is the obvious way to exploit g2-g4. Yet in some previous master games Black had problems after 13...0-0 14 f4 or 13...e5 14 ♘f3 (14...h5 15 g5!).

14 f4

Carlsen allowed 14 ♘f4 ♗h4 15 ♘xg6 fxg6 because f2 would become a target after ...♖f8 or ...0-0.

14 ... hxg4

15 hxg4

Bent Larsen had played 15...♗h7 16 ♘f3 g5, to secure control of e5 after 17 f5 ♘de5 18 ♘xe5 ♘xe5.

Another previous game saw 15...♗h4 16 ♖e3, when 16...♕e7 17 f5 ♗g5 18 fxg6 ♗xe3+ 19 ♘xe3 ♘de5 was also nice for Black.

15 ... ♕c7

Preparing queenside castling was a new move.

16 ♘f3 0-0-0

The plusses and minuses of White's strategy are becoming apparent. He can gain control of e5 after 17 f5 ♗h7 18 d4. But his kingside pawns would be over-extended after 18...♔b8 and ...♘f6.

17 ♘e3

Anand wants to protect his king with pieces (♗g2).

121

17 ... ♘b6

This move is surprising for two reasons.

The first is that the knight would seem better placed on f6 so that ...d5 will have more punch.

After 17...♘f6 18 ♗g2 d5! White should keep the center closed, 19 e5 ♘d7.

But then 20...f6! threatens to favor Black considerably.

After 20 d4 ♗e4! Black prepares 21...cxd4 22 cxd4 f6! with advantage.

18 ♘c4

The second reason 17...♘b6 was surprising is that it prepared 18...c4! – a move that could have been played immediately (17...c4! 18 dxc4? ♗xe4).

The critical line is 17...c4 18 ♘xc4 d5 19 exd5 exd5 when 20 ♘e3 ♕xf4 or 20 ♘a3 ♗d6 exposes the White king.

Also 20 ♘ce5 ♘dxe5 21 ♘xe5 ♘xe5 22 ♖xe5 ♗d6 or 21 fxe5 f6!

would powerfully open up kingside lines.

18 ... ♘xc4

19 dxc4

Anand has stopped ...c4. But he only delayed ...d5.

Carlsen could prepare that powerful push with 19...f6 and 20...♗f7.

If 20 ♗g2 ♗f7 21 f5, he has a strong 21...d5 22 fxe6? dxe4.

19 ... f5!

White cannot allow 20...fxe4 or 20...fxg4.

20 exf5 exf5

21 g5!

Carlsen would have won soon after 21 gxf5 ♗xf5 because he can blow the kingside open with ideas such as 22...d5! 23 cxd5 g5! and 24...gxf4.

For example, 24 ♘xg5? ♗xg5 25 fxg5 ♕h2 mate and 24 fxg5 ♗g4 and ....♗xf3.

21 ... ♗f7!

Anand would have equalized following 21...♗h5 22 ♕d3 g6? 23 ♘h2.

Then the bishop on h5 looks nice but it blocks his play on the h-file.

Carlsen would need a new plan, such as offering a knight with 23...♘e5.

That works after 24 fxe5 dxe5 followed by ...e4/...♗d6.

But 24 ♕d5! is a good reply. White might even get the advantage after ♗g2, ♗e3-f2 and doubling rooks on the e-file.

22 ♕c2

Carlsen's last move made ...d5! inevitable.

22 ... g6

23 ♕f2

His advantage is so great that after 23 ♗e3 he could increase it with either 23...d5! or with 23...♘e5! 24 fxe5 dxe5 and ...e4.

23 ... d5

Anand can keep some lines closed with 24 ♘e5 ♘xe5 25 fxe5.

But after 25...dxc4 26 e6 ♗e8 27 ♗f4 Magnus would insert 27...♗c6! and threaten mate on h1.

He would have at least a two-pawn edge soon after 28 ♗g2 ♗d6.

Giving up the Exchange, 24 ♘e5 ♘xe5 25 ♖xe5 and 25...♗d6 26 ♖xd5 ♗xd5 27 cxd5, is also doomed after 27...♖d7 and ...♖dh7.

24 cxd5 ♗xd5

25 ♗e3

After the game, this was considered the losing move. But the outcome was decided much earlier.

After 25 ♗g2 ♗d6 26 ♕g3 c4! Black opens up another attacking line, a7-g1.

He would win after 27 ♗e3 ♖de8 and ...♖xe3!.

Also, 26 ♘h4 ♗xg2 27 ♘xg2 ♖h3! followed by ...♕h7 or ...♘e7-d5.

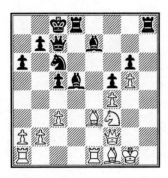

Fans were aware that the players in these tournaments were not really blindfolded.

But few on-line spectators knew that the players could look at a computer screen displaying a diagram with no pieces or pawns on it.

That was a help even in a patternless position like this because, for example, a player could more easily visualize how c7 is on the same diagonal as h2.

25   ...   &xg5!

So that 26 fxg5 &xf3 27 ♕xf3 ♕h2 mate.

Black also wins after 27 &g2 &xg2 28 ♕xg2 ♖h4! and ...♖g4.

26   ♕g3   &e7

Carlsen had to discard false leads such as 26...♕h7? 27 fxg5 &xf3 28 ♔f2, when the game goes on.

27   &g2   g5!

28   ♘xg5   &xg5

Now 29 ♕xg5 ♖hg8 30 ♕xf5+ ♔b8 31 ♖e2 ♕g7 does it.

But 29...♕f7!, as in the game, is simpler.

29   &xd5   ♖xd5

30   ♕xg5

30   ...   ♕f7!

This prepares ...♖g8 but also 31 ♔f1 ♖dd8 and ...♕c4+!.

31   ♔f2   ♖h2+

32   ♔f1   ♖d8!

33   ♕g3   ♕c4+

34   ♔g1   ♖xb2

White resigns

There was no good answer to 35...♖g8.

20
Mentoring Magnus

It was a secret that could not be concealed for long: Garry Kasparov had been hired to tutor Magnus, beginning in 2009. The former world champion was reportedly paid several hundred thousand dollars to refine Carlsen's openings and give him psychological insights into the big-league opponents that Kasparov had known for years. Carlsen said Kasparov even gave him tips about sleeping. They expected to work together at least into 2010.

Magnus-watchers thought they detected Kasparov's influence in his play. He was playing the kind of moves only Kasparov would play in positions that few but Kasparov had mastered, they said. This was an exaggeration but there were traces of Kasparov style in games like this.

Carlsen – Veselin Topalov
Sofia 2009
*Queen's Gambit Declined,
Semi-Slav Defense (D43)*

1	d4	d5
2	c4	c6
3	♘f3	♘f6
4	♘c3	e6
5	♗g5	h6

This forces White to choose between giving up the two bishops (6 ♗xf6) and offering a gambit (6 ♗h4 dxc4 7 e4 g5 8 ♗g3 b5) that was once considered dubious.

The gambit is less sound after 6 ♗f4? dxc4 7 e4 b5 because e4-e5 is not a threat.

6	♗xf6	♕xf6
7	e3	

Databases indicate Carlsen had first played this position in 2008 and scored 4-0 with it in the next few months. It was not a Kasparov specialty.

7	...	♘d7
8	♗d3	dxc4

9	♗xc4	g6
10	0-0	♗g7
11	e4	

All these moves have been played in hundreds of master games and the same positions can arise from different move orders, such as 7...g6 8 ♗d3 ♗g7 9 e4 dxc4 10 ♗xc4 ♘d7.

Black usually seeks ...e5. Then a pawn exchange on d4 or e5 would be fairly equal.

11	...	0-0

This is a provocative move because play becomes sharper if e4-e5 is allowed.

Carlsen had faced 11...e5 in the previous year and got a tiny edge against Sergey Karjakin with 12 d5 ♘b6 12 ♗b3 ♗g4 14 ♖c1 0-0 15 h3 ♗xf3 16 ♕xf3 ♕xf3 17 gxf3.

12	e5

Black would get a better version of that after 12 ♕e2 e5 13 d5 ♘b6 14 ♗b3 ♗g4!.

He would also stand well after 12 h3 e5 13 d5 ♘b6 14 ♗b3 cxd5.

For example, 15 ♘xd5 ♘xd5 16 ♗xd5 ♗e6 or15 exd5 ♗f5 and ...♖ad8.

12	...	♕e7
13	♕e2	b5

This queenside punch is basic to Black strategy in this opening.

In a game at Nanjing six months earlier, Topalov's opponent avoided e3-e4 in favor of 11 ♕c2 ♕e7 12 ♖ad1 0-0 13 ♖fe1.

Topalov got a good game with 13...a6 14 a3 b5! 15 ♗a2 c5 16 d5 c4.

14	♗d3	♗b7

A typical idea in this kind of position is ♘e4 so the knight can go to d6 or, after ♖ac1, to c5

But Topalov was willing to temporarily sacrifice a pawn with 15 ♘e4 c5!.

Then 16 ♘d6? ♗xf3 17 ♕xf3 cxd4 and 16 ♘xc5 ♘xc5 17 dxc5 ♗xf3 18 ♕xf3 ♕xc5 favor him.

White would have no advantage after 16 ♗xb5 cxd4 because the e5-pawn is weak.

15 ♗e4!

This is the best way of delaying ...c5. But it does not threaten 16 ♘xb5 because 16...♘xe5! favors Black (17 dxe5 cxb5 or 17 ♘xe5 cxb5).

15 ...   ♖fd8

The more intuitive way of handling the position is to put Black's rooks at c8 and b8, protect the b-pawn with ...a7-a6 and then push ...c5.

But there is a tactical problem: After ...c5, White could respond ♗xb7/...♖xb7 followed by forking ♘e4-d6.

Topalov has an original use of his rooks in mind.

16 ♖ac1   ♖ab8

17 ♖fd1   a6

If there were a stop-sign that read "Opening ends, middlegame begins," it would be posted here.

Black is ready for 18...c5 because now 19 ♗xb7 ♖xb7 20 ♘e4? favors him after 20...cxd4 21 ♘d6 ♖bb8.

A key point is 22 ♖xd4 ♘xe5! 23 ♘xe5 allows 23...♖xd6, another reason for 15...♖fd8.

18 h4

Carlsen had a variety of good alternatives depending on whether he is focusing on the kingside, the queenside or both.

One option is 18 ♕e3 followed by ♘e2-f4 with a possible h2-h4-h5.

Another looks at the queenside with 18 ♘b1 followed by ♘bd2-b3 and ♖c2.

One of the advantages of 18 ♘b1 is that 18...c5? loses a pawn, 19 ♗xb7 ♖xb7 20 dxc5 (20...♘xc5? 21 ♖xd8+ and ♖xc5).

And 18...♖dc8 19 ♘bd2 c5? is bad for the reason mentioned earlier – the Black rooks make themselves available for a ♘d6 fork after 20 ♗xb7 ♖xb7 21 ♘e4.

18 ...   ♗a8

Topalov was finally ready for 18...c5 19 ♗xb7 ♖xb7 and then 20 d5 exd5 21 ♘xd5 ♕e8 because the e5-pawn is vulnerable.

But his rook is somewhat awkward on b7. Carlsen could have retained a small edge with 22 ♘f4 (22...♘xe5?? 23 ♖xd8 ♘xf3+ 24 ♕xf3 ♕xd8 25 ♕xb7).

127

19 ♖c2

Now 19...c5 20 ♗xa8 ♖xa8 21 d5 exd5 22 ♘xd5 ♕e8? allows 23 ♘c7.

19 ... ♖dc8

With 19...♘b6 Black would be giving up on ...c5 in favor of ...♘c4 or ...♘d5.

That's strategically risky after 20 ♖dc1.

Then 20...♘d5 21 ♘xd5 cxd5 22 ♗d3 shows us one of the virtues of 18 h4. White can play on both wings after 22...♖d7 23 h5! g5 24 ♘h2 and ♘g4.

Applying pressure on both wings was one of the favorite themes of...Garry Kasparov.

20 ♖dc1 ♕f8!

Black protects the c8-rook so that ...c5 is finally coming.

In contrast, 20...c5? 21 ♗xa8 ♖xa8 22 ♘e4! pins the c-pawn (22...c4 23 b3 ♘b6 24 ♘d6).

21 a4?

Playing on both wings has some risks. Black had avoided ...b4 earlier because of ♘a4!.

But now 21...b4! 22 ♘b1 c5 would have been at least equal for Black (23 ♗xa8 ♖xa8 24 dxc5 ♖xc5). In potential endgames the a4- and e5-pawns are weak.

21 ... c5?

Instead, Topalov counted on meeting 22 ♗xa8 with the zwischenzug 22...cxd4.

Then after 23 ♘xb5 ♖xc2 24 ♖xc2 axb5 25 ♗c6 White wins a pawn.

But Black has some compensation following 25...d3! 26 ♕xd3 ♘c5 27 ♕d4 ♘xa4 28 b3 ♘b6 29 ♗xb5 ♘d5. However, White is better.

22 axb5 cxd4!

23 ♘xd4 ♗xe4?

Topalov talked himself out of the routine 23...axb5.

Then if White indirectly swaps pawns, 24 ♘dxb5? ♘xe5 or 24 ♘cxb5 ♖xc2 25 ♕xc2 ♗xe4 26 ♕xe4 ♘xe5, the passed b2-pawn is more liability than asset. He would be worse.

Better is 24 ♗xa8 ♖xa8 But then the position is no more than equal – 25 f4 ♕d8! would threaten 26...♕xh4 as well as 26...♘xe5 27 fxe5 ♕xd4+.

24 ♘xe4!

Magnus must have been tempted by 24 ♕xe4 axb5 25 ♘c6 because 25...♖b6 26 ♘e2 threatens 27 ♘e7+ ♕xe7 28 ♖xc8+.

That gains time for ♘ed4 and kingside ideas such as h4-h5.

But there was a major flaw. Instead of 25...♖b6 Black would have 25...♘c5 26 ♕f3 ♖xc6! 27 ♕xc6 ♘d3.

Then he gets the Exchange with interest after 28...♘xc1 or 28...♘b4.

24	...	♖xc2
25	♖xc2	axb5
26	♘c6	

Also good is protecting the e5-pawn with 26 f4. But 26...♘b6 and ...♘d5 may force a loosening g2-g3. The kingside pawn White would prefer to push is h4-h5.

26	...	♖b6?

After 26...♖a8 27 ♕xb5 White not only wins a pawn but stops ...♘b6-d5.

He would be threatening 28 ♖d2! because 28...♘b8? 29 ♖d8 is fatal.

Nevertheless, this was Black's best. It would have been difficult for White to make his pawn count after 27...♘b8!.

For instance, 28 ♘d6 ♘xc6 29 ♖xc6 ♕e7 30 g3 ♕a7 and ...♕d4.

27 f4!

Now Black's pieces are uncoordinated and threatened by 28 ♕d2!.

Then the only safe move of the knight, 28...♘b8, is bad after either 29 ♘a7 or 29 ♘d8 and 30 ♖c8.

The dancing knights also win after 28...♕e8 29 ♘d6 ♕a8 30 ♘c8! ♖b7 31 ♘d8!.

And after 28...♖b7 29 ♘d6 ♖b6 30 ♘c8! ♖b7 31 ♘a5 and 29...♖c7 30 ♘e7+.

27	...	♕a8
28	♘e7+	♔h7

White's advantage would disappear after 29 ♖c8? ♖b8 or 29 ♘c8? ♖c6 30 ♘cd6 f5! or 30 ♘ed6 b4.

29 h5!

This has a Kasparovian quality.

White threatens 30 hxg6+ fxg6 31 ♕d3! because of 32 ♘g5+! or 32 ♕xd7.

Black would be lost after 31...♘f8 32 ♘g5+! hxg5 33 ♕h3+ and 32...♔h8 33 ♖c8!.

29   ...   ♖a6

The game would have ended immediately after 29...gxh5? 30 ♘g5+! hxg5 31 ♕xh5+ ♗h6 32 ♕xf7+.

The best try was 29...♕d8 30 hxg6+ fxg6.

Then 31 ♘c8 ♖a6 32 ♕d1! maintains a bind. But there is nothing immediate.

Stronger is 31 ♘xg6! ♔xg6 32 ♕d3!, when 33 ♘d6+ and mates is threatened.

Black might hold after 32...♔f7 and 33 ♘d6+ ♖xd6 34 ♕xd6 ♕b6+ 35 ♕xb6 ♘xb6.

But 33 ♖d2! and 34 ♕xd7+ is very close to a technical win (33...♔e7? 34 ♘c5).

So Topalov set a trap.

30   hxg6+   fxg6

31   ♖c7!

It would have worked after 31 ♕d3? ♘xe5! 32 fxe5 ♕a7+ and ...♕xe7.

31   ...   ♖a1+

32   ♔f2

A minor slip. Carlsen thought 32 ♔h2 ♘xe5 would complicate his life (33 fxe5? ♗xe5+).

But 33 ♘f6+! ♗xf6 34 ♘d5+ ♗g7 35 ♕xe5 would have ended the game faster.

32   ...   ♕d8

He could have lasted a bit longer after 32...♖a4 33 ♘c6 ♘f8.

33   ♕d3!   ♕xe7

Or 33...♕xc7 34 ♘g5+ and mates (34...hxg5 35 ♕xg6+ ♔h8 36 ♕h5+).

34   ♖xd7   ♕h4+

35   ♔f3   ♕h5+

36   ♔g3   Resigns

The threat is ♘f6+ and 36...♔h8 37 ♖d8+ ♔h7 38 ♕d7 only delays it.

21
Playability

You can see three Ps in contemporary grandmaster chess – principle, pragmatism and playability. Principled moves are based on general principles: Moving a rook to an open file, seizing the best diagonal for your bishop, doubling enemy pawns, occupying a central outpost with a knight, activating a king in an endgame.

Pragmatic (or practical) moves temper principle with the complicating factors of the clock and tactical risk. Safeguarding your king or overprotecting a piece when there is no immediate threat are examples of pragmatism.

Playability is the variable that weighs how easy or difficult it will be to find good, if not the best, moves in the future. A move may be second-best or third-best in objective (i.e. computer) terms. It may violate general principles. But if it leads to a more "playable" position, it is the pragmatic choice. And, in many cases, it is Carlsen's choice.

Carlsen – Peter Leko
Nanjing 2009
Scotch Game (C45)

1	e4	e5
2	♘f3	♘c6
3	d4	

Carlsen had been playing the Scotch since at least age 12 and scored well with it. But now he was armed with Kasparov's opening database of unused analysis.

3	...	exd4
4	♘xd4	♗c5
5	♗e3	

When he annotated the game, Carlsen awarded the move 3 d4 an exclamation point because of the amount of time his opponent spent in the opening.

In fact, Leko had more experience with the Scotch than Carlsen. But his experience was playing White with 5 ♘b3 or 5 ♘xc6.

5	...	♛f6
6	c3	♘ge7
7	♗c4	♘e5
8	♗e2	

Kasparov preferred 8 ♗b3 in two 2016 speed games against Hikaru Nakamura. But then 8...♛a6 stops 0-0 and might be uncomfortable for White.

8	...	♛g6
9	0-0	d6
10	f4	

Carlsen called this "an old move." In fact, it dates back to a Tchigorin – Schiffers game in 1880, which went 10...♛xe4 11 ♛d2? ♘g4, and White had nothing for his lost pawn.

"Old" moves are often just ones that were abandoned decades ago by masters because they could not prove it leads to a significant edge.

Carlsen may have just been seeking an uncharted middlegame, such as after 10...♘g4 11 ♗xg4 ♗xg4 12 ♛d3.

10	...	♛xe4
11	♗f2	♗xd4!

Black loses his queen after 11...♘5c6? 12 ♗d3 ♛d5? 13 c4 and a piece after 12...♛xf4 13 ♘xc6.

Also bad is 11...♘5g6 12 ♘d2 ♛xf4 13 ♘b5!.

12 cxd4!

White may not have enough for his pawn after 12 ♗xd4 ♘5c6 13 ♘d2 ♛g6, and 13 ♗xg7?? ♖g8 loses.

Instead, Magnus wanted to use a new d4-pawn to gain space.

The perils to Black are apparent after 12 cxd4 ♘5c6? 13 ♘c3 ♛g6 14 d5! ♘d8 15 ♘b5.

12	...	♘5g6
13	g3!	

The most Tchigorinesque of modern grandmasters, Alexander

Morozevich, is credited with this surprisingly good move.

The idea is that Black's knights are restricted by the pawns at f4 and g3 and will be further limited by d4-d5.

The stem game, Morozevich – Kramnik, Dortmund 2001, went 13...♗h3! 14 ♗f3 ♕f5 15 ♖e1 d5 16 ♕b3 0-0 17 ♘c3 c6 18 ♕xb7 and was soon drawn.

White would appear to have compensation after 16...0-0-0 17 ♘c3.

13	...	0-0
14	♘c3	♕f5
15	d5!	

Carlsen aimed for this position when he chose 10 f4. His reasoning was refreshingly modern:

White cannot claim an advantage in the traditional definition. He controls space but Black's only apparent weakness is on c7. That pawn will be safer after his next move stops ♘b5. White's aerated kingside might seem far more vulnerable. And Black does have an extra pawn.

"But I think it is much easier to play White here..." Carlsen said.

Easier to play. This is something computers cannot calibrate and therefore is not part of their evaluation. But it had been a factor in Carlsen's thinking for

some time. He gave a hint of this in his notes to a game with Leinier Dominguez at the 2007 World Cup. It began 1 e4 c5 2 ♘f3 d6 3 d4 cxd4 4 ♘xd4 ♘f6 5 ♘c3 a6 6 ♗e2 e5 7 ♘b3 ♗e7 8 ♗g5 ♗e6 9 ♗xf6 ♗xf6 10 ♕d3 ♗g5 11 ♖d1 ♘c6 12 a3 ♗xb3 13 cxb3 ♘d4 14 b4 ♖c8.

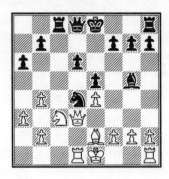

Carlsen – Leinier Dominguez
World Cup 2007

Black has the better-placed minor pieces. If White trades his knight with a later ♘e2, the resulting bishops-of-opposite-color position would seem to favor Black, if only because of a superior pawn structure.

"But during our preparation we had noticed that White, for some reason, has the more pleasant game," Carlsen wrote in *New In Chess*. That's a concept that is invaluable for a human but cannot be measured. It is hard for an engine – or a human – to explain "pleasant."

Yet Black's position slowly worsened for no explainable

reason: 15 0-0 0-0 16 ♗g4 ♖c6 17 g3 g6 18 f4 ♗h6 19 ♖f2 ♗g7 20 f5 ♕g5 21 ♗h3 ♗h6 22 ♖e1 b5 23 ♔g2 ♖a8 24 fxg6 hxg6 25 ♗d7! ♖c4 26 b3 ♖c7 27 ♘d5.

It suddenly became obvious that Black was losing material (27...♖b7 28 ♘f6+ ♔g7 29 h4). He played 27...♖c1 28 h4! ♖xe1 (rather than 28...♕d8 29 ♖xc1 ♗xc1 30 ♕f1!) and eventually succumbed after 29 hxg5 ♗xg5 30 ♗g4.

15	...	a6
16	♖e1	♔h8!

At least one of the knights has a future, at f6 after ...♘g8.

17	♖c1	♗d7
18	♗f3	

This demonstrates Carlsen's confidence that his position will improve with quiet moves, rather than trying to win quickly with 18 h4 and 19 h5.

On 18 h4 ♖fe8 19 h5 ♘f8 20 h6 Black loses immediately after 20...gxh6? 21 ♕d4+ and 22 ♗d3.

But he would have to calculate 19...♘xf4 20 gxf4 ♕xf4 out to a clearcut advantage. The more pragmatic move is 18 ♗f3.

18	...	♖ac8

Black protects c7 but rules out ...♗c8 as a way of protecting the b7-pawn. Computers suggest ...b5 at various points in the last few moves. But then ....♗b7? would allow a strong ♗g4. Leko is learning how hard it is to play this position.

19	♕b3	b5
20	♘e2!	♕h3
21	♘d4	♗g4

This was a good time for the ...♘g8-f6 maneuver.

After 21...♘g8 22 ♗g2 ♕h5 23 ♘c6 ♖fe8 Black is safe (24 ♘a7? ♖xe1+ and 25...♖e8).

Chances would be mixed after 24 ♗d4 ♘6e7 or 24 ♖xe8 ♖xe8 25 ♘d4 ♖c8 25 ♖e1 ♘f6.

22	♗g2	♕h5
23	h4	

23 ... ♘g8?

Once again there is nothing that seems bad enough to be called a losing move. But this is the closest to one.

White was not threatening anything immediate, so a pass, such as 23...h6, made sense (24 ♕a3? ♘xd5).

Carlsen felt that there was no defense to a plan of doubling of rooks on the c-file. But Black would have sudden counterplay after 23...h6 and, for example, 24 ♖c3 ♘f5 25 ♖ec1 ♖fe8.

Then 26 ♖xc7? allows 26...♖xc7 27 ♖xc7 ♘xd4 28 ♗xd4 ♖e1+ 29 ♔h2 ♘xh4 and wins. Or 29 ♔f2 ♖e2+ 30 ♔g1 ♕f5!.

24 ♖c6!

Leko overlooked this move. He had calculated how 24 ♕a3 ♘f6 25 ♕xa6 ♘xd5 26 ♕xb5 c5 would activate his pieces.

For instance, 27 ♘e2? ♖b8 28 ♕d3 ♘b4 and 27 ♘c2 ♗f3.

24 ... ♘f6

25 ♖xa6 ♗d7

There was no way to protect both remaining queenside pawns (25...♖b8 26 ♖a7 ♖fc8 27 ♘c6).

26 ♘xb5 ♖b8

Carlsen was concerned about Black challenging the e-file in the final stages of the game.

Here, for example, 26...♖fe8 would ready counterplay with 27...♖xe1+ 28 ♗xe1 ♕e2.

However, 27 ♖xe8+ ♖xe8 28 ♘xc7 is strong (28...♖e2? 29 ♗f3 or 28...♖c8 29 ♖a8).

27 a4 ♘g4

28 ♗f3!

Another pragmatic move. White's bishops are so useful that there was no reason to allow 28 ♖a7 ♘xf2 29 ♔xf2 ♖fe8.

Computers are confident that 30 ♖xe8+ ♖xe8 31 ♗f3 ♕f5 32 ♖xc7 wins.

With his clock ticking, a human would want to feel sure about

135

32...♕h3 33 ♗g2 ♖e2+ 34 ♔xe2 ♕xg2+ 35 ♔e1, for example.

28	...	♕h6
29	♕c4!	

Carlsen was so sure that his queenside advantage would win that he made this move to discourage 29...♘xf2 30 ♔xf2 ♘xf4.

Leko was so sure that he was losing on the queenside that he made a desperate sacrifice anyway.

29	...	♘xh4!?
30	♗xg4!	

Not 30 gxh4?? ♘xf2 31 ♔xf2 ♕xh4+ and Black wins (32 ♔e2 ♖fe8+ or 32 ♔f1 ♗h3+).

30	...	♗xg4
31	gxh4	♗f3

32 f5

There are many ways to win, such as 32 ♔h2 ♕g6 33 ♖g1 ♕f5 34 ♖a7.

The practical choice is to overprotect the kingside by ruling out ...♕g6(+).

32	...	♕h5
33	♕f4	♗xd5
34	♘xc7	♗b7
35	♖b6	f6
36	♗d4	♕f7
37	♘e6	♖g8
38	♔f2	

Every checking possibility, even an innocuous one such as 38...g6 39 fxg6 ♖xg6+ is prevented.

38	...	♖bc8
39	♗c3	♗d5
40	a5	♖c4
41	♘d4	♗a8
42	♕xd6	♕h5
43	♕f4	♖cc8
44	♖be6	Resigns

Carlsen's performance rating in the tournament was 3001, which became the third highest ever recorded.

22
Rating Number One

"When did you think you were better than everyone else?" Carlsen was asked. "Probably in 2010," he replied. On January first of that year he was the highest rated player in the world. He had long passed Bobby Fischer's peak rating and only Garry Kasparov had achieved one higher.

But January 2010 marked the end of their close collaboration. Magnus was breezing through the annual Wijk aan Zee invitational with a 5½-2½ score, tied with Vladimir Kramnik. He was due to play White against Kramnik in the next round.

Via Skype, Carlsen conferred with Kasparov in Moscow, less than an hour before the game. Kasparov told him to play a different opening than the one he intended. Carlsen appeared overwhelmed with the new information when the game began.

Carlsen stood well in the opening, a Catalan. But he did not seem to be comfortable with the middlegame he got and lost in 38 moves. After the game he decided he and Kasparov played too differently to continue to work together. Kasparov felt Carlsen was unwilling to work hard enough. "I was not in the position to make him change his personality," he told the 'New Yorker.'

Levon Aronian – Carlsen
Melody Amber (blindfold),
Nice 2010
King's Indian Defense,
Taimanov Variation (E98)

1	♘f3	♘f6
2	c4	g6
3	♘c3	♗g7
4	e4	d6
5	d4	0-0
6	♗e2	e5
7	0-0	♘c6

By now Carlsen had abandoned many of the side variations he played as an adolescent, such as 7...♘h5?! 8 g3 ♗g4.

He had gotten inferior positions with inferior openings, then outplayed opponents in the move 15-25 stage. He could not expect to do that against elite players.

8	d5	♘e7

9   ♘e1

The plan of ♘d3/f2-f3 and c4-c5 was powerfully introduced by Mark Taimanov in the 1952 Soviet Championship. That set off a theoretical debate that continues today.

9   ...   ♘d7

10   ♘d3   f5

11   ♗d2

The positions that arise should now be subject to exact evaluation in the computer age. But they aren't.

"That's one of the things I love about the King's Indian," as Carlsen said in *New in Chess*. "In many cases, the computer gives evaluations." But when you go over it and see why the machine analysis differs "it turns out that you're right and the computer is wrong."

11   ...   ♘f6

12   f3

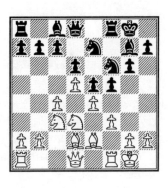

Kasparov, like most Black defenders, usually played 12...f4 and the pawn-storming ...g5-g4.

This a sophisticated wager – that Black can create enough kingside threats to offset White's breakthrough on the queenside from c4-c5!.

A main line runs 12...f4 13 c5 g4 14 cxd6 cxd6 15 ♘f2 ♘g6 16 ♕c2 ♖f7 17 ♖fc1.

Then 17...a6 stops ♘b5-c7 but after 18 a4 h5 19 h3 ♗f8 20 a5 White has had more tournament success.

12   ...   ♔h8

Kasparov had also tried a queenside blockade strategy, 12...♔h8 13 ♖c1 c5. Then the battle shifts to whether White can succeed in opening lines with b2-b4, supported by a2-a3 and ♖b1.

Carlsen knew that. But he admitted after this game that his knowledge of the opening ended with White's next move.

13   g4

If Black can blockade on the queenside with ...c5, why can't White try the kingside version with this move?

He can, as Pal Benko showed more than half a century earlier in a similar position.

Benko played 10 f3 (rather than 10 ♗d2) and then 10...f5 11 g4!.

Pushing pawns in front of your king seemed crazy at the time but Benko explained that White could control key kingside squares.

Or he could seal up the entire wing, e.g. 11...f4 12 h4 g5 13 h5! or 12...h5 13 g5!.

13   ...   c6!

This is quite different from the ...c5 blockade approach and was introduced into master practice by Jan Hein Donner.

Black can open part of the c-file now with ...cxd5. But he also has the option of launching his own queenside attack with 14...b5 (15 cxb5 cxb5 16 ♘xb5? ♛b6+).

14   ♔g2

For instance, 14 ♘f2 b5 is good because 15 cxb5 cxd5! simplifies the center in Black's favor (16 exd5 ♘exd5 17 ♘xd5 ♘xd5).

This attack on the d5-pawn chain had precedents in similar positions. One of the best-known was Petrosian-Fischer, Santa Monica 1966: 1 d4 ♘f6 2 ♘f3 g6 3 g3 ♗g7 4 ♗g2 0-0 5 0-0 d6 6 c4 ♘c6 7 ♘c3 ♗f5 8 h3 e5 9 d5 ♘e7 10 ♘e1 ♗c8 11 e4 ♘d7 12 ♘d3 f5 13 ♗d2 ♘f6 14 ♔h2 c6 15 f3 ♔h8 16 ♖c1 and now 16...b5 17 cxb5 cxd5 18 exd5 ♘fxd5 19 ♘xd5 ♘xd5. A draw was agreed soon after 20 ♘b4 ♗e6 21 ♘xd5 ♗xd5 22 ♗b4 ♗xa2.

14   ...   b5!

15   b3!

Aronian maintains his pawn chain. Now 15...bxc4 16 bxc4 ♗a6? turns out badly after 17 ♘b4!.

15   ...   a5

16   ♘f2

There didn't seem to be any better use of this knight once ♘b4 was ruled out.

If White had played 16 a3, then 16...bxc4 17 bxc4 ♗a6 has more punch.

But Carlsen would jump into the complexities of 16...a4! and 17 bxa4 bxc4 or 17 cxb5 cxd5.

16	...	b4!
17	♘a4	♗b7

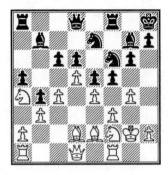

Carlsen was moving quickly and was pleased with the prospect of a knight sacrifice on d5. He considered 18 ♗d3 best.

That bishop can block the crucial long diagonal, 18...fxe4 19 fxe4 cxd5 20 exd5 ♘exd5 21 exd5 ♘xd5 22 ♗e4, leaving chances unclear.

18 ♖c1?

If you had full sight of the board – which the players did not in this "blind" game – you might not suspect that the bishop at b7 is threatening the White king.

Computers do. They look at 18 ♔g1 and then check out 18...cxd5 19 cxd5 ♘exd5! 20 exd5 ♘xd5.

They find that, for example, 21 ♗c4 fxg4 22 fxg4 ♘c7 is excellent for Black in view of ...♕h4 and ...♖f3. Or 22 ♘xg4 h5.

18	...	fxe4

19	fxe4	cxd5
20	exd5	

Black would also sacrifice after 20 cxd5.

20	...	♘exd5!
21	cxd5	♘xd5

Now 22 ♗f3 ♖xf3! 23 ♕xf3 ♘f4+ or 23 ♔xf3 ♘c3+ is over.

22	♔g1

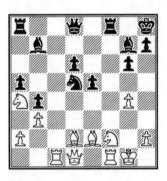

The knight sacrifice on d5 is well-known to grandmasters in similar positions. But the justification is usually an advance of Black's protected center pawns.

Instead, Magnus is looking to overwhelm the enemy king. He could have tried 22...♘f4 so that 23 ♗xf4 ♖xf4 24 ♘d3? ♖d4! threatens ...d5.

Or 23 ♗f3 ♗xf3 24 ♕xf3 d5...

22	...	e4!

...but he had a stronger idea: to unleash the other bishop.

White might have escaped after 22...♕h4 23 ♘e4! and 23...♘f4 24 ♗xf4 exf4 25 ♗f3 or 24...♗xe4? 25 ♗g3.

23   ♘xe4

The main threat was 23...e3. Clearly 23 ♗e1?? ♘e3 was no salvation.

23   ...   ♗d4+

24   ♖f2?

The only way to keep the game going was 24 ♔g2!.

Carlsen said he intended 24...♕h4 so that 25 ♗g5 can be met by 25...♘e3+ 26 ♗xe3 ♗xe4+ and wins.

But after the game he realized 25 ♗f3 is tougher to beat.

He decided 24...♕e7! was right because of 25 ♗f3 ♖xf3! 26 ♕xf3 ♘f6 27 ♖ce1.

Then comes 27...♗xe4 28 ♖xe4 ♘xe4 or 27...♘xe4. He would be close to a win in either case.

24   ...   ♖xf2

25   ♘xf2

Computers point out how 25 ♗g5! threatens the queen as well as ♕xd4+.

Black should still win after 25...♗f6 26 ♗xf6+ ♖xf6 27 ♕d4 ♘f4.

But 24...♗xf2+! 25 ♘xf2 ♕f6 was simpler. "When you play the Classical King's Indian the game is never going to be perfect," Carlsen said.

The rest is a massacre.

25	...	♕h4
26	♕e1	♖f8
27	♗f3	♖xf3
28	♕e4	♕xf2+

White resigns

On his blog, Carlsen told fans, "A very enjoyable win, not least because I spent less than ten minutes on the clock for the entire game."

141

23
When the Opening Ends

Carlsen's opening knowledge often seems like a mighty river –
a mile wide but only a few feet deep. He began Wijk aan Zee 2020
with seven straight draws because he couldn't get an advantage
with White and was regularly worse as Black by move 15 or so.

But there was a silver lining. Once he became a grandmaster,
the opponents he regularly met were so opening-oriented that
their skill level often dropped after the first hour of play. They no
longer tried hard to improve their understanding of the
middlegame or endgame.

A common attitude was expressed by Joel Lautier in 2001
"Once you reach a certain level it doesn't matter if you play much
better than your opponent in other parts of the game," he said
in 'Interview with a Grandmaster.' "...many grandmasters have
stopped working on [other] areas of their game because after a
while it's not very practical."

When confronted by a new opening situation, Carlsen's
opponents often found that it matters very much who plays better
in the middlegame.

Carlsen – Etienne Bacrot
Nanjing 2010
Scotch Game (C45)

1	e4	e5
2	♘f3	♘c6
3	d4	exd4
4	♘xd4	♗c5
5	♘b3	♗b6
6	♘c3	♘f6
7	♕e2	0-0

8	♗g5

This variation was once
considered toothless because of

8...♘d4 9 ♘xd4 ♗xd4. White has to deal with ...♗xc3+/...♖e8.

He would be worse after 10 0-0-0 ♗xc3 11 bxc3 h6 12 ♗h4 ♖e8, for instance.

But as the Scotch was revived in the 1980s it was found that the knee-jerk 9 ♘xd4? was an error.

Instead, after 9 ♕d2! or 9 ♕d3! and 9...♘xb3 10 axb3, White can continue 0-0-0 and f2-f3 and enjoy a spatial advantage that matters.

8 ...   h6

9 ♗h4   a5

This was regarded as a major improvement for Black.

White should avoid 10 0-0-0? a4 11 ♘d2 a3 12 b3 ♗d4.

Or 12 ♘c4 ♗d4 and 12 e5 axb2+ 13 ♔b1 ♘d5!.

10 a4

This is more or less forced because of 10 ♘a4 g5 11 ♗g3 ♘xe4!.

Then 12 ♕xe4?? ♖e8 is out and 12 ♘xb6 cxb6 13 0-0-0 ♖e8 is unpleasant.

10 ...   ♘d4!

11 ♕d3!   ♘xb3

12 cxb3

This was a new position at the time. Bacrot did not appreciate it was already a critical one.

The first thing to notice is that White has sustained more serious pawn damage compared with 8...♘d4 9 ♕d3 ♘xb3 10 axb3.

But the damage is not enough to discourage queenside castling.

For example, after 12...d6 13 0-0-0 ♗e6 14 ♕c2 White threatens 15 e5!.

Black gets the same kind of middlegame, after 14...♕e7 15 ♗c4, as in the game.

12 ...   ♖e8?!

To avoid that Black could shoot for ...c6 and ...d5!.

But to play 12...c6 13 0-0-0 d5 he has to understand that it is a gambit.

After 14 exd5 cxd5 15 ♘xd5 he has 15...g5!.

Then 16 ♘xf6+? ♕xf6 17 ♗g3 ♖d8 gets White killed (18 ♕f3 ♗f5 and ...♖ac8+ or 18 ♕c3 ♖xd1+ 19 ♔xd1 ♗d4).

Black is not worse after 16 ♗g3 ♗e6 or 16 ♕f3 ♘xd5 17 ♖xd5 ♕c7+ 18 ♗c4 ♗e6.

13 0-0-0 d6

14 ♕c2!

Black should begin to sweat when he realizes he cannot play 14...♗e6 because 15 e5 g5 16 ♗g3 wins material.

14 ... ♗d7?

Better is 14...c6 15 ♗c4 ♕e7 16 ♖he1 ♗e6, with a position similar to the note to 12 cxb3.

White can renew the e4-e5 threat with 17 f4.

That would prompt 17...♗xc4 18 bxc4 ♕e6 19 ♕d3.

Then 19...♖ad8 20 f5 ♕e7 21 g4 is the kind of playability position Magnus liked, one that is easier for him to find moves that improve his position (♕g3, ♔c2, ♖e2).

Alternatively, 19...♕g4 gets to an endgame, 20 ♕g3 ♕xg3 21 ♗xg3, again with a position that is more comfortable for White.

15 ♗c4

By now Bacrot knew he was in trouble.

He must have planned to play 15...♗c6 but backed out when he looked at 16 ♖he1 ♕e7 17 f4.

Carlsen would have loved to play the bishops-of-opposite-color middlegame of 17...♕f8 18 ♗xf6 gxf6 19 ♕d3 and 20 ♘d5 ♗xd5 21 ♕xd5.

Inserting 16...g5 17 ♗g3 doesn't help Black because there is still no good defense to e4-e5.

For example, 17...♘h5 18 e5 and 18...♘xg3 19 ♕g6+ or 18...♔g7 19 ♕f5.

15 ... ♗e6

16 ♖he1

Black has lost a tempo, compared with 14...c6, and that's a lot in a position like this.

After 16...g5 17 ♗g3 ♕c8 his queen gets out of the pin. But he would be distinctly worse following 18 h4.

16 ... ♕e7

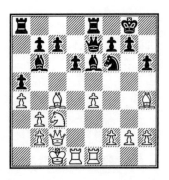

17 e5!

"Obvious move," you might say, "It's Capablanca chess."

This move opens the file leading to the pinned e6-bishop. That forces damage to Black's king position that is much more exploitable than what happened on the queenside.

But Carlsen had to compare the benefits of 17 e5 against that of 17 f4!, which would have made 18 e5 a decisive threat.

On 17...♗xc4 18 bxc4 ♕e6 Black has the same position as in the note to 14...♗d7 but without the extra move ...c6.

That difference means 19 ♗xf6 ♕xf6 20 ♘d5 ♕d8 21 ♘xb6 cxb6 gives him terminally weak pawns.

That is very good for White. But what happens in the game is better.

17 ... dxe5

18 ♖xe5 ♕f8

The chief alternative, 18...g5 19 ♗g3, gives White the strong h2-h4 lever.

For example, 19...♔g7 20 h4 g4 21 ♖xe6! fxe6 22 ♗e5 followed by ♘e4.

On 19...♖ad8 20 ♖xd8 ♖xd8 he wins a pawn with 21 ♗xe6 fxe6 22 ♕g6+.

19 ♗xf6 gxf6

20 ♖e2

Carlsen's superiority would not be so clear after 20 ♖h5 ♖ad8.

After 20 ♖e2 he is ready for ♘e4, ♘d5 or ♖de1.

Black cannot survive 20...♖ad8 21 ♖xd8 ♖xd8 22 ♗xe6 fxe6 23 ♖xe6.

20 ... ♕g7

21 ♗xe6 ♖xe6!

An extra pair of rooks helps White: 21...fxe6 22 ♖d3! ♔h8 23 ♖g3 ♕h7 is like the game.

But this time White has 24 ♕xh7+ ♔xh7 25 ♘e4 ♖f8 26 ♖d2! and ♖d7+ (26...♖f7 27 ♖d7! ♖xd7 28 ♘xf6+).

22 ♖xe6 fxe6

As with 17 e5!, Carlsen has a choice between a good move and a better one. Here 23 ♕e4 forks two pawns. He would have a clear edge after, say, 23...♖e8 24 ♕xb7 ♗xf2 25 ♔b1 and ♘e4.

23 ♖d3! ♔h8

24	♖g3	♕h7

Now 25 ♕xh7+ ♔xh7 26 ♘e4 f5! would throw away his advantage.

25	♕d2	♗c5!

Otherwise 26 ♘e4 and 27 ♘xf6 would win (26...♕xe4 27 ♕xh6+).

26	♘e4	♗e7

Computers claim 27 ♕d7 ♕xe4 28 ♕xe7 is best.

But a pragmatic player would never prefer to play 28...♕e1+ 29 ♔c2 ♕e4+ 30 ♔d2 ♕f4+ 31 ♔e2 ♕e4+ 32 ♖e3 when he can win with simple moves.

27	♖h3

That would be true even though Black can put up better resistance with 27...♖d8! 28 ♖xh6 ♖xd2 29 ♖xh7+ ♔xh7 30 ♔xd2 f5.

White can make slow progress then with 31 ♘c3 ♗c5 32 f3 c6 33 ♔d3 and ♔c4.

Long grinding games did not trouble Carlsen. He defeated nine grandmasters in 2010 in games that lasted more than 60 moves.

27	...	♔g7?

28	♕d7!	♔f7

29	♘g5+!

Also winning is 29 ♘xf6 but the text is much easier to calculate.

29	...	fxg5

30	♖f3+	♔g8

31	♕xe6+	♔h8

32	♖f7	♗d6

Not 32...♕d3 33 ♕xh6+ and mates.

33	♖xh7+	♔xh7

34	♕f7+	♔h8

35	g3	♖a6

36	♔b1

Carlsen does not need his king to win because a White pawn on f6 will be decisive.

36	...	♗b4

37	f4	gxf4

38	gxf4	**Resigns**

24
Berlin Warrior

Every great player (and many a dedicated amateur) has had to deal with the Berlin Defense of the Ruy Lopez since Vladimir Kramnik showed its resilient powers in the 2000 World Championship match. Kramnik's opponent, Kasparov, repeatedly got a slight White endgame advantage by going into the main line of the Berlin. As the match went on, Viktor Korchnoi was certain that Kasparov, with his superior computer power, would find a way to get more. But the Berlin is almost computer-proof.

Jan Smeets – Carlsen
Wijk aan Zee 2011
Ruy Lopez, Berlin Defense (C67)

1	e4	e5
2	♘f3	♘c6
3	♗b5	♘f6
4	0-0	♘xe4

White can play differently after 4...♘xe4 but in the 2010s the best players were so lacking in new ideas that they played for the tiniest of advantages.

For example, they often settled for 5 ♖e1 ♘d6 6 ♘xe5 ♗e7 7 ♗f1 ♘xe5 8 ♖xe5 0-0 9 ♘c3 and 9 d4 ♗f6 10 ♖e1.

The only bid for a major advantage is:

5	d4	♘d6
6	♗xc6	dxc6
7	dxe5	♘f5

8	♕xd8+	♔xd8

White has the better of the pawn structure and much smoother development. Black is compensated with the two bishops.

Tactics are relatively few, so strategy matters more. White's best plan is to mobilize his kingside pawns, such as with h2-h3, g2-g4 and f2-f4-f5.

9	♘c3

Before 2000, it was widely assumed that Black was limited to two continuations. One was 9...h6 so that he could move his king to the queenside without fear of ♘g5xf7. The other way to safeguard f7 was 9...♚e8.

Opening books hardly considered anything after 9...♚e8 aside from 10 ♘e2 ♗e6 11 ♘f4 ♗d5 12 ♘xd5 cxd5. Then the pawn structure is equalized and the two-bishop edge is eliminated. Theory said chances were more or less equal.

Carlsen, and others, took a different approach after **9...♚e8 10 h3 b6**. He liked to play ...♗b7 and, if allowed, ...c5 and ...♘d4!.

At Kristiansund 2010, Judith Polgar tried **11 ♖d1 ♗b7 12 ♗f4 ♖c8 13 a4** and Carlsen replied **13...♘e7? 14 a5! c5.**

Polgar – Carlsen
Kristiansund 2010

Now **15 axb6 axb6 16 ♘b5!** would have made a winning threat of 17 ♖a7.

Black can avert disaster with 16...♗xf3 17 gxf3 ♘c6 but 18 ♖a8 ♖xa8 19 ♘xc7+ wins a pawn.

Instead, Polgar played **15 ♘b5?** and Carlsen recovered with **15...a6! 16 ♘d6+ cxd6 17 exd6 ♘d5**.

Remarkably, Polgar had no advantage. She went for the apparent knockout of **18 c4? ♘xf4 19 d7+ ♚d8 20 ♘e5**.

But Magnus suddenly had the better winning chances after **20...♗e7! 21 axb6 ♘e2+ 22 ♚f1 ♘d4 23 dxc8(♕)+ ♚xc8**. Polgar quickly collapsed and lost.

| 9 | ... | ♗d7 |

Carlsen began playing this move at least as early as 2007, with the idea of ...♚c8 and perhaps ...b6/ ...♚b7.

The bishop looks strange on d7 but it can defend f7 from e8.

| 10 | h3 | b6 |

Now 11 a4 a5! is relatively harmless.

| 11 | b3 | ♚c8 |
| 12 | ♗b2 | h5 |

Carlsen's last move was new. It deters 13 g4? because White would be badly overextended on the kingside after 13...hxg4 14 hxg4 ♘e7.

For example, 15 ♘h2 ♖h4 16 ♔g2 ♘g6. Worse is conceding control of light squares like f5, with 15 g5?.

Note also that Black can answer 13 ♘g5 with 13...♗e7!.

He would be at least equal after 14 ♘xf7 ♖f8 15 e6 ♗xe6 16 ♘e5 ♔b7.

13   g3

Why not 13 ♖ad1 ? Doesn't superior development always matter?

The answer is: *Not in the Berlin Defense.*

After 13 ♖ad1 ♗e7 Black can play ...♔b7 and await events.

White does not have an obvious plan after, for example, 14 ♖d2 ♗e6 and ...♔b7 or 14 ♘e4 c5.

13   ...   ♗e7

14   ♖ad1   a5!

Doesn't Black always need to connect his rooks?

The answer, again: Not in the Berlin Defense.

He can activate the a8-rook where it stands after 15 ♘e4? a4!.

15   a4   ♖e8

Computers say chances remain balanced after a predictable future such as 16 ♖fe1 ♗e6 17 ♘e4 ♔b7 18 ♘eg5 ♗d5.

But Carlsen would have a position with more good moves available to him (...♖ad8, ...g6 and ...c5-c4) than to his opponent.

16   ♖d3?

A rule of thumb for White in the Berlin Endgame is to be wary of any move that puts a piece on a light square because of Black's light-squared bishop.

There is no immediate way to exploit 16 ♖d3, just as there was no way to attack the undefended h3-pawn after 13 g3. But White's likelihood of tactical error is quietly rising.

16   ...   c5!

Some computers recommend 16...♘h6 17 ♔g2 ♗f5 instead. There is nothing wrong with that but an intuitive player would not trust it.

The ...c5 idea is always lurking in the Berlin Defense.

It prepares a strategic plan of pushing ...c4. But here there is also a tactical one of ...♞d4.

For example, 17 ♖fd1 ♞d4! would prompt 18 ♞xd4 cxd4 19 ♖xd4 ♗xh3 – finally taking advantage of the unprotected h-pawn.

That position is solidly in favor of Black for two reasons basic to the Berlin.

It eliminates White's chief asset, his kingside majority, as well as Black's chief liability, the doubled c-pawns.

There is also a benefit for Black's bishops. They grow in power in lines such as 20 ♞d5? ♗c5 21 ♖f4 ♗e6 and ...♚b7/ ...♖ad8.

17   ♞d5

Black usually delays ...c5 in the Berlin until White cannot quickly occupy d5.

This time ♞d5 made tactical sense because after 17...♞d4

18 ♞xd4 cxd4 his knight is not on c3, where it would be under attack, and he can afford 19 h4!.

Chances would be even after 19...♗c5 20 ♗xd4 ♗f5 21 ♖d2 and 21...♗xd4 22 ♖xd4 ♖xe5.

Not 22...♗xc2??, which is beaten by 23 ♖c1!.

17   ...   c4!

By taking precautions against the tactical danger of 16...c5, White made this strategic danger worse. He would grant Black an outside passed pawn with 18 bxc4 ♗xa4.

18   ♖c3!

This stops 18...cxb3?? in view of 19 ♞xb6+ and prepares to take on c4 with the rook.

White would be out of danger after 18...♗c6 19 ♞xe7+ ♖xe7 20 ♖e1 because he threatens 21 ♖xc4! ♗xf3 22 ♖f4, regaining the piece.

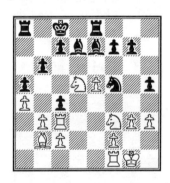

18   ...   ♗c5!

Now 19 ♖xc4! ♗c6 would force 20 ♖d1 ♖d8 21 ♖f4 and allow 21...♞xg3!.

White can avoid losing material with 22 ♘e7+! ♗xe7 23 ♖xd8+ and fxg3.

However, Black's king could make the return trip to defend f7, 23...♔xd8! 24 fxg3 ♔e8.

That is the kind of position Berlin defenders cherish. Black can play without risk, after 25 ♘d4 ♗d7 26 g4 hxg4 27 hxg4 ♖d8, for example.

19 ♔h2?

White was reluctant to walk into a pin after 19 ♔g2 cxb3 20 cxb3 ♗c6!.

But he can get out of it with 21 ♖d1 ♔b7 22 ♔f1.

A likely continuation then is 22...♖ad8 23 ♖cd3 ♘e7! 24 ♘xe7 ♖xd3 25 ♖xd3 ♖xe7, when Black's two bishops give him splendid winning prospects.

19 ... ♗c6

Now 20 ♖d1 ♗xf2 is lost.

20 bxc4 ♗xa4

21 ♖a1

This and White's next move make a bad impression but there was nothing particularly better.

After 21 ♗a3 ♗xa3 22 ♖xa3 ♗xc2 23 ♖e1 White's f1-rook is freed. But Carlsen could win slowly with ...♔b7/...a4.

21 ... ♗c6

22 ♖f1

22 ... a4

Computers want Black to win by calculated craziness such as 22...b5 and 23 ♘g5 ♗d4 24 ♘xf7 a4 or 23 ♔g2 ♘d4 24 ♖d1 ♘e2 25 ♖e3 ♗xe3 26 fxe3. Humans rely on common sense.

23 ♗a3 ♖a5!

The rook will be decisive on c5 (24 ♔g2 ♗xa3 25 ♖xa3 ♖c5 wins the c4-pawn).

24 g4! hxg4

25 hxg4 ♘e7

Computers say 25...♘d4 is faster (26 ♗xc5 ♖h8+! 27 ♔g2 ♖xc5).

26	♘b4	♗b7

And they would grab a pawn here with 26...♗xf3 27 ♔xf3 ♘g6. It hardly matters.

27	♔g3	♘g6
28	♖e1	♗xf3
29	♖xf3	♖xe5

Giving up the bishop made sense now because a trade of rooks (30 ♖xe5 ♘xe5 31 ♖f4)

makes matters easier after 31...♗d6 and ...♖c5.

30	♖d1	♖e4
31	♖xf7	♖xg4+
32	♔xg4	♘e5+
33	♔g3	♘xf7

White resigns

The desperate 34 ♘c6 ♗xa3 35 ♘xa5 is lost (35...bxa5 36 ♖a1 ♗d6+ and ...a3). The threat is ...♘e5 or ...♘d6 and ...♘xc4.

25
The Nakamura Thing

There had been one-sided rivalries of world-class players before. Garry Kasparov's record of 17 wins and no losses against Alexey Shirov is one. But after Hikaru Nakamara declared "I am the biggest threat to Carlsen" it focused unfortunate attention on their record.

At first they were close: Nakamura held a lead of five wins to three losses, with six draws in their first 14 games, at all speeds. This began when Nakamura was the higher rated player but continued after Magnus was.

But beginning in 2010 Carlsen won the next 18 decisive games they played, and allowed 20 draws. In decisive "classical" games his score was 12-0. Nakamura may have been a "threat" to everyone else. But not to Magnus.

Carlsen – Hikaru Nakamura
Medias 2011
Queen's Gambit Declined,
Exchange Variation (D31)

1	**d4**	**d5**
2	**c4**	**e6**
3	**♘c3**	**♗e7**

A move-order war is declared: Black avoids 3...♘f6 4 ♗g5 and tries to prompt ♘f3. That would deny White the option of exchange variations with ♘ge2.

4	**cxd5**	**exd5**
5	**♗f4**	

White counters by trying to exploit 3...♗e7.

If the game had gone 3...♘f6 4 cxd5 exd5 5 ♗f4, Black could equalize easily with 5...♗d6.

But in this move order, 5...♗d6? just drops a pawn, 6 ♘xd5!.

5	**...**	**c6**

Another reason for White's move order:

After 5...♘f6 we would reach what seems like a familiar QGD position, 6 e3 0-0 7 ♗d3 c6 8 ♕c2 ♘bd7 9 ♘f3 ♖e8 10 0-0 ♘f8.

But in the standard version, White's bishop is on g5, not f4. Then it is easier for Black to trade it off after with a well-timed ...♘e4.

153

6 ♕c2

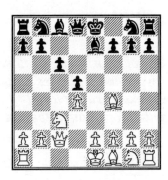

6 ... ♗g4

Among Black's problems in the QGD is the lack of a good square to develop his QB. Nakamura employs an uncommon but solid solution.

7 e3 ♗h5!

Despite the bishop's loss of time, 8 ♘f3 ♗g6! 9 ♗d3 ♗xd3 10 ♕xb3 ♘f6 or 9 ♕b3 ♕b6 is dead even.

8 ♗d3 ♗g6

9 ♗xg6 hxg6

10 0-0-0

Carlsen's move is the first new one, rather than 10 ♘f3 or 10 h3.

The best way to take advantage of Black's kingside pawn structure is to castle on the other wing and consider f2-f3 and g2-g4.

10 ... ♘f6

11 f3 ♘bd7

Carlsen also looked at 12 e4 but rejected it because of 12...♘h5 and 13 ♗e3? ♘g3!.

12 ♘ge2

Now 12...♘h5 13 ♗e5! and 14 g4 is excellent for White (12...f6? 13 ♕xg6+ or 12...♘xe5 13 dxe5 and g2-g4).

12 ... b5

After 12...0-0?, White has a ready-made attack with 13 g4! ♘b6 14 h4 and 15 h5.

Yet 12...b5 doesn't mean kingside castling is off the table.

Rather, it means Nakamura has rejected queenside castling, in lines such as 12...♕a5 13 ♔b1 0-0-0 14 e4.

13 e4

Now 14 e5 could be followed by 15 e6!.

13 ... b4

A good, cautious alternative was 13...♘b6 because 14 e5? ♘h7 and ...♘f8-e6 is solid.

After 14 ♖he1 he can reply 14...0-0!, since White's rook is misplaced for kingside play.

14 ♘a4   dxe4

This move explains his previous one.

Nakamura wanted to exchange on e4 so that if Carlsen pushed e4-e5 he could use the vacant d5-square as a knight outpost.

The downside of ...dxe4 is that Carlsen could get e4 as an outpost for his c3-knight. But now that knight is offsides at a4.

15 fxe4   ♕a5

16 ♔b1   0-0

"Let's take a *fika*," as they say in Oslo when they want to consider the future over a cup of coffee:

On the natural 17 e5 ♘d5, Carlsen would have a choice.

The quiet 18 ♗c1 grants Black at least an equal middlegame after 18...♕b5 and possibly a good endgame after 19...♘7b6 (20 ♘c5 ♕c4).

But if Carlsen tries to force matters with 18 e6, neither 18...fxe6 19 ♕xc6 ♘7b6 nor 18...♘7b6 19 ♘c5 fxe6 20 ♘xe6 ♖f6 is convincing.

17 h4!!

Back at move 14 some computers consider the position after 16...0-0 and rate it as equal.

But when they take another look at it after 17 h4!! they decide 14...b4? was an error.

17 ...   ♖fe8

Carlsen's concept is that once e4-e5 drives the knight from f6 to d5, he can open the kingside with h4-h5.

And if the knight goes to h5, he can embarrass it with ♗g5 and g2-g4.

There are also tactics that favor White after 17...♖ac8 18 e5.

For example, 18...♘d5 19 ♗c1 c5 20 dxc5 ♘xc5? and then 21 ♖xd5 ♕xa4 22 ♖xc5! wins a piece.

18 e5

155

18   ...   ♘d5?

There was another possibility for the attacked knight, 18...♘g4!.

Then 19 e6 fxe6 20 ♕xg6 ♘f2 enters a thicket of survivable complications.

More of a test is 19 h5 ♘f2 20 hxg6!.

Then 20...♘xd1 21 gxf7+ ♔xf7 22 ♕f5+ either mates (22...♔g8 23 ♕e6+) or wins the Black queen (22...♗f6 23 e6+! and ♕xa5).

Better is 19...g5! 20 ♗c1. But 20...♘f2 21 h6! ♘xh1 22 ♖xh1 g6 23 e6! is also strong.

Black's best hope was (after 18...♘g4 19 h5 g5 20 ♗c1) 20...♘b6 21 e6! ♕d5! when he can still fight.

19   h5

Nakamura is looking for a chance to counterattack. But 19...b3 20 axb3 ♘b4 is harmless after 21 ♕e4 or 21 ♗d2.

19   ...   g5

It is time to start looking for knockout punches.

Carlsen thought 20 e6 might be one. But he couldn't see a mate after 20...gxf4! 21 exf7+ ♔xf7 22 ♕g6+ ♔f8! 23 h6 ♗f6.

Also 21 exd7 seemed unclear to him after 21...♖ed8 22 ♕xc6 ♘e3.

There was more to calculate, beginning with 20 ♗c1. That prepares 21 e6 without a piece sacrifice.

20   h6!

But this is simpler. Black could resign after 20...♘xf4? 21 ♘xf4 gxf4 22 hxg7.

After 20...gxf4 21 hxg7 ♘7f6 or 21...♘5f6 White can win with 22 ♘xf4!.

A pretty finish is 21...♘7f6 22 ♘xf4! ♘xf4 23 exf6 ♘g6 24 ♖h8+! ♘xh8 25 gxh8(♕)+ ♔xh8 26 ♖h1+.

Another win is 23...♘h5 24 g4! ♘xf6 25 g5! ♕xg5 26 ♖dg1.

20   ...   g6

At the back of the players' minds for the last few moves was the idea that ...g6 would be met strongly by e5-e6.

Here 21 e6 and 21...gxf4 22 exd7 ℤed8 23 ♕xc6 is good.

Computers claim White still faces a technical task after 19...b3 24 axb3 ℤab8.

21 ♗c1

You may be wondering why White never played h6-h7+. The reason is that the king is safer at h8.

Here White threatens 22 e6 because 22...fxe6?? 23 ♕xg6+ mates.

However, 22 h7+? ♔h8 23 e6 fxe6 would not be easy.

21 ... ♘7b6

If Black uses the other knight, 21...♘5b6, then on 22 ♘xb6 axb6 23 ♕b3 ♕d5! he offers an endgame that is only marginally better for White.

But then 22 h7+ ♔h8 works because of the surprising 23 ℤhf1!.

Believe it or not, 23...♕xa4 24 b3 ♕b5 25 ℤxf7 is winning for White.

A crucial point is that after 25...♘f8 stops ♕xg6 White has 26 ℤh1 and a threat of 27 ℤg7! and 28 ℤg8 mate.

Black's best defense appears to be 23...♕d5 and the inferior endgame of 24 ♘c5 ♗xc5 25 dxc5 ♕xc5 26 ♕xc5 ♘xc5 27 ♗xg5.

22 ♘c5 ♗xc5

Now an attacking player – such as Magnus at age 12 – may say, "Of course, 23 dxc5 is right. Don't trade queens with 23 ♕xc5."

The older, more positional Carlsen should have given greater consideration to 23 ♕xc5 ♕xc5 24 dxc5 because the endgame will be winnable after ♘d4.

23 dxc5?

He was prepared to win after 23...♘d7 24 e6!.

Then 24...ℤxe6 25 ♘d4 (25...ℤf6 26 ♗xg5), for example.

157

23 ... b3!

Nakamura rarely misses a shot like this: 24 axb3?? ♘b4 and Black wins.

24 ♛xb3 ♛xc5

25 ♘d4!

The threats include 26 ♛f3 followed by 27 h7+.

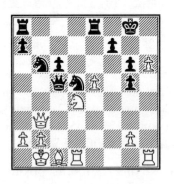

25 ... ♖xe5?

Nakamura had a powerful resource in 25...♖ab8! and then 26...♘c4.

He would have at least a perpetual check after 26 ♛f3 ♘c4 27 h7+ ♚h8 28 ♛xf7 ♘a3+ 29 ♚a1 ♛xd4 and ...♘c2+.

And perhaps more, with 28...♖f8.

White should throw in e5-e6 at some point, such as 25...♖ab8! 26 e6!, so that 26...fxe6? 27 ♛d3 ♚h7 28 ♘f3! wins.

He would have the better chances after 26...f6! 27 h7+ ♚h8 28 ♚a1 followed by ♛d3 and b2-b3.

But the fairly easy win Carlsen had at move 23 would be gone.

26 ♘f3! ♖e2?

Better kingside protection is offered by 26...♖f5.

After 27 ♘xg5 ♛c4! White has an endgame edge but there are technical difficulties.

27 ♘xg5 ♛e7

The difference is that 27...♛c4?? loses to 28 h7+ ♚h8 29 ♘xf7+.

Or 28...♚g7 29 h8(♛)+ ♖xh8 30 ♖xh8 ♚xh8 31 ♛h3+.

28 ♛d3!

This threatens 29 ♖df1 ♖f8 30 ♘xf7! ♖xf7 31 ♛xg6+.

But why not 28 ♖df1 first?

The answer is 28...f6! and the knight is forced back.

For example, 29 ♛d3? fxg5! 30 ♛xg6+ ♚h8 since 31 ♗xg5 or 31 ♖f7 would allow 31...♛e4+!.

28 ... ♖f8

158

29	♖df1	f5
30	g4!	♘a4

Desperation time.

| 31 | ♕d4 |

White could have defended better with 31 gxf5 ♕b4 32 ♕b3 or 31 ♔a1. He wanted to make h7+ a threat.

| 31 | ... | ♕e5! |

| 32 | ♕xe5 |

What Magnus overlooked when he chose 31 ♕d4 is that 32 ♕xa4? allows 32...♘c3+! 33 bxc3 ♖b8+.

Then 34 ♕b3 ♖xb3+ 35 axb3 ♕d5! and the Black queen watches both f7 and b3.

| 32 | ... | ♖xe5 |
| 33 | gxf5 | gxf5 |

Or 33...♖exf5 34 ♖xf5 ♖xf5 35 ♖e1 and 36 ♖e8+ or 36 ♖e6. Nakamura had two minutes left at this point.

34	♘f3	♖e7
35	♖fg1+	♔h7
36	♖g7+	♔h8

It's easy after 36...♖xg7 37 hxg7+ ♔xg7 38 ♗h6+.

| 37 | ♖hg1! |

The main threat is ♘h4-g6 mate.

| 37 | ... | ♖fe8 |
| 38 | ♘h4 | ♖xg7 |

With just two seconds left, **Black resigned** before 39 ♖xg7 ♖e6 40 ♘g6+ or 40 ♘xf5 first.

After the end of his collaboration with Carlsen, Garry Kasparov was hired to give similar tutelage to Nakamura. It ended in 2011 after less than a year and did not end the hex: During calendar 2011, the score was five Carlsen wins, no Nakamura wins and four draws.

26
Annus Mirabilis

The Russian magazine 64 declared 2011 "The Year of Carlsen" because of his stunning string of successes. But it could not explain how he succeeded. The traditional methods, steeped in the Soviet School, did not seem to apply. He did not rigorously study his losses with self-criticism. He did not prepare deep opening systems.

"In what lies his strength?" the magazine asked after reviewing his games from the Tal Memorial in Moscow. "Looking at his first four games: he stood to get 1½ points based on the opening, but out of the middlegame, 3!" Here is his second-round game.

Carlsen – Boris Gelfand
Tal Memorial, Moscow 2011
Slav Defense (D12)

1	d4	d5
2	c4	c6
3	♘f3	♘f6
4	e3	

A minimalist approach, when compared with 4 ♘c3.

4	...	♗f5
5	♘c3	e6
6	♘h4	

If White doesn't try to gain the two-bishop advantage he must acknowledge he's gotten nothing out of the opening.

6	...	♗g6
7	♘xg6	hxg6

Now 8 cxd5 exd5 is a pawn structure similar to that of the last game. But with White's c1-bishop shut in by the e3-pawn he has few prospects for advantage.

8	♗d3	♘bd7
9	0-0	♗d6
10	h3	dxc4

The standard procedure for Black in similar positions, dating back to Mikhail Tchigorin's heyday, is to exchange pawns on c4 and push ...e5.

160

11	♗xc4	♘b6
12	♗b3	e5
13	♕c2	

This is an example of what can be called *pawn structure zugzwang*. Whoever pushes a center pawn quickly will lessen his chances:

Black does not want to exchange on d4 without a good reason, since 13...exd4 14 exd4 frees White's bishop to go to g5.

On the other hand, White does not want to rush dxe5 because it makes e5 and c5 available for Black's minor pieces (...♘bd7-c5, for instance).

13	...	♕e7
14	♗d2	

Black can't castle kingside because of ♕xg6.

He would like to play ...e4 because that creates a nice pawn structure for him, with prospects of ...♗c7/...♕d6-h2 mate as well as ...g5-g4.

But 14...e4 15 f3! opens the center too quickly and 15...exf3 16 ♖xf3 0-0-0 17 e4! shows that White has won the battle of structure zugzwang.

14	...	0-0-0
15	d5?	

Carlsen called this "the only logical move" but at the same time acknowledged it was wrong.

The desirable alternative is 15 dxe5 followed by pushing the f- and e-pawns.

But that runs into tactics: 15...♕xe5 16 f4 ♕e7 17 e4? ♗c5+ 18 ♔h1 ♕d7!, threatening 19...♕xd2 as well as 19...♖xh3+.

15	...	e4!

A stable center, 15...c5? 16 e4, is very good for White,

He could favorably continue a2-a4-a5 and/or ♘b5.

16	dxc6	♕e5

Carlsen foresaw Gelfand's pawn sacrifice and had calculated...

17 f4   exf3

18 ♖xf3

...but he wrongly concluded that Black's best is 18...♕h2+ 19 ♔f2 ♗b4, with unclear complications.

Computers say Black should play 18...♔b8 because it prepares ...g5-g4 and avoids 18...g5? 19 ♕f5+.

18 ...   ♘g4!?

Second-best but still good. Black rules out ♔f2 and thereby makes 19...♕h2+ 20 ♔f1 ♕h1+ a threat.

19 cxb7+

The main tactic is that 19 hxg4 ♖h1+ 20 ♔xh1 ♕h2 is mate. Carlsen is forced to sacrifice the Exchange.

19 ...   ♔b8

20 hxg4   ♖h1+

21 ♔f2   ♖xa1

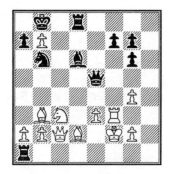

Time for a body count.

The list of casualties says White has two pawns for the Exchange.

But the pawns at b7, g4 and f7 are among the walking wounded.

More immediate is the concern over 22...♕h2!. That would win after 23 ♘e2 ♕h4+ (24 g3 ♕h2 mate).

22 ♘e2   ♗c5

Gelfand wanted to discourage ♘d4-c6+.

23 ♗c3

He also looked for perpetual check, 23 ♘d4 ♖xd4! 24 exd4 ♗xd4+ 25 ♗e3 ♗xe3+ 26 ♖xe3 ♕f4+.

But the position in the last diagram was so unbalanced that it was hard to tell who had the better winning chances.

Most likely it was Gelfand who should have tried for more with 22...♖d7! so that 23 ♘d4 ♕h2! threatens ...♕g1+.

23 ...   ♕e7

Now 24 ♘d4 would be refuted by 24...♗xd4 25 ♗xd4 ♖xd4 (26 exd4 ♕e1 mate) and 25 exd4 ♕h4+.

24 g5!

An oversimplified explanation of what happened in this strange game is that Gelfand began looking for equal or drawable positions beginning with 22...♗c5 – while Carlsen kept looking for a way to win, even when he was worse.

Here he could have sought a draw with 24 ♗xf7 ♖dd1! 25 ♘g3.

But 24 g5! averts ...♕h4+ and gives him more chances to win.

24 ... ♖dd1

After 24...♕xg5 25 ♕e4 he can even play an endgame, 25...f5 26 ♕f4+ ♕xf4 27 ♘xf4, with equal chances.

25 ♘g3 ♗d6

A remarkable position. The Black rooks are close to inflicting mayhem – as they would after 26 ♘e4? ♖ac1! 27 ♕e2 ♖f1+.

If White gives up his queen, 26 ♕xd1 ♖xd1 27 ♗xd1, Black would have excellent winning

chances with 27...♕xg5 followed by ...f5 and/or ...♘c4.

26 ♕e2!

Carlsen learned from all of the modern champions and this looks like a Karpov move.

It threatens 27 ♗xd1. Black's rooks are at their maximum strength so Gelfand is reluctant to liquidate with 26...♗xg3+ 27 ♖xg3 ♖f1+ 28 ♕xf1 ♖xf1+ 29 ♔xf1.

Winning chances would be roughly even after 29...♘d7 and 30...♘e5. Or 29...♘d5 30 ♗xd5 ♕d6.

26 ... ♖g1?

But there was nothing better for Black. Gelfand's move looked good because 27...♕xg5 followed by ...♗xg3+ is a winning threat.

It had a glaring flaw that Carlsen, already in time pressure, did not notice.

27 ♕d3?

He wanted to ensure that 28 ♘e4 would be playable.

But 27 ♕b5! would have made 28 ♖xf7 even stronger.

It would then be too late for 27...♗xg3+ because 28 ♔xg3! wins with its threat of ♗e5+.

27 ... ♗c7!

28 ♘e4

It is still hard to figure out how to use Black's rooks.

After the game 28...♖h1! was shown to be good in view of ...♖h4! and ...♖xe4. He could meet 29 ♖xf7? with 29...♖af1+! and win.

A remarkable draw by repetition of position was possible: 28...♖h1! 29 ♘g3 ♖hg1 30 ♘e4.

28 ... ♖af1+?

Trading rooks usually makes sense when you have won the Exchange. Not here.

29 ♔e2 ♖xf3

There was no alternative now because 29...♖b1, for example, would lose after 30 ♖xf7.

30 gxf3

Gelfand may have expected Carlsen's king to be in greater danger after 30...♖g2+ 31 ♔f1 ♖h2.

For example. 32 ♕d4 ♕e8! 33 ♕xg7?? ♕b5+ mates.

But 33 ♕c5 is safe. And White can do better than 32 ♕d4 with 32 a4!.

30 ... f5!

A similar idea to the last note is 30...♗e5 31 a4!.

The threat is 32 a5 ♘d7 33 ♕xd7! ♕xd7 34 ♗xe5+ ♔xb7 35 ♘c5+.

Then 31...♗xc3 32 ♕xc3 ♕xb7 33 ♔f2 keeps White on top.

31 gxf6 gxf6

Gelfand came up with a fine resource of his own. His queen can go to h7 and then h2 or h1 with effect. He also threatens 32...f5!.

Carlsen could stop that with 32 ♘xf6. Then 32...♗e5! releases much of his pressure.

He would have some winning chances after 33 ♕e4! ♗xf6 34 ♕f4+ ♔xb7 35 ♕xf6.

32 ♗xf6 ♕h7?

It was hard for Black to pass this up since it was one of the reasons for 30...f5. But he needed to stop White's next move with 32...♕e8.

33 ♕b5!

Once again this is strong. Carlsen's threat of 34 ♕e8+ ♔xb7 35 ♘c5 mate should have led to another good endgame for him after 33...♕h5+ 34 ♕xh5.

33	...	♖g2+?
34	♔d3	♕d7+
35	♕xd7	♘xd7
36	♗d5!	

It is the e3-pawn, of all things, that would decide the outcome after 36...♘xf6 37 ♘xf6 a5 38 ♘d7+ ♔a7 39 e4! and 40 e5.

36 ... ♗e5

37 f4?

The methodical 37 ♗xe5! ♘xe5+ 38 ♔d4 would win slowly (or quickly after 38...♘xf3+? 39 ♔c3! and ♘c5!).

But even this late in the game Carlsen plays for tactics.

His move is based on 37...♗xf6 38 ♘xf6 ♘xf6 39 ♗xg2 and the alternative 38...♘c5+ 39 ♔d4 ♖c2 40 b4.

But in this last variation he overlooked the simple 40...♘xb7.

He might have won after 41 ♘d7+ ♔c7 42 ♘f8 a5 but it would not have been easy.

37 ... ♗c7?

38 ♗c6! Resigns

If the attacked knight moves White's knight delivers a deadly check on d7 or a6 in a few moves, e.g. 38...♘b6 39 ♘c5 threatens ♘a6 mate.

27
Seeing the World

When he described his lifestyle to Britain's 'The Telegraph' in May 2011 it didn't sound glamorous. "My main residence is a basement apartment in my parents' home in Baerum, a suburb of Oslo," he said. In his free time he played on-line poker, watched DVDs, downloaded music and rooted for Real Madrid.

But travel intrigued him. "I spend about 200 days a year away from home," he said. "Chess aside, it is a great way to see the world." In this period he was playing in Nice, France, Sao Paulo, Brazil, Sofia and Medias, Rumania and Bilbao and Leon, Spain – as well as the usual venues and against the usual opponents.

Carlsen – Hikaru Nakamura
Wijk aan Zee 2011
Sicilian Defense,
Najdorf Variation (B92)

1	e4	c5
2	♘f3	d6
3	d4	cxd4
4	♘xd4	♘f6
5	♘c3	a6
6	♗e2	e5
7	♘b3	♗e7
8	♗e3	0-0
9	g4!	

If this move could talk it might say: "You should have played the normal 8...♗e6. Then I would get nothing from 9 g4 d5!. But now I can start my attack quicker than usual."

9	...	♗e6
10	g5	♘fd7
11	h4	

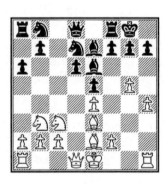

This variation was explored in the 1980s but usually with 11 ♕d2.

One reason to delay the queen move is that it allows White the option of ♗g4.

Then ...♗xg4/♕xg4 would put his queen to work immediately on

166

the kingside and also make ♘d5 stronger.

For example, 11...b5 12 ♗g4 ♘b6? is too slow in view of 13 ♗xe6 fxe6 14 ♕g4.

Better is 12...♘c5, when 13 ♗xe6 fxe6 14 ♕g4 gets White ready for g5-g6.

11 ... ♘b6

But now 12 ♗g4 could be met by 12...♘c4!.

12 ♕d2

At some point White will decide when or whether to seek f2-f4-f5. The immediate 12 f4 exf4 13 ♗xf4 ♘c6! and ...♘e5 eases Black's game.

12 ... ♘8d7

This returns us to more familiar English Attack territory. More enterprising is 12...a5 so that 13 a4 ♘c6 allows Black to play ...♘b4.

The exciting alternative is 13 f4 exf4 14 ♗xf4, which allows the b3-knight to go to d4 when kicked by ...a4.

The exciting part is 13...a4 14 f5 and then 14...axb3 15 fxe6 fxe6 16 ♗g4 d5! 17 ♗xe6+ ♔h8.

Then 18 ♘xd5? ♖xa2! favors Black strongly and 18 ♗xd5 ♘xd5 19 exd5 bxa2 offers some compensation for a pawn.

13 f4

This obvious move was considered a novelty at the time. Instead, 13 0-0-0 ♖c8 14 h5 transposes into a position that was considered difficult for Black to defend in the 1970s – when the variation was strangely forgotten.

13 ... exf4

Black avoids 13...♘c4 14 ♗xc4 ♗xc4 15 f5! because then White's attack (♖g1 or ♕g2) is ahead of schedule.

14 ♗xf4 ♘e5!

15 0-0-0 ♖c8

The same goes for 15...♘bc4 16 ♗xc4 ♘xc4 17 ♕g2 and 18 h5.

16 ♔b1 ♕c7

With his queen on c7 Black has options such as 17...♘bc4 18 ♗xc4 ♘xc4 19 ♕g2? ♘xb2! 20 ♔xb2 ♕xc3+.

17 h5 ♖fe8

Nakamura prepares to safeguard the kingside with ...♗f8.

167

This is one of those positions when you can turn off your computer. It may look at silly moves such as 18 ♕c1 or 18 ♘a5 because it is afraid of 18...♘bc4.

Carlsen makes a move nearly as strange as 18 ♕c1.

18   ♔a1!?   ♗f8

19   ♘d4

But there was a reason for 18 ♔a1:

On 19...♘bc4 20 ♗xc4 ♘xc4 21 ♕d3 he could meet 21...♕b6 with 22 ♗c1! and proceed with his kingside attack because his king is safe.

But if the king were still on b1 this would allow 22...♘a3+ 23 ♔a1 ♕xd4! 24 ♕xd4 ♘xc2+.

Also, with the king on a1, the immediate 21...♘a3 is not check. Black's pieces would just look stupid after 22 ♗d2 ♗c4 23 ♕f3.

19   ...   ♕c5

20   g6!

This is a standard sacrifice, a *priyome*. A master knows that it has opened kingside lines in similar positions so he begins to calculate to see if it works this time.

Here it works after 20...hxg6 21 hxg6 ♘xg6 thanks to 22 ♘xe6 fxe6 23 ♗e3 ♕c7 24 ♗xb6 ♕xb6 25 ♕g5! and wins.

Better is 20...fxg6 21 hxg6 ♘xg6 22 ♘xe6 ♖xe6 but 23 ♗g4 is strong.

That leaves 21...hxg6. The open kingside files allow a deadly attack after 22 ♕e1 and ♕h4.

20   ...   ♘ec4

Putting a knight on c4 is Black's only source of counterplay.

Instead 20...♕a5 threatens 21...♖xc3 and 22...♕xa2 mate.

But 21 ♘b3 forces 21...♗xb3 22 cxb3 and the piece trade makes f7 weaker.

White then threatens 23 gxf7+ ♘xf7 24 h6 and an invasion on the f-file after 24...g6 25 ♗e3 and ♖df1.

21 ♗xc4 ♘xc4

22 ♕d3

From d3 the queen can go to h3 or g3 with an impact. Magnus no longer has ♗g4 but he would win after 22...hxg6 23 hxg6 fxe6 24 ♘xe6 ♖xe6 25 ♕h3!.

22 ... fxg6

Carlsen had threatened 23 h6 since 23...hxg6 24 ♘xe6 fxe6 25 hxg7 and 26 ♕h3 wins again.

For that reason 22...h6 seemed to make sense.

But then 23 ♕g3 would threaten 24 ♗xh6! (24...gxh6 25 gxf7+ ♔xf7 26 ♕g6+).

If allowed, White would follow with 25 ♗xg7! ♗xg7 26 gxf7+ ♗xf7 27 h6.

23 hxg6 h6

Now 24 ♘xe6 ♖xe6 25 ♕h3? ♖xg6 fails.

24 ♕g3

But this threatens 25 ♘xe6 ♖xe6 26 ♕g4! because, with no counterplay to distract him, Carlsen could play ♘d5, post a rook on the f-file and break

through with a timely ♖f7 or ♕f5-f7+.

24 ... ♕b6

25 ♗c1!

The ...♘xb2 sacrifice never worked before and certainly won't now.

25 ... ♕a5?

The power of an impending ♘d5 is so great that Black should have gone for 25...d5!.

Then 26 exd5 ♗d7 provides a more active defense with ...♗d6-e5. Similarly, 26 ♘xd5 ♗xd5 27 exd5 ♗d6.

26 ♖df1 ♘e5

For a crazy moment it looks like 26...♘xb2 27 ♗xb2?? ♖xc3 would have won for Black.

But sanity returns when you see 27 ♘xe6 ♖xc3 28 ♕f2! and he is the one getting mated.

27 ♘d5

Simpler was 27 ♘xe6 ♖xe6 28 ♕h3.

27 ... ♗xd5

28 exd5

Carlsen sets the stage for a final act, such as 29 ♗xh6 gxh6 30 g7 ♗xg7 31 ♘f5 or 30...♗e7 31 ♖xh6.

169

28	...	♕xd5?

The right way to keep the curtains up was 28...♖c4! so that the rook can defend the kingside after 29 ♘e6 ♖g4!.

Or else 29 ♗xh6 gxh6 30 g7 ♗xg7 31 ♘f5? ♘g4! and Black wins.

This means that the crucial test of 28...♖c4 is the forcing line 29 ♘e6 ♖g4 30 ♕f2 ♖xg6.

Then 31 ♘xf8 ♖f6! 32 ♕g2? ♖exf8 throws away all of White's advantage and 32 ♕xf6 gxf6 33 ♘e6 ♘g4 loses most of it.

He could still win with 31 ♖hg1 ♖xg1 32 ♕xg1!.

But more fitting with the theme of the game is 31 ♗xh6!.

For example, 31...gxh6? 32 ♖hg1 or 31...♕xd5 32 ♘c7.

Also 31...♖f6? 32 ♕g2 ♖g6 33 ♗g5! and 34 ♕h2.

29	♗xh6!!

White mates after 29...♕xd4 30 ♗e3 ♕g4 31 ♕h2 or the flashy 31 ♖h8+ ♔xh8 32 ♕h2+.

29	...	gxh6
30	g7	♗e7

Or 30...♗xg7 31 ♘f5 ♖c7 32 ♘xh6+ ♔h7 33 ♘f7+.

31	♖xh6	♘f7
32	♕g6	

White can still go wrong with 32 ♖h8+ ♘xh8 33 gxh8(♕)+ ♔xh8 34 ♖g1? ♕g5! and risk losing. But he would be winning after 34 ♘f5 ♗f6 35 ♕g6.

32	...	♘xh6
33	♕xh6	♗f6
34	♕h8+	♔f7
35	g8(♕)+	

There was even an unclear position after 35 ♖xf6+? ♔e7!.

35	...	♖xg8
36	♕xf6+	♔e8
37	♖e1+	**Resigns**

28
Little Capa

When Isaac Kashdan began to play in Europe in the 1920s he was dubbed "the little Capablanca," because of a similarity in their endgame skill. Since then there have been other "Capablancas." Usually it is a misnomer because the great Cuban did not strive for a queen trade. His proper heirs were players like Anatoly Karpov, Vladimir Kramnik and Vasily Smyslov. But Carlsen played several games with a distinctly Capa quality. Here's one that sent his fans searching for a particular game of the Cuban in the databases.

Teimour Radjabov – Carlsen
Moscow 2012
Scotch Game (C45)

1	e4	e5
2	♘f3	♘c6
3	d4	exd4
4	♘xd4	♗c5
5	♘xc6	♕f6
6	♕f3	

It is Carlsen's opponent who offers an endgame. And with good reason: After 6...♕xf3 7 gxf3 bxc6 he can retain an advantage for many moves.

6	...	bxc6
7	♕g3	d6
8	♘c3	♕g6

Now it is Carlsen's turn to offer a queen trade, again for good reason. White's spatial advantage matters more in a middlegame after 8...♘e7 9 ♗e3 ♗xe3 10 ♕xe3 and 11 0-0-0.

9	♗d3	♘f6
10	♘a4	

White is likely to trade this knight for the bishop at some point and this is a better time than after 10 ♗d2 ♘g4 11 0-0 ♘e5!.

That is a common knight maneuver in similar positions and

it gives Black a comfortable position after 12 ♗e2 ♛xg3 13 hxg3 h5 14 ♘a4 ♗d4! 15 c3 ♗b6.

10	...	♗d4
11	c3	♗b6

Black induced c2-c3 in order to deny White the best square for his bishop, c3.

Eventually ♘xb6 will give White the two-bishop advantage but there will be little he can do with them.

12	0-0	♛xg3
13	hxg3	♘g4

Now 14 ♘xb6 axb6 15 f4 stops ...♘e5. But 15...♗a6! is slightly better for Black.

14	♗f4	f6

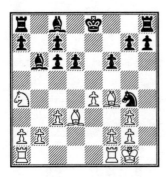

White needs a plan. One possibility is c3-c4-c5 to exploit the b6-bishop.

For example, 15 ♗e2 ♘e5 16 ♖fd1 ♗e6 17 b3 h5 18 c4 ♔f7 and now 19 c5 dxc5 20 ♖ac1 and ♘xc5.

But 18...c5! is fine for Black. If White does not play ♘xb6 at some point, Black's bishop emerges at a5.

15	♖ad1

With more modest ambitions Radjabov could play 15 ♘xb6 axb6 16 f3 and then 16...♘e5 17 ♗xe5 fxe5.

It is hard to play to win after 18 a4 ♗e6 19 b4 ♔d7 – but also hard to lose.

15	...	h5!
16	♗e2	♗e6

In contrast, Carlsen can have serious kingside ambitions.

If Radjabov tries 17 b3 and prepares ♘b2/♗c4, he can counter with 17...g5 18 ♗c1 h4!.

Then 19 gxh4 ♖xh4 will be followed by ...♔f7 and ...♖ah8.

17	♘xb6	axb6
18	a3	♔e7

After this, a Black superiority slowly becomes evident. Where did Radjabov err? There is no single move that deserves a question mark.

19 f3 ♞e5

20 ♔f2 b5!

Now 21 ♔e3? ♞c4+ wins material because 22 ♗xc4? ♗xc4 threatens ...♗xf1 as well as the bishop-trapping ...g5.

If White makes no major changes (with 21 ♖h1, for example) Carlsen can make progress with ...♞f7 and ...♗c4.

Then ♗xc4/...bxc4 will make the b2-pawn a chronic target. If White does not trade bishops, Black advances with ...g5 and then ♗e3/...♞e5.

21 ♗xe5 fxe5

22 ♔e3

White needs counterplay and looks at f3-f4.

For example, 22...♗c4 23 ♗xc4 bxc4 24 f4! since 24...♔e6? 25 fxe5 ♔xe5? 26 ♖f7! favors him.

Better is 25...dxe5 but it is hard to see how Black can improve his position after 26 ♖f5 and ♖df1.

22 ... h4

Carlsen did not want to discourage f3-f4 with ...g5 because it gives up the possible invasion route of ...♔f6-g5.

Here 22...♔f6 23 f4 h4! would help him. Then on 24 fxe5+ ♔xe5 the f7-square is protected by his bishop.

Or 24 gxh4 ♖xh4 25 f5 ♗b3 and ...♖ah8.

But White can pass, 22...♔f6 23 ♖h1 ♗c4 24 ♖df1, and await events.

23 gxh4 ♖xh4

24 ♖h1 ♖ah8

25 ♖xh4 ♖xh4

26 ♖c1!

Radjabov finds a new source of counterplay, c3-c4!.

26 ... ♖h2

27	♔f2	♖h8

Anish Giri said Carlsen was one of the first great players who were willing to admit they had made a mistake and immediately undo it, such as playing ♖c1-c2 on one move then ♖c2-c1 on the next.

With his last move and his next one Carlsen is looking for a Plan B. There was nothing he could accomplish if he got his king to g5.

28	♔e3	g5

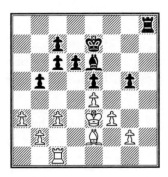

29	♗d3

We've seen Carlsen's opponents play passively in endgames and pay a penalty (Game 8, for example).

Radjabov will have several opportunities to play more actively, such as 29 c4 bxc4 30 ♗xc4 ♗xc4 31 ♖xc4.

Then 31...♔d7 32 ♖c1 ♖b8 33 b4 ♖a8 looks ominous after 34 ♖c3 d5!.

But 34 ♖a1, with the idea of pushing the a-pawn, should hold (34...♖a4 35 ♔f2 d5 36 ♔g3 and ♔g4).

29	...	♔d7
30	♖a1	♗b3
31	♖c1	♔c8
32	♔f2	♔b7
33	♔g3!	♗e6

34	♖a1?

This was another good time for 34 c4.

After a trade of bishops, 34...bxc4 35 ♗xc4 ♗xc4 36 ♖xc4 ♔b6 37 ♔g4!, Radjabov would have his own winning chances.

Black can avoid this with 36...♖h4 but then his king would have to outmuscle the White rook on the other wing without help.

No one is going to win after 37 b4 ♔b6 38 a4 d5 39 a5+ ♔b7 40 ♖c5 or 39...♔b5 40 ♖c5+ ♔xb4 41 ♖xc6, for example.

Of course, there are other Black options, beginning with 34...♔b6.

But with 34 c4 White would at least have active pieces.

34	...	♔b6

35 ♖c1

You might get the impression that Carlsen won this game because he knew his Capablanca and Radjabov did not. Specifically, the endgame Kan – Capablanca, Moscow 1936.

It began: **1 e4 e5 2 ♘c3 ♗c5 3 ♘f3 d6 4 ♘a4 ♗b6 5 ♘xb6 axb6 6 d4 exd4 7 ♕xd4 ♕f6 8 ♗g5 ♕xd4 9 ♘xd4 ♗d7 10 ♗c4 ♘e7 11 0-0 ♘g6 12 a3 0-0 13 ♖ad1 ♘c6 14 ♘xc6 bxc6 15 ♗d2 ♖a4 16 ♗d3 ♘e5 17 ♗c3 f6! 18 f3 ♖e8 19 ♖f2 ♗c8 20 ♗f1 ♗a6 21 ♗xa6 ♖xa6 22 ♗xe5 fxe5 23 ♖d3 b5! 24 ♖fd2 c5 25 ♔f2 ♖a4 26 ♔e3 ♔f7 27 ♖d1 ♔e6 28 ♔d2 ♖b8 29 ♖c3 g5**

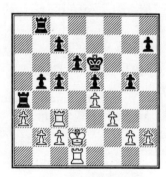

Kan – Capablanca
Moscow 1936

The Cuban had two good plans. One is to push ...g4. The other is to prepare ...d5 with ...c4 and ...c6

Capablanca mixed the two –

30 h3 h5 31 ♖h1 ♖d4+ 32 ♔e2 ♖g8 33 ♖d3 ♖a4 34 ♖hd1 g4

35 hxg4 hxg4 36 ♔e3 ♖h8 37 ♖b3 ♖h2 38 ♖d2 ♖d4 39 ♖e2 c6.

After White passed up 40 fxg4! Capablanca won in impressive fashion, **40 ♖c3? g3 41 ♖d3? ♖h1 42 f4 ♖f1! 43 f5+ ♔f6 44 c3 ♖xd3+ 45 ♔xd3 d5! 46 b3 c4+ 47 bxc4 bxc4+ 48 ♔e3 ♖a1 49 ♔f3 ♖xa3 50 ♔xg3 ♖xc3+ 51 ♔h4 ♖c1 52 g4 ♖h1+ 53 ♔g3 d4 54 ♖a2 d3 55 ♔g2 ♖e1 56 ♔f2 ♖xe4 White resigns**.

Back to Radjabov – Carlsen:

35	...	c5!
36	♖a1	c4!
37	♗c2	♔c5
38	♖e1	c6
39	♗b1	

To win, Black needs ...d5 or ...g4, as Capablanca did. But neither can be achieved quickly.

After 39...d5 40 exd5 ♔xd5 (otherwise ♖xe5) White can be rock solid with 41 ♖d1+ ♔c5 42 ♗e4.

175

The other plan is more appealing. But 39...♖g8 40 ♖h1 g4 41 f4! exf4+ 42 ♔xf4 is also a dead end.

Carlsen finds a way to improve the ...d5 plan, with a better placed king.

39	...	♔b6!
40	♗c2	♔c7
41	♔f2	♔d7

If the king gets to f6, then ...d5-d4 cannot be stopped.

A possible scenario was 42 ♔g3 ♔e7 43 ♗b1 ♔f6 44 ♗c2 d5 45 exd5 cxd5 46 ♗b1 d4 47 ♗e4 ♗f5.

Black is making progress after 48 ♗xf5 ♔xf5. But 48 ♗c6 is not conclusive.

42	a4	bxa4
43	♖a1	♖b8!

White's rook is more active than in the previous note – but Black's rook is more so.

44	♖a2	d5
45	exd5	cxd5
46	♗xa4+	♔d6
47	♗c2	d4
48	♗e4	

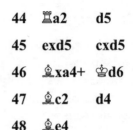

Is it time for 48...g4 ? No, because 49 ♖a6+ ♔e7 50 ♖a7+ ♔f6 51 ♖b7 offers a bishop endgame (51...♖xb7 52 ♗xb7) that is likely drawable.

48	...	♖b6!

White's unfortunately placed rook makes an exchange of pawns, 49 cxd4 exd4, fatal because of ...c3.

49	♔e2	g4!

This hints at 50...g3 and the prospects of a king march to f4.

That's unlikely after 50 ♔d1 g3 51 ♔e2 ♔e7 52 f4, for example. But it forces White's hand.

50	fxg4	♗xg4+
51	♔d2	

Or 51 ♔f2 ♔e6 and 52...♗f5!.

51 ... ♗e6

52 ♔c2?

This frees his rook from the defense of b2. But it is the losing move.

A win is still not evident after 52 ♔e2.

For instance, 52...♗d5 53 ♔f3 and then 53...♔e6 54 ♖a5 or 53...d3 54 g4 d2 55 ♖a1 ♖xb2 56 ♗xd5 ♔xd5 57 ♖a5+!.

52 ... ♗d5!

53 ♗xd5 d3+!

Essential. White can defend after 53...♔xd5 54 cxd4 exd4

55 ♖a5+ ♔e4 56 ♖a8 and ♖e8+.

54 ♔d2 ♔xd5

55 ♔e3 ♖g6!

56 ♖a5+ ♔e6

57 ♔e4

The rook also penetrates after 57 ♔f2 ♖g4 and ...♖e4-e2+.

57 ... ♖g4+

58 ♔f3 ♖f4+

59 ♔e3 ♖f1

White resigns

The win would become obvious after 60 ♖a8 ♖e1+ and 61...♖e2+. Or 60 g3 ♖g1 61 ♔f2 d2.

This was Carlsen's first victory in the tournament and he didn't win again until the last round. But he was the only undefeated player in what was one of the strongest events of the decade. On the final day, tournament leader Fabiano Caruana was defeated, and Carlsen's win, again as Black, gave him the first prize.

177

29

Grindability

Pal Benko liked to talk about his "microscope." He meant his ability to squeeze extra half points out of endgame positions in which he held an advantage that was so minute that annotators called it microscopic.

For Carlsen, the endgames he maximized could be called "grindable." They were also ever-so-slightly advantageous. But if his opponent lacked an obvious source of counterplay, he could grind out a win, even against world-class players.

Carlsen – Fabiano Caruana
Sao Paulo 2012
French Defense (C00)

1	e4	e6
2	d3	d5
3	♘d2	♘f6
4	♘gf3	♘c6
5	c3	♗d6
6	♗e2	0-0
7	0-0	a5

The opening is so innocuous that we can scroll down quickly, without missing anything:

8 ♖e1 e5 9 exd5 ♘xd5 10 ♘c4 ♖e8 11 ♗f1 ♗g4 12 h3 ♗h5 13 g3 ♘b6 14 ♘xb6 cxb6 15 ♗g2 b5 16 a4 b4 17 ♗e3 ♗c7 18 ♕b3 h6 19 ♕c4 bxc3 20 bxc3

20 ... e4?

This is the closest Caruana comes to a losing move, yet it is a move many grandmasters would happily play.

It forces a liquidation that appears to create a drawable endgame.

If, instead, he played a move like 20...♗g6, Carlsen could have tried to slowly improve his position in a middlegame with 21 ♖ed1 and d3-d4.

| 21 | dxe4 | ♗xf3 |

The next three moves are virtually forced.

22 &xf3 &e5

23 ♕e2 &xf3+

24 ♕xf3 ♕d3

Black attacks the c3 and e4 pawns and must win one of them.

The only virtue in protecting the c3-pawn with 25 ♖ac1 is to set a trap: 25...♖xe4? 26 ♖ed1 ♕c4 27 ♖d4! ♖xd4 28 cxd4 skewers the queen and bishop.

White would get something like the position that occurs in the game after 25...♕xe4 26 ♕xe4 ♖xe4 27 &d4.

But the drawback to 25 ♖ac1? is 25...♕c4!. White would have nothing better than 26 ♖a1 and admit that 26...♖ad8 is equal.

This is a position Caruana sought when he chose 20...e4. In that sense, his calculation was perfect. It was his evaluation that was flawed.

25 ♔g2!

When given a choice between a "bookish" ending and a hard-to-define one, Carlsen regularly goes for the latter.

Here he looked at 25 ♖ab1 ♕xe4 26 ♕xe4 ♖xe4 27 ♖xb7 and visualized the kind of rook endgame you will find in almost every endgame textbook.

That is, 27...&e5 28 &d2 ♖xe1+ 29 ♖xe1 ♖c8 30 ♖a7 &xc3 31 &xc3 ♖xc3 32 ♖xa5.

Because his extra pawn is an a-pawn, White's winning chances are iffy. When Peter Leko won a similar position at Linares 2003 it was considered a remarkable lapse by his opponent, Vishy Anand.

What is significant about 25 ♔g2 is that Magnus preferred an endgame with White advantages that are less tangible than that – but with more chances to grind out a win.

25 ... ♕xe4

26 &d4! ♕xf3+

27 ♔xf3

If the Black a-pawn were on its original square this game would be headed for a quick draw.

But Caruana will need to defend the b7-pawn with ...b6 or suffer something like the game, such as 27...♖ab8 28 ♖ab1 ♖xe1 29 ♖xe1 &d6 30 ♖b1 ♔f8 31 ♖b5 &c7 32 ♔e4.

| 27 | ... | b6 |
| 28 | ♖ab1 | ♖ac8 |

Black can use temporary measures to defend the b-pawn (29 ♖xe8+ ♖xe8 30 ♗xb6?? ♖b8).

29 ♖e4!

To win Carlsen will probably need to tie Black up on the queenside and then make inroads on the other wing. Therefore a critical question for Caruana is how to arrange his kingside pawns.

In principle, 29...h5 should be good because it eliminates a potential target.

However, it creates a new way for White to win: 30 ♖b5 g6 31 g4! hxg4+ 32 hxg4 and the possibility of ♖h1-h8 mate.

29 ... g6!

Another principle says Black should avoid putting his pawns on dark squares. But there is another problem with 29...f6.

Caruana's best line of defense is to post a rook on his third rank, where it defends the b6-pawn and stops an eventual king invasion at c6. He will need a pawn on f7 to safeguard ...♖e6!.

30 g4

One of White's mini-plans is ♖b5 and h3-h4-h5, to incur a kingside weakness.

30	...	♔f8
31	h4	♖xe4
32	♔xe4	♖e8+
33	♔d3	

Carlsen would like to play ♔d5-c6 but 33 ♔d5 ♖e6! temporarily stops him.

33 ... ♖e6

34 ♗e3

He rejected 34 ♔c4 because Caruana's rook would become active with 34...♖e4 35 f3 ♖f4.

Then 36 ♔b5 ♖xf3 37 ♗xb6 ♗xb6 38 ♔xb6 ♖xc3 39 ♔xa5 is another difficult version of the rook endgame mentioned in the note to 25 ♔g2!.

A practical endgame player probes other ways to win before he takes such an irrevocable step.

34	...	♔g7
35	♖b5!	♗d8
36	h5	♖d6+
37	♔c4	♖c6+
38	♔d5	♖e6
39	♗d4+	♔f8
40	f4!	

The only secure square for the rook on the third rank is e6 and Black will lose it after f4-f5.

40	...	♗c7
41	f5	♖d6+
42	♔e4	♖c6
43	♖b1!	

The rook is headed to h1 where it will threaten to win the h6-pawn.

If the g-file is opened, 43...gxh5 44 gxh5, it can go to g1 and then g7-h7 with decisive effect.

| 43 | ... | ♔e8 |

If he is denied a kingside file by 43...g5, Carlsen would penetrate on the queenside while watching for a chance for ♗g7xh6.

He could begin with 44 ♔d5 ♖d6+ 45 ♔c4 ♔e7 46 ♔b5 with the idea of winning the b6-pawn but also harassing the bishop.

For example, 46...♔f8 47 ♖e1 ♗d8 loses to 48 ♗e5 ♖d5+ 49 ♔c6 ♖c5+ 50 ♔d7! ♖d5+ 51 ♗d6+ or 50...♗e7 51 f6.

Another version is 46...♔d7 47 ♔a6 ♖c6 48 ♔b7! ♖c4 and now 49 ♗g7!.

Then 49...♖xg4 or 49...♖xa4 loses to 50 ♖d1+! ♗d6 51 ♗e5.

| 44 | hxg6 | fxg6 |
| 45 | ♖h1 | |

Caruana could pose technical problems with 45...gxf5+ 46 gxf5 ♗d8 and then 47 f6! ♗xf6 48 ♖xh6 ♖xc3.

Your computer will probably tell you that 49 &xc3 &xc3 50 &xb6 is a winning +2.00 advantage for White.

But tablebases will tell you what endgame texts have been saying for more than a century: It's a book draw with best play.

White would go instead for 49 &xf6 &a3 50 &h7 &xa4+ 51 &d5. He has no pawns to queen so the only question is whether he can mate.

Normally, in a &+&+&-vs.-&+&, the defender can draw despite many traps.

But this time the Black king is already on its first rank. White has virtually a forced win after 51...&a2 52 &e6 &e2+ 53 &e5 and many more moves.

45 ... &f7

Caruana is surviving on tactics (46 &xh6?? gxf5+ and ...&xh6). White needs another winning plan.

46 &d5 &d6+

47 &c4!

The king hopes to reach b7, via b5 and a6. Then the Black bishop and even the rook begin to run out of squares.

For example, 47...g5 48 &b5 &d8 49 &a6 &c6 50 &h3 &d6 51 &b7 and now 51...&d5? 52 &c6! or 51...&f8 52 f6! and &xh6.

A win would be clear after 51...&e7 52 &c7 followed by &h1-b1xb6 or just &xb6.

47 ... gxf5

48 gxf5 &d8

49 f6!

Now 49...&g6 50 &g1+ &f7 51 &g7+ &e6 52 &h7 and &xh6 wins slowly.

Instead of the endgame cited in the note to 45 &h1, now the liquidation of the kingside pawns allows a winning bishop endgame.

49 ... &xf6

50 &xh6 &e7

51	♖xd6	♗xd6
52	♔b5	♔e6
53	♗xb6	♔d7
54	c4	♔c8
55	♗xa5	

Caruana's last hope is that Magnus will push his c-pawn too quickly and allow ...♗xc5!.

If he is left with an a-pawn and a bishop, Caruana would draw by posting his king near a8. Carlsen would have the "wrong bishop" and the best he can do is force stalemate.

55	...	♔b7
56	♗b4	♗f4
57	c5	♔a7
58	c6	♔b8
59	a5	

Carlsen said he learned the winning technique from a Fischer – Keres game, Zürich 1959. Fischer annotated it in *My 60 Memorable Games*.

Now 76 f5?? ♗xf5 is what Keres had been hoping for. But Bobby won with 76 ♗h5! ♔h7 77 ♗g4! ♗c4 78 f5! and then 78...♗f7 79 ♗h5 ♗c4 80 ♗g6+ ♔g8 81 f6! and Keres resigned because he could see the decisive plan of marching the king to e7 followed by ♗e6+.

59	...	♔a7
60	a6	♔a8
61	♗c5	♗b8
62	♔c4!	♗c7
63	♔d5	♗d8
64	♔e6	♗c7
65	♔d7	♗a5
66	♗e7	**Resigns**

Before 67 ♗d8.

30
Recovery

Simen Agdestein recalled how the very young Magnus was actually better in the opening than in the endgame. "He read opening books constantly and that type of knowledge sticks for those with an iron memory," Agdestein wrote in 'Wonderboy.'

But by the time he was a world-class player, Carlsen was making more opening mistakes than his rivals. He still does. Yet he often wins after committing mistakes. In some cases it seems that his opponents can't believe a world champion would err so early in a game.

For example, **Caruana – Carlsen**, Wijk aan Zee 2015 began **1 e4 c5 2 ♘f3 ♘c6 3 ♗b5 g6 4 ♗xc6 dxc6 5 d3 ♗g7 6 h3 ♘f6 7 ♘c3 b6 8 ♗e3** and now – in a book position – he played **8...e5?**.

His opponent thought for some time before rejecting **9 ♘xe5!**, apparently because of **9...♘xe4**. But that would have allowed a strong **10 ♕f3!** (10...f5 11 ♗f4 ♘xc3 12 ♕xc6+). Carlsen went on to win the game.

What happens in this game is quite different. The then-world champion catches him in a prepared opening with a surprise tactic. Carlsen recovers from the shock and it is his more experienced opponent who quickly goes wrong.

Carlsen – Viswanathan Anand
Sao Paolo 2012
*Sicilian Defense,
Rossolimo Variation (B52)*

1	e4	c5
2	♘f3	d6
3	♗b5+	♗d7
4	♗xd7+	♕xd7
5	c4	

Magnus adopts one of the most conservative ways of dealing with the Sicilian Defense. The middlegame after 5...e5 is stodgy, with a blocked center.

5	...	♘f6
6	♘c3	g6
7	d4	cxd4
8	♘xd4	♗g7

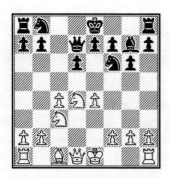

The bishop trade cuts two ways in a Maróczy Bind pawn structure. It eases Black's game because he is less constricted. But it helps White because his light-squared bishop was slightly "bad."

Carlsen had learned how Black can force a change in the structure. If we vary the move order slightly, 5...♘c6 6 d4 cxd4 7 ♘xd4 g6 8 ♘c3 ♗g7, we have his game with Alexander Khalifman from the previous year's Tal Memorial tournament.

Black showed what his position is capable of, 9 ♗e3 ♘f6 10 h3 0-0 11 0-0 a6 12 a4 ♖fc8 13 b3 and now 13...e6 14 ♖c1 d5 breaks the bind.

Carlsen got the upper hand with 15 ♘xc6! bxc6 16 e5 but his advantage soon dissipated.

9	f3	♕c7!?
10	b3	♕a5

Anand's queen maneuver was fairly new and it denies Carlsen a harmonious ♗e3/♕d2 setup.

| 11 | ♗b2 | ♘c6 |

| 12 | 0-0 | 0-0 |

The best square for White's queen is d2. But 13 ♕d2? drops a pawn after 13...♘xe4! (14 ♘xc6? ♕c5+).

Also poor is 13 ♘d5 ♕c5.

| 13 | ♘ce2 | |

This looks awkward but Black would also stand nicely after 13 ♕d3 ♘d7 and ...♘c5.

13	...	♖fd8
14	♗c3	♕b6
15	♔h1	

Carlsen is finally poised to develop his heavy pieces with

185

16 ♕d2 and 17 ♖ad1. But he hadn't neutralized all of Anand's tactics.

15 ... d5!

He would be worse after 16 cxd5 ♘xd5! 17 exd5 ♖xd5 and 18 ♕e1 ♘xd4 19 ♘xd4 ♗xd4 20 ♗xd4 ♖xd4 21 ♕xe7 ♖ad8.

Insufficient is the queen sacrifice 18 ♘xc6 ♖xd1 19 ♘xe7+ ♔h8 20 ♖axd1 ♕e3.

16 ♘xc6 bxc6

After he played 1 d4 ♘f6 2 ♗g5 against Kramnik at Moscow 2013, Carlsen admitted he had problems with his opening knowledge.

"My main concern is how to equalize, even with White," he said.

This is the situation he faces here and would face repeatedly as he met better prepared opponents.

With 17 cxd5 cxd5 18 e5, reminiscent of the Khalifman game, he may barely equalize after 18...♘d7 19 f4 e6.

17 ♕e1

Carlsen seeks more than the south side of equality. He gets his queen off the hot d-file and threatens ♗a5.

17 ... ♖dc8?

Black could have met the threat with 17...a5, which also eyes ...a4.

A key continuation is 18 e5 and 18...♘d7 19 e6! fxe6? 20 ♗xg7

♔xg7 21 ♘f4! with a powerful edge.

But 18...♘e8! is stronger (19 e6 f5! 20 ♗xg7 ♘xg7).

Anand may have seen all that and wanted more than the equality of 18 e5 ♘e8 19 f4 e6 20 cxd5 cxd5 21 ♕d2.

Better is the unbalancing 20...♖xd5! followed by ...♘c7 and a well-timed ...a4.

18 e5 ♘e8

19 e6!?

More enterprising than 19 f4 (threat of 20 f5) e6 20 ♗a5, when White also stands well.

19 ... fxe6?

Anand must have considered 19...f5, so that he can pick off the e6-pawn later on.

Then with 20 cxd5 cxd5 White can seek a drawish endgame with 21 ♖d1!.

For example, 21...♕xe6 22 ♗xg7 ♘xg7 23 ♘f4! ♕xe1 24 ♖fe1 e6 (best) 25 ♘xe6.

Anand vastly overrated his winning chances now.

20 ♘f4!

Now 20...d4? 21 ♕xe6+ ♔h8 22 ♗d2 and it is difficult for Black to defend the e7-pawn. Or 21...♔f8 22 ♗d2 ♘c7 23 ♕h3! ♔g8 24 ♖ae1.

20 ...   ♗xc3

Black's queen can't defend the kingside after 20...♘c7 21 ♗xg7 ♔xg7 22 ♕e5+ ♔f7 23 ♖ae1.

21 ♕xc3   d4

No better is 21...♘g7 22 ♖ae1 because his heavy pieces are no match for White's on the e-file.

For example, 22...♔f7 23 ♕e5 ♕c7 24 ♕g5.

When he looked at 22...♔f7 Carlsen may have noticed 23 ♘h3, with the idea of ♘g5+.

On 23...h6 the knight has a nice maneuver, 24 ♘f4 g5 25 ♘d3 and ♘e5+.

22 ♕d2!

Carlsen had recovered from the shock of 15...d5! and seized the advantage with 20 ♘f4.

He could have regained his pawn with 22 ♕e1. He might not be able to make much progress after 22...c5 23 ♘xe6 a5. But drawing with the world champion after the way this game started could be considered a victory.

Instead, he chooses the most ambitious plan, doubling rooks on the e-file after 23 ♖ae1.

22 ...   c5

23 ♖ae1

On d2 his queen can also land on h6 after ♘d3 – or after ♘h3, the move that arose in calculating 21...♘g7.

This underlines a common feature of a grandmaster's calculation. A potentially good move is not forgotten as the game goes on.

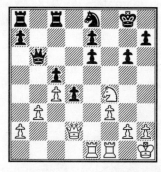

23 ...   ♘g7

Black had to decide whether the knight belongs on g7, defending the e6-pawn, or on f6. There are drawbacks to both.

After 23...♖c6 24 h4 ♘f6, for instance, White breaks through with 25 h5!, e.g. 25...g5 26 ♘d3 h6 27 ♘e5 and ♕c2-g6+.

But on 23...♘g7 24 h4 Black can defend with 24...♕d6 25 h5? ♖f8.

24 g4!

Now that ...♘f5 is ruled out, Anand has to worry about losing the c5-pawn after ♖e5, ♘d3 and ♕g5.

For example, 24...♖f8 25 ♖e5 ♖f6 26 ♘d3 ♖c8 27 ♕g5 followed by ♖xc5.

Better is 25...a5 26 ♘d3 ♖c8 27 ♕g5 a4 with faint counterplay.

24 ... ♖c6?

25 ♘h3!

The ♖e5/♘d3 plan is still strong. But Carlsen points out a greater threat:

Black can get mated after ♕h6/♘g5.

Had Anand chosen 24...♖f8 he could have met 25 ♘h3 with 25...♕c6 and a threat of ...♖xf3.

25 ... ♘e8

This fails but Black would have been losing in the long run after 25...e5 26 ♕h6 g5 27 ♕xg5 and ♖xe5.

26 ♕h6 ♘f6

27 ♘g5 d3

After 27...a5 28 ♖e5 White has another way to win, 29 ♘xh7! ♘xh7 30 ♕xg6+ ♔h8 31 ♖h5.

28 ♖e5 ♔h8

29 ♖d1 ♕a6

30 a4

Magnus will play ♖xd3 and choose a winning plan such as h2-h4-h5. Then ...gxh5 would be met by a deadly ♘f7+.

Black has no counterchances so he **resigned**.

31
Especially Well

By 2012 Magnus was capable of beating the world's best players. This year he won four times apiece against Fabiano Caruana and Teimour Radjabov, for example. In some games he seemed to win without effort. In this one he appears to do nothing special – and does it especially well.

Carlsen – Judith Polgar
London 2012
English Opening,
Symmetrical Variation (A33)

1	c4	c5
2	♘f3	♘c6
3	d4	cxd4
4	♘xd4	♘f6
5	♘c3	e6
6	a3	♗c5
7	♘b3	♗e7

Black will set up the Hedgehog pawn structure, with pawns on e6, d6, b6 and possibly a6. The move order is very flexible. Often ...d6 and ...b6/...♗b7 are played before castling.

8	e4	0-0
9	♗e2	b6
10	0-0	♗b7
11	♗f4	d6

In early Hedgehog games the bishop was played to f4 in the hopes of pressuring the d6-pawn. But Black can blunt that with ...♘e5.

Then ♗xe5?/...dxe5 is an awful trade that gives Black the two bishops and improves his pawn control of the center.

12	♖c1	♖c8

The Hedgehog was once considered prohibitively passive. In the 1970s defenders showed the tactical power of ...d5 and ...b5, even as pawn sacrifices.

When White tried to win quickly he often got crushed by a counterattack in the 1980s and 1990s.

After the turn of the century, the tide swung back in White's favor. Computers steadfastly rate his spatial advantage at +0.30 or more in a typical pre-middlegame position. But he has to have patience.

13 ♖e1 ♘e5

14 ♘d2 ♘fd7

Polgar follows modern Hog thinking by avoiding ...a6.

That move was once routine because Black feared an attack on the d6-pawn with ♕d2, ♖fd1 and ♘b5.

However, ...a6 gives White addtional middlegame plans, such as one directed at b6, by means of ♘b3 and a3-a4-a5.

15 ♗e3 ♕c7

16 b4 ♕b8

Polgar's queen maneuver is also standard. It may go to a8 and threaten the e4-pawn.

If White defends it with f2-f3, the slight new weakness at e3 makes ...d5 stronger.

17 f4 ♘g6

18 g3!

We are still in that curious stage of modern middlegames when both players have available moves that ameliorate their prospects ever so slightly – but only an error changes the evaluation of the position significantly.

For example 18 f5? would leave White overextended after 18...exf5 19 exf5 ♘h4.

18 ... ♖fe8

19 ♗f3 ♕a8

20 ♗f2

A White priority in a Hedgehog is to make sure Black cannot change the structure safely with ...d5.

For example, 20...♘f6 21 ♕e2 d5? and 22 e5 ♘d7 23 cxd5 exd5 is very good for White whether he continues 24 ♘b5 or 24 e6.

20 ... ♘gf8

21 ♕e2 ♕b8

Polgar's last two moves indicate she has exhausted her useful candidates and is waiting for Carlsen to choose a plan, such as ♘b3/a3-a4-a5 or h2-h4-h5-h6.

22 ♖ed1

Black also has priorities in a Hedgehog and perhaps the most important is to make sure White cannot change the structure profitably with e4-e5.

After 23 e5? dxe5 24 ♗xb7 ♕xb7 25 fxe5 White has a vulnerable e5-pawn which can be pressured with ...♘g6/...a6 and ...♕c7.

22 ..   g6?

23 e5!

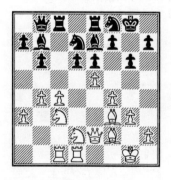

What changed the picture to make this move good?

An obvious answer is the weakness just created at f6. But that is not a factor until the endgame.

More significant is Black's inability to play ...♘g6! as in the last note.

23 ...   ♗c6

24 ♗d4   ♖ed8

25 ♗xc6   ♖xc6

26 ♘f3

Siegbert Tarrasch said the future belongs to the player with the bishops: As pawns leave the board, the opened position favors the player with the better bishops.

But in this game the future belongs to White's superior knights. He could also use them with 26 exd6 followed by ♘ce4/♘f3.

Another good idea is 26 ♖f1 because Black's pieces are not able to defend f7 after an exchange of pawns on e5, for example, 26...dxe5? 27 fxe5 and ♕f3.

26 ...   dxe5

27 fxe5   ♖dc8

28 ♘e4   ♕c7

Strategy is what happens before you have to start calculating. Carlsen's strategy has worked so well he hasn't had to calculate any difficult lines so far.

But he might have started here by 29 ♕f2 with ♖f1/♘fg5 and ♕xf7+ in mind.

That looks promising when he counts out 29...♖xc4 30 ♖xc4 ♕xc4 31 ♘fg5 ♗xg5 32 ♘xg5.

But then he finds there is no knockout after 32...♕c2! 33 ♕xf7+ ♔h8.

Or after 31 ♘fd2 ♕d3 32 ♖f1 ♔h8.

There are other sharp variations to calculate, beginning with 29 ♖f1 and 29 ♘fg5, but none result in a position better than the one Carlsen has now.

29 ♘fd2

By defending the c4-pawn he threatens to trap the c6-rook with 30 b5.

29 ... a6

30 ♘f2!

This points out another reason why 22...g6 deserved a question mark. The hole at h6 matters much more than the one at f6.

Carlsen threatens 31 ♘g4 followed by 32 ♘h6+ and ♖f1.

30 ... ♗g5?

This protects h6 but for only one move.

As ugly as it looks, 30...h5! and 31 ♕e3 ♘h7 would have held the kingside together for the time being.

Carlsen could then turn his attention elsewhere, such as with 32 h4 (to stop ...♗g5) and 33 ♘d3. Then he would be ready for ♘e4 followed by c4-c5.

31 ♖f1!

The threat of 32 ♘fe4! (32...♗h6 33 ♕f2) forces Polgar's hand.

31 ... ♗xd2

32 ♕xd2

192

She has to accept either a losable endgame (after 32...♞xe5) or a lost middlegame (32...♜xc4 33 ♜xc4 ♛xc4 34 ♞g4 and ♞h6+).

It was too late for 32...h5 because of 33 ♞e4 and ♞d6!.

32	...	♞xe5
33	♗xe5	♛xe5
34	♞g4	♜d6!

Without this shot, Black could safely resign, e.g. 34...♛d6 35 ♛c3! e5 36 ♞xe5 or 35 ♞h6+ ♚g7 36 ♜xf7+.

35	♞h6+!	♚g7
36	♜xf7+	♚h8
37	♛f2	♛d4

This is a much better endgame for White than 35 ♛f2? ♛d4 36 ♞h6+ ♚g7 would have been, because of the rook on the seventh rank.

38 c5

To play 38 ♜f1 Carlsen would have had to calculate lines in which he loses his c4-pawn and Black's rooks enter play.

For example, 38...♞d7 39 ♜e7! would win after 39...♛xf2+ 40 ♜xf2 ♜d4 41 ♜ff7!.

But we're not done calculating. Better is 39...♞e5.

The forcing line 40 ♛xd4 ♜xd4 41 ♞f7+ ♞xf7 42 ♜fxf7 ♜dxc4 grants White doubled rooks on the seventh rank.

White is bound to end up a pawn or two ahead, after 43 ♜xh7+ ♚g8 44 ♜eg7+ ♚f8 45 ♜a7 ♚g8 46 ♜hg7+.

But when a human calculates 38 ♜f1 it is impossible to know whether that ending is an easy win, a hard win or a draw. (Engines say it's a win but will take another 20 moves or so before that is clear.)

38	...	bxc5
39	♛xd4+	♜xd4
40	♜xc5	

White would win slowly after 40...♜xc5 41 bxc5 ♞d7 42 c6 ♞b6 43 c7.

40	...	♜cd8
41	♜cc7	♜d1+
42	♚g2	♜1d2+
43	♚h3	♜2d5
44	♞g4	

193

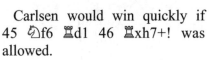

Carlsen would win quickly if 45 ♘f6 ♖d1 46 ♖xh7+! was allowed.

The king threatens to run the rook off the board with 52 ♔d6 and 53 ♔c7 ♖a8 54 ♔b7!.

44	...	♖h5+
45	♔g2	♖d2+
46	♔f3	♖f5+
47	♔e3!	♖xf7

Or 47...♖a2 48 ♘f6 ♖xa3+ 49 ♔d4.

48	♖xf7	♖d8
49	♘f6	♖b8
50	♔f4	h6
51	♔e5	

51	...	a5
52	bxa5	♖a8
53	a6	Resigns

This tournament was conducted with an experimental scoring system, designed to discourage draws. Each victory was worth three points on the scoretable. Each draw was worth one point. The Polgar victory gave him a score of five wins and one draw. Even though this was only a nine-player tournament, it was an almost insurmountable lead. Draws in the final two rounds gave Carlsen first prize by two points.

32
Record Setter

In 1990 Garry Kasparov surpassed Bobby Fischer's record rating of 2785 "I feel I've done something very important for chess," he told 'New In Chess'. "Fischer's name now belongs to the past." Having an active No.1 player, rather than the retired Fischer, holding the record was "a relief for chess."

Carlsen's rating was soaring before he began studying with Kasparov. When they broke up, Kasparov said Magnus had missed a great opportunity. If they had continued, Carlsen might have topped Kasparov's peak rating of 2851, he said.

In fact, Carlsen shattered Kasparov's record in January 2013 and soon reached 2882.

By then the former champion complained that ratings had become inflated. "Today Radjabov, the number four player in ratings, has a rating higher than Fischer 40 years ago," he told the publication 'Argumenty i Fakty.' "This says nothing about the comparison of Fischer and Radjabov. It speaks of the fact that inflation exists."

Carlsen – Pentala Harikrishna
Wijk aan Zee 2013
Ponziani Opening (C44)

1	e4	e5
2	♘f3	♘c6
3	c3	

A first for Carlsen. The Ponziani is largely forgotten although old books say the main lines, such as 3...♘f6 4 d4 ♘xe4 5 d5, tend to favor White slightly.

3	...	♘f6
4	d4	d5!?

If Black feared Magnus' opening preparation, he ended it with this rare move.

5	♗b5

Black would stand quite well after 5 exd5 ♕xd5 6 ♕e2? e4! or 5 dxe5 ♘xe4 6 ♗b5 ♗c5.

5	...	exd4

This is better than 5...♘xe4 6 ♘xe5 ♗d7 7 ♘xd7 ♕xd7 8 0-0 and 9 ♘d2.

6	e5	♘e4

7	♘xd4	♗d7

8	♗xc6	bxc6

9	0-0	

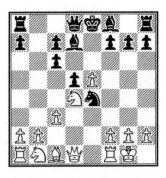

This strongly resembles a sideline of the Two Knights Defense that runs 1 e4 e5 2 ♘f3 ♘c6 3 ♗c4 ♘f6 4 d4 exd4 5 e5 d5! 6 ♗b5 ♘e4 7 ♘xd4 ♗d7 8 ♗xc6 bxc6 9 0-0.

Then White's eyes are directed at the kingside, such as with 9...♗e7 10 f3 ♘c5 11 f4 and then 11...f5 12 b4 or 11...♘e4 12 f5.

9	...	♗e7

White has an extra move, c2-c3 compared with the Two Knights version and this encourages him to fight for control of the c5-square.

If he can occupy it, ideally with a knight, he usually has the greater winning chances.

10	♗e3	0-0

11	♘d2	

In the Two Knights version, without c2-c3, Black could get a serious edge now with 11...♘xd2 12 ♕xd2 c5! and 13...d4.

But that is not possible here. White could retreat 13 ♘b3 and occupy c5 after 13...c4 14 ♘c5.

As long as Black has two bishops, that square is less valuable. The position would be double-edged after 14...♗f5 15 b3.

11	...	♘c5

Enterprising play. Black looks for an advantage from ...♘d3 or ...f6.

His knight seems to be begging for b2-b4 at some point.

White would get the upper hand after 12 f4 f6 13 b4 ♘b7 14 e6 and 13...♘e6 14 ♘xe6 ♗xe6 15 f5! and 16 e6.

Better is 12...a5 because then 13 f5 ♘d3 is again a double-edged game (14 e6 fxe6 15 fxe6 ♗e8).

12 b4

Carlsen would win the struggle for c5 after 12...♘e6 13 ♘2b3 ♘xd4 14 ♗xd4.

12 ... ♘b7

Undoubling his pawns with 12...♘d3 13 f4 c5? is not good enough, as 14 dxc5 ♗xc5 15 ♕e2 and 14...♘xc5 15 ♕f3 show.

But 13...a5! could have led to a promising sacrifice, 14 ♕b1 axb4! 15 ♕xd3 c5.

13 f4

It is important for White to watch both wings. After 13...f6? he would get a big kingside plus with 14 e6 ♗e8 15 ♘f5 and 16 ♕g4.

13 ... a5!

Once again the undoubling of pawns by 13...c5? 14 bxc5 favors White.

For example, 14...♗xc5 15 ♕f3 c6 16 f5.

Better is 14...♘xc5 15 ♕f3 c6 16 f5 when Black can try 16...♘d3.

Then White has a forcing line beginning with 17 ♗h6, which threatens 18 ♕xd3 as well as 18 f6.

Play could go 17...♘xe5 18 ♕g3 ♗f6 19 ♗xg7 ♗xg7 20 f6 and when the smoke clears, 20...♘g6 21 fxg7 ♔xg7 22 ♘2b3!, he has a good knight versus bad bishop matchup.

If White isn't sure about all that, he could try 16 c4!, which is also promising.

14 f5!

If White agrees to fight on the queenside, his chances for a major edge vanish. For example, 14 a3 axb4 15 cxb4 c5.

Or 14 ♕b3 axb4 15 cxb4 c5 16 bxc5 ♘xc5 17 ♕xd5 ♖a3.

14 ... axb4

15 cxb4

After 15...c5 16 bxc5 ♘xc5 17 ♕g4 White would be virtually a tempo ahead of previous positions we considered.

15 ... ♗xb4?!

But it wasn't too late for 15...f6 16 e6 ♗e8 because Carlsen would be temporarily stopped on the kingside.

Black would be in good shape after 17 a3 c5!.

And on 17 ♕c2 ♗xb4 18 ♘xc6 ♗xc6 19 ♕xc6 he has a trick, 19...♕d6!.

The endgame is even after 20 ♕xb7 ♖fb8 21 ♘e4! ♖xb7 22 ♘xd6 ♗xd6.

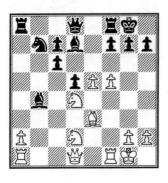

16   ♕g4

Magnus' position is so good that he can choose between promising alternatives. After 16 f6! g6 17 ♕f3 he is close to a major advantage.

He may not have appreciated how strong 17...♖e8 18 ♖ab1! was.

Instead, he preferred 16 ♕g4, which threatens 17 ♗h6 g6 18 e6! with a crushing attack.

16   ...   ♗c3!

Black had an appealing resource in 16...f6 17 e6 c5! and then 18 exd7 ♗xd2 19 ♗xd2 exd4, with an extra pawn.

He would also have the edge after 18 ♘c2 ♗xd2 19 ♗xd2 ♗b5.

But 16...f6? would have allowed Carlsen to switch wings again with 17 ♘e6! ♗xe6 18 ♕xb4!.

Then 18...♗c8 19 e6 gives him a dark-square bind on the queenside (♘b3-c5) as well as a potential kingside attack (♕g4, ♖f3-g3).

17   ♖ac1   ♗xd4

Too fancy is 17...♗b2 18 ♖b1 ♖xa2 because White's initiative rolls on with 19 e6. For example, 19...fxe6 20 fxe6 ♖xf1+ 21 ♖xf1 ♗e8? 22 e7! ♕xe7 23 ♘f5 and wins.

18   ♗xd4

Better was 18 ♕xd4! so that 18...♖xa2? 19 f6! g6? 20 ♕h4 and wins.

White would be winning on the queenside after 18...f6 19 e6 ♗e8 20 ♕b4 and 21 a4.

18	**...**	**♖xa2**
19	**e6**	**f6**

This is the kind of two-front battle Carlsen has been seeking since 16 ♕g4.

Computers want to force matters with 20 ♖ce1 so that 20...♖e8? 21 e7 ♖xe7 22 ♗xf6 wins.

The key continuation here is 20...♖xd2 21 e7 ♕c8 22 exf8(♕)+ ♕xf8.

That looks good for Black but engines find some advantage in 23 ♕f4 because of 23...♕b4 24 ♕xc7! ♕xd4+? 25 ♔h1 and White will regain a piece favorably.

20	**♘b3!**

Even if he had seen all that, preserving tension on both wings is more in Carlsen's "playability" style.

20	**...**	**♗e8**
21	**♘c5**	**♘d6!**

Trading knights is bad. For example, 21...♘xc5? 22 ♗xc5 ♕a8 23 ♗xf8 ♔xf8 24 ♕b4+ ♔g8 25 ♕e7 with no material edge but chances for mate after ♖c3-g3.

22	**♕f3**	**♕e7**
23	**♖f2**	

23	**...**	**♖a5**

In principle Black should preserve his only active piece. But 23...♖xf2 24 ♕xf2 ♗h5 would threaten ...♗g4xf5.

He could keep matters in balance after 25 h3 ♖a8 26 g4 ♗e8.

His position is solid enough to withstand 27 g5 fxg5 28 f6 gxf6 29 ♗xf6 ♕f8.

24	**♘b3**	**♖b5**

This is the first slight slip in what will become a game of minor mistakes.

On b5 the rook makes itself vulnerable to ♘d4 and also occupies a good square for Black's knight.

Correct was 24...♖a4! and 25 ♗c5 ♖e4 or 25...♔h8/...♖g8.

25 ♗c5   ♗h5

26 ♕c3!

When Carlsen has a bind – that is, when his pieces dominate a pawn structure – he is reluctant to liquidate. An example is Game 30 when he declined to win back a sacrificed pawn and instead achieved a bind after 24 g4.

Here he has sacrificed two pawns and would almost certainly get them back after 26 ♕xh5 ♖xb3 27 ♕d1 and ♖fc2 followed by ♗xd6/♖xc6.

But his winning chances would be slim after 27...♖fb8 28 ♖fc2 h6 or 28...g6.

26 ...   ♕e8

Now he had to consider 27 ♘d4 and the reply 27...♘e4.

He could calculate a forced win of the Exchange with the pretty 28 ♘xb5 ♘xc3 29 e7 ♖f7 30 ♘xc7.

But the endgame is likely to be drawn – or at least drawable – after 30...♕xe7 31 ♗xe7 ♖xe7 32 ♖xc3 ♖xc7.

For example, 33 ♖d2 ♗g4 34 ♖xd5 cxd5 35 ♖xc7 ♗xf5 or 35 ♖xc7 ♗xf5.

27 ♕e3

Instead he prepared a stronger version of ♘d4, e.g. 27...♕b8 28 ♘d4 ♖b1 29 h3.

But he missed a good opportunity – 27 ♖f4! would also have threatened to trap the bishop with 28 g4.

After 27...g5 28 ♖a4 ♗e2, for example, his edge would grow with 29 ♗xd6 and 30 ♖e1.

27 ...   ♕a8

28 ♘d4!   ♖xc5!

Better than 28...♖a5 29 ♗xd6 cxd6 30 ♘xc6. Then the White knight is still better than the

200

bishop and Black's f8-rook does not play.

29 ♖xc5 ♘e4?

Surprisingly, 29...♘c4! is much better because ...♕a7! will trap the White rook.

For example, 30 ♕f4 ♕a1+ 31 ♖f1 ♕a7! 32 ♖xc6 ♖c8 and 33...♗e8.

Carlsen could give the Exchange back, 30 ♕c3 ♕a7! 31 ♖xc6 ♖a8 32 ♖xc4 dxc4 33 ♕xc4, but he has no real advantage after 33...♕b6.

30 ♘xc6 ♘xf2

31 ♔xf2!

Not 31 ♕xf2? ♕a1+ 32 ♕f1 ♖a8.

By keeping queens on the board Carlsen assures himself of a substantial advantage, e.g. 31...♕b7 32 ♕d4 ♖a8 33 ♘e7+ and ♘xd5.

That coordination of pieces – a queen on d4, knight on d5 and rook on c5 – ultimately wins the game. But there are a few adventures left.

31	...	♕a2+
32	♔g3!	♖e8
33	h3	♕a6
34	♕c3	♗e2
35	♖xd5	♗b5

The protected e6-pawn is a major trump in endgames. But Black might not reach one because of his vulnerability on g7.

That is shown by 36 ♘d4 c6 37 ♖d7 ♕b6 38 ♔h4!, threatening 39 ♕g3! and ♕xg7 mate.

36	♘b4	♕b7
37	♕c5	♗a4

38 ♖d7!

Rather than the cautious 38 ♖d4 and ♖c4, he wants to win faster. Now 38...♗xd7 39 exd7 ♖a8 40 ♘c6 and wins.

38	...	♕e4
39	♖xc7	h5!
40	♔h2	

There are no checks after 40...♕f4+ 41 ♔g1. Control of the

h2-c7 diagonal is essential to Black's slim hopes.

40	...	♔h7

41	♕f2	

So that 41...♕xb4? 42 ♕g3 wins.

41	...	♖g8

42	♘a6?	

42	...	♗e8?

Black missed his chance with 42...♗b5 and then 43 ♘c5 ♕e5+ 44 ♕g3 ♕xf5.

White would retain winning prospects with 45 e7 but they would not be great.

43	♖c5!	♕d3

44	♘b4	

Trying for counterplay with 44...♕d6+ 45 ♔h1 g6 shortens the game after 46 ♘d5!. For example, 46...♖f8 47 ♖c7+ ♔h8 48 fxg6.

44	...	♕d6+

45	♔h1	♕d1+

46	♕g1	♕d6

Now Carlsen gets that winning piece coordination. But 46...♕d2 47 ♘d5 and 48 ♕e3 would mean a lost ending.

47	♘d5!	♖f8

48	♕d4!	♔h8

49	♖c8!	♗c6?

Black resigned

Before 50 ♘xf6! (50...♕xd4 51 ♖xf8 mate).

33

Champion

The world championship title was devalued in 1993 when Nigel Short and Garry Kasparov broke away from FIDE and placed their championship match outside of official sanction. For the next seven years there were two champions, one recognized by FIDE and one not (Kasparov).

Then it got worse. Kasparov lost a "title" match with Vladimir Kramnik in 2000. But he continued to claim he was the world's number one player, based on rating. Kramnik was not a real champion, he said, because Kramnik "didn't beat an official world champion." FIDE, meanwhile, said its champion was the only legitimate one.

The bizarre situation – three players claiming to be the world's best chessplayer – continued until 2006 when FIDE arranged a "reunification" match. Kasparov ridiculed it, saying it would "trigger chaos." But Kramnik's victory helped end 13 years of confusion. The situation normalized further when Vishy Anand defeated Kramnik and two challengers over a five-year span.

After initially expressing doubt that he wanted to become world champion, Magnus Carlsen qualified to challenge Anand in his hometown of Chennai, India in November 2013. Their best-of-12-game match reached a crescendo in the ninth round.

Viswanathan Anand – Carlsen
World Championship match,
ninth round, Chennai 2013
Nimzo-Indian Defense,
Sämisch Variation Delayed (E25)

1	d4	♘f6
2	c4	e6
3	♘c3	♗b4
4	f3	d5
5	a3	♗xc3+
6	bxc3	c5
7	cxd5	exd5!?

The recapture 7...♘xd5 was considered virtually forced for decades. The reason is that 7...exd5 transposes into a position regarded as too favorable to White since great games of Botvinnik.

203

8   e3

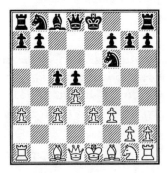

But Nimzo-Indian defenders rallied to find improvements. They settled on a main line of 8...0-0 9 ♗d3 b6! 10 ♘e2 ♗a6 and then 11 0-0 ♖e8 12 ♘g3 ♗xd3 13 ♕xd3 ♘c6 14 ♗b2.

Only then was there a sharp disagreement, between those who favored 14...♖c8 (and a subsequent ...cxd4) and those who felt Black could survive after 14...c4.

8   ...   c4!

This was considered daring for two reasons.

First, it clearly establishes Black's queenside majority, at the cost of ending his pressure on the center.

Secondly, it sharply decreases the chance of a draw that would have helped Carlsen. He led the match by two points so a loss would give Anand a fighting chance to save his title, with three games to play.

9   ♘e2   ♘c6

10   g4!

With no tension in the center, Anand has a free hand to expand on the kingside and prepare, with ♗g2 and ♘g3, for a strong e3-e4-e5!.

10   ...   0-0

11   ♗g2   ♘a5

12   0-0   ♘b3

13   ♖a2

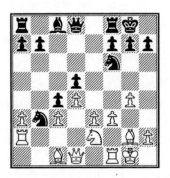

Here 13...h6 would stop g4-g5 and transpose into a Kasparov – Polgar game.

It proceeded with 14 ♘g3 ♗d7 15 ♕e1 ♖e8 and Kasparov found a sound pawn sacrifice, 16 e4! dxe4 17 fxe4 ♘xg4 18 ♗f4.

That seemed to put a nail in the coffin of 8...c4.

Anand, well aware of the evolving theory, was playing quickly. He still had 111 of his allotted 120 minutes at this point.

13   ...   b5!

Carlsen had 32 minutes less than him now.

14 ♘g3   a5

Carlsen seemed to be telling Anand, "Come and get me." His queenside pushes are at least three moves away from generating counterplay.

But 14...a5 was also a defensive move because it allowed him to safeguard some kingside squares with ...♖a6!.

15 g5

After the match, annotators wondered if Anand missed his best chance to remain champion around here. He could have played a sacrifice 15 e4 and 15...dxe4 16 ♗g5.

But his compensation is not evident after 16...e3 17 ♘h5 ♖e8 18 ♖e1 ♖a6, for example.

15 ...   ♘e8

16 e4

Anand's basic plan is e4-e5 followed by f3-f4-f5. That mass of pawns would allow him to go for mate, such as with ♕h5/♖f4-h4.

16 ...   ♘xc1

Carlsen took 23 minutes on this move, his longest "think" of the game.

He likely spent some of it considering whether to accelerate his counterplay with 16...♘c7 17 e5 b4. Then on 18 axb4 axb4 his a8-rook is protected.

The crucial question is how to evaluate 19 ♖xa8 ♘xa8 20 cxb4 ♘xc1 21 ♕xc1 ♕b6 22 ♕d2 ♘c7 and ...♘b5.

He would be a pawn down but with plenty of compensation and no dangers on the kingside.

17 ♕xc1   ♖a6

He preferred to play for a bigger edge, since ...♘c7 and ...b4 will not cost a pawn now.

18 e5!

As he edged into time trouble, Magnus had to make a major decision about his knight: kingside or queenside?

18 ...   ♘c7

The way to stop f4-f5 was 18...g6 19 f4 ♘g7.

But he was concerned about Anand taking the fight to the queenside, with 20 ♕b1 ♖b6 21 ♖b2.

Then Carlsen's knight could no longer defend the b5-pawn with ...♘c7. He would drop a pawn after 21...♗d7? 22 ♗xd5.

205

Almost as bad is 21...♗a6 because White is free to play 22 h4 followed by 23 f5!.

But when Carlsen calculated this he underestimated 21...♕d7!.

Then 22 f5 ♘xf5 23 ♘xf5 gxf5 seems dubious in view of 24 ♗h3 ♕e7! and 24 h4 ♕e7.

His queen would also help out in 24 a4 b4! 25 cxb4 c3 26 ♖b3 ♕xa4!, with a big edge.

19   f4   b4!

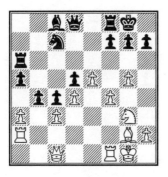

GMs – and computers – had a field day second-guessing Anand here.

Some wanted him to keep the queenside closed, with 20 a4 and then 20...b3 21 ♖af2.

Others wanted an all-out bid for mate, such as 20 f5.

They looked at 20...♘b5 21 axb4 axb4 22 ♖xa6 ♗xa6 23 f6 g6 24 ♕f4 followed by ♕h4-h6.

But computers find defenses in these continuations, such as 24...♕b6 25 ♕h4 h5 and 26 ♘xh5 bxc3! 27 ♘f4 ♘xd4 and ...♘f5!.

20   axb4

There was also something to be said for 20 ♖af2 and 20...♘b5 21 axb4 axb4 22 cxb4 ♘xd4 23 f5 But again, nothing is clear (23...♗b7).

20   ...   axb4

21   ♖xa6   ♘xa6

With 21...♗xa6 Black's knight can jump to b5 next move. But his compensation for a pawn would be questionable after 22 cxb4!.

22   f5!   b3!

Since ...♘b5 is not available, 22...bxc3 lacks bite.

White would have the upper hand after 23 f6 g6 24 ♕xc3 followed by ♖b1 and ♘e2-f4.

Then Carlsen would have a passed c4-pawn – his goal since 8...c4!. But he has to be constantly concerned about ♕h3-h6 and mate.

23   ♕f4

Anand spent 45 minutes on this move, an amount he later called "irresponsible" because he ran short of time in two moves.

He wanted to play f5-f6 at the right moment:

The immediate 23 f6 would prompt 23...g6 because Black's knight can rush back to the kingside, 24 ♕f4 ♘c7 25 ♕h4 ♘e8.

Then ♕h6-g7 mate can be forgotten. But Black's rook is useless and his knight is frozen in place.

Can White play for something other than mate? Yes, as we'll see.

23 ... ♘c7

Some of Anand's time was wasted in calculating 23...♔h8.

Then he might have won in brilliant style, 24 f6 g6 25 ♕h4 ♖g8 26 ♖f4! followed by 27 ♕xh7+! ♔xh7 28 ♖h4 mate.

But this is a mirage. Black does not have to play ...♖g8 until ♕h6.

He would have good winning chances after 25...b2! 26 ♕h6? ♖g8.

In any case, play proceeded:

24 f6

Carlsen considered committing heresy here by opening the kingside with 24...gxf6.

The reason is that 24 gxf6 ♔h8 and ...♖g8 would be safe.

But he had second thoughts when he looked at 24 ♘h5

(24...fxe5?? 25 ♘f6+ and ♕h4).

However, he also saw 24...fxg5! 25 ♘f6+ ♔h8 would have been harmless.

Nevertheless, when calculation conflicted with his intuition, he went with intuition.

24 ... g6?!

25 ♕h4 ♘e8

Forced, since 25...♔h8 26 ♕h6 ♖g8 27 ♖f4 sets up that ♕xh7+! mating combination. Or 26...♘e6 27 ♖f4!.

26 ♕h6?

This is the same position we considered in the note to 23 ♕f4. All that has changed is the clock status.

That was significant. Anand had gone from being a half hour ahead of Carlsen at move 22 to 17 minutes behind him here.

With more time he most likely would have found the stronger idea of ♘e2-f4, threatening the d5-pawn.

For example, 26 ♘e2! ♝e6 27 ♘f4 ♕a5.

Then he would have a choice. One path goes 28 ♝h3 ♝xh3 29 ♕xh3 b2!.

Black would seize the initiative after 30 ♖b1? ♕a2 31 ♕f1 ♘c7.

Instead, 30 ♘e6! would win after 30...fxe6?? 31 ♕xe6+ ♚h8 32 ♕e7!.

The same for 30...♕a1! 31 ♘xf8 ♚xf8 32 e6! b1(♕) 33 ♕h6+ ♚g8 34 exf7+.

But 32...♘d6! finishes with a dramatic perpetual check after 33 ♕h6+ ♚e8 34 exf7+ ♘xf7! 35 ♕h3! ♚d8 36 ♕g2!, according to engines.

It was impossible to see all that in Anand's time pressure – or to see that he had a better policy at move 28.

He could have reversed field with 28 ♘xe6 fxe6 29 ♕f2! with continuations such as 29...♖f7 30 ♝h3 ♘g7 31 ♕b2! and ♖a1.

26   ...   b2!

The match tension was getting to both players. In an interview with Shortlist.com several months later Carlsen recalled the final games.

"Usually I meticulously place the pieces in the center of the squares," he said. "And I wasn't even close to doing that."

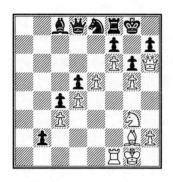

27   ♖f4

Anand felt his move was forced and played it instantly. He thought he had a forced win.

However, Kasparov pointed out 27 ♘e2! would have created more problems.

For example, 27...♕a5 28 ♘f4 ♝b7? 29 e6! or 28...♕a1? 29 ♘xd5 and ♘e7+.

Black could play 28...♝e6 after which 29 ♘xe6 fxe6 30 ♝h3 is similar, but not as good as the 26 ♘e2 line we examined in the last note.

27   ...   b1(♕)+

On-line fans wondered if they were watching one of the most

brilliant world championship victories.

28 ♘f1?? ♛e1!

White resigns

And so what happened? Anand explained:

Several moves earlier he had visualized the position after 27...b1(♛)+ and calculated 28 ♗f1.

Then Carlsen could only stop ♖h4/♛xh7 mate by giving up his extra queen, with 28...♛d1! 29 ♖h4 ♛h5 30 ♘xh5 gxh5.

A remarkable position occurs after 31 ♖xh5 ♗f5! defends h7.

White would reply 32 g6! ♗xg6 33 ♖g5. Black has an extra piece but may not be able to use it because he is so tied up.

After seeing this, Anand looked for an improvement. He found 28 ♘f1.

Once again the threat of ♖h4/♛xh7 mate seems to force 28...♛d1 29 ♖h4 ♛h5.

Anand had seen that this would lose to 30 ♖xh5 gxh5 31 ♘e3!.

What might have been

For example, 31...♗e6 32 ♗xd5 ♗xd5? 33 ♘f5! and ♘e7+.

Carlsen would have enough material for the queen after 32...♛xd5 33 ♘xd5 ♗xd5. But he can't move his king, rook or knight.

Anand would win with a remarkable king march, ♔f2-e1-d2-c2-b2-a3-b4-c5!.

What he overlooked was that after 28...♛e1! Carlsen would again have to give up his queen – but with 29 ♖h4 ♛xh4 30 ♛xh4 ♛a5. Then 31 ♘e3 ♛a1+ is much too slow.

When Anand resigned, Carlsen needed only a draw to become world champion. He got that the next day, in 65 moves.

209

34

Good, Ugly Moves

Carlsen's defeat of Anand in his first world championship match confirmed his supremacy over the older generation. But not all of the veterans approved of his play. Viktor Korchnoi disliked Carlsen's style. "He wins with the ugliest of moves," he said.

Younger players were more approving. "There isn't too much of a mystery to Carlsen," Fabiano Caruana said at Shamkir 2014. "He plays good moves and that's why he wins." Caruana and Carlsen were tied for the lead when they met in the final round.

Carlsen – Fabiano Caruana
Gashimov Memorial,
Shamkir 2014
King's Indian Defense, Irregular Fianchetto Variation (A49)

1	d4	♘f6
2	♘f3	g6
3	g3	♗g7
4	♗g2	c5

Caruana signals that he is willing to reach a standard KID position that arises after 5 0-0 cxd4 6 ♘xd4 0-0 followed by ...♘c6, e.g. 7 c4 ♘c6 8 ♘c3 ♘xd4 9 ♕xd4 d6.

5   c3!?

"Carlsen doesn't have any openings," Korchnoi said before the 2013 world championship. "No openings!" This move seems to confirm that.

5   ...   d5

Now 6 0-0 cxd4 7 cxd4 creates a symmetrical position in which the advantage of playing the first move of the game has become tiny.

6   dxc5!?

This move, "giving up the center," could be considered ugly. It is also fairly original and certainly a way to sharpen the position.

Efforts by Black to regain the c5-pawn immediately will backfire.

210

6	...	0-0

7	0-0	

For example, 7...♕c7 8 b4 a5 9 ♗f4 or 7...♘a6 8 b4 ♘e4 9 ♘d4 e5? 10 ♘b5.

7	...	a5!

This discourages b2-b4 and keeps ...♘a6xc5 in reserve.

8	♗e3	

Both players were calculating at a much earlier point than they were used to in a game.

Caruana could get his pawn back with 8...♘a6 9 ♗d4 ♕c7 and ...♘xc5.

But he could see how 10 ♘a3! ♘xc5 11 ♘b5 ♕d7 12 a4! is unpleasant.

The most forceful variation to calculate begins with 8...♘g4, because ...♘xe3 would offer compensation for a pawn.

That suggests 8...♘g4! 9 ♗d4 and the more or less forced 9...e5! 10 h3! exd4 11 hxg4 dxc3 12 ♘xc3 ♗xg4.

White regains his extra pawn with 13 ♕xd5 but 13...♘a6 14 ♕xb7 ♘xc5 is full "comp" for Black.

8	...	♘c6?

This move gives up on regaining the pawn with ...♘a6 and commits Black to playing gambit style.

9	♘a3!	a4!

A broad pawn center alone is not enough to equalize, e.g. 9...e5 10 ♘b5 and later ♘d6.

10	♕c1	

Another "ugly" move. But 10 ♘b5 ♕a5 11 ♘fd4 e5 12 ♘xc6 bxc6 offers obvious compensation and so does 11 ♘bd4 ♘e4.

10	...	e5

Carlsen's last move prepared ♖d1!.

For example, 10...♘g4 11 ♖d1! ♘xe3 12 ♕xe3 lets him try to exploit the d-file with ♘c4 and ♘b6.

11	♖d1!	

He would also exploit the d-file pin with 11...♘e4? 12 ♘xe5! and 13 ♗xe4.

11 ...   ♕e7

Caruana relies on solid, principled moves. If now 12 b4 axb3 13 axb3 he would have active play with 13...♘e4 14 ♖xd5 ♗e6.

Better is 14 ♘b5 with a middlegame similar to what occurs in the game, 14...♖xa1 15 ♕xa1 f5 16 b4 f4 17 ♗c1!.

12 ♘b5

This knight may land on d6 and discourage ...♘e4. But Black has another attractive idea for the next few moves, ...e4.

For example, 12...e4 13 ♘fd4 ♗g4.

Then 14 ♗f4 ♕xc5 15 ♗d6 allows 15...♘xd4! 16 ♗xc5 ♘xe2+ (17 ♔h1? ♘xc1 favors Black).

Instead, 17 ♔f1 ♘xc1 18 ♗xf8 ♘d3! 19 ♗xg7 ♔xg7 would be an Exchange-up endgame. White is better, but not by much.

12...♗e6

In the last note there were too many promising alternatives for White, such 15 ♘c7 (instead of 15 ♗d6) and, earlier, 13 ♘g5 (instead of 13 ♘fd4).

Instead of trying to make that work, Caruana can rely on solid moves – until he runs out of them.

13 ♘g5   ♗g4

14 ♘d6

Now 14...♗xe2 would have been met by 15 ♖xd5! ♗xd5? 16 ♗xd5.

Then the pressure on f7, and potentially b7, gives White the upper hand (16...♘d8 17 ♕c2! ♗a6 18 ♖d1 or 17...♗g4 18 ♕e4).

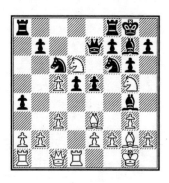

14 ...   h6!

Caruana would like to use his center pawns but 14...d4? 15 cxd4 exd4 16 ♗xd4 ♕xe2 17 ♖d2 ♘xd4 18 ♖xd4 is a pawn-down dead end.

15 ♘f3   ♔h7

16 h3

On the other hand, White would like to solidify his extra pawn with b2-b4 or give his extra pawn back in return for positional goodies.

For example, 16 b4! axb3 17 axb3 e4 18 ♘d4 turns out nicely after 18...♘xd4 19 ♗xd4 ♗xe2 20 ♖e1 ♗d3 21 b4!.

16 ... ♗e6

17 b4?

Carlsen was playing quickly to avoid the time pressure that had been troubling him.

He may have rejected 17 ♘e1 – with the idea of ♘c2-b4 or ♘c2-a3-b5 – because it would require a lot of calculation after 17...♘e8!.

Computers find these matters simple. They claim a solid edge for White after 18 ♗xd5 ♗xd5 19 ♖xd5 ♕e6 20 ♘xe8! ♖fxe8 21 ♖d6 or 20...♕xd5 21 ♘xg7!.

17 ... axb3

18 axb3 ♖xa1

19 ♕xa1 ♘e4!

Magnus misjudged this move.

With ...f5-f4! in mind, Caruana has battled back to equal chances. He would be happy with 20 ♘xe4 dxe4 21 ♘d2 f5.

20 ♘d2!

This is the game's most critical moment.

Caruana saw that 20...♘xd6 21 cxd6 ♕xd6 22 ♘c4 would be bad for him.

He may have noticed 21...♕d7! but had doubts about 22 ♔h2 d4 23 ♗xc6 ♕xd6.

However, 22...e4!, instead of 22...d4?, would have made for an interesting time pressure scramble.

Then White's knight is misplaced and he can easily get the worst of 23 ♗c5 f5 24 e3 ♖c8 and ...♗e5.

20 ... f5?

Since 8...♘c6 Caruana has sought compensating play based on his pawn center. After rejecting

...e4 at various points he now bets the house on ...f4.

What he didn't appreciate was the shocking 20...d4!.

Carlsen could have captured on e4 in three ways but the reply 21...dxe3 would give Black strong chances.

For instance, 21 ♘2xe4 fxe3 22 fxe3 f5 23 ♘d2 e4!.

The desperado 21 cxd4 exd4 22 ♗xh6 is also good for him after 22...♘xg3!.

21   ♘2xe4   dxe4

22   ♕b1   f4

On-line fans looked at 22...♘a5 23 b4 ♘c4 24 ♘xc4 ♗xc4 – until computers showed them 25 c6! and ♗c5.

23   ♗d2   e3

24   ♗e1!

Carlsen has called Caruana's bet. As a practical matter, this is much easier to play than 24 fxe3 fxg3 25 ♗e1 ♕g5.

24   ...   ♗f5

25   ♕c1   h5

Black cannot allow the line-closing 26 g4.

26   fxe3   fxg3

27   ♗xg3   ♕g5

Carlsen's king is relatively safe and he can allow 28 ♔h2 h4 29 ♗e1 e4 because ....♗e5+/♔h1 is harmless. Winning would then be a slow process.

He decides, instead, to end Caruana's initiative with forcing moves.

28   e4!   ♕xg3

29   ♖d3!

The Black queen would be better off on g6, after 29 exf5 gxf5 30 ♖d3 ♕g6, although 31 e4! is still strong.

29   ...   ♕h4

30   exf5   gxf5

31   e4!

Here 31...♗h6 32 ♕f1 fxe4 33 ♗xe4+ and ♖f3 makes matters easy.

31	...	fxe4
32	♗xe4+	♔h8
33	♕e3	♖f4
34	♗g2	♕e7

Carlsen can convert his various advantages with b3-b4-b5.

35	♕e2	♕h4
36	b4	e4!

The best try, allowing the c6-knight to play, in a lost position.

37	♘xe4	♘e5
38	♖d5	♔g8
39	b5!	

After 39...♖f8 White can take his time with safety-moves like ♔h1.

Or he can plow ahead with 40 c6 bxc6 41 bxc6 because 41...♘xc6 42 ♕c4 sets up ♕xc6 as well as a deadly discovered check.

39	...	♖f5

40	c6	bxc6
41	bxc6	♕e7
42	♘d6	♖g5
43	♘b5	♕e6
44	♖d8+	♔h7
45	♕e4+	♖g6
46	c7	♕a6
47	c8(♕)	♕a1+

Last chance: 48 ♔h2?? ♘f3+! mates (49 ♗xf3 ♕g1 mate or 49 ♕xf3 ♗e5+).

If you don't believe crazy tactics can work like that in a Caruana – Carlsen game, wait until Game 44.

48	♔f2	♕b2+
49	♔e1	Resigns

"How long do you think your peak will last?" Carlsen was asked by *Esquire* magazine in 2014. "I think your peak comes when you have the right combination of experience, brainpower and energy," he replied. "I don't think I'm quite there yet."

35

Small Chess

After Boris Spassky famously beat Bobby Fischer with the King's Gambit, he admitted that the gambit promises White very little. But neither does the Ruy Lopez, Spassky felt.

In the decades that followed, Spassky and Fischer showed that there really were ways for White to obtain a solid plus after 1 e4 e5. But after the turn of the century, leading players began to feel that the era of significant opening advantages was closing. All you could expect from the first stage of the game is some chances to exert pressure.

"That's the most you can ask for these days, making your opponent feel uncomfortable," Hikaru Nakamura said in 2019. "Ask Magnus, ask anyone, that's pretty much what they'll tell you." The new era, the era of 'small chess', had arrived.

Carlsen – Viswanathan Anand
World Championship Match,
second game, Sochi 2014
Ruy Lopez, Berlin Defense (C65)

1	e4	e5
2	♘f3	♘c6
3	♗b5	♘f6

By coincidence, this game was played on the 25th anniversary of the fall of the Berlin Wall.

Magnus-watchers were wondering what he had come up with to defeat the Berlin Defense.

4	d3	♗c5
5	0-0	d6
6	♖e1	

His last move is very rare but the main alternatives, 6 c3 and 6 h3, hadn't shown much either. This is *small chess*.

6	...	0-0
7	♗xc6	

Conventional Berlin wisdom says that if Black carries out the maneuver ...♘e7-g6 he would be close to equality.

7	...	bxc6
8	h3	♖e8

Some grandmaster-spectators thought 6 ♖e1 was designed to support 9 ♗e3 ♗xe3 10 ♖xe3.

But with the weakening of h2-h3, that would permit Black to

seize the initiative with 10...♘h5! and ...♘f4/...♖e6-g6.

9   ♘bd2

This move indicates that Carlsen will not try to change the pawn structure with c2-c3 and d3-d4, at least for a while.

9   ...   ♘d7

If White isn't going to change the center structure, should Black? This is his last good chance for 9...d5.

This would be out of character for Anand because it is positionally risky – 10 exd5 ♕xd5 (10...cxd5 11 ♖xe5) ruins his pawns.

But there are tactical benefits – 11 ♘c4 e4! favors Black.

The best test seems to be 11 ♘b3 ♗-moves 12 ♗g5, to stop ...e4.

10   ♘c4

Carlsen hints at a modest plan of ♘a5 or ♗d2 followed by b2-b4.

10   ...   ♗b6

This rules out ♘a5 but allows ♘xb6.

11   a4   a5

12   ♘xb6!

This was compared by some surprised GMs with Bobby Fischer's unexpected trade of a superior knight for Tigran Petrosian's bishop in the 1971 Candidates match.

12   ...   cxb6

13   d4

Carlsen's advantage is tiny – and it would be non-existent without this move. It forces Anand to evaluate the future:

If pawns are traded on e5, the position would be more or less symmetrical. With bishops of opposite color, wouldn't a draw be certain? Does that mean Black should play quietly?

13   ...   ♕c7

An active alternative is 13...c5. It follows the familiar formula of putting pawns on the color of the enemy bishop, when there are opposite-colored bishops.

Anand would have good piece play after 14 dxe5 ♘xe5! 15 ♗f4 ♕f6 or 14 dxc5? ♘xc5 and ...♗b7.

A closed center, 14 d5, might favor White but only if he can avert ...f5!.

The position would be roughly even after 14...♘f8 15 ♘d2 ♘g6 16 ♘c4 ♖f8 and 17...f5.

14   ♖a3!

A more orthodox approach is 14 b3 and 15 ♗b2.

After 14...♘f8 15 ♗b2 ♘g6 the d-file is of little immediate value to White.

For example, 16 ♕d2 ♗e6 17 ♖ad1 f6 18 dxe5 dxe5 19 ♕d6 ♕c8! with prospects of ...♗xh3.

Instead, 14 ♖a3! prepares to swing the rook to g3 and do battle on g7.

For instance, 14...c5 15 d5 ♘f8 can now be met by 16 ♘h4 and ♖g3.

White isn't significantly better after 14 ♖a3!. But a draw is less likely.

14   ...   ♘f8

After 14...♗a6, Black's rooks would be connected. But his bishop isn't really in the game. White can proceed, undistracted, with 15 ♘h4 and ♖g3/♗h6.

Better is 14...♗b7 so that 15 ♘h4? exd4 16 ♕xd4 c5! targets the e4-pawn.

Instead, 15 dxe5 dxe5 16 ♘h4 is a better version of what happens in the game. Worse is 15...♘xe5 16 ♘d4 and f2-f4.

15   dxe5   dxe5

16   ♘h4

The difference in bishops makes White stronger than Black on dark squares.

Anand could try to block that bishop with 16...g6 17 ♖g3 ♘e6 18 ♘f5 ♘f4.

But 18 ♕h5 ♘f4 19 ♕h6 is stronger, with ♘f3 and ♘g5 or h3-h4-h5 in mind.

16   ...   ♖d8

17   ♕h5

The speed of White's attack is shown by 17...♗e6 18 ♖g3 when he already threatens 19 ♖xg7+! ♔xg7 20 ♗h6+ ♔h8 21 ♕g5.

For example, 21...♘g6 22 ♕f6+ or 21...f6 22 ♕xf6+ ♔g8 23 ♖e3.

17 ... f6

If any kingside pawn had to be pushed, this was the one: Now g7 is defended by the queen and, if necessary, can get help from the rook on a7.

18 ♘f5

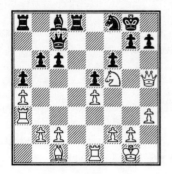

18 ... ♗e6

After the game, analysts declared that 18...♕f7 would have equalized.

But 19 ♕e2 turns White's attention to the queenside and d-file.

For example, 19...♘g6 20 ♖d3 and ♖ed1. Or 19...♘e6 20 ♕c4! ♕c7 (20...♘d4 21 ♘h6+! gxh6 22 ♖g3+) 21 ♖c3.

This points out that the pawn structure is not exactly symmetrical. Black's c- and b-pawns are slightly weak and this will be a factor in the rest of the game.

19 ♖g3 ♘g6

Black, along with on-line analysts, has been thinking that this knight belongs on g6, not e6. However, White's next move challenges that notion.

20 h4 ♗xf5?

Small chess exploits small errors and this is one of them.

After the game, the clever defense of 20...♔h8 21 ♖xg6 ♕f7! was pointed out.

Then 22 ♗h6 ♗xf5? 23 exf5 favors White strongly.

But 22...gxh6 23 ♖xh6 ♕xh5 24 ♖xh5 ♖d2 isn't as bad.

More enterprising is 22 ♖h6!? because White would have compensation for the Exchange after 22...gxh6 23 ♕xf7 ♗xf7 24 ♗xh6.

However, the position is no more than equal after 24...♖g8 25 ♖d1! b5! 26 ♖d6 bxa4 27 ♖xf6 ♗g6 28 ♖xc6 ♗xf5.

21 exf5 ♘f4

Anand counted on this, rather than 21...♘f8? 22 ♗h6 ♖d7 23 ♕g4 – although that is still only a moderate White advantage.

22 ♗xf4 exf4

23 ♖c3!

The former world champion badly misjudged this position when he burned bridges with 20...♗xf5.

The biggest factors now are:

(a) the vulnerable f4-pawn and queenside pawns,

(b) the powerful effect of ♖e6! and,

(c) the problems Anand has on his first rank (23...♖d4? or 23...♖d6? allow 24 ♖e8+).

23 ... c5

No better was 23...♖ac8 24 ♖e6 ♕d7 in view of 25 ♖d3 ♕c7 26 ♕e2 and ♕e4.

24 ♖e6 ♖ab8?

Reduced to passive moves, Anand should have eliminated the first-rank danger with 24...h6. Then 25 ♖c4 ♖d4 would postpone a crisis.

This confuses some computers so much that they start recommending 24 ♖a3?! followed by ♖a1-e1.

Much better is 24 ♕f3 so that after 24...♖ab8 or 24...♖ac8 White can retain a sure edge with 25 ♖c4 ♖d4 26 c3! ♖xc4 27 ♕d5! and ♕xc4.

25 ♖c4

Black faces a new danger, ♖ce4 and ♖e7.

25 ... ♕d7

26 ♔h2! ♖f8

Anand's bid for 25...♕d1+ was stopped and the rest is surprisingly easy. Or it should have been.

27 ♖ce4

If he seeks counterplay with 27...b5? and 28 ♖e7 ♕d8 29 axb5 ♖xb5? he loses immediately, 30 ♕g4 ♖f7 31 ♖e8+.

27 ... ♖b7

Carlsen might have finished more efficiently now with 28 ♕f3 b5 29 ♕xf4.

28 ♕e2 b5

And here 29 ♖e7 ♕d6 30 f3 ♖xe7 31 ♖xe7 would have saved energy because the endgame is lost after 31...bxa4 32 ♕e4.

29 b3

This is super-safe. The desperate 29...c4!? 30 axb5 cxb3 could be refuted by 31 c4 a4 32 ♖e7.

There is a more complex win, 31 b6! b2 32 ♕c4 and 33 ♕b3 because 32...b1(♕) would have allowed mate with 33 ♖e8+ ♕f7 34 ♖xf8+.

29 ... bxa4

30 bxa4

Black would have tactical chances after 30 ♖xa4 ♖b4 31 ♖xa5? f3! and ...♕c7+.

30 ... ♖b4!

31 ♖e7 ♕d6

32 ♕f3?

Much simpler is 32 f3!. Now Anand can dream of survival.

32 ... ♖xe4

33 ♕xe4 f3+

34 g3

34 ... h5?

35 ♕b7! Resigns

Annotators had nearly as much to say about the finish as about anything that preceded it. They pointed out that Anand would have been close to drawing after 34...♕d2!.

Then 35 ♕e6+ ♔h8 36 ♕f7 is a common mating pattern (36...♖xf7 37 ♖e8+ and 36...♖g8 37 ♖e8).

But 36...♕xf2+ 37 ♔h3 ♕f1+ 38 ♔g4 h5+! creates luft so that 39 ♔xh5?? ♖xf7 is taboo.

What is surprising is that 39 ♕xh5+ ♔g8 is not a win. Black has a checking square at c4, 40 ♕g6 ♕c4+! 41 ♔xf3 ♕f1+ or 41 ♔h5 ♖f7.

Of course, Carlsen would not have to rely on that mating pattern. After 35 ♕xf3 ♕xc2 36 ♖a7 or 36 ♔g2 he will win a queenside pawn (36 ♖a7 ♕xa4?? again loses to 37 ♕b7).

But Black may be able to eliminate all the queenside pawns and force Magnus to try to win a queen or rook endgame with just kingside pawns. Then this 35-move game might have been doubled in length.

Anand avenged this loss the very next round. The outcome of the match remained in doubt until the 11th round when Carlsen outplayed him in another Berlin Defense. Carlsen became the first player since Emanuel Lasker to win two world championship matches in a year.

36
Miraculous

Carlsen's domination of Hikaru Nakamura continued to amaze. Magnus defeated him in good positions, in equal positions, even in bad positions. Fans had gotten used to the hex he had over the American. But what happened in the third round at Zürich 2014 shocked everyone. To turn a +6 White advantage into a Black win is one thing. To turn a +11 edge into a win is astonishing.

Hikaru Nakamura – Carlsen
Zürich 2014
Nimzo Indian Defense,
Kmoch Variation (E20)

1	d4	♘f6
2	c4	e6
3	♘c3	♗b4
4	f3	d5
5	a3	♗e7

Carlsen varies from the high-risk 5...♗xc3+ he played against Anand in their world title match (Game 33).

His move invites Nakamura to over-extend his center, 6 cxd5 exd5 7 e4 dxe4 8 fxe4 c5!, when Black has good play on dark squares (9 d5 ♗d6 and ...♘bd7-e5).

6	e4	dxe4
7	fxe4	e5

Now 8 dxe5? ♕xd1+ favors Black (9 ♔xd1 ♘g4).

8	d5

8	...	♗c5

On the face of it, the last move was obvious. If White is allowed to develop smoothly, such as after 8...0-0 9 ♘f3 ♘bd7 10 ♗d3 ♘c5 11 ♗c2 and 0-0, his advantage in space begins to matter.

But there is a back-story:

When Anand was preparing for his 2008 world championship match with Vladimir Kramnik he studied the 4 f3 variation. He secretly enlisted the help of Carlsen and they played training games.

Carlsen did well in those games with 8...♗c5, a favorite move of his friend Jon Ludwig Hammer, and before that, of Paul Keres. Among the merits is that Black can plant the bishop on d4 and may inflict pawn damage with ...♗xc3+. So Carlsen had confidential experience with the move.

9	♗g5	0-0
10	♘f3	♗g4
11	h3!	♗xf3
12	♕xf3	

He may have known that 12...♗d4 would discourage 13 0-0-0 by means of 13...♗xc3 and 14 ♕xc3? ♘xe4.

But 13 ♗xf6 and then 13...♗xc3+ 14 bxc3 ♕xf6 15 ♕xf6 gxf6 gives both players doubled pawns.

Then ...♘a6-c5 seems solid. But it is easier to play for a win with the White pieces than with the Black ones.

12	...	♘bd7
13	0-0-0	♗d4
14	♘e2!	c5

This is a sound pawn offer, 15 dxc6 bxc6 16 ♘xd4 exd4 17 ♖xd4 ♕b6! and 18 ♖d2 ♘c5 or 18 ♖d6 ♖ab8!.

| 15 | g4 | |

But around here Carlsen must have suspected that anchoring the bishop on d4 was not enough to offset Nakamura's kingside initiative with ♘g3-f5.

| 15 | ... | a5? |

The best chance for queenside counterplay is 15...a6 and 16...b5, even at the cost of a pawn. Carlsen overestimated the impact of ...♖a6-b6.

16	♔b1	♖a6?
17	♘g3	

His initiative would end soon after 17...♖b6 18 ♖h2.

For example, 18...a4 19 ♘f5 ♖b3 20 ♖d3 ♕b6 21 ♗c1. Then it is White's turn for attack with g4-g5 and h3-h5-h5.

17	...	g6
18	h4	a4
19	♖h2	♕a5

The queen does little on a5. But at least this move frees the pinned knight for ...♘e8-d6.

| 20 | ♗d2 | ♕c7 |

223

21	g5	♘e8

22 h5!

White is just a few moves (♗c1, ♗d3, ♖dh1, ♕g4) away from an overwhelming position.

22	...	♖b6
23	♗c1	♖b3
24	♕g4!	

He is ready to win on the h-file with 25 hxg6 hxg6 26 ♕h4.

Or 25...fxg6 26 ♕e6+ ♔g7 27 ♕e7+ ♖f7 28 ♖xh7+!.

He also has a slower knockout plan of ♗d3 and ♗c2, followed by ♖dh1 and hxg6.

24	...	♘b6

25 ♗e2!

And he has yet another winning idea, getting his bishop into the game via g4 and e6.

For example, 25...♕d7 – a reasonable move in case of 25 ♗d3? – would walk into 26 ♕h4 ♘d6 27 ♗g4!.

Then 27...♕e7 28 hxg6 fxg6 29 ♗e6+ ♔h8 30 ♖dh1 is a win.

Nakamura's advantage has been hovering around +2 in computer terms but begins to shoot up. In other words, it is swindle time.

25	...	♘d6!

Carlsen knew he was losing. That can be a weapon in the hands of a swindler because he is freer to try desperate, trappy moves.

Here the bait is 26 hxg6 fxg6 27 ♕e6+. White can see brilliancy-prize finishes:

(a) 27...♘f7 28 ♖xh7! or 28 ♘f5! (threat of 29 ♘h6+ and mate) gxf5 29 g6!, and

(b) 27...♔g7 28 ♖xh7+! ♔xh7 29 ♖h1+ ♔g7 30 ♕h3!, and

(c) 27...♖f7 28 ♘f5! gxf5 29 g6 hxg6? 30 ♖dh1, and

(d) 27...♔h8 28 ♖xh7+! ♕xh7 29 ♕xd6! and ♕xf8+ or ♖h1.

Finishes like that could make up for some of Nakamura's previous losses to Magnus.

But the trap would be sprung by 27...♕f7! 28 ♕xd6? ♘c8!.

That would turn the game around after 29 ♕f6? ♕xf6 30 gxf6 ♖xg3.

Or it might end in a draw after 29 ♕b8 ♘b6 30 ♕d6 ♘c8.

The worst Carlsen would face is 29 ♕b8 ♘b6 30 ♘f5!, based on 30...♖xb8 31 ♘h6+.

He would be lost after 30...gxf5 31 ♕d6 ♘c8 32 ♕h6 ♖b6 33 ♕h3. But he wouldn't be ready to resign.

26   ♖dh1!

26   ...   ♗xb2!

Computers try to minimize Black's inferiority with 26...♕d7 27 ♕h4 ♖xg3.

Then 28 hxg6 fxg6 29 ♕xg3 ♘xe4 30 ♕g2 is better than what happens in the game – but only in a mathematical sense.

27   ♗xb2   ♘bxc4

28   ♗xc4   ♘xc4

29   hxg6!   ♕b6

Now 30 gxh7+?? ♔h8 is a file-closing blunder that loses the game.

But the g-pawn has two other moves and both win.

After 30 gxf7+! ♖xf7 31 ♘h5 Black is helpless in the face of ♘f6+, e.g. 31...♖xb2+ 32 ♔a1.

He would face a +7 disadvantage after 32...♕g6 33 ♖xb2. Nakamura wanted more. He deserved it.

30   g7!   ♖d8

31   ♕h4

And not 31 ♖xh7?? ♖xb2+ 32 ♔a1 ♖a2+! and mates.

Now 31...♕g6 32 ♘f5 is hopeless so the next few moves are forced on both sides.

31	...	♖xb2+
32	♔a1	♖xh2
33	♖xh2	♕g6
34	♘f5	♖e8

In 2014 Nakamura felt he had been playing better than Magnus. Some fans scoffed. But in this game he was proving it.

He just needed to find the forced win that everyone watching the game felt must be there. It lies in three winning motifs.

One is to push the d-pawn and threaten ♘e7+. But 35 d6? ♘xd6 36 ♘xd6 allows Black to get back into the game with 36...♖d8!.

The second motif is to exploit the Black queen's tie to h7. With 35 ♕g4 White threatens 36 ♖h6.

The third motif is the hardest to detect – a sacrifice on h7.

After 35 ♕f2! White's main threat is 36 ♖xh7! ♔xh7 37 ♕h4+ and mates.

Or 36...♕xh7 37 ♘h6+ ♔xg7 38 ♕xf7+ ♔h8 39 ♕xe8+ and mates.

35   ♕g4   ♕b6!

Carlsen's threat of mate on b2 prevented 36 ♖h6 or 36 ♖xh7.

White can settle for winning with 36 ♘h6+ ♔xg7 37 ♕d7!. But once again he found the best move.

36   ♕h3!   ♕g6

37   d6??

If Nakamura had played 37 ♕f1! annotators would congratulate him on finding an improved version of 35 ♕f2. It improves because he would threaten 38 ♕xc4 as well as 38 ♖xh7!.

37   ...   ♘xd6

38   ♘xd6   ♖d8!

Back at the previous diagram Nakamura must have looked at 35 d6 and seen that 35...♘xd6 36 ♘xd6 ♖d8! defends.

For example, 37 ♘f5?? ♖d1+ and mates (38 ♔b2 ♕b6+ or 38 ♔a2 ♕e6+).

Why, then, did he allow the same idea now?

39   ♘c4?

Once again 39 ♘f5?? gets mated.

White would have no more than a draw after 39 ♘b5 ♛xe4 40 ♘c3 ♛e1+ 41 ♘b1 ♛e4.

But because his queen is on h3 he still had winning chances after 39 ♘c8!, taking away the checking square at b6.

A long endgame would follow 39...♔xg7 40 ♘e7 ♖d1+ 41 ♔a2 ♛e6+ 42 ♛xe6. White's advantage will have dropped from +12 to barely +1. But at least he is still better.

39 ... ♛xe4

40 ♛h5?

No better was 40 ♛f1? ♖d3 41 ♖h4 ♖xa3+ 42 ♘xa3 ♛xh4 with an ending like the game.

But 40 ♘e3! ♛d3! 41 ♘f5 or 41 g6 would force Black to deliver perpetual checks.

40 ... ♖d3

41 ♖h4 ♛f5

42 ♛e2

Black has enough pawns to more than offset the knight in an ending but the outcome depends on what kind of ending.

The rook version, 42 g6 ♛xg6 43 ♛xg6 fxg6, is lost. Nakamura goes into a queen ending.

42 ... b5

43 ♘d2 ♛xg5

44 ♛xd3 ♛xh4

Alone, the knight is helpless, e.g. 45 ♛xb5 ♛d4+! 46 ♛b2 f5 47 ♛xd4 cxd4 48 ♘f3 d3 49 ♔b2 e4.

45 ♘e4 ♔xg7

46 ♛f3 ♛f4

The same goes for 47 ♛xf4 exf4 48 ♔b2 f3 49 ♔c2 f5. The rest is methodical but can be done in various ways:

47 ♛g2+ ♔f8 48 ♔b2 h5 49 ♘d2 h4 50 ♔c2 b4 51 axb4 cxb4 52 ♛a8+ ♔g7 53 ♛xa4 h3! 54 ♛b3 h2 55 ♛d5 e4! 56 ♛h5 e3 57 ♘f3 e2 58 ♔b3 f6 59 ♘e1 ♛g3+ 60 ♔a4 ♛g1 61 ♛xe2 ♛a7+ White resigns

Nakamura tried to forget the game and 37 d6?? that night. "But when I went to sleep, the position came into my head and wouldn't leave," he said.

37
Harmony

Carlsen's propensity to win long endgames by nursing a pawn to victory led some fans to assume he was a materialist. But his former trainer Simen Agdestein said he "loves harmony more than material."

"Harmony" was a favorite word of Vasily Smyslov, a world champion Carlsen closely resembles. Here is a Smyslov-style victory.

Take note of the knight play. Early on Black establishes d4 as an ideal outpost. But only one of his knights can occupy it. The other one is "redundant" as Mark Dvoretsky would say. Carlsen's knights just seem to be massed together on the kingside. But suddenly at move 19 all of his pieces are working together – harmoniously.

Carlsen – Radoslaw Wojtaszek
Olympiad, Tromsø 2014
*Sicilian Defense,
Closed Variation (B26)*

1	e4	c5
2	♘c3	d6
3	g3	♘c6
4	♗g2	g6
5	d3	♗g7
6	♗e3	

This is how the old-school method of development, with 7 ♕d2 or 7 ♘ge2, begins. But that doesn't promise White much and it was supplanted in the 1960s by 6 f4 followed by ♘f3.

| 6 | ... | e5 |

| 7 | ♘h3 | |

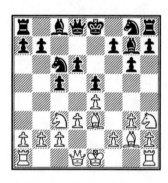

This development of the knight is more common after 6 f4 e5 7 ♘h3.

The difference between that and 7 ♘ge2 or 7 ♘f3 is illustrated by (6 f4 e5 7 ♘h3) ♘ge7 8 0-0 0-0 9 f5!.

This thematic advance is justified by 9...gxf5 10 exf5 ♗xf5 11 ♖xf5! ♘xf5 12 ♗e4.

228

There are finishes such as 12...♘fe7? 13 ♗xh7+! ♔xh7 14 ♕h5+ ♔g8 15 ♘g5 and wins.

7	...	♘ge7
8	f4	

This is an uncommon position. Not a favorable one, just a different one.

8	...	♘d4
9	0-0	0-0
10	♕d2	

Another benefit of not putting the knight on e2 or f3 is that Black is denied an early piece trade that can ease his game.

If it were on e2 here, then 10...♗e6 11 ♘d1 ♕d7 12 c3 ♘xe2+! 13 ♕xe2 turns out well for him after 13...exf4 14 ♗xf4 d5 or 14 gxf4 ♖ae8 and ...f5.

10	...	♗d7

There was nothing wrong with 10...♗e6 because Black could meet 11 ♘g5 with 11...♗d7 and 12...f6.

But 10...♗g4!? might have made Carlsen wonder what he had done when he played ♘h3.

For example, 11 ♘d1 ♕d7 12 ♘df2 looks like piece "harmony."

But 12...♗e2 13 ♖fe1 ♗f3 is fine for Black.

11	♘d1	♕c8

Now 12 ♘hf2 is inconsistent with 11 ♘d1. Black would have a fine game after 12...b6 13 c3 ♘bc6 followed by ...♗e6/...d5.

12	♘df2	

Carlsen's knights aren't doing anything yet. But they don't get in each other's way.

In contrast, Black has one ideal square for his knight, at d4, and both knights cannot occupy it. Neither can after 12...♘ec6? 13 c3!.

White would have an evident edge after 13...♘e6? 14 f5! ♘c7 15 ♗h6.

12	...	♘dc6

But 12...f5 13 c3 ♘e6 would be approximately even.

Play might go 14 ♖ae1 ♕c7 15 fxe5 dxe5 16 exf5 gxf5! 17 ♘g5 ♖ae8 and it is easier to find good moves for Black.

13 c3

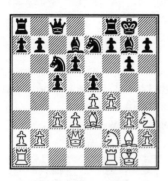

13 ... b5

Instead, Black pursues the traditional Closed Sicilian strategy of trying to soften up the enemy dark squares with ...b4. But this is where his position begins to sour.

If he had overprotected the c5-pawn with 13...b6, he can prepare for ...d5 with ...♕c7 and ...♖ad8.

Computers even say that after 13...b6 White should admit ♘h3 was wrong and play 14 ♘g5 and 15 ♘f3.

14 fxe5!

Black cannot play 13...dxe5 14 ♗xc5.

14 ... ♘xe5

Carlsen gets an outpost at f4 for his unemployed h3-knight.

In return, Black temporarily gets e5 for a knight. But it can be ousted by d3-d4.

15 ♗h6!

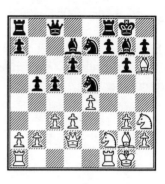

15 ... ♘7c6

He tries to delay d3-d4 with this knight.

Computers suggest that goal is better served by getting his queen onto dark squares, 15...♕a6 and ...♕b6.

That works well after 16 ♗xg7 ♔xg7 17 ♘f4 ♕b6 18 d4? ♘c4.

An endgame, 18 b3 b4 19 cxb4 ♕xb4 20 ♕xb4 cxb4 21 d4 ♘5c6, would also be acceptable to Black.

But White has another plan, 18 ♘d1! and 19 ♘e3 followed by ♘ed5 or just ♖f2/♖af1.

16 ♗xg7 ♔xg7

17 ♘f4 ♕d8

The queen can also get to dark squares this way, 18 b3 ♕a5 and deter 19 d4.

18 ♖ad1 ♖c8

But 18...♕a5 19 ♕e2 followed by 20 d4! cxd4 21 cxd4 ♘c4 22 b3 would point out the traffic jam of Black's minor pieces.

And 19...♕xa2? loses the queen to 20 ♖a1 and 21 ♖a3.

19   ♕e2!

What has seemed like a quietly even game will change sharply after 20 d4!.

19   ...   h5

20   d4   cxd4

21   cxd4   ♘g4

This was the point of 19...h5. White allows a knight trade.

But his remaining pieces have much more... well, harmony... than Black's.

22   h3   ♘xf2

23   ♕xf2

Computers initially prefer 23 ♖xf2. But when they see the maneuver ♖d3-f3 they appreciate how much trouble Black is in.

For example, now 23...b4 24 d5? ♘e5 25 ♕xa7 ♖a8 is fine for Black.

But 24 ♖d3! is not, for example, 24...♗e8?? 25 ♘e6+.

23   ...   ♘e7

24   ♖d3!

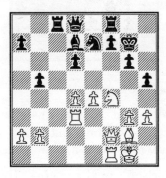

Once the rook reaches f3 White will have a threat of ♘xh5+! followed by ♖xf7+.

24   ...   b4

This prepares ...♗b5 and safeguards the queenside pawns, which can become a new battleground.

For example, 24...♘g8 25 ♖f3 ♘h6 would overprotect f7.

However, then 26 ♕d2! threatens 27 ♘xh5+! gxh5 28 ♖f6! and wins.

And when Black defends with 26...♘g8, he has no good defense of his a7-pawn after 27 ♖a3!.

For example, 27...♖a8 28 e5 or 27...♕c7 28 ♘d5.

| 25 | ♖f3 | ♕e8 |

26 g4!

With 26 d5 White wins a pawn (26...a5 27 ♕b6). But this is not nearly as good as a mating attack.

Carlsen recalled how Garry Kasparov had been watching this game. When Kasparov saw 26 g4! he moved on to watch the other boards.

| 26 | ... | hxg4 |
| 27 | hxg4 | ♗b5 |

Of course, 27...♗xg4 28 ♖g3 is suicidal (28...♗d7 29 ♘h5+). But so is allowing the pawn to reach g5.

28 ♖e1

Computers recognize that 29 ♕h4 and 30 ♕g5/♘h5+ is an immediate danger. And 29 g5 and ♗h3 is a long-term problem.

28	...	♕d8
29	g5!	♕b6?
30	♗h3	♖cd8

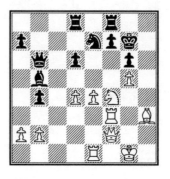

31	♗e6!	♗e8
32	♘d5	♘xd5
33	♗xd5	**Resigns**

There is no defense to doubling heavy pieces on the h-file.

38
Younger Generation

As 2015 began, Carlsen was becoming dominant in big-time chess. In his previous 30 tournaments he had scored 18 first prizes, finished second nine times and placed third three times – none lower. He had not had a bad tournament since he finished sixth at Dortmund 2007, when he was still 16.

But so far his strongest opponents had been older players. They were members of a generation that was used to the leisurely pace of a time control of 40 moves in two and a half hours. The faster new control – 40 moves in 100 minutes with 30-second increments – was difficult for some of them to handle. "Almost all of the players are united on this," GM Michael Adams said in 2001, "I don't think that any players are interested in this new time control."

Within a decade "almost all" of the top players were happy with it. They were members of the Fischer clock generation and Carlsen was their champion.

But by 2015 he was the older generation and was meeting members of the somewhat newer one, led by Wesley So.

Carlsen – Wesley So
Sinquefield Cup, St. Louis 2015
Sicilian Defense,
Najdorf Variation (B90)

1	e4	c5
2	♘f3	d6
3	d4	cxd4
4	♘xd4	♘f6
5	♘c3	a6

Carlsen and So had only played twice before. They had an uneventful draw at Wijk aan Zee 2015 and a hard-fought one three months later at the Gashimov Memorial.

6	♗e3	e5
7	♘b3	♗e6
8	f3	♘bd7

When Sicilian variations with ...e5 were new, classically trained players assumed Black would be equal if he eliminated the pawn center hole with ...d5.

But 8...d5? 9 exd5 ♘xd5 10 ♘xd5 is too early.

233

This is shown by 10...♕xd5 11 ♕xd5 ♗xd5 12 0-0-0 and 10...♗xd5 11 c4 ♗b4+ 12 ♔f2! ♗e6 13 ♕xd8+ ♔xd8 14 ♘c5.

9	♕d2	b5

10	0-0-0

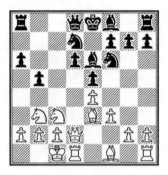

The aggressive battle array, with ♗e3, ♕d2, 0-0-0, f2-f3 and g2-g4-g5, became popular in the 1980s at the amateur and master level. It is easy to find White's candidate moves and they can be used against several forms of the Sicilian Defense, including Scheveningen and Taimanov lines.

10	...	♗e7

An early 0-0-0 seems to give Black a queenside to attack before ...♗e7/...0-0 grants White a target on the other wing.

However, experience has shown that White scores well after, for example, 10...♘b6 11 ♕f2 ♘c4 12 ♗xc4 ♗xc4 13 g4.

The same goes for 12...bxc4 13 ♘c5. Even 13 ♘a5 works because 13...♕xa5? 14 ♗b6 traps the queen.

11	g4

Now on 11...0-0 12 g5 Black can't retreat to the occupied d7 square.

True, he can play 12...b4 because 13 gxf6? bxc3 14 ♕xc3 ♘xf6 is fairly even.

But 13 ♘e2 ♘h5 14 ♘g3 is unpleasant because 14...♘xg3? 15 hxg3 opens the h-file for ♕h2.

And 13...♘e8 14 f4 is also good for White.

11	...	b4
12	♘d5	

But now 12 ♘e2 would allow Black the first punches at the enemy king with 12...a5! and ...a4.

And 12 ♘a4 ♖b8 leaves the knight at risk of ...♕c7-c6.

12	...	♗xd5
13	exd5	♘b6

Black could stop White's next move with 13...a5.

But there's a trick, 14 g5 ♘h5 15 ♗b5! a4? 16 ♘c5! so that 16...dxc5 17 d6 with a sizable White edge.

Better is 15...0-0, e.g. 16 ♔b1 a4 17 ♘c1 when ♗c6 should only favor him slightly.

14	♘a5!

Not 14 ♕xb4 ♘fxd5 when Black enjoys excellent play.

14	...	♘bxd5

Otherwise 15 ♘c6 ♕c7 16 ♘xb4.

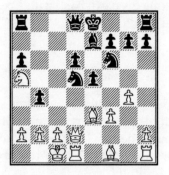

15   ♘c4!?

This first new move of the game confused on-line spectators. Didn't White play ♘a5 in order to go 15 ♘c6 ?

Yes, but after 15 ♘c6 ♕c7 he would be worse following 16 ♘xe7 ♘xe3! 17 ♕xe3 ♔xe7 and only equal after 16 ♘xb4 ♘xb4 17 ♕xb4 0-0.

15   ...   ♘xe3

Forced, in view of White's threat of 16 g5 ♘xe3 17 gxf6! ♘xd1 18 fxe7 or 17...♘xc4? 18 fxe7.

16   ♘xe3

Now the picture clarifies: Carlsen sacrificed a pawn in order to dominate the light squares, especially d5. He can defend his king position with ♗c4 and attack Black's with ♘f5.

16   ...   0-0

If Black controls f5 with 16...g6, his king has no safe haven after h2-h4-h5.

For instance, 17 h4 h6 18 ♗c4 ♔f8 19 h5.

17   ♗c4

Quite wrong is 17 ♕xb4? d5! when Black's bishop comes alive and he is better (18 ♕a4 ♗c5 or 18 ♕b7 ♖b8 19 ♕a7 ♖c8 and ...♗c5).

17   ...   ♘d7

This move is a comment about the pawn sacrifice. It says "I don't believe it."

If So appreciated the dangers in the position he would have played 17...d5.

Then 18 ♗xd5? ♘xd5 19 ♕xd5 ♗g5! favors him.

And 18 ♘xd5 ♘xd5 19 ♕xd5 (19 ♗xd5?? ♗g5) ♕c7 is equal.

18   h4   a5

19   g5   ♖c8

Computers don't believe it either. Some engines regard Black as better if he plays ...♔h8 soon.

20   ♗d5   ♘b6

21　♔b1

Carlsen did not want to trade knights, as he might have done with ♗b3 and ♘d5. Instead, he allows ...♘xd5/♘xd5 because his knight will be much better than Black's bishop.

21　...　♕c7

22　♖hf1!

Since 14 ♘a5! was prepared in advance, this was likely Carlsen's first major decision of the game:

He delays the most natural plan, ♖dg1 and h4-h5, in favor of f3-f4.

If Black stops f4-f5-f6 with, for example, 22...♕c5 23 f4 exf4, he cannot defend f7 for long, after 24 ♖xf4.

He also has to meet the threat of 25 ♖f5! and 26 ♗xf7+ or 26 ♗e6.

But if Black gives back his extra pawn, 24...♔h8!, White's advantage is minimal.

22　...　♘xd5

23　♘xd5

This gives White the option of getting his pawn back with ♘xe7+ and ♕xd6.

23　...　♕b7

24　f4!

But that would be an admission that his pressure is waning. Black would be at least equal after 24 ♘xe7+? ♕xe7 25 ♕xd6 ♕xd6 26 ♖xd6 f6!.

Instead, Carlsen looks toward pushing his h-pawn to h6. If Black keeps the files closed with ...g6, White can exchange pawns on e5 and play a strong ♕e3!.

24　...　f5

By exchanging on d5, Black made possible this move and tries to neutralize the f-file.

But the counter-intuitive 24...f6! was better.

It looks wrong because White's queen can invade on light squares, such as 25 ♕d3 ♔h8 26 ♕f5.

Then on 26...fxg5 27 ♕e6 Black would pay the price for opening his king position after 27...♗d8? 28 fxe5 or 27...♖ce8 28 fxg5.

But computers point out the counter-sacrifice 27...gxh4!.

Black would have the superior chances after 28 ♕xe7 ♕xe7 29 ♘xe7 ♖ce8.

Or 28 ♘xe7 ♖fe8! 29 ♘g6+ hxg6 30 ♕xg6 ♔g8.

25   ♕e3!

Now 25...♖c5 26 fxe5! ♖xd5? 27 ♕b3 is lost.

This means that the threat of fxe5 forces Black to freeze the center.

25   ...   e4

So badly misevaluated his chances in what follows – but so do computers.

26   h5   ♖c5!

He badly needs counterplay and would get it from 27 ♕b3 ♔h8 28 a3 ♖fc8!.

27   h6!

Much better than 27 g6 h6, when White would have to hunt for a way to win.

27   ...   g6

28   ♕b3

The specter of a last-rank mate hovers over the next stage.

For example, 28...♔h8 29 ♖d2 ♖fc8 30 ♖fd1 threatens to win with 31 ♘xe7 and 32 ♖xd6.

Black cannot allow 30...♗f8 31 ♕e3 and ♕d4+/♘f6(+).

And he would be in for a surprise after 30...♗d8 31 ♘xb4!.

Then 31...axb4 32 ♖xd6 ♗e7 33 ♕f7! or 31...♕xb4 32 ♕f7!.

28   ...   ♖f7

29   a4

Carlsen can play "without an opponent."

Among his options is ♖d4/♖hd1 followed by either ♘xe7 or ♘e3-c4xd6.

But first he makes luft and rules out a tactical ...a4.

29   ...   ♗d8

30   ♖d4   ♔f8!

So had to meet the danger of 31 ♖fd1 followed by 32 ♘f6+! ♗xf6 33 ♖xd6! and ♖d7. His king is much safer on f8.

31   ♖fd1

This is such a natural preparation for ♘e3-c4 that the value of 31 ♘e3! wasn't appreciated.

31	...	♖c6
32	♘e3	♗b6
33	♘c4!	

This is where the game is decided. Black could try 33...♖xc4!.

Then 34 ♖xc4?? falls into a trap because 34...♖d7! and 35...d5 snares the c4-rook.

After 34 ♕xc4! ♗xd4 35 ♕xd4 ♕c7 36 ♕h8+? ♔e7 Black is safe.

Critical is 36 ♕xd6+ ♕xd6 37 ♖xd6 ♖a7 and ...♔e7, when Black's rook is passive but he has survival chances.

33	...	♗xd4?

But there was also 33...♕c7!.

Then 34 ♘xb6 ♕xb6 35 ♕e6 ♖e7! is a surprising dead end (36 ♕f6+ ♖f7).

And 34 ♘xd6? ♗xd4 35 ♘xf7 ♕xf7 is worse.

The key continuation is 34 ♖xd6! ♖xc4 35 ♖d8+ ♔e7 36 ♖1d7+ ♕xd7 37 ♖xd7+ ♔xd7 38 ♕xc4.

Then White has a material edge but after 38...♖e7! the passed e-pawn should be enough to draw.

This is why 31 ♘e3! would have been more exact.

34	♘xa5	♕b6
35	♘xc6	♗c5!

Black could have safely resigned after 35...♕xc6 36 ♖xd4 and ♖xb4.

36	♕d5!	e3!
37	a5	

The a-pawn becomes a winner after 37...♕c7 38 a6 and 39 a7.

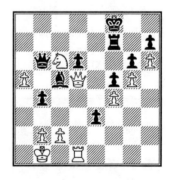

37	...	♕b5

A pretty finish to the game would now have been 37...♕b7 38 ♕xc5! e2 39 ♖xd6 e1(♕)+ 40 ♔a2.

Then the threat of ♖d8 mate would prompt 40...♖e7 and 41 ♖d8+ ♔f7 42 ♘e5+ ♕xe5 (42...♖xe5 43 ♕f8+ mates) 43 fxe5.

Black would soon have to give up another queen to avert 43 e6+! and mate.

But this is unnecessary because 39 ♕xd6+ would win without effort.

38	♘d8!	♖a7
39	♘e6+	♔e8
40	♘d4	

This move would have been the best after 39...♔e7 because of 40 ♘d4 ♕d7 41 ♘c6+ and ♘xa7.

With the king on e8 that is not possible. That's why 40 ♘xc5! and 41 ♕g8+/42 ♕xh7+ would have won faster now.

40	...	♕xa5
41	♕g8+	♔d7
42	♕xh7+	♔c8
43	♕g8+	♔b7
44	c3	

Definitely not 44 ♘b3?? ♕a2+ 45 ♔c1 ♕a1+! and mates.

44	...	bxc3
45	♕b3+	♕b6

| 46 | ♕xb6+ | |

There was no reason to be cute with 46 ♕xc3 when you can have an endgame with a protected passed pawn two squares from queening.

46	...	♔xb6
47	bxc3	♗xd4
48	♖xd4	♔c6
49	♔c2	♖a2+
50	♔d1	♖f2
51	♔e1	♔d7
52	♖a4	

There were several ways to win and some (52 ♖d3 ♖f3) to drag it out.

52	...	♔e6
53	♖a8	♖h2
54	c4	♔f7
55	♖b8	

Zugzwang: 55...♖h4 56 ♔e2 or 55...♖f2 56 h7.

55	...	♔e6
56	♖g8	**Resigns**

39
The Carlsen Exchange Sacrifice

Sacrifices of the Exchange have become steadily more popular in recent decades as masters appreciated how great a role that an extra minor piece can play in a middlegame. The extra enemy rook on the other side often does not become a significant factor until queens are traded.

Carlsen does not offer the Exchange more often than his leading rivals. But he appears to use slightly different criteria for evaluating the sacrifice. Here's an example.

Carlsen – Arkadij Naiditsch
Baden Baden 2015
Sicilian Defense,
Najdorf Variation (B91)

1	e4	c5
2	♘f3	d6
3	d4	cxd4
4	♘xd4	♘f6
5	♘c3	a6
6	g3	

One of Carlsen's first impressive Exchange sacrifices also came out of this opening. His opponent, Evgeniy Perman, sidestepped theory with 6...g6.

The game, from the 2003 European Under-14 Championship, went **7 ♗g2 ♗g7 8 0-0 0-0 9 h3 ♘c6 10 ♘de2 ♗d7 11 ♔h2 b5 12 f4 ♖c8 13 ♘d5 ♘xd5 14 exd5 ♘a5 15 c3 ♘c4 16 b3 ♘b6 17 ♗e3 b4**. Then came **18 c4! ♗xa1 19 ♕xa1** with more than

enough compensation because of Black's severely weakened kingside and dark squares.

He won after **19...f5 20 ♘d4 h6 21 ♕e1 a5 22 g4 ♔h7 23 gxf5 gxf5 24 ♘f3 ♗e8 25 ♕h4! ♗f7 26 ♘g5+ ♔g6** and **Black resigned** before 27 ♗f3 and ♖g1.

6	...	e5
7	♘de2	♗e7
8	♗g2	0-0
9	0-0	♘bd7
10	a4	b6

For more than 70 years Najdorf Variation players have been wrestling, in various positions, with a fundamental question: Should he allow a4-a5?

He would get play along the b-file after 10...♖b8 11 a5 b5 12 axb6.

But it isn't much play after 13 b3! regardless of how he captures on b6.

11 ♘d5 ♘xd5

12 ♕xd5

Not 12 exd5? a5, when the pawn structure favors Black.

He can make progress with ...f5/...♘c5 but White cannot make anything out of the holes at b5 and c6.

12 ... ♖b8

Black might have spared himself ...♖b8 by means of 12...♕c7 and 13...♗b7.

Then the queen sacrifice, 13 ♕xa8 ♗b7 14 ♕xf8+ ♘xf8, is at best even because the Black queen matters before the White rooks do.

For instance, 15 c3? ♕c4 or 15 ♘c3 ♘e6 and ...♘d4.

13 ♘c3 ♘f6

14 ♕d3 ♗e6

This was Black's new idea. Usually the bishop is developed on b7 but exerts little pressure on the e4-pawn then. Now it can go to c4.

If White stops that, Black may force him to play ♘d5.

For example, 15 b3 ♕c8 16 ♗b2 ♖d8 17 ♖fd1 ♕b7 prepares 18...b5!.

The position after 18 ♘d5 ♘xd5 19 exd5 ♗g4 is slightly better for White.

15 ♕xa6! ♕c7

This was an "Armageddon" tiebreaker game. Carlsen had six minutes for all of his moves, while Black began with five. Magnus would lose the playoff if the game were drawn.

With more time he might have chosen 16 ♖e1 ♗c4 17 ♘b5.

But to play it he would have to be confident that 17...♕c6 – which threatens ...♖a8 – could be met safely by 18 b3 ♖a8 19 ♘d4! exd4 20 ♕xc4.

He may also have had doubts about 16 ♘d5.

241

Then 16...♘xd5 17 exd5 ♗d7 18 ♕d3 ♖a8 19 b3? b5! is unclear.

But there may be significant advantage in, for example, 19 ♗e3 ♗xa4 20 c4.

16   ♕e2!

In contrast, he could feel certain, with little calculation, that this is a sound Exchange offer.

16   ...   ♗c4

17   ♕f3   ♗xf1

18   ♗xf1

What made the Exchange sacrifice so attractive was that:

(a) it was forcing,

(b) it ensured great control of several light squares and,

(c) the next several moves will be easier for White to play, compared with Black.

Often when Carlsen sacrifices the Exchange his minimum expectations are an extra pawn and superior "playability."

His game with Fabiano Caruana at Biel 2011 was typical:

After **1 e4 e5 2 ♘f3 ♘c6 3 d4 exd4 4 ♘xd4 ♗c5 5 ♘xc6 bxc6 6 ♗d3 ♕h4 7 ♕e2 ♘e7 8 ♘c3 0-0 9 ♗e3 ♗b6 10 0-0 d5 11 exd5 ♘xd5 12 ♗d2 ♗d4 13 ♖ae1 ♘b4 14 ♕e4 ♕xe4 15 ♗xe4 ♗a6 16 ♘e2 ♗c5 17 a3 ♘d5 18 b4 ♗d6** he chose **19 ♘d4! ♗xf1 20 ♔xf1**.

Carlsen – Caruana
Biel 2011

Once he wins the c6-pawn the position is only slightly better for White, e.g. 20...♘e7 21 ♘xc6 ♘xc6 22 ♗xc6 ♖ad8.

However, it was easier for Black to make bad mistakes.

This was evident after **20...♘b6 21 ♘xc6 ♖fe8 22 a4 ♔f8 23 a5 ♘c4 24 ♗c1 a6 25 f4**

Caruana failed to find 25...♘e3+! 26 ♖xe3 ♗xf4, which should have drawn.

Instead, he lost after **25...♖e6?? 26 ♗d5! ♖f6 27 ♖e4 Resigns**.

A comparable situation arose in Bacrot – Carlsen, Biel 2008 after **1 d4 ♘f6 2 c4 e6 3 ♘c3 ♗b4 4 ♘f3 b6 5 ♗g5 ♗b7 6 ♘d2 h6 7 ♗h4 ♘c6 8 a3 ♗xc3 9 bxc3 ♕e7 10 e3 g5 11 ♗g3 d6 12 h4 0-0-0 13 ♗e2 ♘d7 14 ♘b3 f5 15 ♕c2 ♖hf8 16 f3 e5 17 hxg5 hxg5 18 0-0-0 ♖de8 19 ♗d3 ♕f7 20 ♖h6 ♗a6 21 ♘d2 exd4 22 exd4 ♘a5 23 ♖dh1 ♖e7 24 ♕a4 ♖e3 25 ♖h7 ♕e8 26 ♕c2 ♘f6 27 ♖7h6 ♔b7 28 ♗f2**

Bacrot – Carlsen
Biel 2008

With **28...♖xd3! 29 ♕xd3 ♘d5 30 ♖e1 ♕a4 31 ♕c2 ♕xa2+** he temporarily secured two pawns for the Exchange but also domination of the light squares.

One of his extra pawns was the outside passed a-pawn and he nursed it with **32 ♕b2 ♕xb2+ 33 ♔xb2 ♘xc4+ 34 ♘xc4 ♗xc4 35 ♗e3 g4 36 fxg4 fxg4 37 ♖g6 a5 38 ♖xg4 a4**

He gave it back to win back the Exchange, **39 ♖g3 a3+ 40 ♔xa3 ♖a8+ 41 ♔b2 ♖a2+ 42 ♔c1**

♘xc3 43 ♗d2 ♘e2+ 44 ♖xe2 ♗xe2, and the outcome was in little doubt. **White resigned** 18 moves later.

Back to Carlsen – Naiditsch:

| **18** | **...** | **d5!** |

Carlsen was poised to improve his position with simple moves, 19 b3 and 20 ♗c4.

Black can temporarily stop that with 18...♖fc8.

But 19 ♗a6 ♖-moves 20 ♗d2 and ♖d1/b2-b3 has to be better for White.

| **19** | **exd5** |

Naiditsch has two tactical ideas to work with. He can push ...e4 and he can play against the d5-pawn with ...♗b4 and ...♖fd8.

He stands worse but his disadvantage would be more manageable after 19...♗b4 20 ♗d2 e4.

Or after 20 ♘e4 ♘xe4 21 ♕xe4 ♗c5.

| **19** | **...** | **e4?** |

Now it begins to look like the speed game it was.

| **20** | **♕f5?** |

After 20 ♘xe4! Black would be losing (20...♕xc2 21 ♗d3 or 20...♘xd5 21 c4 ♘-moves 22 ♗f4).

| **20** | **...** | **♖bd8** |

| **21** | **♗f4** | **♕c5** |

Black can quickly develop chances on dark squares. For example, 22 ♗e3 ♛b4 23 ♖b1? g6!.

Then he would stand well after 24 ♛e5? ♘g4 25 ♛xe4 ♛xe4 26 ♘xe4 ♘xe3 27 ♘xe3 ♖xd5.

Or 24 ♛g5 h6 25 ♛xh6 ♘g4 26 ♛f4 f5.

22   ♖d1   ♛b4

The same 22...g6! works here:

23 ♛g5 ♘h5 or 23 ♛e5 ♘g4 24 ♘xe4 (24 ♛xe4 ♛xf2+) ♛xc2 offers Black some chances.

23   ♗e5!

Suddenly it becomes simple. Carlsen sets the table for 24 ♗d4 and 25 ♘xe4.

The game could end with 23...♛xb2? 24 ♘xe4 ♛xc2 25 ♘xf6+ ♗xf6 26 ♛xc2 resigns.

23   ...   ♗c5

The last try was 23...♘d7.

Then 24 ♗d4? ♗f6! would be roughly balanced.

Also, 24 ♗c7 ♘f6 25 ♗xd8 ♖xd8 is confusing enough to give

him practical chances from ...♗c5 and ...e3.

But 24 ♘xe4 ♘xe5 25 ♛xe5 should be enough to win.

24   ♗xf6   gxf6

25   ♘xe4   ♛xb2

There was no defense (25...♗e7 26 d6 ♖xd6 27 ♖xd6!).

26   ♗d3   ♖fe8

27   ♘xf6+   ♔f8

It is mate after 27...♔g7 28 ♛g5+ ♔h8 29 ♛h6.

28   ♘xh7+   ♔e7

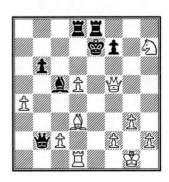

Among the knockout moves are 29 ♗b5 and 29 d6+, both followed by 30 ♖e1+. Carlsen chooses the easiest win to calculate.

29   ♖e1+   ♔d6

30   ♛f4+   ♔xd5

31   ♘f6+   ♔c6

32   ♘xe8   Resigns

40
Mystery Moves

Every great player has made moves that at first left their fans stumped. Even those with a seemingly transparent style – Capablanca, Tarrasch, Smyslov, Fischer and Anand – occasionally played the inexplicable. Only after a few moves was the mystery solved. It took longer in this game.

Carlsen –
Maxime Vachier-Lagrave
Shamkir 2015
Réti Opening (A05)

1	♘f3	♘f6
2	g3	b5
3	♗g2	♗b7
4	♘a3	a6

This seems like a loss of a tempo because Black will play ...a5 three moves later.

But there was no better way to protect the attacked b-pawn.

After 4...b4 5 ♘c4 Black has to spend a tempo to discourage 6 ♘a5!.

He would be slightly worse after 5...c5 6 0-0 e6 7 a3, for example.

5	c4	b4
6	♘c2	e6
7	d4	

White is ready to attack the b4-pawn, such 7...♗e7 8 a3.

Then 8...bxa3 8 ♘xa3 favors him a bit.

So does 8...a5 9 axb4 axb4 10 ♖xa8 ♗xa8 11 ♗d2 ♘a6 12 ♕a1.

7	...	a5

Now on 8 a3 ♘a6! 9 axb4 ♘xb4 Black's queenside is in good shape.

8	0-0	♗e7
9	d5!	

Carlsen gains an advantage in space with a sound gambit: 9...exd5 10 ♘fd4 c6 11 cxd5 is nice for him after 11...cxd5 12 ♘f5.

It is more than nice after 11...♘xd5 12 e4! ♘c7 13 ♘f5 0-0 14 ♕g4.

9	...	♘a6
10	♘fd4	♘c5
11	♖e1	0-0
12	e4	e5

This takes d4 away from White but gives him f5.

That is a major concession but 12...d6 13 ♘b3! could be worse.

After 13...♘xb3 14 axb3 White threatens 15 dxe6 fxe6 16 e5 ♗xg2 17 exf6.

Black would be slightly worse after 14...♘d7 15 ♘d4 ♘c5 16 ♗e3 ♗f6.

13	♘f5	d6

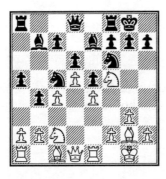

Vachier-Lagrave expected to approach equality after ...♗c8xf5.

White can't claim much of an edge after 14 ♗e3 ♗c8 15 ♗xc5 dxc5 16 ♘ce3 ♗d6, for example. Only a Karpov would feel he has good winning chances then.

14	♗g5!

Carlsen hints at kingside pressure with f2-f4 and ♖f1.

His move required not only exact calculation but solid evaluation.

First, what is happening after 14...♗c8 15 ♘ce3 ?

Then 15...h6 16 ♗h4 ♔h7 would threaten to trap the bishop with 17...g5.

A likely continuation is 17 f4! ♗xf5 18 ♘xf5 ♘g8, when Black breaks the pressure on f6.

But 19 ♘xe7 ♘xe7 gives White the two bishops and, despite the closed position after 20 f5, he could play for g3-g4-g5.

14	...	♘xd5

Carlsen had foreseen 15 cxd5? ♗xg5 and 15 ♘xe7+? ♘xe7.

15	♗h6!

This was not hard for a master to spot or to calculate 15...♘f6? 16 ♗xg7.

More difficult was evaluating the position that comes after the next three forcing moves.

15	...	gxh6
16	♕g4+	♝g5
17	cxd5	♔h8
18	h4	♝f6

Carlsen has a small and apparently long-term positional advantage. There is no rush to regain a pawn with ♘xh6.

But he needs a plan – or a mini-plan – before Black develops counterplay with ...♝c8 followed by ...♝xf5 and ...♜c8/...c6.

19 ♘ce3

A good plan would be 19 a3 to soften up the queenside.

After 19...b3 20 ♘ce3 he could double rooks (♖ec1-c3 and ♖ac1) and even consider an Exchange sacrifice on c5.

19	...	♝c8
20	♕f3	♝g7

21 ♗h3

But Carlsen prefers a mini-plan, maneuvering his bishop to h5 where it attacks Black's weakest point, f7.

21	...	♖g8
22	♗g4!	♕f6
23	♗h5	

23 ... ♝xf5

It is easy to criticize this no-turning-back move, particularly because Vachier-Lagrave had surprising resources after 23...♖f8.

For example, 24 ♘g4 ♕d8 25 ♘gxh6 seems to demonstrate progress by White.

But then comes 25...♝xh6 26 ♘xh6 f5!.

Black would suddenly have the edge after 27 exf5 ♕f6! 28 ♕e3 ♝xf5 and ...e4.

If White takes the Exchange, 27 ♘f7+ ♖xf7 28 ♗xf7, the position is double-edged after 28...fxe4.

For example, 29 ♕h5 ♕f6 or 29 ♕e3 ♕f6 30 ♗h5 ♗b7 and ...♖g8.

24 ♘xf5   c6?

This could be called the losing move because of Carlsen's ruthless technique. Vachier-Lagrave should have prepared the push with 24...♖gc8.

Then 25 ♕d1? allows 25...♘xe4! 26 ♖xe4 ♕xf5.

Better is 25 ♖ed1 c6 26 ♖ac1 ♗f8 when Magnus would have to find a good plan, not just a mini-plan.

25 dxc6   ♖ac8

26 ♕d1!

Vachier-Lagrave must have missed this move. Now 26...♘xe4 27 ♗g4! cost him material (27...♘c5 28 ♘xg7).

26 ...   ♖xc6

27 ♕d5!   ♖gc8

28 ♖ad1   ♗f8

29 ♕xf7

One of those Magnus moves that, at first, makes even masters

wonder if they are playing the same game as him. A trade of queens seems to make a draw more likely.

But he had to take on f7 before it was defended (29 b3? ♖8c7).

When you take a longer look you see that 29 ♗xf7 ♘a4! also leads to an endgame, after 30 ♖d2 ♘b6 31 ♕b3 a4 32 ♕e6.

29   ...   ♕xf7

30 ♗xf7

Now we can see Carlsen's conception: After ♗d5 and ♘e3-c4, perhaps supported by b2-b3, both the a5- and d6-pawns will be vulnerable.

If Black defends them, he can then turn to the kingside with a rook maneuver such as ♖e3, ♖de1, ♖f3, ♖ee3, ♖f5 and ♖ef3. That would stretch Black's pieces to the breaking point.

30   ...   ♘a4

Vachier-Lagrave correctly reasons that a trade of rooks will help him.

31	♖e2

It is harder to win after 31 b3 ♘c3.

31	...	♖c1
32	♖xc1	♖xc1+
33	♔g2	♘c5
34	b3	♖c3
35	♔h3	

Carlsen hints at ♔g4.

35	...	♘d7

Black has the more active rook but using it to swap the queenside pawns is doomed.

For example, 35...a4 36 bxa4 ♘xa4 37 ♔g4 ♘c5 38 ♗d5 b3? 39 axb3 ♘xb3 40 ♖b2 ♘c5 and now 41 ♖b8 ♘d7 42 ♖d8 ♖c7 43 ♗e6 wins a piece.

36	♗e6	♘c5
37	♗d5	♘d7
38	♘e3	♘f6
39	♗e6	♖c5
40	♘c4	♔g7

41	f3	♘e8
42	♖d2	

Once again, trading pawns would give White what he needs most, a file for his rook.

For example, 42...a4 43 ♗d7 axb3 44 axb3 ♘f6 45 ♗e6 ♘e8 46 ♖a2 and ♘e3/♖a7+.

41	...	♘c7
43	♗g4!	

Now 43...♘e8 44 ♗d7! ♘f6 45 ♗e6 ♘e8 seems to protect everything.

But 46 ♖d5! would trade off the only Black piece that can defend the a5-pawn.

Then the desperate 46...♖xc4 47 bxc4 ♘c7 would fail after 48 ♖xa5 ♘xe6 49 ♖b5 followed by ♖xb4.

43	...	a4!
44	♘xd6	♗xd6
45	♖xd6	a3
46	♗d7!	♖c2

249

47 &c6!

It wasn't too late to throw the win away with 47 &f5 ♘b5!, when Black wins the a2-pawn.

47 ... ♖xa2!?

The best practical try. After 47...♔f8 48 ♖d8+ and 49 ♖d7+ the knight falls. White was also bound to win after 47...♘a6 48 &d5.

48 ♖d7+ ♔f6

49 ♖xc7 ♖c2

50 ♖xh7!

So that 50...♖xc6 51 ♖xh6+ and ♖xc6.

The endgame would have lasted much longer after, for example, 50 ♔g4 a2 51 ♖a7 ♖xc6 52 ♖xa2 h5+ and 53...♖c3.

50 ... ♔g6

51 ♖c7 ♔f6

52 h5!

The rook endgame, 52...a2 53 ♖a7 ♖xc6 54 ♖xa2, is hopeless.

52 ... ♖c1

Black threatens to draw with 53...a2.

53 ♖h7 a2

54 &d5! Resigns

It's mate: 54...a1(♕) 55 ♖f7+ ♔g5 56 ♖f5.

This was played in the second memorial tournament dedicated to the talented Azerbaijani grandmaster Vugar Gashimov, who died of a brain tumor at age 27.

41
Grand

The genesis of the Grand Chess Tour can be traced to the 2014 Sinquefield Cup. Mega-sponsor Rex Sinquefield said he would like to link four or five super-tournaments of classical chess together, like the pro tours in tennis and golf. The winner would be recognized as the number one player in the world. "In some sense the world championship isn't necessary," Sinquefield said. "We only have to go back a couple of years to see two people contesting the world championship who were nowhere near the top." (Whether he was referring to Anand vs. Topalov in 2010 or Anand vs. Gelfand in 2012 was unclear.)

The Grand Chess Tour kicked off in 2015. Carlsen took the $215,000 overall prize by winning the final event, in London. He drew his first six games in that tournament before this game.

Carlsen – Hikaru Nakamura
London 2015
Slav Defense (D12)

1	d4	d5
2	c4	c6
3	♘f3	♘f6
4	e3	♗g4
5	h3	♗h5
6	cxd5	

This is a low-risk, but also low-benefit, way of handling the position, compared with 6 ♘c3 e6 7 ♕b3.

6	...	cxd5
7	♘c3	e6
8	g4	♗g6

9	♘e5	

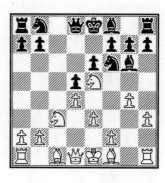

9	...	♘fd7!

Nakmura evades the only trap in this variation – 9...♘bd7? 10 h4! and 11 h5.

For instance, 10...♘xe5 11 dxe5 ♘d7 12 h5 ♗e4 13 f3.

10	♘xg6	hxg6
11	♗g2	♘c6

Traditional thinking held that the half-opening of the h-file for Black should offset his loss of kingside pawn flexibility.

That view was supported a year before, when Vishy Anand demonstrated how 12 0-0 f5! and ...♗d6 can give Black excellent chances.

12	e4	dxe4
13	♘xe4	♗b4+
14	♘c3	♘b6

Traditional thinking also indicates that the opening of the center should benefit White's two bishops. But it also made the d4-pawn a target.

Black would be equal after 15 ♗e3 ♘d5 and better after 15 ♗xc6+? bxc6 16 ♕f3 ♕d5.

| 15 | 0-0 | 0-0 |

Carlsen gets to trade off his only weakness now. If Nakamura had any worries about that he would have tried 15...♘xd4 16 ♗xb7 ♖xh3!.

It would then be foolhardy to accept the sacrifice of 17 ♗xa8? ♕xa8 18 f3 ♕b8.

16	d5	exd5
17	♘xd5	♗c5
18	♘c3	♗d4
19	♕f3	♕f6

Team Carlsen saw this move as an indication that Nakamura was seeking a quick draw.

The two players had made such draws before, of 12, 21 and 25 moves – when Nakamura was White.

| 20 | ♕xf6 | ♗xf6 |
| 21 | ♗f4 | ♖ad8 |

But the previous seven games in which Nakamura was Black averaged more than 70 moves. He scored four draws and three losses.

| 22 | ♖ad1 |

Piece and pawn trades are inevitable. Which exchanges are good and which bad?

A trade of queenside pawns is almost certain to help Black.

For example, 22...♘c4 23 ♗c1 ♘b4! 24 ♗xb7 ♗xc3 25 bxc3 ♘xa2 would likely draw.

A swap of knights may help White, e.g. 23 b3 (instead of 23 ♗c1) ♗xc3 24 bxc4 ♘d4 25 ♗g5 and ♗d5.

22	...	♗xc3!?

A daring decision, characteristic of Nakamura's style.

He may have been concerned about 22...♖fe8 23 ♘e4 and then 23...♗xb2 24 ♘d6.

Then 24...♖e7 25 ♘xb7 ♖xd1 26 ♖xd1 ♖xb7? 27 ♗xc6 ♖e7 leads to another kind of exchange – of rooks, 28 ♖d8+ ♔h7 29 ♖e8! ♖xe8 30 ♗xe8.

White would have good winning chances because his king can centralize faster than Black's.

23	bxc3	♘a4
24	c4	♘c3

The next few moves hold White's advantage to a minimum.

25	♖d2	♖xd2
26	♗xd2	♘e2+
27	♔h2	♖d8
28	♗e3	♘c3
29	a3	

29	...	♖d3

As long as Black can force matters, his knights match up well with the bishops. Nakamura may have done better with 29...♘d1 30 ♗f4 ♖d4!.

But it was hard to evaluate 30 ♗c5 ♘a5 31 ♗xa7 ♘xc4 32 ♗c5 b6 33 ♗b4 ♖d4. White would be better but not by much.

30	♖c1	♘d1
31	♗e4	♖d7
32	♗c5	♘b2
33	♖c2	♘a4
34	♗e3	♘b6
35	c5!	

Two bishops often beat two knights in an endgame when the knights are restricted by pawns.

253

This is the first restricting move and leads to a favorable trade of rooks.

35	...	♘d5
36	♖d2	♘f6
37	♖xd7	♘xd7
38	♔g3	♔f8
39	f4	♘f6
40	♗f3	♔e7
41	f5!	

An alternative plan is 41 g5 followed by preparing f4-f5. Then ...gxf5 would give White an opportunity to create a passed h-pawn.

Carlsen's plan is more sure-handed. He wants his king on g5 and the prospect of h4-h5-h6.

41	...	gxf5
42	gxf5	♔d7
43	♔f4	♘e8
44	♔g5	

Black's c6-knight can be traded off when White wants to.

On 44...♘f6 he might try 45 ♗xc6+ ♔xc6 46 ♗d4! in order to make his h-pawn a winning passer.

For example, 46...♘e4+ 47 ♔f4 ♘xc5 48 ♗xg7 and h3-h4-h5.

Or 46...♘e8 47 h4 ♔d5 48 ♗b2 ♔xc5 49 h5 f6+ (else 59 f6!) 50 ♔g6 ♔d6 51 a4! followed by ♗a3+ and ♗f8.

44	...	♔e7
45	♗f4	a6
46	h4	♔f8
47	♗g3	♘f6
48	♗d6+	♔e8
49	♔f4	♘d7
50	♗g2	♔d8
51	♔g5	♔e8
52	h5!	

Another version of that is 52...♘de5? 53 ♗xc6+! ♘xc6 54 f6! and wins.

Similar is 52...♘f8 53 f6! ♘h7+ 54 ♔f5 ♘xf6 55 ♗xc6+ bxc6 56 h6.

254

52	...	♘f6
53	h6	♘h7+
54	♔h5	♘f6+
55	♔g5	♘h7+
56	♔h4!	

This forces an exchange of pawns and allows his king to reach g7.

56	...	gxh6
57	♔h5	♘f6+
58	♔xh6	♘g4+
59	♔g7!	

Now the f7-pawn is a target (60 ♗d5 f6 61 ♗f3 or 60...♘d8 61 ♗f4 ♘f2 62 ♗g5 and ♗xd8).

Nakamura is forced to use the piece he hasn't touched in the last 47 moves.

59	...	♘d4
60	♗e4	♘f2
61	♗b1!	♘g4
62	♗f4	f6

This move is another concession. But Nakamura's knights would slowly run out of safe squares after 62...♘e2 63 ♗c7 ♘c3 64 ♗c2.

63	♗e4	♘f2
64	♗b1	♘g4
65	♗e4	♘f2
66	♗xb7!	♘d3

Fans watching the game on-line were puzzled by Carlsen's next move. The ever-present computers assured them that 67 ♗d6 wins.

They gave 67...♘xf5+ 68 ♔xf6 ♘xd6 69 ♗c6+! as proof. White has more than a +2.00 advantage after 69...♔d8 70 cxd6.

But the engine analysis soon reaches a point where no progress is possible.

For example, 70...♘b2 71 ♔e6 ♘c4 72 a4 a5 73 ♔d5 ♘e3+ 74 ♔c5 ♘g4! and then 75 ♔b6 ♘e5 76 ♗b5 ♘f7.

Here Stockfish 9 saw that 77 d7 ♘e5 and ...♘xd7 is a draw. Therefore, it examined 77 ♔c5 for 40 uneventful moves and concluded White is still close to a win. He isn't.

67	♔xf6!	♘xf4
68	♔e5!	♘fe2
69	f6??	

Nakamura could have resigned after 69 c6! because of 69...♔d8 70 f6 ♘f3+ 71 ♔d6.

69	...	a5

70	a4	

Seventy moves appeared to have been wasted by Carlsen's blunder. There is no win after 70 c6 ♘b5! 71 a4 ♘a7, e.g. 72 ♔d6 ♘c3 73 c7 ♔f7 and ...♘xa4.

70	...	♔f7

71	♗d5+	♔f8

72	♔e4!	

But this is a stunningly simple conception: Carlsen threatens to corral one of the knights with 73 ♔e3 and 74 ♗c4, followed by ♗xe2.

72	...	♘c2

73	c6!	

Earlier this advance would have permitted Black to sacrifice a knight (...♘xc6/♗xc6) and draw. Now Black doesn't get a chance.

73	...	♘c3+

74	♔e5	♘xa4

75	♗b3!	♘b6

76	♗xc2	a4

77	c7	♔f7

78	♗xa4	

Black resigns

What happened? Wasn't Black drawing after 69 f6??.

Yes, he was. But he had to find 71...♔g6 so that 72 c6 ♘xc6+ 73 ♗xc6 ♔f7! is another book draw.

The final position is lost in view of 78...♔f8 79 ♔e6 followed by ♗d7 and c8(♕)+.

The Grand Chess Tour did not grow into a super-league of classical chess as was hoped. It began with three tournaments in 2015. But one of them, the Norway Chess, dropped out in 2016 and Carlsen did not play in the only two "classical" tournaments that remained. The tour was reformulated each year after that. By 2020 it was a series of two "classical" events and three speed tournaments. The annual winners were not recognized as the world's best player.

42
Open

No world champion had played in an open tournament in more than 40 years, since Boris Spassky entered the 1971 Canadian Open. Anatoly Karpov, among others, did not like Swiss System tournaments and felt playing non-elite players would hurt his game. Magnus felt differently and entered an open tournament of 132 players in 2015. He also played in other opens, such as the 2017 and 2019 Isle of Man masters. In this game he needed a win to stay in first place.

Carlsen – Li Chao
Qatar Masters, Doha 2015
Neo- Grünfeld Defense (D70)

1	d4	♘f6
2	c4	g6
3	f3	

This move sidesteps the main lines of the Grünfeld Defense (3 ♘c3) and tries to steer Black into the Sämisch Variation of the King's Indian Defense (3 f3 ♗g7 4 e4 d6 5 ♘c3).

When Carlsen faced 3 f3 as Black he often went for rarely tried lines such as 3...♘c6, 3...d6 4 e5 e5 and even the gambit 3...e5!? 4 dxe5 ♘h5.

3	...	d5
4	cxd5	♘xd5
5	e4	♘b6
6	♘c3	♗g7
7	♗e3	0-0
8	♕d2	

Li Chao's decision to stay in the Grünfeld family creates a position similar to one that often arises after 3 ♘c3 d5 4 cxd5 ♘xd5 5 e4 when Black avoids 5...♘xc3! and plays 5...♘b6.

Then 6 ♗e3 ♗g7 7 ♕d2 0-0 would transpose in the game after 8 f3. But more common is 8 ♖d1 or 8 0-0-0.

What this means is that Carlsen has gotten a somewhat freer version of a Grünfeld sideline (5...♘b6?!) that has a somewhat dubious position. That should benefit him substantially.

8	...	♘c6
9	0-0-0	

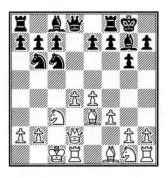

In the one time he reached this position as Black, Carlsen went for 9...♕d6 and 10 ♘b5 ♕d7 and ...♖d8. His pressure on d4 was not enough to equalize.

9	...	f5!

Black would appear to equalize with 9...e5 because of 10 d5 ♘d4.

But the centralized knight can be undermined immediately with 11 f4 and 11...c5 12 fxe5 ♗xe5 13 ♘f3.

10	e5

Since ...f5 weakens the king position slightly, White would like to hit back quickly with h2-h4-h5.

But 10 h4 fxe4 11 fxe4? drops a pawn (11...♘xd4! 12 ♗xd4 ♕xd4 13 ♕xd4 ♗xd4 14 ♖xd4 ♖xf1+).

Instead, White can make it a gambit with 11 h5!. Tournament experience has been mixed with that.

10	...	♘b4
11	♘h3	

A center outpost, even a splendid one like d5, does not create a middlegame plan. Black needs one before White overwhelms his kingside with ♘f4 and h2-h4-h5.

For example, 11...♘4d5 12 ♘f4 ♘xe3 13 ♕xe3 and 14 h4 is unpleasant.

11	...	♕e8

The same goes for 11...♗e6 12 ♔b1 ♕d7 13 ♘f4 and then 13...♘c4 14 ♗xc4 ♗xc4 15 h4.

Or 13...♗c4 14 ♗xc4+ ♘xc4 15 ♕e2 ♘xe3 16 ♕xe3 with the idea of 17 d5.

Black's last move was new and prepares 12 ♘f4 ♕f7.

He would have counterplay after 13 a3 ♘a2+.

On e8 the queen also watches h5 so that 13 ♔b1 g5 14 ♘h5?? is not possible – and 14 ♘h3? allows 14...f4! and ...♗f5+ .

Better is the double-edged 14 e6! ♗xe6 15 ♘xe6 ♕xe6 16 ♗xg5 ♖ad8 and 16 a3 f4.

258

12 ♔b1!

Carlsen does not get enough credit for his prophylactic moves, such as 18 ♔a1 and 25 ♗c1 in Game 27.

Now 12...♕f7? 13 ♘g5 ♕e8 14 h4 sets Black back.

Or 12...♘a4 13 ♘xa4 ♕xa4, when 14 ♗c4+ ♔h8 15 ♗b3 ♕b5 16 ♗g5 shows that Black has misplaced his pieces.

12 ... a5!

Li Chao needs time to prepare ...♗e6/...♕f7. He played this move so that if Carlsen tries to drive the b4-knight back with a2-a3, he will ignore it.

Then axb4/...axb4 is almost certainly a sound knight sacrifice.

And since 13 ♘f4 would again be met by 13...g5!, Carlsen temporarily shelved the kingside attack plans.

13 ♗e2 c6

14 ♖c1 ♔h8

This creates room for ...♗e6-g8! and ...♕f7.

For example, 15 ♘f2 prepares the g2-g4 push. Black's attack comes alive after 15...♗e6 16 a3 ♗g8!.

He would hold the edge after 17 g4? ♕f7 18 h4 ♘a2!.

15 ♔a1!

This is both a waiting move and prophylaxis.

It is waiting for 15...♗e6 16 ♘f4! ♗g8 17 h4, when 17...♕f7 18 h5! is winning because of 18...g5? 19 ♘g6+!.

At the same time it ensures that a ...♗xa2 capture will not be a check.

15 ... ♗e6

Black could have reverted to exploiting the d5-square with 15...♘4d5 but he presses on with his queenside attack.

16 ♘f4 ♕f7

Still bad is 16...♗g8 17 h4!.

Some computers initially recommend continuing 17 ♘xe6 ♕xe6 18 h4.

But given more time they concede that 18...♖fd8 means counterplay for Black (...♗xe5 or ...c5).

17 h4! ♗xa2?

That last note indicates Black should play 17...♖fd8! and exploit the position of the White queen (...♗xe5).

The queen is needed on d2 to make his attack come first, as 18 ♕e1 ♗xa2! shows.

If White solves his ...♗xe5 problem with 18 ♘xe6 ♕xe6 19 f4, Black can end his own kingside fears with 19...h5!, with near equality.

18 h5

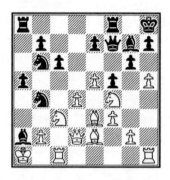

18 ... ♔g8

Of course, both players saw 18...g5 19 ♘g6+! because this trick has been in the air since move 15.

They must also have evaluated 19...♔g8 20 ♘xf8 ♗xf8 21 ♗xg5 as bad for Black.

But did they see the zwischenzug 20...f4 ?

Then 21 ♗f2 ♗xf8 is actually playable for Black. He has a pawn for the Exchange and the initiative after ....♗b3/...♘c4 or ...a4-a3.

The flaw in this clever defense is 21 ♘xh7! and then 21...♔xh7 22 h6 ♗f8 23 ♗d3+.

Or 21...fxe3 22 ♕xe3 ♔xh7 23 h6.

19 hxg6 hxg6

20 g4!

The game seems over in light of 20...g5 21 ♘h3 f4 22 ♗f2 and ♘xg5 (22...♕g6? 23 ♘xa2).

20 ... ♗b3!

But Black found survival chances, 21 gxf5 ♕xf5 22 ♖hg1? ♘c2+.

21 ♗d1!

Suddenly the threat of mate with ♕h2! seizes back the reins.

For example, 21...♗xd1 22 ♕h2! ♖fd8 23 e6 ♕f6 24 ♕h7+ ♔f8 25 ♘xg6+ and mate soon.

21 ... a4!

Black has one resource left, ...a3xb2+.

22 ♕h2 ♖fd8

23 ♕h7+ ♔f8

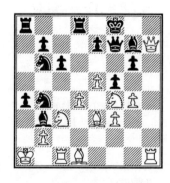

Now 24 ♘xg6+ ♔e8 25 gxf5 becomes problematic after 25...a3!

because Black threatens mate after 26...♘c4! or 26...♘d3!.

White's only forcing reply, 26 e6, allows 26...axb2+ 27 ♔xb2 ♗xe6 28 fxe6 ♘c4+ 28 ♔b3.

After 28...♛xe6 he has nothing better than perpetual check – and would lose after 29 ♔xb4?? ♘xe3 threatens 30...♛c4 mate.

24   d5!!

A beautiful example of the interference theme of problemdom:

If Black takes the pawn with a knight, White wins with 25 e6 followed by ♘xg6+.

If he takes with the pawn or bishop, 25 ♗xb6 wins.

24   ...   ♘c4

25   ♘xg6+   ♔e8

But Black still has a mating idea, 26 gxf5 a3!.

26   e6   a3!

27   exf7+   ♔d7

There is another remarkable mate after 28 bxa3?? ♖xa3+ 29 ♔b1 ♗c2+!.

One neat finish is 30 ♗xc2 ♖a1+! 31 ♔xa1 ♗xc3+ 32 ♔b1 ♘a3 mate.

Another is 30 ♖xc2 ♖b3+ 31 ♔a1 ♘xc2+.

28   ♘e5+!   ♗xe5

29   ♛xf5+   ♔c7

White only draws after 30 bxa3 ♖xa3+ 31 ♔b1 ♗a2+! 32 ♔a1 ♗b3+.

30   ♛xe5+!

But he is so far ahead in material he can afford this.

30   ...   ♘xe5

31   ♗xb3   axb2+

32   ♔xb2   ♘bd3+

33   ♔b1   ♘xc1

34   ♖xc1

The dust settles and Magnus has a winning material edge and a powerful f7-pawn (24...♘xf7 25 dxc6 ♘e5 26 ♘b5+ and mates).

34   ...   ♔c8

35   dxc6   bxc6

36   f4   Resigns

43
Confidence Game

*"I don't think there is such a thing as overconfidence in chess,"
Carlsen said in a 2014 interview with 'Esquire' magazine. "It's
always better to be too confident than too reluctant."*

*When an amateur hears this he wonders: How does it help you
win when you have no more than an even position? This game is
an illustration of how.*

*When Carlsen pushed his a-pawn to the sixth rank, beyond his
natural ability to defend it, he couldn't possibly know that he
would have sufficient compensation if it were captured. Then, at
move 25, when his opponent was blowing up the center, he could
have reached a safe haven. But he played to win, with that
a-pawn.*

*Again, he couldn't be sure he was winning (and he wasn't). But
he believed he could outplay a former world champion (and he
did).*

Viswanathan Anand – Carlsen
Baden-Baden 2015
*Dutch Defense,
Stonewall Defense (A90)*

1   d4

Let's see: What haven't we
played against one another? After
some 20-plus games in which he
opened with 1 e4, Anand tries to
test Carlsen in something else.

1   ...   f5

And in games in which Anand
opened 1 d4 Carlsen tried 1...d5
as well as the Grünfeld Defense
and Nimzo-Indian and Queen's
Indian. The Dutch starts a new page.

2	g3	♘f6
3	♗g2	e6
4	c4	c6

This is a transpositional finesse
that means a lot to grandmasters
but to few others. Black delays a

decision about his d-pawn until he sees what the g1-knight does.

Now on 5 ♘h3 and ♘f4, he can try to kick it back with 5...d6 and ...e5. He couldn't do that if he played the routine 4...d5.

5   ♘f3   d5

But with the knight on f3 he reverts to a traditional Stonewall setup and will fight for control of e5 with ...♗d6.

6   0-0   ♗d6

For many years, theory recommended 6...♗e7 and rated the position as distinctly favorable to White.

The bishop was supposed to be misplaced on d6 because 7 ♗f4 ♗xf4 8 gxf4 would trade off his good bishop.

But the verdict of theory was reversed when Black got good kingside play later with ...g5.

7   b3   ♕e7

8   ♘e5

More finesses: Black's last move stopped another bishop trade, 8 ♗a3. White's reply allows him to favorably meet 8...b6 with 9 cxd5 and then 9...cxd5 10 ♘c4!.

That threatens to capture Black's better bishop. The tactical basis is 10...dxc4? 11 ♗xa8.

8   ...   0-0

9   ♘d2   a5

White developed his knight at d2 because he wants to reinforce its brother with ♘gf3. But this gives Black the option of opening the queenside with ...a4 (which 9 ♘c3 would have made difficult).

10   ♗b2

White can stop the Black a-pawn with 10 a4 but then ...♘a6-b4 eases his game.

10   ...   ♘bd7

11   ♕c2   a4

12   ♘df3

A Black capture on e5 will now be positionally dicey – whereas 12 c5? ♗xe5! 13 dxe5 ♘g4 would win the c5- or e5-pawn.

12   ...   ♘e4

13   e3

A dicey version is 13...g5 14 ♖ac1 g4 15 ♘e1 ♘xe5 16 dxe5 (16...♗xe5?? 17 ♗xe5) which is nice for White.

13   ...   a3!

This is actually part of the battle for control of e5.

After 14 ♗c1 g5! Black threatens 15...g4, since 16 ♘e1 ♘xe5 17 dxe5 ♗xe5 would drop a pawn.

White can avoid that with 15 ♘d3 g4 16 ♘fe5.

But he would be worse after 16...♘xe5 17 ♘xe5? c5! and no more than equal after 17 dxe5 ♗c7.

Of course, White can avoid those problems with 15 ♘xd7 ♗xd7.

But 16 ♗d2 g4 is another version, 17 ♘e5 ♗xe5 18 dxe5 c5 and ...♗c6 is excellent for Black.

14 ♗c3

Black usually needs knights to make the Stonewall pawn structure work well.

Therefore 14...♘xc3 15 ♕xc3 should be dubious and this is verified by 15 ...g5 16 ♘d3.

White has the superior prospects (16...b6 17 ♘fe5 or 16...b5 17 c5).

14 ... ♘xe5

Earlier Carlsen had the option of ...b6/...♗d7 Now he opts for a standard maneuver, ...♗d7-e8-h5.

15 ♘xe5 ♗d7

The consensus view for most of the 20th century was that this kind of position guarantees White a small, lasting plus.

That seems to be the case after 16 ♗e1 ♗e8 17 f3 ♘f6 18 ♖b1 followed by 19 b4! and c4-c5.

But today's Dutch players are much more willing to loosen the bricks in the Stonewall.

After 18 ♖b1 or 18 ♖c1 Black gets good play from 18...c5! and ...♖c8/...b6.

White can avert that with 18 c5 and offer a pawn, 18...♗xe5 19 dxe5 ♘d7 20 f4!.

That can lead to a drawish endgame, 20...♕xc5 21 ♕xc5 ♘xc5 22 ♗b4 b6 23 ♗xc5 bxc5 24 ♖ac1.

16 ♘xd7 ♕xd7

Black's minor pieces are at least as good as White's. The trade ♗xe4?/...fxe4 should favor Black and the other swap, ...♘xc3/♛xc3 may also be good.

17 c5   ♗c7

18 b4

Anand signals that he intends 19 ♖ab1, 20 ♗e1 and the capture of the a3-pawn after ♖b3 or the push b4-b5.

18 ...   h5!

The kingside counts more after 19 ♖ab1 h4. Black could follow with ...g5 and ...♛h7 and make threats long before White achieves anything on the queenside.

19 ♗e1

Anand shoots for 20 f3 ♘f6 21 b5 rather than investigate 19 b5 cxb5 20 ♗b4 ♛c6.

19 ...   e5

The main drawback of 16 ♘xd7, exacerbated by 19 ♗e1, was the loss of control of what should have been White's strongest center square, e5.

20 dxe5

Computers can't panic. But they like the extreme measure 20 f3 ♘f6 21 b5!.

They suggest 21...cxb5 22 ♖b1 ♖a4 23 ♛d3 ♖c4 24 ♗h3 g6 25 ♛xa3 is a favorable main line. But humans would find White's position hard to handle.

20 ...   ♗xe5

21 ♖d1   ♛e6!

Anand threatened 22 f3! ♘f6 23 ♗h3 because of 23...g6 24 e4!.

22 f3   ♘f6

23 ♗h3   g6

24 e4

This makes a good impression based on a general principle: Open the center when you have the two bishops.

24 ...   dxe4

25 fxe4

It is also based on simple tactics (25...♘xe4? 26 ♛xe4! fxe4 27 ♗xe6+).

If Carlsen had less confidence, he would meet the threat of

26 exf5 with 25...♘g4, after calculating 26 exf5 ♖xf5! 27 ♖xf5 gxf5.

Then Black's kingside pawns look weak but his minor pieces are strong (...♘e3, ...♗d4+).

Chances would be roughly balanced after 28 ♗f2 and ♖e1 because 28...♗b2 29 ♖e1 ♕xa2?? would lose to 30 ♗f1! and ♗c4+.

25 ...   ♗b2!

Carlsen declares his intent to win with ...♕xa2 followed by promoting the a-pawn.

26 exf5

Since 26 ♕b1? ♘xe4! is very bad for White, the position will become tactically sharp. The complications are too great to be sure of the outcome. Risk-taking is inevitable if Black is playing to win.

26 ...   ♕xa2

"What would you do if you weren't a chessplayer," Carlsen was asked on Chess24.com in 2016.

"I'm so glad I don't have to find out anytime soon!" he replied. "Hypothetically maybe I'd be a gambler of some sort."

27 ♗f2

The other way of meeting the threat of 27...♗d4+ was 27 ♖f2!.

It has the benefit of preparing ♗f1-c4!.

But it disconnects White's rooks and that encourages 27...♖ad8, with a threat of 28...♖xd1 29 ♕xd1 ♕d5 and ...a2.

A likely continuation would be 28 ♖xd8 ♖xd8 29 ♗c3 ♕c4 and the endgame of 30 ♗xb2 ♕xc2 31 ♖xc2 axb2 32 ♖xb2.

That looks much better for White but turns out to be balanced after 32...g5!.

27 ...   g5!

28 ♖fe1   ♕f7

Now Magnus threatens to win after 29...♘g4! and ...♕xf5.

Anand may have counted on ♗f1-c4 but now saw that 29 ♗f1

♘d5 30 ♗c4 ♕xf5 is closing in on a win.

29 ♖e6!

You also have a king, Anand says with this move.

Carlsen may be perfectly safe after 29...♘d5 30 ♖g6+ ♔h7.

But 31 ♕e2 g4 32 ♕d2 ♗g7 33 ♗f1 would be getting risky after ♗d4, ♗c4 or ♗d3.

29 ... ♘g4!

Now 30 ♖g6+? ♔h7 31 ♖xg5? ♗f6! is over (32 ♖g6 a2).

30 ♗xg4 hxg4

31 ♖g6+ ♔h7

Anand undoubtedly looked at 32 ♖dd6 and saw that there is no real threat. Black wins after 32...a2! 33 ♖h6+ ♔g8 34 ♖dg6+ ♗g7.

That suggested he needed something more forceful and he chose:

32 ♖d7 ♕xd7

33 f6!

He threatens to mate with 34 ♖g7+. It is also mate after 33...♔h8 34 ♖h6+ ♔g8 35 ♕g6+.

33 ... ♕d1+!

34 ♕xd1 ♔xg6

But now he is out of bullets and ...a2 will queen.

35 ♕d3+ ♔h6

36 h4 gxh3

White resigns

Carlsen was right when he bet on being the better tactician after 25...♗b2!.

After the game Anand discovered that he might have drawn with 32 ♖e6! (rather than 32 ♖d7??)

... and threaten 33 ♖e7 ♕xe7 34 f6+.

On 32...♗f6 he would have 33 ♖xf6! ♕xf6 34 ♖d7+.

Then 34...♔h6? 35 ♖d6 and 34...♔g8? 35 ♗d4 are bad.

And 34...♖f7 35 ♗d4 forces 35...♕xd4+! 36 ♖xd4 a2 37 ♖d1

a1(♕) 38 ♖xa1 ♖xa1+ 39 ♔g2 with a likely draw.

This means that following 32 ♖e6! Black could:

(a) accept a draw by repetition, 32...♔g8 33 ♖g6+ ♔h7 34 ♖e6,

or

(b) allow perpetual check after 32...♕xf5 33 ♖d7+ ♔h8 34 ♖h6+ ♔g8 35 ♖g6+, or

(c) take his chances with 32...♖fe8!.

Carlsen would most likely have chosen (c) – because he was confident he was the better tactician.

44
Clock-think

We know anecdotally that great players of the past were in severe time trouble when they played some of their most famous games. We know the winner was sometimes determined by clock-think, a better sense of the remaining time for each of the players.

But we don't know details. Did Alexander Alekhine have minutes or just seconds left in the final stage of his brilliancies? Even in some of the great time scrambles of Mikhail Tal and Garry Kasparov we have only the word of spectators.

Today there is an accurate historical record on-line and we can appreciate spectacular clock scrimmages more. The following should become legendary.

Fabiano Caruana – Carlsen
Sinquefield Cup, St. Louis 2015
Ruy Lopez,
Archangel Variation (C78)

1	e4	e5
2	♘f3	♘c6
3	♗b5	a6
4	♗a4	♘f6
5	0-0	b5
6	♗b3	♗b7

The early ...b5 was considered premature until the 1960s, when exciting lines were analyzed after 7 ♖e1 ♗c5 8 c3 d6 8 d4 ♗b6 9 ♗g5 h6 10 ♗h4 g5 and ...0-0-0.

The analysis, some of it extensive, wasn't refuted. Instead, White players decided they had better chances of advantage with d2-d3 than with d2-d4.

Then Black's b7-bishop may turn out to be misplaced and he has given up on neutralizing the a2-f7 diagonal with ...d6/...♗e6.

7	d3	♗e7
8	♘c3	0-0
9	a3	

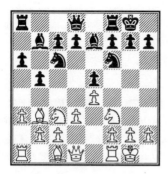

This quiet move, allowing the bishop to retreat to a2 when necessary, competed with 9 ♗d2 (and 9...d6 10 ♘d5) for status as the main line.

9 ... d6

In later games Carlsen preferred 9...♘d4 because 10 ♘xe5 ♘xb3 11 cxb3 d5! is a promising gambit.

But what about 10 ♘xd4 exd4 11 ♘d5 ♘xd5 12 exd5 ? Shouldn't Black be significantly worse in a nearly symmetrical position?

No, because after 12...c5! he has an advantage in space.

Carlsen quickly won a 2016 Paris rapids game from **Maxime Vachier-Lagrave**: 13 dxc6 dxc6 14 ♖e1 c5 15 a4 ♗d6 16 ♕h5 ♕c7 17 c3? c4! 18 ♗c2 g6 19 ♕h3 dxc3 20 axb5 ♖fe8 21 ♖e3? cxb2 22 ♗xb2 c3 23 ♗c1 axb5 24 ♖xa8 ♖xa8 25 ♗b3 ♗f4 26 ♖e1 ♖a1 **White resigns.**

10 ♖e1 ♕d7

11 ♘e2

Both players quietly reposition their queenside knights. It is hard to imagine this will turn into a nail-biting time scramble.

11 ... ♘d8

12 ♘g3 ♘e6

13 ♗a2

They are still hiding their cards, compared with the committal 13 c3 c5 14 d4.

13 ... ♖fe8

14 ♘g5

This, too, is fairly innocuous. After 14...♘xg5 15 ♗xg5 Black can offer a roughly equal endgame with 15...♕g4 (16 ♕xg4 ♘xg4).

White should not refuse, 16 ♕d2? ♘xe4! 17 ♘xe4 ♗xe4.

14 ... d5!?

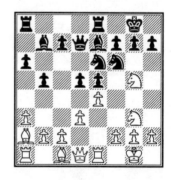

This is where the game really begins. Carlsen's move looks risky because 15 exd5 ♘xd5 would favor White slightly after 16 ♘xe6 ♕xe6 17 ♕f3.

But 15...♗xd5! is sound. The pawn cannot be taken, 16 ♖xe5?, since 16...♗xa2 17 ♖xa2 ♗d6

270

18 ♖e1 ♗xg3 19 hxg3 ♘xg5
20 ♗xg5 ♕d5! forks two pieces.

15 ♘xe6 ♕xe6

One of the benefits of 14...d5 was to shut out the a2-bishop.

That would be undermined by 16 ♕f3 dxe4? 17 dxe4.

Black is worse after 17...♕g4 18 ♕b3! ♕g6 19 f3 or 17...♕c6 18 ♘f5.

But a good answer to 16 ♕f3 is 16...c5 and ...c4.

16 ♗g5 h6

17 ♗xf6 ♗xf6

18 ♕f3

Caruana tries to force 18...dxe4 19 dxe4 and 19...♕b6 20 ♘h5.

18 ... c6

19 c4! ♖ad8

His superiority would be evident after 19...bxc4? 20 dxc4 d4, despite the passed d-pawn.

For example, 21 c5 ♕d7 22 ♘f5 and ♘d6, or 21...♕e7 22 ♘f5 ♕xc5? 23 ♕b3 and wins.

20 cxd5 cxd5

Now 21 exd5? ♗xd5 would leave White with a weak d3-pawn.

21 ♘f5

He would like to play 21 ♖ac1 but then the bishop is unprotected (21...dxe4 22 dxe4? ♕xa2).

Caruana would have the first real advantage of the game if he can play 22 ♕g3 and 23 ♘e3!.

21 ... ♗g5!

But now 22 ♘e3? ♗xe3 is excellent for Black (23 ♕xe3 ♕g6 and ...♖d7).

22 h4

Now 22...♗f4 is attractive because it would threaten to get the better endgame with 23...dxe4 24 dxe4 ♕xf5!.

The critical test is 23 g3. Then 23...♗d2 and 24 ♖e2 dxe4 25 dxe4 ♕f6 would put Carlsen a tempo behind what happens in the game.

Caruana could use that extra tempo with 26 ♖d1 ♗a5 27 ♗d5.

22 ... ♗d2

But Carlsen could have played 22...♗f4 if he had confidence in 23 g3 dxe4!? and then 24 ♕g4 ♕f6 25 gxf4 exd3.

He would then have good compensation for a piece and a threat of 26...♗c8.

But the outcome of, for example, 26 ♖ec1! ♗c8 27 ♖xc8 or 26...d2 27 ♗xf7+! ♔h8! was beyond accurate evaluation in what was becoming a time trouble battle.

23	♖e2	dxe4
24	dxe4	♕f6
25	g3!	

Carlsen wanted to play ...g6 now without allowing ♘xh6 with check.

If he prepares that with 25...♔h7, White has 26 ♗d5 and then 26...♗xd5 27 exd5.

Then 27...e4? 29 ♖xe4 ♖xe4 30 ♕xe4 sets up a discovered check by the knight.

| 25 | ... | ♔f8? |

But he called this over-finesse a "stupid" move.

26 h5!

There wasn't much in 26 ♗d5 ♗xd5 27 exd5 because of 27...e4! 28 ♖xe4 ♖e5.

The principal point of 26 h5 is to discourage ...g6 – although 26...g6 27 hxg6 fxg6 was playable.

But to play it Carlsen would have to calculate 28 ♕b3! gxf5 29 ♕g8+ ♔e7 and be convinced that the worst result is perpetual check, 30 ♕h7+ ♔f8 31 ♕g8+ ♔e7.

White could not play 31 ♕xb7?? because of the queen trapping 31...♖e7!.

26	...	♗g5
27	a4	b4

Carlsen is playing the safest moves. Here he ruled out a queen check at a3.

But 27...bxa4 28 ♕a3+ ♔g8 29 ♕xa4 ♗c8! or 28 ♗d5 ♗xd5 29 exd5 g6 30 hxg6 fxg6 31 ♕a3+ ♔g8 were nothing to fear.

| 28 | a5! | ♔g8 |

An embarrassing move to make but Caruana threatened to take on b4 with check after 29 ♕b3.

29	♗c4	♖d7?
30	♖a4!	

Carlsen realized too late that what he needed was another king move, 29...♔h8!.

Then 30 ♖a4? would lose material to the 30...g6! trick that he has been trying for.

| 30 | ... | ♔h8! |

The players were dealing with a somewhat unusual format: The time control was 40 moves in 120 minutes, twenty minutes more than usual. But there was no 30-second increment until move 40.

That meant if they spent more than 30 seconds on a move they would not immediately get it back.

Nevertheless, Carlsen spent a good part of his remaining time here because he knew it would take a swindle to save him.

31 ♖xb4 g6

32 hxg6 fxg6

One of the traps he set was 33 ♖b6? ♛xf5! and Black wins.

33 ♛b3!

Caruana was also short of time and it cost him 40 badly needed seconds to find this move.

No true swindler would consider 33...gxf5 34 ♖xb7 ♖xb7 35 ♛xb7.

Carlsen would have drawing chances in the bishops-of-

opposite-color endgame, 35...f4 36 ♛xa6 ♛xa6 37 ♗xa6 ♖a8 but it would be a hard slog.

33 ... ♗c6!?

He also rejected 33...♗xe4 reluctantly.

It would have reduced his deficit after 34 ♖xe4 gxf5.

But he feared the desperado 34 ♘xh6!.

Then 34...♗xh6 35 ♖xe4 would have provided Caruana with good winning chances, 35...♖f8 36 ♖e2 ♖d2 37 ♖b6! ♛f5 38 ♖b8!.

The exciting alternative is 34...♖d1+! 35 ♛xd1 ♛f3.

That seems to win for Black – until you see 36 ♘f7+ ♚g7 37 ♖xe4 ♛xd1+ 38 ♚g2. Then White has material compensation for the queen and, what's equally important, more tactics than Black.

34 ♘e3 ♗xe4

Now Caruana rejected 35 ♗b5 ♖b8!, apparently because pressing his advantage would become harder.

35 ♗d5!

He intended to answer 35...♛f3 with 36 ♖xe4! ♛xe2 37 ♘c4 with ♘xe5 to come. But he had only 20 seconds left to play five moves.

35 ... ♗xd5

The chief alternative was 35...♗f3 and then 36 ♘g4 ♗xg4 37 ♖xg4 ♖ed8.

White's winning chances remain strong after 38 ♗g2.

36 ♘xd5 ♕c6

The best reason to prefer 35...♗xd5 is that Caruana's time trouble made it difficult to find best moves. His winning chances would disappear after 37 ♘e3? ♕f3.

37 ♘c3!

Best but costly. Caruana only had eight seconds now.

The practical move was 37 ♖b8!. The reason is that 37...♖xb8 38 ♕xb8+ ♔h7 39 ♘c3 would get him to within one move of the time control.

Since Carlsen would have has no forcing 39th move, Caruana could quickly play some safe move, such as 39...♗f6 40 ♖e4, and relax with a new hour to spend.

37 ... ♕f3

Carlsen had 12 seconds after this move. It threatens...nothing.

38 ♕c2

There were safe moves, such as 38 ♖be4 and 38 ♕c4, that over-protect pieces. Also good is the forcing 38 ♖b8.

Caruana spent only three seconds on 38 ♕c2 and didn't appreciate how good it was.

38 ... ♖ed8

This looked scary because 39...♖d2 seemed to be a threat.

It wasn't: White could have replied to it with 40 ♕e4! and have good winning chances.

39 ♖be4?

Because there was no increment, Caruana played this immediately. There was no time to calculate 39 ♕e4!.

It looks like a blunder that loses to 39...♖d1+ 40 ♘xd1 ♖xd1+ and ...♖h1 mate.

But that is a mirage. White has 41 ♖e1! ♕xe4 42 ♖bxe4.

39 ...   ℤd2!

Even with more time to see 39...♗f4 Carlsen might have rejected it because 40 gxf4 leads only to perpetual check (40...♕g4+ 41 ♔f1 ♕h3+). He is playing to win.

Each player had four seconds to play their final move of the time control.

Any of three moves of the White queen, to b1, b3 or a4, would have been safe.

The cautious 40 ♕b1 makes doubly sure ...ℤd1+ doesn't work. It also threatens 41 ℤxe5.

But White would have no advantage after 40...ℤ8d4! because 41 ℤxe5 ℤh4! leads to perpetual check.

The most interesting try is 40 ♕b3 and then 40...ℤd1+ 41 ℤe1.

Now 41...ℤ8d2? would lose to 42 ♕b8+ (42...♔h7 43 ♘xd1!).

Instead, Black could offer to repeat the position with 41...ℤ1d2.

That sets a devilish trap, 42 ℤ4e2 ♗e3! and he would win.

But with a fresh hour on his clock, Caruana would surely have spotted it.

He would also have seen that 42 ℤ1e2 is an offer of a draw (41...ℤd1+).

A better try is 42 ♕b6!. But with his own fresh hour, Carlsen would have found 42...ℤ8d3!.

What might have been

Black threatens 43...♗e3! so that 44 ℤ4xe3 ♕xf2+ mates.

The other point is 43 ℤxe5 allows a remarkable draw by repetition, 43...♕xg3+! 44 fxg3 ℤxg3+.

However, the game ended in an anti-climax because Caruana moved instantly.

40   ℤxd2?? ℤxd2

White resigns

45
Closer to the Start

As Magnus turned 25 he became more self-critical. His games at the 2016 version of the Norway Chess super-tournament were "complacency riddled," he said. He felt he did not make bold decisions.

Garry Kasparov, in a Russian edition of one of his Great Predecessors books, said some world champions "stalactified" after they won the title. Their style had become rigid, like a calcium deposit in a cave. Their greatest achievements were past.

Carlsen said in 2016, "I feel that I have been in the game a long time." But he added "I think if you do the right things you can be good for a very long time. I feel that I am closer to the start than to the end of my prime."

Carlsen – Wesley So
Bilbao 2016
Ruy Lopez, Berlin Defense (C67)

1	e4	e5
2	♘f3	♘c6
3	♗b5	♘f6
4	d3	♗c5
5	♗xc6	

Until recently, this capture was a 19th century antique.

White can safely keep an extra pawn after 5...bxc6? 6 ♘xe5. But why should he stand better after 5...dxc6 than if he had played a delayed ♗xc6 ?

Nevertheless, Vishy Anand, hardly an unambitious player, has held the White side of 5...dxc6 at least 30 times since 2009 and achieved a plus-five score.

5	...	dxc6
6	♕e2	

Not 6 ♘xe5? ♕d4 and 7 ♗e3 ♕xe5 8 d4 ♕xe4 9 dxc5 ♕xg2.

6	...	♕e7
7	♘bd2	

This is how a new anti-Berlin strategy evolves. White can attack

276

the e5-pawn with ♘c4 and force either ...♗g4 or ...♘d7/...f6.

Then the position resembles the Doubly Delayed Exchange Variation of the Ruy Lopez, 1 e4 e5 2 ♘f3 ♘c6 3 ♗b5 a6 4 ♗a4 ♘f6 5 0-0 ♗e7 6 ♗xc6 dxc6 7 d3. That is not a fearsome opening but it poses a different set of early middlegame problems for Black.

7	...	♗g4
8	h3	♗h5
9	a3	

At the turn of the century, conservative treatments of 1 e4 e5 openings came into fashion. These were *small chess* versions of the Giuoco Piano and the Ruy Lopez, with an unprovoked h2-h3 or a2-a3 – or both – in the first ten moves.

Garry Kasparov said that if this was the way his young opponents were thinking, he might delay his retirement for some time.

Magnus spent 20 minutes on 9 a3 and admitted afterwards that playing h2-h3 and a2-a3 on successive moves amused him.

9	...	♘d7

But there was a valid reason for 9 a3. If Black stops 10 b4 with 9...a5, queenside castling would be riskier.

Then 10 ♘f1 ♘d7 11 ♘g3 ♗g6 12 0-0 is a bit more pleasant for White than Black.

10 b4!

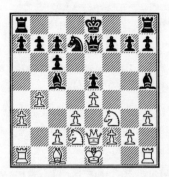

Wesley So thought 20 minutes on this move. It is a major decision because the bishop is well placed after 10...♗d4.

But after 11 ♖b1 White threatens 12 g4 ♗g6 13 ♘xd4 with advantage.

Trading a bishop for a knight with 11...♗c3 12 0-0 ♗xd2 13 ♗xd2 or 11...♗xf3 12 ♘xf3 ♗c3+ 13 ♗d2 ♗xd2+ 14 ♕xd2 would give White the kind of superior pawn structure he wants in all Lopez exchange variations without any offsetting Black compensation.

10	...	♗d6

Carlsen said afterwards he could not dispute computers who said 10...♗b6 is best. Levon Aronian played it two years later against him in a speed game and achieved equality after 11 ♘c4 a5! 12 ♖b1 axb4 13 axb4 ♖a2.

11	♘c4	f6

The ...f6 move is played in so many similar positions that it is easy to overlook Black's more forceful options. One is 11...♘f8 so that ...♘e6 is available.

Carlsen felt that after 11...♘f8 12 ♘a5 there was no comfortable way to avert 13 ♘xb7.

He was assuming that 12...0-0-0 is too dangerous but that is hardly certain.

More forcing is 11...♕f6 with a possible endgame, 12...♗xf3 13 ♕xf3 ♕xf3.

If White averts that with 12 g4 ♗g6 13 ♗g5 ♕e6 he has to deal with ...h5 (or 14 ♘h4 ♗e7!).

12 ♘e3   a5!

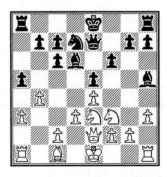

Carlsen's approach to chess was revealed when he gave 12...a5 a question mark in his annotation of the game. He wasn't evaluating its objective value. It is the most principled move. But it is "certainly not the most practical option," he wrote in *New in Chess*.

13 ♘f5

He could claim a minor success: He got to play ♘e3-f5 without allowing ...♗xe3. But Black has greater counterplay from ...a5 than if his bishop were on b6.

13 ...   ♕f8

Again, the most principled move.

After 13...♕f7 White is not forced into 14 bxa5. He can play 14 ♖b1 axb4 15 axb4 because the b4-pawn is adequately protected.

But 15...0-0 16 0-0 ♖fc8 would have been fairly balanced.

A recurring tactical trick in similar positions is 16 ♗h6 (16...gxh6?? 17 ♘xh6+). But here 16 ♗h6? allows 16...♕a2!, winning material.

14 bxa5   ♖xa5

15 0-0   ♕f7

Wesley So spent a tempo (...♕f8-f7) to force a favorable change in the queenside pawn structure. But he can't castle because of that ♗h6 trick.

16 a4

Carlsen might have offered a pawn, 16 ♗d2 ♖a4 17 ♖fb1 b5

18 ♗e3 ♗xa3 but there was no particular reason to.

Now the positionally desirable 16...♗b4 and ...c5 would encourage 17 ♖b1! ♖xa4 18 c3!.

Then 18...♗xc3? 19 ♕c2 or 18...♗c5 19 ♖xb7 favors White.

16 ... ♘c5

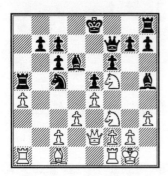

By targeting the a4-pawn So must have calculated the forcing 17 g4 ♗g6 18 d4.

Then 18...♘e6 allows White to steal the queenside initiative, with 19 ♗d2 ♖a8 20 dxe5 fxe5 21 ♖fb1.

More consistent – and principled – is 18...exd4 19 ♘3xd4 ♖xa4 20 ♖xa4 ♘xa4.

But 21 ♘e6 is a bit unpleasant (21...♕xe6? 22 ♘xg7+).

Instead, the pragmatic path is 19...0-0 20 ♗h6 ♘e6! with equal chances (21 ♘xe6 ♕xe6 22 ♗xg7 ♖e8).

17 ♕e1

This is good but so is 17 ♗d2.

For example, 17 ♗d2 ♖xa4 18 g4 ♗g6 19 d4 with play similar to the last note.

White wins after 19...exd4 20 ♖xa4 ♘xa4 21 e5! fxe5? 22 ♘xe5 ♗xe5 23 ♕xe5+ ♔f8 24 ♗b4+.

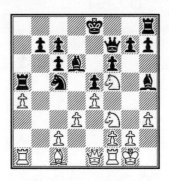

17 ... b6

Black loses material after 17...♖xa4? 18 ♖xa4 ♘xa4 19 ♕a5!.

Another reason for 17 ♕e1 is that it freed the pinned f3-knight.

For instance, 17...♖a7 18 ♘3h4 followed by f2-f4 or ♘xd6+/♘f5.

18 ♘d2!

On c4 this knight will attack the rook but also the d6-bishop.

Black would be lost after 18...0-0 19 ♘c4 ♖xa4 20 ♖xa4 ♘xa4 because of that 21 ♗h6! trick.

Retreats turn out badly, e.g. 18...♖a8 19 ♘c4 ♗e7 20 f4.

18   ...   ♖xa4!

19   ♘c4

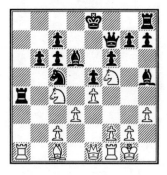

At first it appears that 19...♗e7 loses to the simple 20 ♗e3.

One forcing line runs 20...0-0? 21 ♗xc5 ♖xa1 22 ♘xe7+!.

Another goes 20...♖xa1? 21 ♕xa1 0-0 22 ♗h6! ♘e6 23 ♗xg7.

Or if 21...♘e6 then 22 ♕a8+ (22...♗d8? 23 ♘cd6+ and 22...♘d8 23 ♗xb6!).

However, 20...♔d7! is remarkably safe.

The only forcing line, 21 ♘xb6+ cxb6 22 ♗xc5 ♖xa1 23 ♕xa1 ♗xc5 is worth no more than perpetual check, 24 ♕a7+ ♔e6! 25 ♕a2+ ♔d7 or 25 ♘xg7+ ♔d6 26 ♘f5+.

Carlsen said that if So had found 19...♗e7! he would probably have gone for 20 ♖xa4 ♘xa4 21 f4. Then he would have ample compensation for a pawn and a small plus.

19   ...   ♗f8?

20   ♗e3!

The threat is 21 ♗xc5 ♖xa1 22 ♕xa1 ♗xc5 23 ♕a8+ and ♕xh8.

20   ...   ♔d7

The best defense that computers can find is 20...♖g8!? so that the rook is protected.

White could then choose between 21 f4 and 21 ♕c3, which threatens 22 ♘xb6 as in the game. His edge would be substantial in either case.

21   ♕c3!

If this had occurred with the bishop on e7 (19...♗e7! 20 ♗e3 ♔d7! 21 ♕c3) Black would have fairly equal winning chances following 21...♖ha8!.

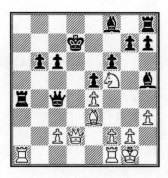

But as it stands, Carlsen threatens 22 ♘xb6+ cxb6 23 ♗xc5 ♖xa1 24 ♖xa1 ♗xc5 25 ♖a7+.

So's position would pancake after 21...♖xa1 22 ♖xa1 b5 23 ♘a5.

He could sacrifice the Exchange with 21...♖xc4 22 dxc4.

But he lacks compensation after 22...♘xe4? 23 ♕d3+ ♘d6 24 g4 ♗g6 25 ♖fd1 and 26 c5 or 26 ♖a7.

He gambled on:

21	...	♘xe4
22	♘xb6+!	cxb6
23	dxe4	♕c4
24	♕d2+	

Now 24...♔e8 25 g4 ♗g6 26 ♖fd1 is better than in the game.

For example, 26...♗xf5 27 exf5 ♔f7 28 ♖xa4 ♕xa4 29 ♕d7+ ♗e7 30 ♕e6+ ♔f8.

Then the artistic finish of 31 ♗c5! bxc5 32 ♖d7.

24	...	♔c7

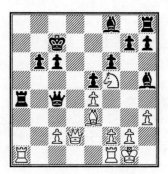

25	g4!	♗g6
26	♖fd1	**Resigns**

46
Most Watched

Sergey Karjakin was born 11 months before Carlsen. When fans first began to take notice of the two shooting stars, they saw that Karjakin was well ahead: He outrated Carlsen by nearly 250 points as 2003 began. But Carlsen overtook him in 2006 and held the lead since.

As Carlsen's fame grew, Karjakin faded slightly into the background. He was never rated higher than number four in the world. When Magnus was asked in 2014 to predict his next world championship challenger, he named three players, Fabiano Caruana, Levon Aronian and Alexander Grischuk. But Karjakin won the 2016 Candidates by defeating Caruana in the final round.

The following may be the most-watched chess game of all time. Web sites that gave move-by-move coverage reported record numbers of on-line spectators. Fans continued to argue about it long after Karjakin resigned. Chessgames.com received 53 pages of reader posts within the first two days after it was played.

The reason for the intense interest was simple. Magnus trailed by one point and needed a win in one of his three final games of this 12-round match to save his title.

Carlsen – Sergey Karjakin
World Championship match,
10th game, New York 2016
Ruy Lopez, Berlin Defense (C65)

1	e4	e5
2	♘f3	♘c6
3	♗b5	♘f6
4	d3	♗c5
5	c3	0-0
6	♗g5	

This is a favorite move of Alexey Shirov, who used it against Carlsen at Biel 2011.

6	...	h6
7	♗h4	♗e7!

A trade of dark-squared bishops after a move of the f6-knight helps Black. Shirov lost to Carlsen after 8 ♘bd2 d6 9 ♘f1 ♘b8!? 10 ♘e3 ♘g4!.

8	0-0

White cannot win a pawn with 8 ♗xc6 bxc6 9 ♘xe5 because

of 9...♞xe4! (10 dxe4 ♗xh4 or 10 ♗xe7 ♛xe7).

8	...	d6
9	♞bd2	♞h5
10	♗xe7	♛xe7

Carlsen had to ask himself whether to take risks in this game or take his chances in the two remaining scheduled games of the match. He also had to decide whether he wanted a game dependent on calculation or one in which he could rely mainly on his intuition. And specifically, whether he should seek center tension, such as 11 d4 ♞f4 12 ♖e1 ♛f6.

11	♞c4	♞f4
12	♞e3	♛f6
13	g3	

The answers are: No early risks today, not a lot of calculation and no quick change in the pawn structure.

13	...	♞h3+
14	♔h1	♞e7!

On g6 the knight will ensure that f2-f4 is off the menu.

15	♗c4	c6
16	♗b3	♞g6
17	♛e2	a5
18	a4	♗e6
19	♗xe6	

Now 19...♛xe6 20 ♖ae1 is nice for White.

Black can get into trouble after 20...♛b3? 21 ♞c4! ♛xa4 22 ♞xd6 or 21...♖fd8? 22 ♖a1! and 23 ♖a3.

19	...	fxe6!

The rules out ♞f5. But the much greater benefit is pressure on the f-file – which was underestimated by both players.

20	♞d2	

Defending the attacked knight by 21 ♔g2?? loses to 21...♞hf4+!.

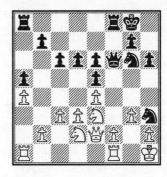

20	...	d5

This is a perfectly good move and yet one of the most costly errors of the match.

Why? Because 20...♘xf2+! would have forced a repetition of moves, 21 ♔g2 ♘h4+! 22 ♔g1 ♘h3+ 23 ♔h1 ♘f2+.

Both players overlooked that 22 gxh4 would lose to 22...♕g6+.

Drawing this game would have made Karjakin a heavy favorite to win the match and become the 16th undisputed world champion.

21 ♕h5   ♘g5

Relying on intuitive moves should have cost Carlsen again:

Karjakin could still force a draw with 21...♘xf2+ 22 ♔g2 ♕f7 (threat of ...♘f4+) 23 ♕e2 ♘h4+! as in the last note.

Worse for White is 22 ♔g1? ♕g5! 23 ♕xg5 ♘h3+.

22	**h4**	**♘f3**
23	**♘xf3**	**♕xf3+**
24	**♕xf3**	**♖xf3**
25	**♔g2**	**♖f7**
26	**♖fe1**	

Carlsen could have tried 26 h5 and then 26...♘f8 27 ♘g4 ♘d7 28 ♖fe1 ♖e7 29 ♖e2 d4 or 28 b4/29 ♖fb1.

But he still seemed to be avoiding moves based on calculation.

26	**...**	**h5**
27	**♘f1!**	**♔f8**

28	**♘d2**	**♔e7**
29	**♖e2**	**♔d6**
30	**♘f3**	

After the trade of queens he has another grindable position, one that he could improve imperceptibly with "little" moves. He can already claim a positional success by inducing 26...h5. That handed him an outpost square, g5, for his knight.

30	**...**	**♖af8**
31	**♘g5**	**♖e7**
32	**♖ae1**	**♖fe8**
33	**♘f3**	**♘h8**

But now he's at a dead end. He cannot achieve anything further by pressuring the e5-pawn.

He has two other plans. One is to target the b7-pawn with 34 b4! and 35 ♖b1. He preferred:

34	**d4**	**exd4**
35	**♘xd4!**	

The main point of his last two moves is that from now on Black's king is a potential target.

He threatens 36 exd5 (36...exd5?? 37 ♘f5+ or 36...♔xd5?? 37 ♘f5).

Or 36...cxd5 37 c4! dxc4 38 ♖d2.

35	...	g6
36	♖e3	♘f7
37	e5+	♔d7

This is another pivotal moment. Carlsen has been delaying b2-b4 in order to get the maximum out of his pieces first. This was a good time for 38 b4!.

38 ♖f3!

But this move is a good example of the kind of mind game that goes on in world championship matches.

Carlsen is allowing Karjakin two chances for counterplay. But they require irrevocable steps that could lose the game.

One is 38...g5 and then 39 hxg5 ♘xg5 40 ♖f6. This looks bad because ♖h1xh5 is coming.

But Black has 40...h4! and 41 gxh4 ♘e4.

His pieces get to play after 42 ♖g6? ♖f8 43 f3 ♘c5 or 42 ♖f4! ♖g7+ 43 ♔f3 ♖h8.

However, White is still better and, considering the match situation, Karjakin's rejection of 38...g5 makes sense.

38 ... ♘h6

The other irrevocable step was 38...c5.

Karjakin turned it down in view of 39 ♘b5 ♖g8 40 ♖f6 and then 40...♘h6 41 ♘d6 and 42 f3.

39 ♖f6 ♖g7

Magnus's last two moves pushed Karjakin further into passivity. Now 40 c4! dxc4? 41 ♖d1 would have been deadly.

And allowing 41 cxd5 cxd5 42 ♖e3 and ♖b3 would have made it nearly impossible to defend the queenside.

40 b4!

This is also good. With one rook and the king defending the e6-pawn Black can't afford 40...♖a8? 41 ♘xe6 or 40...b6 41 bxa5 bxa5 42 ♖b1.

40	...	axb4
41	cxb4	♘g8
42	♖f3	♘h6
43	a5!	

Carlsen readies ♘b3-c5+.

Black's window of kingside opportunity has closed, e.g. 43...g5? 44 ♖f6 ♘g8? 45 hxg5! ♘xf6 46 exf6 ♖f7 47 f4 or 47 ♘f3 is paralyzing.

43 ... ♘f5

44 ♘b3 ♔c7

45 ♘c5

Karjakin would like 45...b6 46 axb6+ ♔xb6 because his king becomes a fighting piece (...♔b5) and he can try to seize the open file with 47...♖a7.

But 46 ♘a4! bxa5 47 bxa5 would have made queenside matters much worse.

For example, 47...♖a8 48 ♘c5 ♖xa5? 49 ♘xe6+.

What is particularly impressive in this game is the way Carlsen exploits weaknesses on both wings.

In that last line, Black should play 48...♖e7 (instead of 48...♖a5?) but then comes 49 ♖a3 and a threat of ♖b1-b7+.

After 49...♘d4 50 ♖b1 ♘b5 he would switch back to the kingside, 51 ♖f3! ♖xa5 52 ♖f6 and win with captures on e6 and g6.

45 ... ♔b8

46 ♖b1

Carlsen has three targets. Capturing one of them would be sufficient for victory.

The e6- and g6-pawns can be simultaneously attacked by a knight after ♘d3-f4 The third target is the king, after b4-b5.

One of many winning scenarios is 46...♖ee7 47 ♖d3 (stopping ...♘d4) ♖gf7 48 b5! cxb5 49 ♖xb5 ♔a7 50 ♖b6! ♘g7 51 ♖3b3 and 52 a6.

46 ... ♔a7

47 ♖d3 ♖c7

48 ♖a3 ♘d4

49 ♖d1

Carlsen is taking his time. If Karjakin stops his queenside plan with 49...♘b5, he goes back to the kingside, 50 ♖f3 ♖g7 51 ♖f6 ♘c7.

With Black tied up there he can prepare a decisive g3-g4 with 52 f4 and ♔f3-e3/♖g1.

49	...	♘f5
50	♔h3	♘h6
51	f3	♖f7
52	♖d4	♘f5
53	♖d2	♖h7

Karjakin had another thing to worry about, g3-g4, which would have driven his knight into passivity.

54	♖b3	♖ee7
55	♖dd3	♖h8
56	♖b1	

Despite White's many knockout plans, Karjakin – the "Russian Minister of Defense" – has stopped them so far.

After a "pass" like 56...♔a8 White appears to be winning with 57 b5 cxb5 58 ♖xb5 ♖c8 and then 59 g4! ♘h6 60 ♖db3.

But both 60...♘f7 and 60...♖c6 (61 ♘xb7 hxg4+ 62 fxg4 ♖ec7 and ...♖c3+) may defend.

56	...	♖hh7?
57	b5!	cxb5
58	♖xb5	

Now 58...♖h8 59 ♖b6 ♘g7 60 ♖db3 and 61 ♖xb7+ or 61 a6 would win.

58	...	d4
59	♖b6	♖c7
60	♘xe6	♖c3

61 ♘f4!

No swindle today: 61 ♖xc3? dxc3 and Black holds (62 ♖b3 ♖e7 63 ♘c5 c2 or 62 ♖c1 ♖e7 63 ♘c5 ♖c7).

After 61 ♘f4! White is prepared to start pushing Black back with ♖bb3 and win slowly. Karjakin goes for broke.

61	...	♖hc7

Computers say 62 ♖xg6 is best now.

But that requires the kind of faith in your calculation you may not be comfortable with when the world championship title is at stake.

On 62...♖xd3 63 ♘xd3 ♖c3 Carlsen could have thrown away hours of work with 64 ♘e1? ♖e3! 65 ♘g2 ♖xf3.

He could even lose, 64 ♘f4 ♖xf3 65 ♔g2?? ♖xf4! 66 gxf4 ♘xh4+.

Instead, 64 ♖f6! would have won, e.g. 64...♘e3 65 ♘f4 d3 66 ♖d6!. But once again Magnus made the practical choice.

62	♘d5	♖xd3
63	♘xc7	♔b8
64	♘b5	

He had seen this far and knew it is a definite win (64...♖b3 65 a6!).

64	...	♔c8
65	♖xg6	♖xf3
66	♔g2	♖b3
67	♘d6+!	♘xd6
68	♖xd6	

Now 68...d3 69 e6! is over.

But 68...♔c7 69 ♖xd4 ♖b5! would have forced Carlsen to work further.

A position that you might find in an endgame textbook could arise after 70 e6 ♖xa5 71 e7 ♖e5 72 ♖d5! ♖xe7 73 ♖xh5.

If Black can play ...b5 and ...♖b7 he may survive.

For example, 73...♔c6 74 ♔f3? b5! makes a draw likely.

But White will win if his rook is the one behind the passed pawn.

That means 74 ♖h6+ ♔c5 75 ♖h8! b5 76 ♖b8 wins.

Also lost for Black is 74...♔c7 75 h5 b5 76 ♖f6 b4? 77 ♖f4 b3 78 ♖b4.

68	...	♖e3
69	e6	♔c7
70	♖xd4	♖xe6
71	♖d5!	

The difference between the passive Black rook and active White one makes it easy.

71	...	♖h6
72	♔f3	♔b8
73	♔f4	♔a7
74	♔g5	♖h8
75	♔f6	**Resigns**

47

Overtime

Thanks to that victory, the 2016 world championship match turned out to be one of the closest matches for the title. Carlsen was trailing by one point when he won the tenth game and forced Karjakin into overtime.

The third playoff game was hardly the best played game of the match. But after winning it, Carlsen had "draw odds" going into the final game. In effect, this game won Carlsen his third world championship title.

Sergey Karjakin – Carlsen
World Championship match,
third playoff game,
New York 2016
Ruy Lopez (C78)

1	e4	e5
2	♘f3	♘c6
3	♗b5	a6
4	♗a4	♘f6
5	0-0	♗e7
6	d3	

This modest move had been overshadowed by 6 ♖e1, 6 ♕e2, 6 ♗xc6 and 6 d4 for decades. But it became a major variation after the turn of the century.

As usual when White protects his e4-pawn in the Lopez, he is threatening ♗xc6 and ♘xe5.

6	...	b5
7	♗b3	d6
8	a3	0-0

9	♘c3	

Paul Keres used an early ♘c3 in the Lopez with the idea of ♘d5. Here 9...♗e6 10 ♘d5 would give White a slight pull.

Black can also develop his bishop on g4 and prepare ...♘d4. But Maxime Vachier-Lagrave has shown that 9...♗g4 10 ♗e3 ♘d4 11 ♗xd4 exd4 12 ♘d5 is excellent for White.

9	...	♘a5
10	♗a2	♗e6
11	b4	

Usual is 11...♗xa2 12 ♖xa2 ♘c6 13 ♗g5, seeking a minimalist edge with ♗xf6 and ♘d5.

11	...	♘c6

As obvious as it is, this was virtually a novelty. Now on routine moves (i.e. 12 ♗e3) Black equalizes with 12...♗xa2 and 13...d5.

12   ♘d5!

This is the drawback to 11...♘c6 Black cannot play 11...♘xd5? because of the 12 exd5 fork.

12   ...   ♘d4!

White was preparing 13 c3 and a3-a4.

13   ♘g5

Less than a month later, GM Dmity Andreikin achieved nothing with 13 ♘xd4 exd4.

Then 14 ♘xf6+ ♗xf6 15 ♗xe6 fxe6 and 16 a4 ♕d7 17 ♗d2 c5!.

Nor is there much to 14 ♘xe7+ ♕xe7 15 ♗b2 in view of 15...♗xa2 16 ♖xa2 c5.

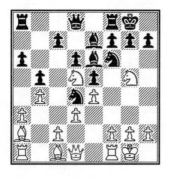

Karjakin aims at an advantage after 14 ♘xe7+ ♕xe7 15 c3!.

For example, 15...♗xa2 16 cxd4! ♗e6 17 ♘xe6 ♕xe6 18 d5 ♕d7 19 ♗g5 and 20 ♖c1 signifies lasting pressure on the c-file.

13   ...   ♗xd5

His superiority on light squares would be also significant after 13...♘xd5 14 ♘xe6 fxe6 15 exd5 or 14...♘xe6 15 ♗xd5 ♖b8 16 a4.

What required calculation in that line was 14...♘c3 15 ♘xd8 ♘xd1.

Then 16 ♘xf7 ♘c3! leads only to perpetual checks at h6 and f7, since 17 ♘xe5+? ♘xa2 is bad for White.

But he may secure a pull with 16 ♘c6! ♘xc6 17 ♖xd1 and then 17...♘d4 18 ♗b2 and 19 c3 (18...♘xc2? 19 ♖ac1).

14   exd5

Carlsen has three sources of counterplay. They are on the queenside (...a5), on the kingside (...f5-f4) and in the center, attacking the d5-pawn.

14   ...   ♘d7

After 14...a5! 15 c3! he has to block the f-pawn with 15...♘f5.

Then 16 ♗d2 ♕c8 17 ♘e4 makes winning the d5-pawn problematic.

15   ♘e4

With 15 ♘h3 White prevents 15...f5? in view of 16 c3.

But after 15...♘f5 Black can go back to the ...a5 plan. White doesn't have an active idea since the f2-f4 break will be strongly met by ...exf4 and ...♗f6.

| 15 | ... | f5 |

However, 15...a5 16 f4! would work well: 16...exf4 17 c3 ♘f5 18 ♗xf4. Or 16...f5 17 c3!.

| 16 | ♘d2 |

This was a rapid game. With more time, Karjakin might have given more consideration to the forcing 16 c3 fxe4 17 cxd4.

Then 17...exd3 18 dxe5 ♘xe5 19 ♗b1! prepares to regain the pawn favorably after f2-f4.

| 16 | ... | f4 |
| 17 | c3 | ♘f5 |

| 18 | ♘e4?! |

When he returned to Russia, Karjakin must have wondered if his conservative play – in the tenth game and with this too-principled move – cost him a world championship title.

Instead, 18 ♖e1! would have created the possibility of a strong d3-d4 sacrifice.

For example, 18...♕e8 makes sense because it begins a queen transfer to g6, as in the game.

But 19 d4! exd4 (20...♕g6 21 ♗b1) 20 cxd4 ♘xd4 21 ♗b2 ♘f5 22 ♖c1 would have granted White excellent pressure on c7 and prospects of sinking a knight or rook onto e6. He would have a solid advantage.

Black has other ideas besides 18...♕e8. But 18...♘b6 19 d4! exd4 20 cxd4 ♘xd4? 21 ♘e4 is similar.

| 18 | ... | ♕e8! |

Carlsen takes aim at g2 with ...♕g6 and ...f3 or ...♘h4.

| 19 | ♗b3 |

There was no immediate benefit to 19 a4 ♕g6 20 axb5 axb5 because White can't easily attack the b5-pawn or trade rooks.

He would have to avoid 21 ♗d2? ♘h4 22 g3 ♘f6!, when his kingside is crumbling.

| 19 | ... | ♕g6 |
| 20 | f3 |

This reinforces the e4-knight, denies ...f3 and allows him to answer ...♘h4 with the lateral defense of g2, ♖a2.

But it also weakens e3 and makes possible Black tactics such as ...♗h4/...♕h5 and ...♗g3!?.

A good alternative was 20 ♔h1 so that 20...♘h4 21 ♖g1.

Carlsen could test him on the other wing as well, 20 ♔h1 a5! 21 ♗d2 axb4 22 axb4 ♖xa1 23 ♕xa1 f3 24 gxf3? ♘h4, for example.

20   ...   ♗h4

21   a4!

It is too late for 21 d4 because 20 f3 weakened the dark squares so much.

For example, 21...exd4 22 cxd4 ♗f6! 23 ♘xf6+ ♕xf6 and ...♕xd4+.

Similarly 22 ♗xf4 dxc3 23 ♘xc3 ♗f6 24 ♕d2 ♘d4 25 ♗a2 ♘e5, also with a solid plus for Black.

21   ...   ♘f6

Now 22 axb5 axb5 23 ♖xa8 ♖xa8 24 ♕e2 was much safer. Allowing ...♖a1 is a minor concession.

22   ♕e2   a5!

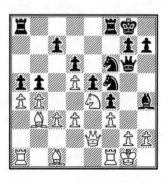

An indication of how this two-wing pressure matters is 23 bxa5 ♖xa5 with the intent of ...♖fa8 and ...bxa4.

A natural defense is 24 ♖a2 ♖fa8 25 axb5? ♖xa2 26 ♗xa2.

But that loses to 26...♘xe4! 27 dxe4 ♘g3! 28 hxg3 ♗xg3 and the threat of ...♕h6-h2 mate.

23   axb5   axb4

Carlsen fights for control of c3 or e3 for his knight.

For example, 24 ♖xa8 ♖xa8 25 cxb4 ♘d4 26 ♕d1? ♖a1 threatens 27...♖xc1 28 ♕xc1 ♘e2+.

Then 27 ♔h1 ♕h6! sets the stage for ...♘f5/...♘f6xe4 and ...♘g3+.

24   ♗d2   bxc3

25   ♗xc3   ♘e3

26   ♖fc1

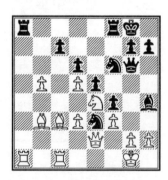

The d5-pawn is weak but not in immediate danger.

White can turn the tables after 26...♘fxd5? with 27 ♕xe3!

fxe3 28 ♗xd5+ and 29 ♗xa8. Or 26...♖xa1 27 ♖xa1 ♘fxd5? 28 ♕a2! ♕f7 29 ♗d2 and ♗xe3.

Black can safeguard the a2-g8 diagonal with 26...♔h8.

But he would not be winning after 27 b6! cxb6 28 ♘xd6 or 27...♘xe4 28 dxe4 cxb6 29 ♗a4 and ♗c6!.

26 ... ♖xa1

Carlsen goes after the b5-pawn, with ...♕e8.

27 ♖xa1

If 27 ♗xa1 ♕e8! Karjakin can have too many unprotected pieces (28 ♖xc7 ♕xb5 29 ♗c4? ♕b1+).

Carlsen could also swing back to the kingside after 28 ♖c6 ♘xe4 29 dxe4 ♖f6! and ...♖g6.

27 ... ♕e8

Given what was at stake, it was much too risky to see what happens after 27...♖b8 28 ♗c4 ♘fxd5!?.

28 ♗c4 ♔h8!

29 ♘xf6

This capture can be criticized for three reasons.

First, the threatened White pawns could be protected more cheaply, with 29 ♕a2.

Second, the capture granted Carlsen a new way to win on the kingside, 29...gxf6! followed by ...♖g8.

For instance, 30 ♔h1? ♖g8 31 ♖g1 ♗g3!. Then 32...♕h5 33 h3 ♕h4 and 34...♗f2 would win.

Better is 30 ♗d2 with hopes of ♗xe3 Black's initiative would continue after 30...♘c2 31 ♖a2 ♘d4 32 ♕d1 ♕h5 and ...♗g3.

29 ... ♗xf6

30 ♖a3 e4!

And this is the third reason. The exchange of knights freed the e4-square for this thematic way of trading dark-squared bishops.

The pawn sacrifice could not be prevented, e.g. 30 ♖a7 e4! 31 ♗xf6 gxf6! and ...♕e5!.

293

Computers say 30...e4 is not the best move, maybe not the second best in the position. But it is another good example of pragmatism. For the rest of the game, White's moves will be harder to find and the likelihood of a Karjakin blunder escalates.

31	dxe4	♗xc3
32	♖xc3	♕e5

Under normal conditions a draw could be expected after 33 ♕d2! ♖a8 34 ♖c1.

But Karjakin had left himself with only seconds to reach move 40. He could also have recovered with 34 ♕d2 and 35 ♕d2 as the game goes.

33	♖c1	♖a8

If a computer makes White's moves it will draw a position like this 100 percent of the time. A human short of time will lose it the vast majority of the time.

34	h3	h6
35	♔h2	♕d4!

Now 36 ♗d3 ♖a3 37 ♗b1 ♖c3 would set a trap, 38 ♕b2 ♖xc1 39 ♕xd4 ♘f1+ 40 ♔g1 ♘g3+ mates.

But after 39 ♕xc1 – or 38 ♖xc3 earlier – it is not clear how Black can win.

Besides, there is no reason to trade an active rook for a passive one.

36	♕e1?

Karjakin sets his own trap, 36...♘xc4? 37 ♕b4, when he would regain the piece and steal the winning chances.

36	...	♕b2!

Now 37 ♗e2 ♖a2 looks hopeless for White. But there is a miracle move: 38 e5!!.

What might have been

Then 38...♕xe2 39 ♕xe2 ♖xe2 40 b6! and White is not losing.

He even gets the advantage after 40...cxb6? 41 exd6.

Another point is that 38...♕xe5 allows 39 b6! so that 39...cxb6?? 40 ♖c8+ ♔h7 41 ♕b1+! and ♕xa2.

Best, after 38...♕xe5 39 b6, is 39...♕g5!.

Then 40 ♕f2 ♕g3+! 41 ♕xg3 fxg3+ 42 ♔xg3 ♖xe2 temporarily wins a piece.

But Black would have to give it back: 43 bxc7 ♖xg2+ 44 ♔f4! ♘xd5+ 45 ♔e4 ♘xc7 46 ♖xc7, "and the rook endgame can be held, even against Magnus," as Sergei Shipov put it.

That leaves 38...dxe5. Then 39 b6? ♕xb6 is lost.

But again there is a stunning resource, 39 d6! cxd6 40 ♖c8+ ♔h7 41 ♗d3+ g6 42 ♖c2!!.

White would win after 42...♘xc2?? 43 ♕e4. He would draw by perpetual check after 42...♕b3 43 ♕h4!.

37 ♗f1 ♖a2!

At this point Carlsen had seven minutes to play three moves.

Karjakin had twenty seconds – and a margin of error of zero.

There are a variety of tricks at Black's disposal after 38 ♖b1 ♕d4.

For example, 39 ♔h1 ♕f6! threatens ...♕g5 and would win a pawn after 40 ♗e2 ♕g6 41 ♕f2 ♘xd5!.

Better is 39 ♕h4 ♖d2 (threat of 40...♖d1) 40 ♕e1.

He could try for zugzwang with 40...♔h7 since 41 ♗e2 ♘c2 42 ♕f1 ♕e3 43 ♗c4 ♕c5 44 ♗e2 ♘e3 45 ♕e1 ♕c2 wins.

But White can pass, 41 ♔h1!.

Magnus has said he doesn't believe in fortresses but he would have had to recognize that 40...♖f2 41 ♕xf2! ♘g4+ 42 hxg4 ♕xf2 is a draw.

White can even win then after 43 e5! dxe5?? 44 d6! or 43...♕c2?? 44 b6!.

Nevertheless:

38 ♖xc7?? ♖a1

White resigns

This win meant that Carlsen only needed a draw to retain his title in the fourth playoff game. Karjakin took the risks that time. The match ended with a dramatic queen sacrifice by Magnus, the only time that happened in a world championship match.

48
True to his Style

Certain world champions – Alexander Alekhine, Mikhail Botvinnik, Tigran Petrosian – won games that left amateurs impressed but confused. They made chess look hard.

Other champions – José Capablanca, Max Euwe, Vishy Anand – won with a much more understandable style. They made chess look elegant but simple.

After a win from Levon Aronian at the Paris blitz/speed tournament of 2016, Peter Heine Nielsen said, "Magnus has been playing true to his style...he has made chess look simple." It was another game against his old rival and friend that stood out.

Carlsen – Levon Aronian
Paris Blitz 2016
Ruy Lopez, Berlin Defense (C65)

1	e4	e5
2	♘f3	♘c6
3	♗b5	♘f6
4	d3	♗c5
5	♗xc6	dxc6
6	h3	

Another *small chess* move that Carlsen used repeatedly to defeat world-class players.

Fabiano Caruana played 6...♘d7 against him at Zürich 2014 and play went 7 ♗e3 ♗d6 8 ♘c3 c5 9 0-0 ♘f8 10 ♘d2 ♘g6 11 ♘c4 ♗e6 12 ♘e2 ♕d7.

Then 13 ♘xd6+ cxd6 14 f4! gave White an advantage. He went on to win, thanks to another Carlsen Exchange sacrifice.

In the Paris 2016 blitz tournament, Vladimir Kramnik varied with 7...0-0 and eventually lost after 8 ♕d2 ♖e8 9 ♘c3 a5 10 ♗xc5 ♘xc5 11 0-0-0 f6 12 ♕e3 ♕e7 13 d4.

6	...	♗e6

In another game from the Paris blitz tournament, Hikaru Nakamura went for 6...0-0 7 ♘c3 ♖e8 8 ♗e3 ♗xe3 9 fxe3 ♘d7 10 0-0 ♘f8 11 ♕e1 f6.

He was equal after 12 g4 ♘g6 13 ♕g3 h6 14 ♖f2 ♕e7 15 ♖af1 ♗e6 16 h4 ♕d7 17 ♖g2 ♖f8. But he also lost.

7   ♘c3   ♕d6

With his bishop on e6, 7...♘d7 invites 8 ♘g5 and ♘xe6. The "two bishops" are Black's main compensation for a slightly inferior pawn structure.

8   ♘a4!   ♗b6

White's chances are preferable after 9...♗b4+ 10 c3 ♗a5 11 0-0 and 12 b4.

9   0-0   0-0

Aronian's king would be insecure after 9...0-0-0 10 ♘xb6+ axb6 11 ♗d2 and 12 a4/13 a5.

10   b3   h6

He wants to play ...♘d7 without fear of ♘g5xe6.

11   ♗b2   ♘d7

12   ♘xb6   axb6

13   d4!   exd4

14   ♘xd4

Carlsen will have better chances in a bishops-of-opposite-color middlegame than in the ending after 14 ♕xd4 ♕xd4 15 ♘xd4 ♘c5 16 ♘xe6?! ♘xe6.

14   ...   c5

But his edge would have been slight after 14...♘c5!.

For example, 15 f3 ♗xh3! 16 gxh3 ♕g3+ is a perpetual check.

Or 15 ♕f3 ♖fe8 16 ♖fe1 ♗d7 (threatening ...♕e5 and ...♘xe4) 17 ♘f5 ♗xf5 18 ♕xf5 ♕d2!.

15   ♘b5   ♕c6

Now the endgame, 15...♕xd1 16 ♖fxd1, is more problematic for Black because of White's play along the d-file, 16...♖fc8 17 ♖d2, followed by a2-a4 and ♖ad1.

No better is 15...♕f4 16 ♕c1! ♕xc1 17 ♗xc1! c6 18 ♘c7 or 17...♖fc8 18 ♗f4.

16 c4!

16 ...   f6

This and Black's next move are based on the common-sense idea of blocking the b2-g7 diagonal.

Yet they constitute a serious positional error because the diagonal can be blown open by an eventual e4-e5.

At first 16...f5 looks suspicious because that diagonal will remain open and because of 17 ♕d3 fxe4? 18 ♕g3 ♘f6 19 ♘xc7.

But 17...f4! and ...♖f7/...♘f8 is not at all bad.

Or 17 exf5 ♗xf5 18 ♖e1 ♖f7 and ...♘f8.

17 f4   ♖fe8?

18 ♕f3   ♖e7

It's too late for 18...f5? 19 exf5 ♗xf5 20 ♕xc6 and ♘xc7.

19 a4   ♘f8

20 ♘c3   ♕e8

Aronian was worried about 21 ♘d5. But of greater concern was ♕g3 followed by f4-f5.

For example, 21 ♕g3! ♗f7 22 f5 ♖d8? loses to 23 ♘b5!.

If 22...c6, White can reposition his bishop powerfully, 23 ♗c1! ♔h8 24 ♗f4 followed by ♖ae1 and e4-e5!.

21 ♖ae1   c6

22 f5!   ♗f7

23 e5!

An echo of the classic game Lasker – Capablanca, St. Petersburg 1914. Getting his knight to e4 is more than worth a pawn.

23 ...   fxe5?

This position is strategically lost. Aronian needed to try 23...♖xe5 even if it means sacrificing the Exchange.

He would lose after 24 ♘e4! ♖e7? 25 ♗xf6 or 25 ♘xf6+ gxf6 26 ♕g3+.

But 24...♘d7 25 ♗xe5 ♘xe5 26 ♕g3 ♔h7 was a fighting chance.

White would win slowly, such as with 27 ♘f2 and a trade of knights via ♘d3 or ♘g4.

24   ♘e4

Now 24...♘d7 25 ♕g3 and 26 f6 does the job.

For example, 25...♕f8 26 f6 ♖e6 27 ♖d1!.

The attacked knight can't move safely, 27...♗e8 28 f7+.

Or 27...♖d8 28 fxg7 ♕xg7 29 ♕h4 and 28...♕e7 29 ♖xd7! ♖xd7 30 ♗xe5, threatening ♘f6+.

24   ...   ♘h7

25   ♕g3   ♖d7

There was no defense in 25...♔h8 because of 26 f6 gxf6 27 ♘xf6 ♘xf6 28 ♖xf6, e.g. 28...♔h7 29 ♕h4 ♗g6 30 ♗c1.

26   ♗xe5   ♕f8

27   ♔h2

It is hard to tell what Carlsen was afraid of when he made this cautious move. The immediate 27 f6 g6 28 ♗d6 ♕d8 29 h4 and ♕f4 was good enough to win.

27   ...   b5?

28   ♘xc5   ♖d2

29   ♘e6!   Resigns

Carlsen and Levon Aronian were good friends when they were intense rivals. This was one of more than 120 games, at all speeds, from 2004 to 2020.

49
Opening Surprise

Carlsen often surprises opponents with his choice of opening. Sometimes it is a variation he had never played before – or a variation almost no one had ever played before.

Yet afterwards his moves are copied by players around the world. For example, Carlsen defended a Catalan Opening against Pavel Eljanov at Wijk aan Zee 2016.

It began **1 d4 ♘f6 2 c4 e6 3 ♘f3 d5 4 g3 ♗b4+ 5 ♗d2 ♗e7 6 ♗g2 0-0 7 0-0 ♘bd7 8 ♕c2 ♘e4 9 ♗f4 c6 10 ♘c3** and he opted for the rare **10...g5!?**.

He stood well after **11 ♗e3 ♘d6! 12 b3 ♘f5!** because of **13 ♗d2 g4! 14 ♘e1? ♘xd4**. After he won, his original play became a model for masters and amateurs.

A rematch a year later with Eljanov was also instructive.

Pavel Eljanov – Carlsen
Isle of Man Masters,
Douglas 2017
Owen's Defense (B00)

| 1 | ♘f3 | b6! |

The move 1...b6 is considered somewhat dubious against 1 d4, 1 e4 or 1 c4 – because White can defend his e4-pawn with ♗d3 or f2-f3. For example, 1 e4 b6 2 d4 ♗b7 3 ♗d3 e6 4 ♘f3 ♘f6 5 ♕e2.

| 2 | e4 | ♗b7 |
| 3 | ♘c3 | |

But in this move order White cannot play f2-f3 and does not have enough time to avoid a pin of this knight.

| 3 | ... | e6 |

| 4 | d4 | ♗b4! |
| 5 | ♗d3 | ♘f6 |

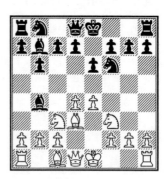

The ...♘xe4 threat tries to force White into a concession.

| 6 | ♕e2 | |

For example, 6 e5 ♘e4! threatens ...♘xc3.

Black would be at least equal after 7 ♗d2 ♘xd2 8 ♕xd2 ♗xf3 9 gxf3 ♘c6.

He should not fear the dubious gambit 7 0-0!? ♘xc3 8 bxc3 ♗xc3 9 ♖b1 ♘c6.

6 ... d5

Transposition to a kind of Sicilian Defense, 6...c5 7 0-0 cxd4 8 ♘xd4, is not good (8...♘c6 9 ♘xc6 and 10 e5).

7 exd5

If Black's knight becomes anchored in the center, 7 e5 ♘e4 8 ♗d2 ♗xc3, we can call his opening experiment a success (9 bxc3 c5).

7 ... ♕xd5

Sharpest. White would have a tiny pull after 7...♘xd5 8 ♗d2 ♘xc3 9 bxc3 and 10 0-0.

8 0-0

One of the benefits of 7...♕xd5 is that the queen will be useful on h5.

For example, 8 ♗d2 ♗xc3 9 bxc3 ♘bd7 10 0-0 0-0 11 c4 ♕h5! and ...♗xf3.

Or 12 ♘g5 ♕xe2 13 ♗xe2 e5.

8 ... ♗xc3

A necessary trade. White would be better after 8...♕h5 9 ♘e4! and 9...♘bd7 10 ♗f4/11 c3.

9 bxc3 ♘bd7

The a2-pawn can be left hanging as a sound gambit (10 ♖b1 ♕xa2 11 ♖b3 ♕a5 12 ♗f4).

10 c4

A major alternative is 10 a4 0-0 11 a5.

Then 11...bxa5? 12 ♗f4 is too hot to handle.

For instance, 12...♖fc8 13 ♖fb1 ♖ab8 14 ♖b5 ♕c6 15 c4.

Or 13...♗c6 14 c4 ♕h5 15 d5! and ♖xa5.

Black should ignore 11 a5 with 11...♖ac8. A double-edged position arises after, for instance, 12 axb6 axb6 13 ♖a7 c5.

10 ... ♕h5

11 ♗f4 ♖c8

Not 11...c5 12 d5!.

Safer but still a bit risky is 11...0-0-0 12 a4!.

12 a4

Eljanov wants to induce ...a5 so that Carlsen's queenside will be more vulnerable if he seeks counterplay with ...c5.

12 ... a5

At various points Carlsen can try for a double-edged endgame with ...♗xf3.

For example, 12...♕g4 13 ♗e3 ♗xf3 14 ♕xf3 ♕xf3 would be a roughly even battle between two bishops and two knights.

But there is also a possible gambit in 13 ♗g3 ♗xf3 14 gxf3 ♕xd4. Carlsen decides to keep ...♗xf3 as an option for later.

13 ♖ab1

White can avoid the ...♗xf3 scenarios with, for example, 13 ♘d2 ♕xe2 14 ♗xe2.

Then 14...0-0 15 ♖fe1 ♖fd8 is balanced and 16 ♗f3? ♗xf3 17 ♘xf3 c5! would turn in Black's favor.

13 ...   0-0

In an endgame ...♗c6xa4 would be strong. But a middlegame is different, as 14 ♖fe1 ♗c6 15 c3 ♗xa4? 16 ♕d2 and ♘e5! shows.

For example, 16...♗c6 17 ♘e5 ♘xe5? 18 ♖xe5 ♕h4 19 ♗g5 ♕g4 20 d5! exd5 21 h3 and White wins (21...♕d7 22 ♗xf6).

14 ♖b5

It is tempting to play this move before ...♗c6 makes it impossible.

Now Black would be relatively solid after 14...♗xf3 15 ♕xf3 ♕xf3 16 gxf3 ♖fe8 or 16...♖fd8.

But his winning chances would be slim, even after ...c5/c2-c3.

14 ...   c5!

This is the best way to play for a win. But it is risky after 15 ♗d6.

Then on 15...♖fe8 16 dxc5 Black cannot recapture with his rook or b-pawn.

This explains why White wanted to induce ...a5.

He would have the better chances after 16...♘xc5 17 ♖xb6 ♘fe4 18 ♗xc5 or 17...♗xf3 18 ♕xf3 ♕xf3 19 gxf3 ♘xa4 20 ♖b5.

Better than 15...♖fe8 is 15...♗c6. Then White's edge would be minimal after 16 ♗xf8 ♗xb5 17 ♗xc5 ♗xc4! or 17 ♗xg7 ♔xg7.

But there would also be a good opportunity for a Carlsen Exchange sacrifice, 16...♔xf8!.

After 17 ♖b2 ♗xf3 18 ♕xf3 ♕xf3 19 gxf3 cxd4 Black has plenty of compensation and an easier position to play.

15 dxc5   ♖xc5

16 ♗d6   ♖xb5

17 cxb5?

Strangely, it was better to allow Black a protected passed a5-pawn with 17 axb5!.

For example, 17...♖c8 18 ♖d1 or 17...♗xf3 18 ♕xf3 ♕xf3 19 gxf3 ♖c8 20 ♖d1 is comfortable for White because his queenside pawns are safer.

17 ...   ♖c8

Now 18 ♘e5? drops a pawn (18...♕xe2 19 ♗xe2 ♖xc2) and 18 ♘d4?? ♕d5 loses a piece.

18 c4?

The a4-pawn would also be vulnerable after 18 ♖d1 ♗xf3 19 ♕xf3 ♕xf3 21 gxf3 ♘c5.

18 ...   ♘c5

Now 19 ♖a1? ♗xf3 forces 20 gxf3, when 20...♖d8! gives Black a solid plus.

19 ♗c2

When he chose 18 c4, Eljanov may have expected to reach the

equality of 19 ♗xc5 ♖xc5 20 ♘d2!.

But Carlsen would insert the zwischenzug 19...♗xf3!.

Then 20 ♕xf3 ♕xf3 21 gxf3 ♖xc5, is much better for him in view of ...♘h5-f4.

19 ...   ♘ce4!

A new tactical nightmare for White is 20...♘g5, after 20 ♗g3 or 20 ♗e5.

20 ♗f4?

The other way of stopping ...♘g5 was 20 ♗xe4 ♘xe4 21 ♗e7!.

That looks artificial but 21...f6 would allow 22 ♕e3! and ♕xb6.

Instead, 21...♘c5 22 ♗xc5 ♗xf3! or 22 ♖a1 ♗xf3 23 ♕xf3 ♕xf3 24 gxf3 f6 and ...♔f7 are promising for Black.

20 ...   ♘c3!

Now 21 ♕e3 ♗xf3 22 ♕xf3? ♕xf3 23 gxf3 ♘e2+ and ...♘xf4 is lost.

So is 21 ♕e5 ♕xe5 22 ♗xe5 ♖xc4.

21 ♕d3

A slower loss was available after 21 ♕d2 ♗xf3 22 ♕xc3 ♘d5! 23 ♕xf3 ♕xf3 24 gxf3 ♘xf4.

| 21 | ... | ♕g4 |

The simplest win was 21...♗xf3! 22 gxf3 ♕g6+ 23 ♕xg6 hxg6 because both ...♘e2+ and ...♖xc4 would be threatened.

22 ♗e5?

The only way to make the remainder of the game interesting was 22 ♕xc3!.

White may have rejected it because of 22...♘d5 23 ♘e5 and the combination 23...♕xg2+ 24 ♔xg2 ♘xf4+! 25 ♔g3 ♘e2+ 26 ♔h3 ♘xc3.

But 27 ♖e1 and 28 ♖e3 offered some drawing prospects.

More likely, Carlsen would have kept the pressure on with 22...♕xf4.

The threat of ...♘g4/...♗xf3 could lead to 23 ♘d2! ♕g5 24 g3 ♕d5! 25 f3 ♕c5+ 26 ♖f2! h5 when he is clearly better but far from a win.

22	...	♕xc4
23	♕xc4	♖xc4
24	♗d3	

Or 24 ♗b3 ♖c8 25 ♖a1 ♘d7 26 ♗g3 ♘dc5.

| 24 | ... | ♖c8 |
| 25 | ♖a1 | ♘fd5 |

Black would make steady progress now after 26 ♘d4 f6 27 ♗g3 ♘b4 28 ♗f1 ♔f7 followed by ...g6 and ...e5.

| 26 | ♘d2 | f6 |
| 27 | ♗d6 | ♘b4! |

Now 28 ♗xb4 axb4 29 ♗c4 ♗d5 30 ♗xd5 exd5 and ...♖a8xa4.

| 28 | ♗c4 | ♗d5 |
| 29 | ♗f1 | ♘ba2! |

White resigns

After the a4-pawn dies, the rest would be routine.

50
Magnus versus Magnus

One of the challenges for the elite grandmasters of the 21ˢᵗ century is how to play both sides of an opening. Like his rivals Fabiano Caruana and Hikaru Nakamura, Magnus found himself repeatedly trying to defeat the Ruy Lopez when he had White and then trying to defend the same opening as Black.

This phenomenon had occurred in some previous generations, such as in the 1920s when virtually all the top players played the Queen's Gambit Declined as White and Black. What was new nearly a century later was that the battlegrounds were among the most innocuous openings.

Carlsen – Ding Liren
Champions Showdown,
St. Louis 2017
Ruy Lopez (C78)

1	e4	e5
2	♘f3	♘c6
3	♗b5	a6
4	♗a4	♘f6
5	0-0	♗e7
6	d3	b5
7	♗b3	d6
8	a3	

This is the same position as in Game 47 as well as two other games from the 2016 World Championship match. Carlsen was Black in all three.

Ding Liren was one of the world's experts in this variation. Carlsen must have noticed that a year before the Chinese grandmaster had gotten into trouble against Caruana after 8...♘a5 9 ♗a2 c5 10 ♘c3 ♗e6 11 ♘h4 c4 12 ♘f5!.

8	...	0-0
9	♘c3	♘a5
10	♗a2	♗e6

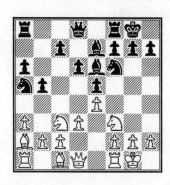

11 b4!

There is nothing to 11 ♘d5 in view of 11...♘xd5 12 ♗xd5 ♗xd5 13 exd5 c5.

Then Black's knight is temporarily out of play but he would have the better middlegame plan in ...f5.

11 ... **♗xa2**

12 ♖xa2

Another way to start the middlegame is 12 ♘xa2 ♘c6 13 c4 and 14 ♘c3.

White has the better pawn structure after 13...bxc4 14 dxc4 (and would fork the knights after 14...♘xe4? 15 ♕d5).

White is slightly better after 13...♕d7 14 ♘c3 ♘d4 15 ♗e3, for example.

12 ... **♘c6**

Carlsen can try to improve the pawn structure with 13 ♘d5 ♘xd5 14 exd5 ♘b8.

But 15 d4? e4! turns out badly and 15 ♖e1 ♘d7 16 c4 f5 or 16 d4 ♗f6 are relatively harmless.

13 ♗g5

Now a trade of bishops, 13...♘d7 14 ♗xe7 ♘xe7, would ease Black's position.

Better is 14 ♗d2 or 14 ♗e3 so that after 14...♘f6 White will have gained a tempo.

The tempo matters after 14 ♗d2 ♘f6 15 ♘d5.

For example, 15...♘xd5 16 exd5 ♘b8 17 a4 ♘d7 18 c4 and 18...♘b6? 19 a5!.

13 ... **♕d7**

14 ♗xf6!

Carlsen had to upset the symmetry or find he had the worst of 14...a5!.

14 ... **♗xf6**

15 ♘d5 **a5!**

This was a 20-minute game and it really began with this new move.

It is tempting to damage the Black kingside with 16 ♘xf6+ gxf6.

But the d5-knight was White's best piece and he has to meet the threat of 17...axb4.

He can't play 17 c3? axb4 18 cxb4 ♘xb4!, for example.

Betting on kingside success with 17 bxa5 ♖xa5 18 ♘h4 or 17...f5 18 ♘h4 is not Carlsen's style. He opts instead to keep some control of the queenside.

306

16 c4!

So that 16...axb4 17 cxb5 ♞e7 18 a4! or 17...♞a7 18 b6, when White is clearly better.

16 ... ♞e7!

Now 17 cxb5? ♞xd5 18 exd5 ♛xb5 is great for Black.

There is nothing much for White in 17 bxa5 ♞xd5 18 cxd5 ♜xa5 or 17 ♞xf6+ gxf6 18 cxb5 axb4 19 a4 c6.

17 ♜c2

Vachier-Lagrave later tried 17 ♛b3 against Ding Liren but Black was at least equal after 17...bxc4!.

For example, 18 dxc4 ♞xd5! 19 cxd5 axb4 20 axb4 ♜xa2 21 ♛xa2 ♛b5!.

Instead, the game continued 18 ♞xe7+? ♝xe7 19 dxc4 axb4 20 axb4 ♛c6 and Black was better.

17 ... ♞xd5

Since several world-class players played this opening it was inevitable that improvements would be found. One is 17...axb4! 18 axb4 bxc4 when Black is close to equality (19 ♞xf6+ gxf6 20 dxc4 ♞g6).

18 cxd5 axb4

19 axb4 ♜a4

In effect, Black is saying:

Yes, it's true that I have a backward c7-pawn and I can't easily dissolve it with ...c6. And maybe your knight is better than my bishop.

But your b4-pawn will also be a target. And I'm going to own the only open file after ...♜fa8.

I don't have great winning chances. But where are yours?

20 ♛d2 ♜fa8

21 ♜fc1

The best answer to his question is d3-d4.

Black must have considered defending his c7-pawn with 21...♜8a7.

Then on 22 d4 exd4 23 ♘xd4 he should not allow ♘c6. So 23...♗xd4! 24 ♕xd4 is best.

After both sides make luft, 24...h6 25 g3, White can shoot for e4-e5.

That works if Black passes, for example, 25...♕e7 26 ♔g2 ♕d7?, because of 27 e5! dxe5 28 ♕xe5.

Then 28...♖xb4 29 ♖xc7 ♖xc7 30 ♖xc7 ♕d8? 31 ♖e7! and ♖e8+.

But if Black takes precautions such as 26...f6 it is not evident how White can make progress.

21 ... ♗d8

22 h3

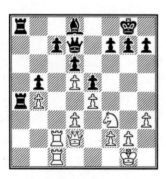

Another problem for Carlsen is that his e4-pawn would be exposed after 22...h6! 23 d4 exd4 24 ♘xd4 ♕e8.

Then Black's bishop comes alive, e.g. 25 f3 ♗g5 26 f4 ♗f6 (27 ♖xc7 ♕xe4).

The same for 25 ♖e1 ♖a1 26 ♖cc1 ♗g5.

Note also that 22...h6! would prepare ...f5 (because ♘g5-e6 is no longer possible. Once Black achieves ...f5 he can transfer his queen to g6 and may stand slightly better.

22 ... ♖a1?

23 ♖xa1!

Another case of Magnus's superior powers of evaluation. His opponent misjudges a trade of a pair of rooks.

23 ... ♖xa1+

24 ♖c1

Trading both rooks is even better for White. After 24...♖xc1+ 25 ♕xc1 Black would not have to worry about ♖xc7 any more. But White would no longer have to defend his b4-pawn.

Then the board's most glaring weakness is Black's b5-pawn, e.g. 25...g6 26 d4 exd4 27 ♘xd4 and ♕f1.

Black can avoid that with 26...♗f6 27 dxe5 dxe5. But the ♕+♘ -vs.- ♕+♗ endgame favors White after 28 ♕c3.

The same goes for the pure queen endgame after 27...♗xe5 28 ♘xe5 dxe5 29 f3. Black would be in for a long, dismal evening in either case.

24 ... ♖a4

Another misjudgment. The b4-pawn never faces real danger now.

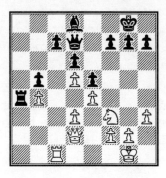

25 d4! exd4

No master wants to accept as passive a position as 25...f6 but it was Black's best.

26 ♘xd4 ♗f6

27 ♘c6

The knight protects the b4-pawn. Now 27...♕e8 28 ♕e2 would threaten ♕xb5.

There is another winning idea: After 28...♖a8 White would have a strong 27 f4 and 28 e5!.

27 ... ♕c8?

28 e5!

So that 28...♗xe5?? 29 ♘e7+.

28 ... dxe5

29 d6!

Now 29...cxd6? 30 ♘e7+ costs the queen and 29...♕d7 30 ♘e7+! ♗xe7 31 ♖xc7 is also lost.

29 ... ♖a8

30 ♘e7+!

Faster than 30 d7 ♕f8 31 ♖d1 ♗d8 32 ♕e2.

30 ... ♗xe7

31 dxe7 Resigns

It is lost after, for example, 31...g6 32 ♖d1 ♕e8 33 ♕d8 or 33 ♕g5.

51

Unbalancing Act

When a very young Carlsen defeated a grandmaster with Black it was often a back-and-forth struggle in which his opponent went out of his way to avoid drawing with a boy.

As he reached chess-maturity, Carlsen had to deal increasingly with GM opponents who would be content to draw with him and knew how to play for a draw with the White pieces. How do you play to win with the Black pieces against an experienced seen-it-all grandmaster? Let us count the ways.

Alexey Dreev – Carlsen
World Cup, Tbilisi 2017
*Queen's Gambit Declined,
Ragozin Variation (D38)*

1	d4	d5
2	c4	e6
3	♘c3	♗b4!

One way: Get him out of his comfort zone.

When Alexey Dreev faced a Nimzo-Indian Defense, he usually played 4 ♕c2 or 4 f3.

This position is similar. But if Dreev tried to transpose into a Nimzo after 4 ♕c2 ♘f6 or 4 f3 ♘f6, Carlsen could create a sharper and thoroughly unfamiliar position with 4...dxc4! and ...b5.

4	♘f3!	♘f6

You can't trick a veteran out of *all* of his openings. Dreev has transposed into the Ragozin

Variation of the Queen's Gambit Declined, an opening he knew well.

5	♗g5	h6
6	♗xf6	♕xf6

Carlsen had some experience on the White side of 7 ♕a4+ ♘c6, which stops ...c5.

7	♕b3	c5!

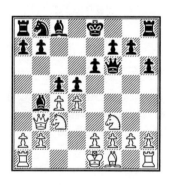

8	cxd5	

Experience has shown that Black has no problems after 8 dxc5 ♗xc3+ 9 ♕xc3 ♕xc3+

10 bxc3 dxc4. Or after 9 bxc3 dxc4 10 ♕xc4 0-0.

8	...	exd5
9	a3	

It pays White to force matters before Black plays the thematic ...c4.

A relatively ancient example, played by Vyacheslav Ragozin himself, went 9 e3 ♘c6 10 ♗e2? c4! and Black won with his queenside majority (versus Pirc, Saltsjöbaden 1948).

9	...	♗xc3+
10	♕xc3	c4!

This unbalancing move sidesteps drawish positions such as 10...♘d7 11 ♕e3+ ♕e7 and 10...b6 11 e3 0-0 12 dxc5 ♕xc3+ 13 bxc3 bxc5 14 c4.

11 b3

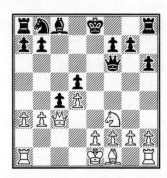

Carlsen invested time in the c4-pawn so he should not allow 11...b5 12 a4! (12...bxa4 13 bxc4 or 12...a6 13 axb5 axb5?? 14 ♖xa8).

The only alternative is the risky 12...♗d7 13 axb5 ♗xb5.

Then 14 e4 dxe4 15 ♘e5 followed by bxc4 or ♗xc4 would point out how far behind in development he is.

11	...	♗e6

This allows Carlsen to protect the c4-pawn indirectly, 12 e3 0-0 13 bxc4 dxc4 14 ♗xc4? ♖c8.

He would achieve the unbalanced middlegame he wanted after 14 ♗e2 ♘d7 15 0-0 ♗d5 and ...b5.

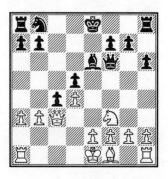

12 ♘e5

This leaves "book." The critical test is 12 bxc4 dxc4 13 e4 0-0 14 ♗e2 so that after 14...♘d7 15 0-0 Black doesn't get to play 15...♗d5!.

His queenside pawns would become a liability after 15...b5 16 a4! a6 17 ♖fb1.

Mostly likely Carlsen would have solved this problem with 14...b5! (instead of 14...♘d7).

One difference is that 15 0-0 ♘c6! enables him to meet 16 a4 with 16...b4! and enjoy two connected passed pawns.

The other difference is that 15 a4 allows a sacrifice, 15...b4! 16 ♕xb4 ♘c6.

Black would get enough for his pawn after 17 ♕c3 ♖ab8 and ...♖b3.

That also seems to be true of 17 ♕c5 ♖ac8 and ...♖fd8 or ...♗g4.

12 ... 0-0

Another pawn offer is 13 bxc4 dxc4 and 14...♘d7!.

For example, 14 e3 ♘d7 15 ♘xd7 ♗xd7 16 ♗xc4 ♕g5 favors Black (17 0-0 ♗h3 or 17 g3 ♖ac8 18 ♕b4 ♕f5 and ...♕e4.

Also 16 ♕xc4 ♖ac8 17 ♕b3 ♕g6.

13 e3 ♘c6

Now on 14 ♘xc6 bxc6 15 bxc4 ♕g6! White cannot complete his development smoothly (16 ♗e2? ♕xg2).

He would be in grave trouble after 16 g3 ♕e4 17 ♖g1 dxc4

18 ♗xc4 ♗xc4 19 ♕xc4 ♖ab8 and ...♖b1+ or ...♖b6/...♖fb8.

14 ♗e2

It's a similar story after 14 bxc4 ♘xe5 15 dxe5 ♕g6 (16 c5 ♖ac8).

Perhaps AlphaZero will claim 16 0-0-0 is good because of White's superior "king mobility." Yeah, right.

14 ... ♘xe5

15 dxe5 ♕g6

16 0-0

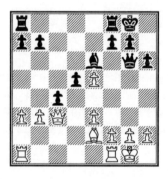

Dreev, an excellent defender, seems to have minimized the damage.

After the thematic 16...b5 he would avoid 17 a4 b4! 18 ♕xb4 ♖ab8 and ...♖xb3.

Instead, he could blockade the queenside with 17 b4! and be ready to equalize with 18 a4.

16 ... d4!

17 exd4 cxb3

This required quite a bit of calculation because White will

have opportunities to push d4-d5 or capture on b7.

18   ♗f3   ♖ac8

Now 19 ♕b4 a5 20 ♕xb7? ♖b8 is lost because of ...b2/...♗f5.

19   ♕e3!

The initiative would turn traitor after 19...b6? 20 d5!.

19   ...   ♕g5!

Now 20 ♕xg5 hxg5 21 ♗xb7 ♖b8 22 ♗e4 b2 23 ♖ad1 appears to defend.

But Black can improve slowly with 23 ♖ad1 ♗b3! 24 ♖b1 ♗c4 so that 25 ♖fd1? ♗a2 wins.

Also 25 ♖fe1 ♖fd8 26 ♖bd1 ♗b3 27 ♖b1 ♗a2 28 ♖bd1 a5.

20   ♖ab1

Or 20 d5 ♕xe3 21 fxe3, when 21...♗f5 runs into 22 e4!.

The bishop works better after 21...♗d7 22 ♖ab1 ♗b5!.

Then 23 ♖fd1 a5 and 24...a4 allows Black to protect his passed pawn (based on 24 ♖xb3? ♗a4!).

Similar to the game is 23 ♖fe1! ♖c3 24 d6, with good drawing prospects.

20   ...   ♕xe3

21   fxe3   ♖fd8

22   ♗xb7   ♖c3

23   d5

Passive defense, 23 ♖fe1!, was best.

Then 23...♖b8 24 ♗e4 b2 25 d5! holds.

Instead, Black can build slowly with 23 ...♔f8 and ...♔e7.

But a draw is likely after 24 ♖b2.

23   ...   ♗d7

24   ♖f4!

Dreev saw that Carlsen's threat of 24...♖b8 (25 ♗a6 b2 and ...♖xa3) could now be met by 25 ♖b4!.

Then 25...♖xe3 26 ♖4xb3 ♖xb3 27 ♖xb3 ♗c8 fails to 28 d6! ♗xb7 29 d7.

| 24 | ... | a5! |

| 25 | ♔f2? |

The final mistake. White should try 25 d6 ♗e6 26 ♖d4! with the idea of trading bishops with ♗d5!.

For example, 26...♖b8 27 ♗d5 ♗xd5 28 ♖xd5 b2? 29 d7! ♖c1+ 30 ♖d1.

Instead, Carlsen would retain good winning chances with 28...♔f8 so that 29 d7 ♔e7 or 29 ♔f2 ♖c2+ 30 ♔f3 ♔e8.

| 25 | ... | ♖b8 |
| 26 | ♗c6 | |

Also lost was 26 ♗a6 b2.

26	...	♗xc6
27	dxc6	♖xc6
28	♖d4	

And here 28 ♖b2 ♖c1 and ...♖a1.

28	...	♖c2+
29	♔f3	b2
30	♖dd1	♖b5!

| 31 | a4 | ♖xe5 |
| 32 | ♖d8+ | ♔h7 |

Dreev may have counted on 33 ♖b8 but now saw how hopeless 33...♖f5+ and ...♖ff2 would be. So: **White resigns**.

52

Regrets, he had a few

When Veselin Topalov started his 2006 world championship match with two losses, he was asked how he was able to retain his composure during the remaining games. It was easy, he said. "Generally, I am good at forgetting."

One of the ailments that plagues amateurs is the realization that they missed a strong move. When they know they have spoiled the game, they become discouraged and hobbled by regret.

Carlsen doesn't forget his mistakes. But he manages to focus. He may have just missed a winning shot. But if he still has good opportunities before him, he recovers. All that matters is the position on the board. "Try to pull yourself together" is one of his messages he gives himself. "You are not going to lose this game like an idiot. Try to pull yourself together."

Carlsen – Radoslaw Wojtaszek
Gashimov Memorial,
Shamkir 2018
Sicilian Defense, 4 ♕xd4 (B23)

1	e4	c5
2	♘c3	d6
3	d4	cxd4
4	♕xd4	♘c6
5	♕d2	

When this move appeared on the computer screens of on-line spectators, they scoured through databases for examples of 5 ♕d2. There were virtually none.

Grandmasters were also surprised. "Chess wisdom suggests to move each piece only once in the opening, especially the queen," commented a Russian GM, Igor Khenkin. "However, the world champion seems to have his own rules."

Actually, 5 ♕d2 is similar to book positions that occur after 1 e4 c5 2 ♘f3 d6 3 d4 cxd4 4 ♕xd4 when Black avoids 4...♘c6 5 ♗b5.

Instead, the game may go 4...a6 or 4...♗d7 and then 5 c4 ♘c6 6 ♕d2 when White has a favorable pawn structure. The loss of time with the queen is a minor concern.

Of course, Carlsen can't play c2-c4 because 2 ♞c3 blocked the c2-pawn. But he has a new approach – a queenside fianchetto and 0-0-0.

5	...	♞f6
6	b3	

Now on 6...g6 7 ♝b2 ♝g7 a reasonable way to start the middlegame is 8 0-0-0 0-0 9 f3 ♛a5 10 ♚b1 followed by ♞ge2 or g2-g4.

6	...	e6
7	♝b2	a6!

The d-pawn would be a long-term liability after 7...d5 8 exd5 ♞xd5 9 ♞xd5 ♛xd5 10 ♛xd5 exd5 11 0-0-0!.

Or 8...exd5 9 0-0-0 ♝e6 10 ♞ge2.

8	0-0-0	b5
9	f3	

Here's an admittedly over-simplified way of evaluating the position:

First, just look at the top half of the diagram.

The Black pieces and pawns are on the same squares they could be on in other balanced Sicilian positions, such as in the Richter-Rauzer or Scheveningen variations.

Now look at the bottom half of the diagram. White's pieces and pawns are uncommon but coordinated. The worst thing you can say is that he has no obvious plan except a kingside attack, begun by pushing his g-pawn.

Now let's consider specifics. After 9...♝e7 White must avoid 10 g4? because 10...♞xg4! 11 fxg4? ♝g5! loses his queen.

Instead, 10 ♚b1 0-0 11 g4 and then 11...♞d7, perhaps followed by ...♞c5 and ...b4 would have the double-edged nature of a typical Sicilian.

9	...	h5

This move strikes many amateurs as bizarre but it is a common way for masters to stop g2-g4.

For example, 1 e4 c5 2 ♞f3 d6 3 d4 cxd4 4 ♞xd4 ♞f6 5 ♞c3 e6 6 ♝e3 a6 7 f3 b5 8 ♛d2 h5 is a "book" line.

Then White has nothing he can easily attack on the kingside. It is difficult to organize center play with f3-f4.

Black has stood well in games that continued 9 0-0-0 ♗b7 10 ♔b1 ♘bd7 11 ♗d3 ♖c8, for example.

10   ♘h3!

Unlike that example, Carlsen's knight was at g1 not d4. Now it will stand quite well on g5.

10   ...   ♗e7

11   ♘g5

This knight is not enough to boast of a White advantage. But it gives Carlsen good reason to pursue a plan of f3-f4 and ♗e2-f3.

11   ...   h4?

Black's ninth move limited some of his own options but for a good reason, to stop 10 g4. This move limits him more and for no good reason.

Engines initially look at alternatives such as 11...♗b7 12 ♔b1 ♕b6 13 ♗e2 0-0.

But when they examine 14 f4 further they recognize a major White advantage.

On the other hand, queenside castling, 13...♖f8 14 f4 0-0-0, isn't appealing either after 15 ♗f3.

Question: So where will Black's king spend the middlegame?

12   f4   ♗b7

13   ♔b1   ♖c8

Answer: In the center.

That's a dangerous policy in the Sicilian when White can play e4-e5. Here Black can deter that push.

14   ♗e2   ♕c7

But e4-e5 isn't the only arrow in White's quiver. One alternative is f4-f5.

The threat of fxe6 would virtually force ...e5 and give White the prospect of ♘d5/ ...♘xd5/exd5.

15   ♖he1

But much more dangerous is ♘d5 as a sacrifice.

For example, 15...♘d7 16 f5 is good but 16 ♘d5! exd5 17 exd5 is stronger.

Black could resign after 17...♘cb8 18 ♗xg7 ♖g8 19 ♗h5! and ♗xf7+ or ♘e6.

15   ...   ♘h7

Black might have tried 15...0-0 and hoped for counterplay after 16 ♗f3 b4 17 ♘a4 e5 and ...♘d4.

White can play for mate after 18 ♕f2. For example, 18...exf4 19 ♘b6! ♖cd8? 20 ♗xf6 and ♘d5.

But better is 17 ♘d5! exd5 18 exd5 ♖a7 19 ♖e2!.

16   ♘xh7   ♖xh7

Black is ready to safeguard his kingside with 17...♔f8!. He would have a playable game after ...♔g8 and ...♖h6.

17   g4?

"Attacking without Sacrificing" is the name of a well-received video series Carlsen launched in 2020. He showed how some of his positions were so good that he could win with solid moves that do not give up material.

Here he has an impressive plan based on 18 g5 followed by ♗g4 and g5-g6 or f4-f5.

He acknowledged after the game that 17 ♘d5! exd5 18 exd5

would have been good. But he didn't appreciate how good.

After 18...♘d8 he would have had a choice of winning with 19 ♗d3 or 19 ♗g4.

For instance, 19 ♗d3 g6 20 f5 or 19...♖h5 20 ♖xe7+ ♔xe7 21 ♕e2+ and 20...♕xe7 21 ♖e1.

Black could keep the game going by giving back the piece, 18...♔f8! 19 dxc6 ♗xc6.

But Carlsen's pressure would be relentless after 20 ♗g4 ♖d8 21 ♖e2 and 22 ♖de1, for example.

17   ...   hxg3

18   hxg3   ♗f6!

Black is not out of the woods. But after 19 ♕xd6 ♕xd6 20 ♖xd6 ♘b4 he would have active pieces and only be a pawn down (21 e5 ♗e7 22 ♖d2 ♖h3).

19   ♗d3

Again, Carlsen relies on simple moves rather than a standard Sicilian Defense sacrifice, 19 e5! dxe5 20 ♘e4.

Black cannot afford 20...♗e7 21 fxe5 (21...♘xe5? 22 ♗xe5 ♕xe5 23 ♕d7+) or 20...♖d8 21 ♘d6+.

White would retain a substantial edge after 20...♘d4 21 ♗d3.

But Carlsen's move is also quite good.

19	...	♖h8

20	g4

This advance was positionally valid, since 21 g5 would again be strong. It is tactically based on 20...g6? 21 ♘d5! exd5 22 ♗xf6 and wins.

Computers said 20 ♖h1 ♖xh1 21 ♖xh1 would be stronger.

For example, 21...♔e7 22 e5! dxe5 23 ♘e4 is again strong.

Or 22...♘xe5 23 fxe5 ♗xh1 24 exf6+ gxh6 25 ♕h6.

20	...	♘d4!

Carlsen underestimated the threat of ...♘f3.

21	♖e3

It is too late for 21 ♖h1 ♖xh1 22 ♖xh1 in view of 22...♘xb3! 23 axb3 ♗xc3.

21	...	♔f8!

22	♘e2!	♘xe2

23	♖xe2

"Despite his earlier errors..." is a phrase that often occurs in notes to Carlsen games.

Usually it is followed by "...Magnus had reason to be optimistic."

That is the case here. Black's king is still the board's most vulnerable target. This would become clearer after 23...♗xb2 24 ♔xb2 and 25 g5!.

23	...	♗c3

24	♗xc3	♕xc3

25 ♕e3!

A trade of queens greatly helps Black. He may have expected to continue forcing play with 25...♕c5.

But after 26 ♕g3 he has to find an answer to 27 g5 and 28 g6.

Extreme measures (26...g5 27 ♖f1) don't work.

On 26...e5 White can target f7 with 27 ♖f2. For instance 27...exf4 28 ♖xf4 ♖e8 29 g5.

25	...	♖c5
26	e5!	dxe5

The kingside is opened fatally after 26...d5 27 f5.

Carlsen's pressure would also mount after 26...♖d5 27 ♕a7.

Then 27...♗c8 28 exd6 ♖xd6 29 f5 is strong. For example, 29...♖d7 30 ♕a8 e5 31 g5 with the idea of 32 f6 and 33 ♖h1!.

27 fxe5

Carlsen prepares to crash through on the f-file with his heavy pieces, aided in some cases by g5-g6.

With 27...♖c7 Black would be offering a pawn – 28 ♗xb5 ♕xe3 29 ♖xe3 because 30 ♖d8+ is threatened.

But Carlsen would be justified in disdaining it in favor of 28 ♖f1! and then 28...♕c5 29 ♕f4 and ♖ef2.

For example, 29...♔g8 30 ♖ef2 ♕e7 31 ♕d4 ♖d7 32 ♕b6 prepares 33 g5 and 34 g6.

It is not a forced win after 32...♕e8 33 g5 g6 34 ♖f6. But it is getting close.

27 ... ♖h1?

This is the kind of oversight that grandmasters make when they see how lost other moves are.

Black could try to reach a rook endgame with 27...♖d5 and ...♕d4.

A crucial continuation is 28 ♖f1 ♕d4 29 ♗g6! and the forced 29...♕xe3 30 ♖xf7+ ♔g8 31 ♖xe3 ♖h6! 32 ♖xb7 ♖xg6.

White should win eventually by creating passed queenside pawns, e.g. 33 ♖e4 ♖g5 34 ♖b6 ♖gxe5 35 ♖xe5 ♖xe5 36 ♖xa6 and a2-a4.

28	♖xh1	♗xh1

29 ♖h2!

Now 29...♗d5 30 ♖h8+ ♔e7 31 ♕g5+ is a mate.

29	...	♖xe5
30	♖h8+	♔e7
31	♕a7+!	**Resigns**

53

Everyone wants to draw...

... with the World Champion, that is. When Tigran Petrosian was champion he found that the title could be a huge asset. If he found himself with a lost position against a weaker player he could offer a draw. His opponent often accepted – even if he knew he was winning.

But there was a downside to being champion, Petrosian found. His opponents sometimes made clear they wanted to split the point. He found it difficult to maintain tension in the position, and therefore winning chances, without also creating losing chances. So he often drew against good but not great players.

Carlsen faced a similar problem when playing draw-minded opponents. But he managed to win much more often than Petrosian, by extending the length of the game.

Baskaran Adhiban – Carlsen
Wijk aan Zee 2018
Four Knights, Scotch Variation
(C47)

1	e4	e5
2	♘f3	♘c6
3	♘c3	♘f6

The younger Carlsen met 4 ♗b5 with 4...♘d4, the Marshall-Rubinstein Variation. But that allows White to head towards a notoriously drawish endgame after 5 ♘xd4 exd4 6 e5 and 6...dxc3 7 exf6 ♕xf6 8 dxc3 ♕e5+ 9 ♕e2 ♕xe2+.

Instead, Carlsen opted for 4...♗b4 and 4...♗d6!?.

4	d4	exd4

5	♘xd4	

This transposes into a drawish Scotch Opening variation that is usually arrived at via 1 e4 e5 2 ♘f3 ♘c6 3 d4 exd4 4 ♘xd4 ♘f6 5 ♘c3.

Carlsen's opponent can claim a minor psychological victory: In the Scotch move order Carlsen often avoided this by playing 4...♗c5, rather 4...♘f6. Now he is on a less familiar playing field.

5	...	♗b4
6	♘xc6	bxc6

He has little choice here because he would have no compensation for an inferior pawn structure after 6...dxc6? 7 ♕xd8+ ♔xd8 8 f3.

321

7   &d3   d5

Carlsen had a non-game in the last round of Wijk aan Zee 2020 when Wesley So played 8 &d2.

After 8...0-0 So took seconds – and Carlsen took little more than that – to continue 9 0-0 &xc3 10 &xc3 dxe4 11 &xf6 ♕xf6 12 &xe4 ♕xb2 13 &xc6 ♖b8 14 ♖b1 ♕xb1 15 ♕xb1 ♖xb1 16 ♖xb1. Less than an hour later the board only contained the two kings. Draw.

8   exd5   0-0!

The book move is 8...cxd5 and then 9 0-0 0-0. The drawback is that this allows 9 ♕e2+.

It is not a bid for a significant advantage because the 9...♕e7 endgame is even. But White might not be averse to a drawish endgame.

9   0-0!

Accepting the gambit, 9 dxc6, is dangerous after 9...&g4.

Carlsen would be much better after 10 &e2? ♕e8! 11 0-0 ♖d8

and have a nice game after 10 f3 ♖e8+ 11 &e2 ♕e7.

White could explore 10 ♕d2 ♖e8+ 11 ♔f1 &c5 or 10...♕e8+ 11 ♔f1 ♕xc6. But Adhiban preferred to transpose back into the dead-even book line.

9   ...   cxd5

10   &g5   c6

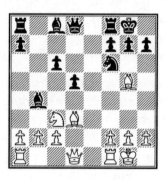

11   ♕f3

Databases indicate Carlsen had never played this position before.

Instead he had faced 11 ♘a4 and replied 11...&d6, against Nakamura at Zürich (blitz) 2014.

He stood better after 12 c3 ♖e8 13 &h4 &g4 14 f3? &h5 15 ♕c2 &g6 16 ♖ae1 ♕c7 17 g4 &xd3 18 ♕xd3 ♘d7 and he won after 19 ♕c2 ♘f8 20 ♖xe8 ♖xe8 21 ♖e1 ♖b8 22 ♔g2 ♘e6 23 &g3 c5 24 b3 c4!.

11   ...   &d6

Somewhat more popular is 11...&e7. That leads to very

balanced positions after, for example, 12 ♖ae1.

A quick draw by perpetual check is possible after 12...♖b8 13 ♘d1 h6 and now 14 ♗xh6! gxh6 15 ♕e3 ♗d6 16 ♕xh6 and ♕g5+.

The main difference between 11...♗e7 and 11...♗d6 is that Black is now willing to go into an endgame with doubled pawns after ♗xf6/...♕xf6/♕xf6.

12   ♖ae1   ♖b8

For example, 13 ♘d1 h6 14 ♗xf6 ♕xf6 15 ♕xf6 gxf6 16 b3 is very similar to what happens in the game.

The White knight can get to f5 in two moves. If Black captures it (♘f5/...♗xf5/♗xf5) the bishops of opposite color make the endgame – for lack of a better expression – drawisher and drawisher.

The doubled Black f-pawns matter very little after, for example, 16...f5 17 ♘e3 f4 18 ♘f5 ♗xf5 19 ♗xf5 ♔g7 and ...♔f6.

13   b3   a5

Carlsen's move is natural but very rare, according to databases.

14   h3   h6

This prompts an endgame because 15 ♗h4 ♗b4! is unpleasant and 15 ♗f4 ♗e6 allows Black to use his mobile center, ...c5, as in the Nakamura – Carlsen game.

15   ♗xf6   ♕xf6

16   ♕xf6   gxf6

Now on 17 ♘a4 Black can begin a good plan with 17...♗e6 and ...c5-c4!.

17   ♘e2!   c5

Only White would have winning chances after 17...a4 18 ♘d4!.

18   ♘g3   ♖d8

Ideally, he would like to trade bishops with 19 ♗f5 and ♗xc8.

But 19...♗a6! 20 ♗d3 c4 is the flaw (21 bxc4 dxc4 22 ♗e2 ♖b2).

19   ♘f5

An illustration of how the two bishops can offset an inferior pawn structure is 19 ♘h5 ♗e5 20 f4 ♗c3 21 ♖e7 ♗d7 and ...♚f8.

19 ... ♗f8

Computers say that if Black avoids 19...♗xf5 he will be worse. They are right. But only very slightly worse and the position would be double-edged enough to allow Carlsen significant winning chances.

He now threatens 20...c4 (20 c3 c4! 21 bxc4 bxc4 22 ♗e4 ♖b2).

Adhiban might have tried 20 g4 and then 20...♗e6 25 ♘g3 c4 26 ♗f5 ♖b6, when chances remain even.

20 ♘e7+

This leaves him with the better remaining bishop but the advantage is largely optical.

20 ... ♗xe7

21 ♖xe7 ♗e6

There is nothing in 22 ♖a7 ♖a8 23 ♖xa8 ♖xa8 24 f4 f5, for instance.

22 ♖d1!? c4

23 ♗e2

Now White does threaten 24 ♖a7 because 24...♖a8 25 ♖xa8 ♖xa8 26 ♗f3! cxb3 27 cxb3 ♖d8 28 ♚f1 and ♖d4/♚e1 would be unpleasant for Magnus to defend.

He must have looked at 23...d4 because of 24 ♖a7? d3!.

Then 25 cxd3 cxb3 26 axb3 ♗xb3 creates a powerful passed pawn, 27...a4.

But he would have seen that the rook endgames that could arise after (23...d4) 24 ♗xc4 ♗xc4 25 bxc4 are sterile.

For example, 25...♖b2 26 ♖e4 ♖xa2 27 ♖exd4 ♖xd4 28 ♖xd4 ♖xc2 29 ♖d8+ ♚g7 30 ♖a8.

23 ... a4!

The rook at e7 would be badly out of play after 24 bxc4? dxc4 25 ♖xd8+ ♖xd8 and ...♖d2.

Also 25 ♚f1 ♖xd1+ 26 ♗xd1 ♖b2 or 26...c3.

24 bxa4

324

How can Carlsen play to win?

The natural 24...♖b2? fails to 25 ♗xc4 ♖xc2 26 ♗b3 and White is on top.

Better is 24...♔f8 25 ♖c7 ♖b2. Then 26 ♖xc4 dxc4! 27 ♖xd8+ ♔e7 and ...♖xc2 could make the passed c4-pawn dangerous.

But chances are equal after 26 ♗xc4! ♖xc2 27 ♖c6! and 28 ♗b5.

24 ... ♗f5

He could have tried to improve on those variations with 24...d4 with a threat of 25...♔f8 26 ♖c7 ♖b2! because then the pin after 27 ♗xc4 ♖xc2 is lost.

White would need counterplay after 24...d4. The best resource is 25 f4, with a threat of 26 f5 (26...♗xf5 27 ♗xc4 or 26...♗d5 27 ♖xd4).

The position would again become drawish after 25...f5 26 g4! fxg4 27 ♗xg4 ♗xg4 28 hxg4 ♖b2 29 ♖e4!.

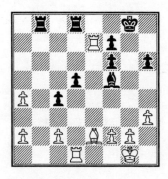

25 ♗f3?

Adhiban must have looked at 25 c3 and worried about 25...d4.

Carlsen's c-pawn would win after 26 ♖xd4?? ♖xd4 27 cxd4 ♖b1+ 28 ♔h2 c3 and ...c2.

Or after 26 ♗xc4 dxc3 27 ♖xd8+ ♖xd8 28 ♖xf7?? c2.

But he frightened himself: 28 ♗b3 c2 29 ♖e1 is better for White in that variation.

After 25 c3! Carlsen would likely have played 25...♖a8 25 ♖c7 ♗e6 with 26...♖db8 and ...♖b2 in mind.

He would not be winning after 26 f4! f5 but not losing either.

25 ... d4!

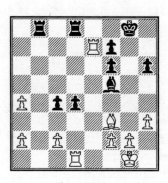

Now he is inching closer to a win. For example, 26 ♖c7 c3 27 ♖c1 ♖b2.

26 a5

A more intricate alternative is 26 ♖e2 ♖b2 27 ♖ed2 d3!.

Then 28 c3 ♖b6 and ...♖a6xa4 may be lost.

But White has the ingenious 28 cxd3! c3! 29 ♖xb2 cxb2 30 ♖b1 ♖b8 31 ♗e4 ♗e6 32 a5!.

The point is that 32...♗xa2 33 ♖xb2 ♖xb2 34 a6 may create a fortress after 34...♖b1+ 34 ♔h2 ♖a1 35 a7 ♗d5 36 ♗xd5 ♖xa7 37 g4.

26	...	♗xc2
27	♖c1	

Instead of that, Adhiban figures that a5-a6-a7 will distract Carlsen (27...d3 28 a6!).

27	...	♖b1!
28	♖xb1	♗xb1

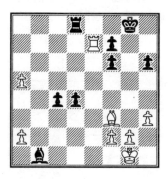

The a-pawn is as fast as the c-pawn. But it can't beat two connected pawns:

Black wins after 29 a6 c3 30 a7 c2 31 ♖c7 d3!.

29	♖c7	c3
30	♗d1	

Or 30 a6 c2 31 ♖xc2 ♗xc2 32 a7 d3 33 a8(♕) ♖xa8 34 ♗xa8 d2.

30	...	♖a8!
31	♖c5	♗xa2

32	♗c2	

Stiffer resistance comes from 32 ♗f3 and then 32...♖d8 33 a6 ♗b1 34 ♔f1.

Black's rook should stay on the a-file – 32...♖a7 threatens 33...♗b1 and 34...c2.

He would be winning slowly after 33 ♗e4 ♔f8 and ...♔e7-d6.

For example, 34 f3 ♔e7 35 ♔f2 ♔d6 36 ♖c6+ ♔d7.

Then 37 a6 f5! or 37 ♖c5 ♖c7!.

32	...	♗e6
33	♔f1	♖c8!
34	♖xc8+	♗xc8
35	♔e2	♗a6+
36	♔f3	d3

White resigns

54
The New Lasker

Remember Alexander Nikitin? He was the former trainer of Garry Kasparov who tested Carlsen's talent when he visited Moscow in 2004. Nikitin studied his career after that and 14 years later he detected the spirit of Emanuel Lasker in the following, shocking game.

Carlsen could have resigned after 17 moves when he lost a piece. But following Luskerian principles, he navigated his way from a -2.00 evaluation to one with even chances in seven moves. Then the real miracle begins.

Carlsen – Gawain Jones
Wijk aan Zee 2018
Sicilian Defense,
Dragon Variation (B83)

1	e4	c5
2	♘f3	d6
3	d4	cxd4
4	♘xd4	♘f6
5	♘c3	g6
6	♗e3	♗g7
7	f3	♘c6
8	♕d2	0-0
9	0-0-0	

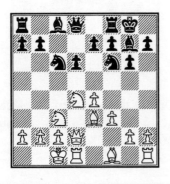

This position, rather than 9 ♗c4 ♗d7, became the prime Dragon battlefield in the first decades of the new century.

9	...	d5

For decades, books have claimed a White advantage now with 10 exd5 ♘xd5 11 ♘xc6 bxc6 12 ♘xd5 cxd5 13 ♕xd5 or 12 ♗d4 ♗xd4 13 ♕xd4 ♕b6 14 ♘a4.

10	♕e1	

But many masters are unconvinced by that. They try unusual recipes such as 10 ♔b1 ♘xd4 11 e5.

With 10 ♕e1 White lines up his rook against the enemy queen and discourages 10...dxe4? 11 ♘xc6.

10	...	e5

Leaving the center tension intact, such as with 10...e6, frees White to pursue h2-h4-h5.

For example, 11 h4 ♛c7 12 ♞db5 and 12 h5 have been popular.

11 ♞xc6 bxc6

12 exd5 ♞xd5

Carlsen appreciated Black's problems ten years previous when he played 12...cxd5? in a rapids match with Peter Leko and found his center under pressure after 13 ♝g5 ♝e6 14 ♝c4!.

13 ♝c4

The promising candidate moves ♞e4, ♝c5, ♝c4, h2-h4 and even ♚b1 suggest themselves. White's task is finding the proper move order.

The immediate 13 ♞e4 releases pressure on d5 and Black may be OK after 13...♛c7 14 ♝c5 ♜fd8.

Worse is 13 ♝c5? because of 13...♝h6+! 14 ♚b1 ♞xc3+.

13 ... ♝e6

The main line is 14 ♞e4 ♛c7 15 ♝c5 ♜fd8. But White has not proven a major advantage with 14 g4, 14 h4 or 14 ♛h4.

14 ♚b1

Carlsen tries a relatively new idea. He allows Black to liquidate two pairs of pieces with 14...♞xc3+ 15 ♛xc3 ♛e7 and a swap of bishops. Then the potential weakness of Black's a7- and c6-pawns grows.

Black would like to get out of the d-file pin but his queen does not have a good move: 14...♛c7 15 ♞xd5 is an unsound pawn sacrifice and 14...♛d7 invites 15 ♞e4 and ♞c5.

14 ... ♜e8

Gawain Jones, a Dragon expert, had had some success with 14...♜b8, which offers the a-pawn.

But here he plays another principled move, lining up his rook against the e1-queen.

15 ♞e4

One of the points of 14...♜e8 is that 15 h4 ♛c7 is now a sound sacrifice, 16 ♞xd5 cxd5 17 ♝xd5 ♝xd5 18 ♜xd5 e4!.

By opening the long diagonal Black threatens 19...♕b7.

He would stand well after 19 fxe4 ♖xe4, e.g. 20 ♖d3 ♖ae8 and 20 ♕d2? ♗xb2! 21 ♔xb2 ♕b7+ and 22...♖xe3.

15	...	f5
16	♘g5	

This prepares to weaken the Black kingside with 17 ♘xe6 and 18 g4!.

This is better than 16 ♘c5 ♗f7!, when 17...e4! would threaten to make the e-file dangerous to White.

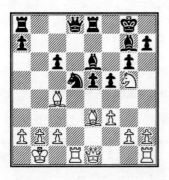

16	...	♗c8!

Jones blitzed off all of his moves in four minutes and this is a good one.

At first it seemed that he had made 17...h6 a serious threat.

For example, 17 h4 h6 18 ♘h3? ♗e6 followed by ...♕b8 is excellent for Black.

But 18 ♘e4! is playable because 18...fxe4? 19 fxe4 regains the

knight favorably. Instead, 18...♗e6 19 ♘c5 ♗f7 would be balanced.

For example, 20 g4 e4 21 fxe4? ♕b6!, threatening mate on b2.

17	g4??

What happened was so shocking that on-line spectators hunted for a deep reason why 17...f4 doesn't win a piece. There was none.

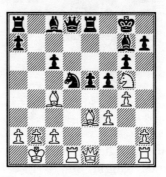

17	...	f4!

At first, the combination 18 ♗xf4 exf4 19 ♖xd5 looks good.

White would then indeed win after 19...♖xe1+ 20 ♖d1+! ♔h8 21 ♘f7+ or 20...♔f8 21 ♘xh7+ ♔e7 22 ♖hxe1+.

But 19...cxd5! is the simple refutation.

Then 20 ♗xd5+ ♕xd5 21 ♕xe8+ ♗f8 (22 ♘xh7 ♔xh7 23 ♕xf8 ♗e6) and wins.

Carlsen admitted afterwards that he had simply blundered.

"Resignation would in principle be a viable option for White," said his trainer Peter Heine Nielsen.

18   h4

It took Magnus eight minutes to recover and play this.

18   ...   fxe3

19   ♕xe3

He still had pressure on the pinned knight and a threat of 20 ♕b3!.

Jones took 15 minutes to consider two ways to meet it.

He would have a solid advantage after 19...♗e6 20 ♕e4 ♖b8!.

For example, 21 ♗b3 ♕f6 and 22 ♘xe6 ♕xe6 23 ♖xd5? ♖xb3!.

19   ...   h6!

But this is better. Carlsen would have scant compensation for the lost bishop after 20 ♕b3 hxg5 21 ♖xd5 cxd5 22 ♗xd5+ ♔f8 23 ♗xa8 ♗e6.

The same for 20 ♕e4 hxg5 21 ♖xd5 cxd5 22 ♗xd5+ ♗e6.

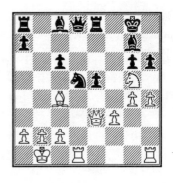

20   ♕c5!

Nikitin, in the Russian magazine *64*, felt Carlsen was following Lasker's advice of what to do in lost positions:

Don't panic, don't despair. Your opponent expects you to resign soon. That's good. He may become careless.

20   ...   ♗b7!

Or sloppy, as with 20...hxg5?!.

That sharply diminishes his advantage after 21 ♕xc6 ♗e6 22 ♗xd5 ♗xd5 23 ♖xd5 ♕b6 24 ♕c4!.

Black might have to try to win, after 24...♕e6 25 hxg5 e4! 26 fxe4 ♖ac8, in an endgame battle of three extra pawns against Black's bishop, 27 ♕a4 ♕xe4 28 ♕xe4 ♖xe4.

21   ♘e4

Now 21...♗f8 22 ♕g1! could be followed by 23 g5 and 24 ♘f6+.

That poses the kind of problem that allowed Lasker to escape so often from lost positions: Should Black give back some of his extra material?

For example, 22...♕b6 23 ♘f6+ ♔h8 24 ♘xe8 ♖xe8 would win after 25 ♕e1? ♘e3.

But Black's chances of winning an endgame after 25 ♖d3 ♕xg1+ 26 ♖xg1 would not be great.

Computers prefer 22...♔h8 and then 23 g5 h5 24 ♘f6 ♖e7.

But Black still has to untangle his pieces after, for example, 25 ♗b3 ♕b6 26 ♕e1 and ♕e4.

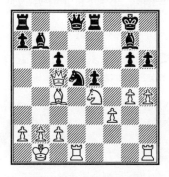

21 ... ♖e6?!

Like 21...♗f8, this move stops ♘d6. However, Black's greatest problem since move 15 was having his king sit at the end of the c4-bishop's diagonal.

He could solve that with 21...♔h8!.

Then 22 ♘d6 ♕e7 looks awkward. But Black threatens to liquidate with 23...♖ed8 or 23...♗f8.

Carlsen would be out of tactical surprises and facing another

difficult endgame after 23 ♗b3 ♗f8 24 ♘xb7 ♕xc5 25 ♘xc5 ♗xc5 26 ♗xd5 cxd5 27 ♖xd5 ♗e3 and ...♗f4.

Black does not have to give up a pawn and may prefer 23...♖fd8 24 ♘xb7 ♕xb7 and ...♘f4, again with a likely win.

22 h5! ♕b6?

This stops the ♕g1 idea. But much better was 22...g5, or 22...♗f8 first.

For example, 22...g5 23 ♗b3 ♗f8 24 ♕f2 would threaten 25 c4.

Black still has work to do after 24...♕b6 25 ♕h2 ♕c7 but Carlsen would be running out of tactics.

23 g5!

He can allow a trade of queens, 23...♕xc5 24 ♘xc5, because of 24...♖e7 25 ♘xb7 ♖xb7 26 ♖xd5! cxd5 27 ♗xd5+.

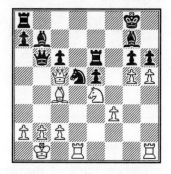

23 ... hxg5?

Lasker won lost positions when his opponents panicked after most of their edge evaporated. That's the case here.

Black would remain somewhat better after 23...♗f8 24 ♕xb6 axb6 25 gxh6 gxh5.

The same goes for 24 ♕g1 ♕xg1 25 ♖dxg1 ♗e7!.

Black has good winning chances in the endgame (26 gxh6 g5! 27 ♘xg5 ♖xh6!). But it would no longer be the easy win that seemed inevitable four moves ago.

24   ♕a3!

Played instantly. Carlsen now threatens 25 ♘xg5 ♖ee8? 26 ♕d6 and wins.

Nikitin pointed out that since 27 g4??, Jones had spent 68 minutes and Carlsen spent only 15 minutes. Magnus was doing the blitzing now.

24   ...   ♖b8

His biggest think of the game, 13 minutes, came here.

The reason is that on 25 ♘xg5 ♗f8 26 ♕d3 ♗a6! Black seems to be making progress with his threat of ...♕xb2 mate.

But after 27 b3 ♗xc4 28 ♕xc4 ♖d6 neither side can improve significantly.

For example, 29 ♘e4! ♖e6 30 ♘g5 ♖e7 31 ♕d3! ♘f4 32 ♕c4+ ♘d5.

That means Carlsen has battled back to rough equality. He was thinking of playing for more.

25   b3!

Nikitin felt this move was pure Lasker. Black's tactics on the b-file are over and Carlsen is preparing 26 ♕c1! and ♕xg5.

25   ...   ♕d8?

Now it was Jones' turn to pass up possible equality.

After 25...gxh5 26 ♖xh5 ♖g6 White could seek a draw by repetition, 27 ♕e7 ♕d8 28 ♕c5 ♕b6 29 ♕e7.

That looks like his best, because 27 ♕c1 ♕d8 28 ♖g1 ♕e7 29 ♖hxg5 ♖xg5 30 ♖xg5 ♖f8 is looking good for Black again.

26   ♕xa7!

Carlsen's queen maneuvers in this game are a testament to the remarkable geometry of the chessboard.

He takes the meaningless a-pawn so his queen can go strongly to g1!

For example, 26...♖e7 27 ♕g1 and 28 hxg6 or 28 ♕xg5.

Another illustration is 26...♔f8 27 ♖dg1 ♕c7 28 ♖xg5 ♖a8 29 ♕g1! with crushing pressure.

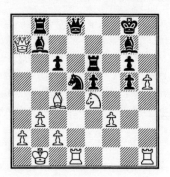

26 ... gxh5?

One of the prettiest wins comes after 26...♗h6 27 hxg6 ♔g7.

Black has gotten his king to apparent safety and will reinforce it with 28...♖xg6.

But White has 28 f4!!.

Engines show that 28...exf4 29 ♕d4+ ♔xg6 loses to 30 ♖xh6+ ♔xh6 31 ♖h1+ ♔g6 32 ♗d3!.

They also find a win in 28...gxf4 29 ♖dg1, e.g. 29...♖xg6 30 ♖xg6+ ♔xg6 31 ♕g1+ ♔g5 32 ♗d3!.

27	♖xh5	♖g6
28	♖xg5!	♖xg5
29	♘xg5	

Black is lost because his queenside pieces are immobile (29...♖a8? 30 ♕xb7; 29...♗a8 30 ♕f7+).

29	...	♕c8
30	♖g1	♖a8
31	♕b6	♖a6
32	♕c5	

There are various final scenarios, such as 32...♕f8 33 ♘e6 ♕xc5 34 ♖xg7+ ♔h8 35 ♘xc5.

32	...	♕d7
33	♘e4	♔h8
34	♕f2	♕e7

Black stops 35 ♕h4+ ♔g8 36 ♘f6+ and makes his hopelessness obvious. The rest needs no comment:

35 ♗xa6 ♗xa6 36 ♕h2+ ♔g8 37 ♕h6 ♕a7 38 ♕e6+ ♔f8 39 ♖g5 ♘e3 40 ♕d6+ ♔f7 41 ♘c5 ♗c8 42 ♖xg7+ Resigns

Everyone knows how to play well in good positions, Nikitin concluded, quoting Lasker. What you need to learn is how to play well in bad ones.

333

55
Favorably with Fischer

When Carlsen turned 29 in November 2019, the renowned chess columnist Leonard Barden noted that he had won eight elite tournaments that year. Barden said this compared favorably with Bobby Fischer's four great tournament wins in 1970 and Garry Kasparov's four in 1988. Carlsen added two more big tournament wins before 2020 began. His string of 2019 successes began where it often did, on the North Sea coast.

Jorden van Foreest – Carlsen
Wijk aan Zee 2019
Sicilian Defense,
Sveshnikov Variation (B33)

1	e4	c5
2	♘f3	♘c6
3	d4	cxd4
4	♘xd4	♘f6
5	♘c3	e5
6	♘db5	d6

7 ♘d5

This was once a major alternative to 7 ♗g5. But that was when this opening, once called the Lasker, then the Pelikan and then the Chelyabinsk variation, was just coming into popularity as the Sveshnikov.

But 7 ♘d5 fell into disuse, for no particular reason, while 7 ♗g5 was analyzed well past move 20. Carlsen knew the theory for Black.

For example, one of his 2003 games went 7 ♗g5 a6 8 ♘a3 b5 9 ♗xf6 gxf6 10 ♘d5 f5 11 c3 ♗g7 12 exf5 ♗xf5 13 ♘c2 0-0 14 ♘ce3 ♗e6 15 ♗d3 f5 16 ♗c2 f4! 17 ♕h5 ♖f7 18 ♗xh7+ ♔f8 19 ♗f5 ♕e8 20 ♗xe6 ♕xe6 21 ♕g4 ♕h6 22 ♘f5 ♕e6.

This is all "book" and had been played dozens of times before. Carlsen won after 23 ♘fe3 ♕h6 24 ♘c2? e4!. The over-analysis of 7 ♗g5 led to revived interest in 7 ♘d5.

7 ... ♘xd5

The threat of a knight check on c7 enables White to change the pawn structure so that he gains queenside space.

8   exd5

Black's biggest decision of the opening comes here: What should he do with the attacked c6-knight?

The best middlegame squares for it would be d4 and c5. Whether he can carry off the maneuvers ...♘e7-f5-d4 or ...♘b8-d7-c5 can depend on what White does.

8   ...   ♘e7

There are tactical differences between the two knight moves.

For example, now 9 c4 a6?? 10 ♕a4! wins material with the threatened discovered check.

With 8...♘b8 this does not work because of 10...♘d7!.

9   c4

There are also tactical benefits to 9 c3. One is 9...♘g6 10 ♕a4 ♗d7 when White has 11 ♕b4 ♕b8 12 ♕c4! and threatens ♘c7+.

If Black has to play ...♗xb5 he will be seriously weak on light squares.

But 9 c3 has fallen out of favor because of 9...♘f5. Then 10 ♕a4? ♗d7 is harmless.

9   ...   ♘g6!?

As the 7 ♘d5 variation evolved, it was found that getting this knight to d4 does not solve Black's problems.

For example, 9...♘f5 10 ♗d3 ♗e7 11 0-0 0-0 12 ♔h1 removes the White king from the g1-a7 diagonal and makes f2-f4 safer.

After 12...a6 13 ♘c3 ♘d4 he can assure himself of the better prospects with 14 f4!.

But with the knight on g6, he is hesitant to play a middlegame based on f2-f4 because of his weakness on dark squares after a double exchange on f4.

10   ♕a4

A traditional middlegame strategy in this pawn structure is to engineer c4-c5 and create a passed c- or d-pawn.

To do this White usually needs the support of ♗e3 followed by ♖c1, b2-b4 and ♘a4.

But Black generates quick counterplay from ...f5. For example, 10 ♗d3 ♗e7 11 0-0 0-0 12 ♗e3 a6 13 ♘c3 f5!.

Then 14 ♘a4 ♗d7 15 ♘b6 ♖b8 is bad and 14 f3 ♗g5 15 ♗f2 ♘f4 is no more than equal.

10   ...   ♗d7

11   ♕b4

Carlsen had prepared the Sveshnikov Variation for the 2018 World Championship match and found himself in this position five times over a period of a few months.

In one of the match games he defended the d6-pawn with 11...♗f5 and was worse after 12 h4 h5. He repeated this against Caruana at Karlsruhe 2019. He drew both games.

11   ...   ♕b8

12   h4

Since Black's future middlegame counterplay will most likely come from ...f5, it will be riskier if he stops 13 h5 with 12...h5.

12   ...   h5

But this is safer than 12...♗e7 13 h5 or even 12...a6 13 h5!

(13...axb5 14 hxg6 fxg6 15 cxb5 followed by a2-a4-a5).

13   ♗e3

Van Foreest makes a positional threat of 14 c5 as well as a tactical threat of 14 ♕a5 and ♘c7+.

For instance, 14 ♕a5 b6 15 ♗xb6! axb6 16 ♕xa8 ♕xa8 17 ♘c7+.

13   ...   a6

14   ♘c3   f5

Carlsen's last move was the first departure from "book." In one of the dramatic playoff games of the championship match, he drove the White queen back with 14...a5 15 ♕b3 a4 16 ♕d1.

But that made ♗e2xh5 a threat. He was clearly worse until Caruana rushed c4-c5 and lost.

15   0-0-0   ♗e7

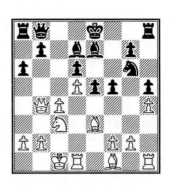

16   g3

Black should not be troubled by 16 ♘a4 f4 17 ♗b6 0-0.

But computers point out 17 ♗d3! ♘xh4 18 ♗b6 is trickier.

They find the complications tending to benefit White after 18...♘xg2 19 ♗a5 ♗g4 20 c5! ♗xd1 21 ♔xd1.

16 ...   0-0

Carlsen had drawn 21 straight games in "classical" time controls before this and was expected to take greater risks against his much-lower-rated opponent.

Castling is risky because he is more or less offering the h5-pawn as a sacrifice.

But after a move like 16...e4 White can proceed favorably on the queenside with 17 ♘a4 and ♘b6.

For example, 17...b5 18 ♘b6 bxc4 19 ♕xc4 ♗b5 20 ♕b3 ♖a7 21 ♗xb5+.

Or 19...♖a7 20 ♔b1 0-0 21 ♘xd7 ♖xd7 22 ♗d4, with balanced chances.

17 ♗e2

Carlsen could have met 17 ♘a4 b5 18 ♘b6 bxc4 19 ♕xc4 favorably with 19...♗b5.

For instance, 20 ♕b3 ♖a7 21 ♗xb5 axb5 22 ♕xb5 ♖xa2 or 22 ♔b1 ♖b7.

17 ...   e4

18 ♗d4

His young Dutch opponent talked himself out of 18 ♗xh5 ♘e5.

He may have seen 19 ♗e2 b5! and detected dangers in 20 cxb5 axb5 21 ♗xb5? ♗xb5 22 ♕xb5 ♕c8! and ...♖b8/...♘c4.

But 21 ♗g5 or 21 ♔b1 ♗f6 22 ♗g5 is a better way of trading dark-squared bishops than what happens now.

18 ...   ♗f6

Now 19 ♗xh5 ♘e5 gives Black dark-square compensation after 20 ♗xe5 ♗xe5 and ...♕a7.

Or after 20 ♔b1 ♘d3 and 20 ♗e2 ♘d3+ 21 ♗xd3 ♗xd4.

Better, in the last line, is 21 ♖xd3! exd3 22 ♗xf6 dxe2 23 ♗d4, with unclear chances after 23...b5.

19 ♗xf6   ♖xf6

The bishop swap didn't solve White's dark-square problem, e.g. 20 ♗xh5 ♘e5 21 ♗e2 ♕c7.

Then ...a5/...♕c5 is one good option and 22...♖c8 (23 b3? b5) is another.

20   ♕b6!

Carlsen would have seized the advantage after 20 ♔b1 ♕a7!.

20   ...   ♘e5

Chances would again be equal after 21 b3 and 22 ♔b2.

21   ♔b1   ♗e8!

Carlsen prepares ...♗g6/...f4 as well as ...♘d7 to drive the queen back.

22   ♖d2   ♘d7

23   ♕d4   ♕c7

The position remains balanced but Black has more ways to improve his chances.

One is to threaten the c4-pawn with ...♘e5 and ...♖c8. If White defends it with b2-b3, he makes ...b5! possible.

A second way is to play for ...f4, after ...♘e5, ...♗g6 and ...♖af8.

But Black has to make sure that ...f4 cannot be safely met by ♘xe4.

The third way is to trade queens, such as with ...b6 and ...♕c5. That makes the ...f4 plan more feasible.

24   ♘d1

White is concerned with Carlsen's first option, an attack on the c4-pawn from ...♘e5/...♖c8. The right way to anticipate that is to play a rook to c1 or c2 and then b2-b3.

24   ...   ♘e5

25   ♘e3?   f4!

White's knight can no longer answer this with ♘xe4.

26   gxf4   ♖xf4

The f2-pawn is doomed now and perhaps the h4-pawn as well.

After 27 ♘d1 ♗g6 28 ♔a1 ♖af8 Black would threaten 29...♘f3 30 ♗xf3 exf3 31 ♕-moves ♖xc4. He also has a strong ...♘d3.

White cannot block the f-file with 27 ♘g2 ♖f6 28 ♕e3 ♗g6 29 ♘f4 because of 29...♖xf4! 30 ♕xf4 e3+.

338

Carlsen would be close to a win after 31 ♖c2 exf2 32 ♕xf2 b5!.

27	♖g1	♗g6
28	♔a1	

White is approaching the desperation stage. He might have tried 28 ♖xg6 ♘xg6 29 ♘g2 ♖f6 30 ♕xe4.

But it doesn't quite work after 30...♕e7 and loses after 30...♖af8 31 ♗xh5 ♘f4.

28	...	♖af8

There was nothing wrong with 28...♖xf2. But in sharp positions Carlsen tends to prefer moves that keep his pieces mutually protected. Now 29 ♘d1 b5! is strong.

29 c5!

A swindle try in the style of the young Magnus.

White would rebound after 29...♕xc5 30 ♕xc5 dxc5 31 ♖g5!.

The deeper idea was 29...dxc5 30 ♕c3 and 31 d6.

If Black blocks the d-pawn with 30...♕d6, White can try 31 ♗xh5! ♗xh5 32 ♘c4 since 32...♘xc4?? 33 ♕xg7 is mate.

But 32...♕f6 33 ♘xe5 ♖xf2 wins, since 34 ♖xf2 ♖xf2 35 ♖xg7+ ♔xg7 36 ♘g4+ fails to 36...♕d4.

29	...	♖xf2
30	♕c3?	

There were still swindling chances in 30 c6!.

After 30...bxc6 31 dxc6 the d5-square is freed for his knight and the b3-g8 diagonal is opened.

White would be back in the game after 31...♘xc6? 32 ♕d5+.

For example, 32...♖8f7 32 ♗c4 or 32...♗f7 32 ♕g5. He even wins after 32...♔h7?? 32 ♖xg6!.

Nevertheless, Carlsen should still have won after 31...♕xc6 32 ♘d5 ♕b7 or 32...♖f1+ 33 ♖d1! ♖xd1+ 34 ♖xd1 ♖f7.

30	...	♕xc5
31	♕xc5	dxc5
32	d6	♔h7
33	d7	♘f3!

White resigns

It was lost anyway (33 ♖c2 ♖d8 and ...♖xd7).

56
Sound Blunder

Judith Polgar used the following game to illustrate the sophisticated grandmaster sense of "blunder." It does not mean hanging the queen or allowing checkmate as in an amateur game. Rather, it is a minor oversight. In this case, Magnus's mistake turned out to be a sound pawn sacrifice that led to a pyrotechnic finish.

Carlsen – Richard Rapport
Wijk aan Zee 2019
Sicilian Defense,
Taimanov Variation (B47)

1	e4	c5
2	♘f3	e6
3	d4	cxd4
4	♘xd4	♘c6
5	♘c3	♕c7
6	g3	

Another rare-for-Magnus move, instead of 6 ♗e3.

6	...	a6
7	♗g2	♘f6
8	0-0	d6

Black's move seems obvious but 9...♗e7 10 ♖e1 has been considered the main line for decades.

9	♘xc6

After instead 9 ♖e1, theory recommends 9...♗d7 10 ♘xc6 ♗xc6.

A major reason is that 9...♗e7?! allows 10 ♘xc6 bxc6 11 e5! dxe5 12 ♖xe5!.

Thanks to tactics (12...♕xe5? 13 ♗xc6+) this leaves Black with weakened queenside pawns.

That may not sound like much but in grandmaster chess it is a significant advantage.

9	...	bxc6
10	♘a4	

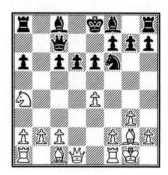

This begins a common *priyome*, a positional plan, of c2-c4 followed by b2-b3, ♗b2 and ♖c1.

White can get a strategic advantage after routine moves

340

such as 10...♗e7 11 c4 0-0 12 b3
♗b7 13 ♗b2 and now 13...d5?
14 cxd5 cxd5 15 ♖c1 or 14...exd5
15 cxd5 cxd5 16 ♖c1.

10	...	♖b8
11	c4	c5
12	b3	

Another obvious move but a
new one, in place of 12 ♘c3 and
12 f4.

12	...	♗e7
13	♗b2	0-0
14	♕e1	

Not a move many grandmasters
would make. He seeks a positional
advantage from 15 e5!.

But 14 f4 serves the same
purpose, since 14...♗b7 15 e5
♘e8 16 ♕e2 is an evident
advantage.

14	...	♘d7
15	♖d1	♗b7

16	♕c3

Magnus-watchers wondered if
he chose 14 ♕e1 because he
intended 16 ♗c3 and 17 ♗a5.

That isn't at all bad as 16...♗c6
17 ♗a5 ♕b7 18 ♘c3 ♘f6 19 ♕e2
indicates.

Then a trade of bishops,
19...♗d8 20 ♗xd8 ♖fxd8, allows
White to pressure the d6-pawn
with 21 ♖d3 and ♖fd1 while
Black shoots for ...a5-a4.

16	...	♗f6

Another unfavorable pawn
structure for Black arises from
16...♘f6 17 e5.

17	♕d2	♗e7
18	♕c3	♗f6
19	♕d2	♗e7
20	f4	

After a curious repetition of
moves, Carlsen threatens 21 e5!,
based on 21...♗xg2 22 ♔xg2
dxe5? 23 ♕xd7. This idea
apparently stuck in his mind and
led to his oversight at move 25.

20	...	e5

The chief alternative is
20...♘b6.

Then on 21 ♘xb6 ♕xb6 Black can become fatally passive after 22 f5 exf5? 23 exf5.

But 22...e5 is better. White would be better after 23 ♗c3 and ♗a5. However, he may have preferred to keep wood on with 21 ♘c3 because...

21	♗c3!	♗c6
22	♗a5	♕b7
23	♘c3	

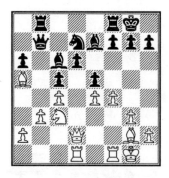

...his chances are greater with knights on the board. Now he can watch for any opportunity for a strong ♘d5.

For example, 23...♖be8 24 f5 ♕b8 25 ♘d5 ♗xd5 26 ♕xd5 is very good for him (and 24...♕a8 25 ♗c7 costs a pawn).

If Black just passes, such as with 24...♖c8, White has to decide whether to prepare g3-g4-g5 or go straight for ♘d5 followed by exd5 after Black captures the knight. He would have splendid winning chances.

| 23 | ... | exf4? |

24 gxf4

Exchanging pawns is a strategic error that forces Black to be constantly aware of e4-e5 now.

For example, 24...♘f6 25 e5 dxe5 26 ♗xc6 ♕xc6 27 fxe5 ♘e8 28 ♘d5 leaves him in bad shape.

| 24 | ... | ♖fe8 |

As ugly as 24...♘b6 is, it has one benefit: It can't be refuted quickly.

25	e5!	♗xg2
26	♕xg2	dxe5

This was Carlsen's "blunder." He thought he was winning a pawn because ...dxe5 would leave the d7-knight hanging (as it would be after 26...♕xg2+? 27 ♔xg2).

27 ♘d5

"I sat there for one minute cursing myself," he said later. Then he saw how strong this is.

Now 27...♗f6 28 ♗c7 ♖bc8?? 29 ♘xf6+ loses Black's queen and 28...exf4 29 ♗xb8 ♕xb8 30 ♕g4 and ♕xf4 would be insufficient compensation for the Exchange.

Similarly, 27...♔h8 28 fxe5 ♘xe5 29 ♗c7.

This was "pure luck," Carlsen said. "because realistically I wouldn't have played e5 if I'd known that it loses a pawn."

27   ...   e4

Carlsen also calculated 27...♗d6 28 ♘c7! so that 28...♗xc7 29 ♕xb7 ♖xb7 30 ♖xd7 again wins the Exchange.

28   ♗c3

There is no precise definition of a "bind" but this is an illustration. Black has no counterplay and faces a powerful buildup of White pieces.

28   ...   f6

For example, 28...♗f8 29 f5 would be followed by an unstoppable ♖de1-e3 and ♖f4-g4.

29   ♔h1   ♔h8

30   ♖g1   ♗f8

31   ♘e3!

Magnus has so much attacking capital that he should not sell it cheaply with 31 ♘xf6 ♘xf6 32 ♗xf6.

31   ...   ♕c6

His winning idea is ♖d5-h5 and ♕h3 or ♘f5xg7.

Black can stop that with 31...♘b6 but 32 ♗xf6! will be followed by ♗c3, ♘f5 and f4-f5-f6.

32   ♖d5!   ♕e6

33   ♖h5   ♕f7

Otherwise 34 ♘f5 and ♘xg7.

34   ♕h3   g6

On 34...h6 35 ♘f5 ♔h7 Black stops the immediate ♘xh6.

But he is helpless to stop 36 ♖h4 followed by 37 ♖hg4.

35   ♖h4

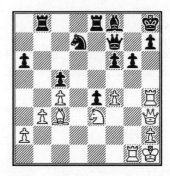

Now 35...♔g8 36 ♖xg6+! ♕xg6 37 ♖g4 is lost because his attack continues, e.g. 37...♖e7 38 ♖xg6+ hxg6 39 ♕g4 ♖g7 40 ♕e6+ and ♘d5.

35 ...   ♖b6

No better is 35...♕g7 36 ♘d5 when White threatens 37 f5 g5 38 ♖xg5+! and wins (38...♕xg5 39 ♖xh7+ ♔g8 40 ♖xd7 ♗g7 41 ♘xf6+ and mates).

36 f5   ♘e5

37 ♘d5

37 ...   ♖d6

A slower death is 37...g5 38 ♖xe4 ♖d6 39 ♗xe5 ♖xe5 40 ♖xe5 fxe5 41 ♖xg5.

38 fxg6   ♘xg6

39 ♗xf6+   ♖xf6

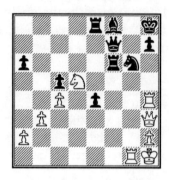

40 ♖xh7+! Resigns

In view of 40...♕xh7 41 ♕xh7+ ♔xh7 42 ♘xf6+ and ♘xe8(+).

57
Swindlee

After winning so many games by swindles early in his career, Magnus increasingly found himself on the other side of the board – holding substantial middlegame advantages against opponents who wanted to swindle him, as in Game 55.

His opponent in this game, Peter Svidler, has been one of his most difficult opponents. By 2008 Carlsen outrated him. But he didn't win one of their classical time limit games until five years later. He equalized their score – two wins apiece and sixteen draws – in this game.

Peter Svidler – Carlsen
Baden-Baden 2019
Sicilian Defense,
Closed Variation (B30)

1	e4	c5
2	♘f3	♘c6
3	♘c3	e5

This is a Nimzovichian blockade move. It rules out transpositions to normal Sicilians by 4 d4.

A drawback is surrendering pawn control of d5. If White's king's knight were on e2 – say, after 2 ♘c3 ♘c6 3 ♘ge2 e5 – he could reinforce a knight on its outpost, 4 ♘d5 ♘f6 5 ♘ec3.

4	♗c4	♗e7

White's domination of d5 was once considered good enough for a solid plus. But after the inevitable trade of knights and the likely swap of dark-squared bishops (...♗e7-g5), only computers can detect a meaningful edge.

5	d3	d6
6	♘d2	

This is another way (♘f1-e3) of reinforcing control of d5.

At one time, 6 0-0 ♘f6 7 ♘g5 was considered favorable. But 7...0-0 8 f4 ♗g4 and 9...exf4 10 ♗xf4 ♘d4 proved to be an antidote.

6	...	♘f6

White has greater opportunities for favorable complications after 6...♗g5 7 h4 (7...♗xh4? 8 ♕h5).

7	♘f1	♘d7
8	♘d5	♘b6
9	♘xb6	axb6!?

The queen would be misplaced after 9...♕xb6 and likely to return to d8 soon.

There are also tactical reasons for 9...axb6.

10 c3

One is 10 ♘e3 b5! 11 ♗xb5? ♕a5+.

After 11 ♗b3 ♘d4 Black would have the better set of doubled pawns following the exchange 12...♘xb3 13 cxb3.

He would also have the better middlegame plan after 12 c3 ♘xb3 13 ♕xb3 ♗d7 followed by ...0-0/ ...♔h8 and ...f5.

Of course, 12 ♗d5 preserves the bishop. But that takes away the best square for his knight. You can't have everything.

10	...	0-0
11	♘e3	♗g5

A trade of dark squared bishops is virtually inevitable.

12 0-0

Engines say 12...♗e6 13 ♘d5 ♗xc1 14 ♕xc1 or 12...♗xe3 13 ♗xe3 ♗e6 14 ♗xe6 favors White slightly.

12	...	♔h8

Signalling that ...f5 is coming.

The natural 13 ♘d5 ♗xc1 14 ♕xc1 f5 15 f4 helps White after, for example, 15...♗e6 16 fxe5 ♘xe5 17 exf5 because of that knight on d5.

13 a3?!

By protecting the a-pawn, Svidler can retake with his rook on c1 later on.

After the natural 13 ♗d2 f5 we get a position like the game after 14 ♘xf5 ♗xd2 15 ♕xd2 ♗xf5 16 exf5 d5 17 ♗b3 ♖xf5 except that he can play 18 f4! more safely.

13	...	f5!
14	♘xf5	

When he chose 13 a3 Svidler may have intended 14 ♘d5 ♗xc1 15 ♖xc1 and 16 ♕b3.

But 15...f4! would threaten 16...f3 and 17...♕g5.

It is risky to try 16 ♕b3 f3 17 g3 ♕d7 18 ♔h1 ♘e7!.

For example, e.g. 19 ♘xb6?? ♕h3 20 ♖g1 ♖f6! and mates.

Chances would be roughly equal after 19 ♘e3 ♖f6 20 g4 ♕d8 but that's not the kind of middlegame Svidler intended.

14 ... ♗xc1

15 ♖xc1

Dead even is 15 ♕xc1 ♗xf5 16 exf5 d5 17 ♗a2 ♖xf5 or 17 ♗b5 ♖xf5 18 f4 ♘a7 19 ♗a4 ♘c6.

15 ... ♗xf5

16 exf5 d5

17 ♗a2 ♖xf5

With his queen on d1 rather than c1, Svidler has options such as ♕b3 or ♕g4.

His problem is that Carlsen can improve his position with simple moves, ...♕d6, ...♖af8 and ...♘e7. Then he could begin to think about mate after ...♖5f6-h6!.

That indicates that time is on Black's side and that Svidler should change the pawn structure before it is too late.

For example, 18 ♕b3 ♘e7 19 ♖ce1 ♕d6 20 d4.

That looks good after 20...exd4 21 cxd4 cxd4? 22 ♕d3 and ♕xd4.

But it favors Black after 21...c4!.

18 ♕g4

Instead, Svidler tries to open the position with forcing moves. His heavy pieces would get into play after 18...♘e7 19 ♖ae1 ♕d6 20 f4! (20...exf4? 21 ♖xe7).

18 ... ♖f6

Computers look at strange continuations such as the queen maneuver 18...♖f4 19 ♕e6 d4 20 ♕b3.

347

But 18...♖f6 threatens to stop f2-f4 with 19...♕d6. This makes it much easier to calculate the next few moves and come to a favorable conclusion.

19   f4   exf4

Now 20 ♖xf4?? allows 20...♘e5 21 ♕g3 ♖xf4 22 ♕xf4 ♘xd3.

20   ♕g5!

This was the first time in the game that Magnus *had* to calculate.

His d-pawn is attacked and 20...♘e7? 21 ♖xf4 would give White what he wants.

A crucial line to work out was 20...d4 21 ♖xf4 dxc3.

This wins after 22 ♖xf6? gxf6 or 22 ♖xc3? ♘d4!.

Carlsen would have an extra pawn after 22 bxc3 ♖xa3 23 ♗c4. Is there anything better?

20   ...   ♕f8!

He must have also considered 20...f3, and seen that it could lead into endgames that are either balanced or slightly favorable.

For example, 21 ♖xf3 ♖xf3 22 ♕xd8+ ♖xd8 23 gxf3 d4 or 23...g5.

But with 20...♕f8! Magnus judges that his f4-pawn is his most valuable asset and it pays to keep it.

21   ♕xd5   ♖d8

His attack would roll on now after 22 ♕e4 ♖e8 23 ♕f3 ♘e5 24 ♕-moves f3.

22   ♕f3

Svidler will try to turn Carlsen, a master swindler, into a swindlee.

One way was 22 ♕g5 ♖xd3 23 ♖ce1.

That sets a trap of 23...♖d2? 24 ♖xf4! ♖xf4 25 ♕xf4 and 25...♕xf4?? 26 ♖e8+ and mates.

Svidler might hold a pawn-down endgame, such as after 23...♖d8 24 ♖e6 ♖d6 25 ♖xd6 ♕xd6 26 ♕d5 ♕xd5 27 ♗xd5.

Carlsen would elude traps with 23...h6 24 ♕h5 g6 but then he is miles from winning. Svidler had a deeper trap in mind.

22 ...   ♞e5

23 ♕e4

He is trying to lure Magnus into 23...♞xd3 and then 24 ♖cd1!.

Then 24...♕d6?? 25 ♗c4 walks into a losing pin – while 24...♖fd6 25 ♗b1 balances the chances (25...♞xb2?? 26 ♕xh7 mate).

The key continuation after 24 ♖cd1! is 24...♞xb2 25 ♗b1 g6 (forced) 26 ♖xd8 ♕xd8 and then 27 ♕e2! ♞a4 28 ♖d1!.

The swindle unfolds after 28...♕f8 29 ♖d7 and 30 ♕e5! (or 29...♞xc3 30 ♕d3 and ♖d8).

Better is 28...♕g8. Then 29 ♕e7 or the trappier 29 ♖d6 would draw.

But 29 ♕b5 ♞xc3 30 ♕b2! wins a piece (30...♞xd1 31 ♕xf6+ ♕g7 32 ♕d8+ and ♕xd1).

23 ...   ♞g4!

Carlsen tightens his kingside bind. Besides ...♞e3 he threatens 24...♖e8 25 ♕f3 ♞e5 26 ♕-moves f3.

24 ♖ce1   ♞e3

25 ♖f2

White could try for a fortress with 25 ♖xf4 ♖xf4 26 ♕xe3 followed by ♗d5/c4 if allowed.

For instance, 26...♕f6 27 ♗d5 ♖xd5? 28 ♕xf4!.

But Black could make progress on dark squares after 26...♕d6 27 ♗d5 ♖ff8 28 c4 ♕f6!.

That is clear following 29 b3 ♕b2 or 29 ♕e2 ♕d4+ 30 ♔h1 h6 and ...♖f2.

25 ...   ♖e8

26 ♕xb7?   g5!

His plan is ...g4 followed by either ...f3 or ...♕h6/...♖ef8 and ...g3.

For example, 27 h3 g4 28 hxg4 ♘xg4 29 ♖xe8 ♕xe8 30 ♖f3 ♕e1+ 31 ♖f1 ♕e3+ and mates.

To keep the game going Svidler had to play 26 ♕f3! g5 27 h3.

Then Black has to build slowly towards a knockout, for example with 27...♖e7 and ...♕h6 or ...♕e8.

27	♖fe2	g4
28	♖f2	♕h6
29	♕c7	

This covers g3 but does not stop 29...g3 in view of 30 hxg3 ♖ff8! 31 ♖xf4 ♘g4! and wins.

29	...	♖ef8

30	h3	gxh3
31	g3	fxg3
32	♖xf6	

Grandmaster humor.

Even the second best move, 32...♕xf6 (33 ♕xg3 c4! and ...♖g8), and the third-best move, 32...♖xf6 (33 ♕b8+ ♕f8 34 ♕xf8+ ♖xf8 35 ♖xe3 h2+), would win.

32	...	h2+
33	♔h1	g2 mate!

This win helped push Carlsen's performance rating for the tournament to 2990, one of the highest ever recorded.

58
Must Win

Carlsen found himself in a rare situation after nine rounds of the 2019 Sinquefield Cup. He had drawn all of his previous games and was tied for fifth through seventh place. It would take a remarkable chain of events for him to be in contention for first prize.

But fortune provided the chain. Many of the great players before him had been in a situation when they needed to win with Black in the final game of a match or tournament. Very few succeeded.

Maxime Vachier-Lagrave – Carlsen
Sinquefield Cup, St. Louis 2019
Sicilian Defense,
Rossolimo Variation (B31)

1	e4	c5
2	♘f3	♘c6
3	♗b5	g6
4	♗xc6	bxc6!

Recapturing with the b-pawn was new for Carlsen. It offers greater winning chances than the static middlegame that often comes after 4...dxc6 and its main line, 5 d3 ♗g7 6 h3 ♘f6 7 ♘c3 0-0 8 ♗e3 b6 9 ♕d2.

5	d4	

This open treatment of the center is also a surprise, rather than 5 0-0 followed by ♖e1 and c2-c3 and d2-d4.

5	...	cxd4
6	♕xd4	

This leads to a position resembling the Sicilian sideline that runs 1 e4 c5 2 ♘f3 d6 3 d4 cxd4 4 ♕xd4 ♘c6 5 ♗b5 ♗d7 6 ♗xc6 bxc6 7 c4.

In that version 7...♘f6 8 e5 offers White a small plus.

6	...	f6

Similar would be 6...♘f6 7 e5!. By avoiding that Carlsen commits to developing his g8-knight at h6.

7	0-0	d6
8	c4	

8	...	c5!

This is the pawn structure Carlsen wanted. It denies White the positionally desirable c4-c5.

An illustration of that break is 8...♗g7 9 ♘c3 ♘h6 10 c5 when Black's center pawns are under pressure.

White can offer the temporary sacrifice of 8...♕b6 9 c5 and then 9...dxc5 10 ♕c3 and ♗e3 followed by ♗xc5, with the advantage.

9	♕d3	♗g7
10	b3	♘h6
11	♘c3	

This position could have come about via 10 ♘c3 ♘h6 11 b3, a more forthright move order. Is there a reason Vachier-Lagrave chose this one?

Yes, he may have wanted Carlsen to try 10 b3 f5 and then 11 e5.

That would favor White big time after 11...dxe5? 12 ♕xd8+ and 13 ♗b2.

More double-edged is 11...♗b7! so that 12 ♗b2 dxe5 13 ♕xd8+ ♖xd8.

But much more dangerous to Black is 13 ♕e2! and 13...♕c7 14 ♘xe5 or 13...♗xf3 14 gxf3! ♕c7? 15 f4.

11	...	♖b8

Carlsen has the luxury of not having to think about the middlegame: He still has solid moves (...♘f7, ...0-0) that he can play automatically.

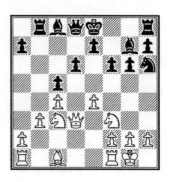

12	♗d2	

But the onus is on Vachier-Lagrave to choose a plan soon.

He could follow general principles with ♗b2 and putting rooks on d1 and e1.

For example, 12 ♗b2 ♘f7 13 ♖ad1 0-0 14 ♖fe1 ♗d7 and it is easier to see what Black is doing (...a5-a4) than to detect White's path forward.

Instead of the routine 14 ♖fe1, Vachier-Lagrave might try 14 ♘h4 followed by f2-f4.

That risks loss of dark-square control after 14...e6! 15 f4 g5!.

For example, 16 fxg5? fxg5 17 ♘f3 g4 is very good for Black (18 ♘d2 ♗d4+ 19 ♔h1 ♘e5).

12	...	0-0
13	♖ae1	♘f7

With the bishop on d2, the 14 ♘h4 e6 15 f4 plan works better.

Then after 15...g5 16 ♘f3! he can retake 16...gxf4 17 ♗xf4.

More Magnus-like is 15...f5, which would lead to a flexible position after 16 ♘f3 ♗d7 and ...♕f6.

14 h4!

Vachier-Lagrave wants to create a kingside target with h4-h5xg6 and ♘h4.

He would stand well after 14...♗g4 15 ♘h2 ♗d7 16 h5.

Is Magnus willing to stop this by an extreme measure, 14...h5 ? Then he would have to defend the g6-pawn after 15 ♘h2 and 16 ♕g3.

14 ... ♖b7

Carlsen's trainer Peter Heine Nielsen said this move "would never have entered my mind."

But after ...♗b7 or ...♗d7 the rook has no middlegame work to do on b8.

On b7, it adds power to a far-reaching plan of ...e6 and ...f5 because the rook can swing over to the kingside.

15 h5 g5

Now 15...gxh5? 16 ♕d5 e5? 17 ♘h4 and 18 ♘f5!.

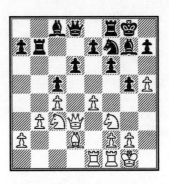

16 ♘h2

The "programmed" move is 16 ♘e2 and not just because it is recommended by computers.

In the heyday of Akiba Rubinstein and Aron Nimzovich, the potential hole at f5 almost demanded ♘e2-♘g3. In addition, the knight would defend the h-pawn against ...♕e8xh5 and also anticipate ...e6/...f5.

But MVL should be trying to change the pawn structure, not just manage it.

After 16 ♘e2 a5 17 ♘g3 e6 18 ♗c3 ♗d7 Carlsen has something to do (...a4) but White does not.

16 ... ♘e5

17 ♕g3

MVL clearly prepares f2-f4 and that can give him – or Carlsen – a big edge.

For example, 17...e6 18 f4! gxf4 19 ♗xf4 threatens 20 h6.

17   ...   ♔h8!

This avoids 17...♕e8 18 h6! ♗xh6 19 f4 ♘f7 20 e5!, with the kind of complications that White needs.

For example, 20...dxe5? 21 fxg5 ♘xg5 22 ♘f3! and 21...♗xg5 22 ♘e4! (22...h6? 23 ♖xf6! and wins).

18   f4?

The threat was 18...♕e8 and 19...♕xh5 MVL could batten down the hatches with, for example, 18 ♕e3 and 19 g4. But he was still optimistic about the kingside.

18   ...   gxf4

19   ♗xf4   ♖g8

Otherwise 20 h6!.

20   ♖e3

White cannot protect the h-pawn for long and faces a long-term threat on the g-file.

For example, 20 ♖e2 ♗h6 21 ♕h4 ♗xf4 22 ♕xf4 ♕e8 23 ♕h4 ♖g5 dooms the pawn.

20   ...   ♘c6

21   ♕f2

The greater problem is that White's pieces are becoming tactically vulnerable, as 21 ♕h4? e5! 22 ♗g3 ♗h6 shows.

Then Black wins because the main threat is 23...♗g5!.

21   ...   f5

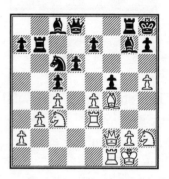

Computers wanted Black to trade bishops with ...♗h6, with ...♕f8 support if necessary.

Carlsen preferred to weaponize the a1-g7 diagonal and threaten ...♗d4.

22   ♘f3?

Saving the Exchange this way was not necessary.

White can afford 22 exf5 ♗d4 23 ♘b5 ♗xe3 24 ♗xe3 because of ♕b2+ or ♗c1-b2+.

Better is 22...♗xf5 and then 23 ♖g3 ♕e8.

But 24 ♗h6! ♗d4 25 ♖xg8+ ♕xg8 26 ♗e3 is fairly equal.

22   ...   ♗xc3!

23   ♖xc3

MVL prepared to meet 23...fxe4 with 24 ♗h6!.

Then 24...exf3? 25 ♖xf3 and the threat of ♖f8 wins (25...♗e6 26 ♕e3!).

Black can avoid disaster with 24...♗f5 25 ♘g5 e6. But he would be worse after 26 ♖g3 and ♕e3/♘xe4.

23 ... e5!

Now 14...♖b7 looks like a genius move because the rook is headed to g7 with powerful effect.

For example, 24 ♗c1 f4 25 ♕h4 ♖bg7 26 ♖c2 ♕xh4 27 ♘xh4 ♘d4 and ....♗b7.

24 ♖d3!

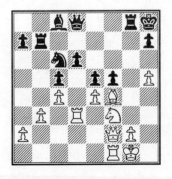

An excellent swindling try.

White would win after 24...fxe4?? 25 ♘xe5!.

He would get back into the game following 24...♕f6? 25 ♗g5 ♖xg5 26 ♘xg5 ♕xg5 27 ♖xd6.

24 ... exf4!

It took confidence in his calculation to play this because Carlsen would likely have won with the safer 24...♕f8.

For example, 25 exf5 ♗xf5 26 ♖d5 ♗e4 or 25...exf4 26 ♕b2+ ♘e5.

25 ♕b2+ ♖bg7

26 h6 fxe4

Now 27 hxg7+ ♖xg7 28 ♘e5 is tempting (28...exd3 29 ♘f7+).

But it loses to 28...♘xe5 29 ♕xe5 exd3.

27 ♖d2 exf3

28 hxg7+ ♖xg7

29 ♖xf3 ♕g5

There are a variety of ways of finishing off, such as 29...♘d4 30 ♖xf4 ♕e7, with finishes such as 31 ♖f1 ♕e3+ 32 ♖df2 ♘f3+ and 32 ♔h2 ♖g4.

30 ♖df2 ♘d4

31 ♖xf4

As a general rule, a player with a rook, bishop and knight against two rooks does not want to trade rooks.

In this case, having a rook means Black has tactics directed at g2 (unlike after 31...♕e5 32 ♖f8+ ♖g8 33 ♖xg8+).

31 ...   ♗f5

But he also has to beware tricks such as 31...♗h3? 32 ♖xd4!.

Then he loses: 32...cxd4 33 ♖f8+ ♖g8 34 ♕xd4+ and gxh3 after a trade of queens and rooks.

32	b4	♗e6
33	♖f8+	♗g8
34	bxc5	dxc5
35	♕b8	♕e3
36	♕d6	♕c1+
37	♔h2	♕g5
38	♕d5	

A queen swap also helps because then Black has to try to win with pawns that are disappearing from the board, 38...♕xd5? 39 cxd5 ♖d7 40 ♖2f4! ♔g7 43 ♖c8! and ♖xc5 (not 43...♖xd5? 44 ♖g4+).

38	...	♕h4+
39	♔g1	♕e7

Computers have been screaming for ...h6 and ...♔h7 for several moves.

But a pragmatic player doesn't like to create a potential weakness like that until he needs to.

His minor pieces can outplay the rooks in lines such as 40 ♕d8 ♕e1+ 41 ♔h2 ♘e6!.

40	♕h5	♕e3

Now on 40 ♕d1 one of the winning plans is 40...♖g6, 41...♔g7, 42...♗xc4 and 43...♘e2+.

41	♕h4?	♘e2+
42	♔h1	♕c1+
43	♖f1	♘g3+
44	♔g1	♕e3+

White resigns

59
Mind Game

Magnus' first game with Anish Giri was a disaster. He lost in 22 moves, with White. It began with a minor error, then a more serious one. He didn't realize his position had become inferior. He moved quickly, choosing a piece-losing blunder after two seconds thought, he told New In Chess. "If I had taken another two seconds, I would have found something else to defend my position."

Over the next several years Carlsen and Giri carried on an amiable feud on social media. The vast majority of their classical games were draws. But their next four decisive games were Carlsen wins. He was happy after this game to describe how he exploited his opponent psychologically.

Anish Giri – Carlsen
Zagreb 2019
Sicilian Defense,
Rossolimo Varation (B30)

1	e4	c5
2	♘f3	♘c6
3	♗b5	e6

Carlsen reverts to an old favorite way of meeting 3 ♗b5. It prepares 4...♘ge7 and 5...a6.

| 4 | ♗xc6 | bxc6 |

This recapture is better than the somewhat sterile 4...dxc6 5 0-0 ♘f6 6 d3.

| 5 | d3 | ♘e7 |

The reason is that Carlsen can seek a nice pawn structure with ...♘g6 and ...e5!.

White can foil that plan with e4-e5, e.g. 6 0-0 ♘g6 7 e5.

But Giri had once gotten a bad game after 7...f6! 8 exf6 ♕xf6 9 ♘c3 d5.

| 6 | h4 |

Giri tries another idea, 6...♘g6? 7 h5!.

| 6 | ... | h5 |
| 7 | e5 |

357

If the h-pawns had not been moved, then 6 e5 ♘g6 and ...f6! is promising for Black.

Giri indicated he would have greater kingside prospects now if Carlsen continued in that style, 7...♘g6.

For example, 8 ♘bd2 f6 9 ♘c4 and 9...♗a6 10 0-0!? ♗xc4 11 dxc4 fxe5? 12 ♕d3!.

Or 11...♘xe5 12 ♘xe5 fxe5 13 ♕d3 ♕f6? 14 ♗g5.

7   ...   d6

If Black is going to accept doubled isolated c-pawns, a better version would be 7...♘f5 8 ♘bd2 f6 9 ♘e4 d5!? 10 exd6 e5.

8   exd6   ♘g6

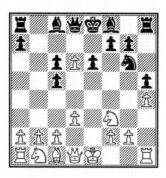

Carlsen shows remarkable faith in the spatial advantage he would get after ...e5.

Later this year at the St. Louis rapids/blitz his game with Caruana varied earlier with 6 b3 and then 6...♘g6 7 h4 h5 8 e5 f6 9 ♘bd2.

Then instead of 9...fxe5 10 ♘c4 d6 he played 9...d6!? 10 exd6 e5 with a position that computers rate as dubious. Caruana seriously weakened his light squares with g2-g3 and was soon worse (but eventually won).

9   ♘fd2

The straightforward 9 ♘bd2 ♗xd6 10 ♘c4 ♗e7 11 ♕e2 makes a better impression.

9   ...   ♗xd6

Not 9...♘xh4? 10 ♘e4 when ♗g5 is threatened, and 10...♘g6 11 ♖xh5 is awful.

10   ♘c4   ♗e7

11   ♘c3

Giri's ninth move was based on the premise that knights at c4 and c3 are better than at c4 and f3.

That would be proven true by, for example, 11...e5 12 ♕e2 ♕c7 13 ♗g5! f6 14 ♗d2 and 0-0-0.

11   ...   ♗a6

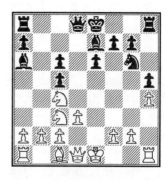

"He surprised me in the opening," Carlsen recalled to the

Guardian newspaper later in the year.

"And I just decided that I was going to play something very dubious since I knew that was going to be unpleasant for him psychologically."

He didn't indicate what his dubious move was. But this was the best position Giri had in the game.

12 ♕f3?

Much better is 12 ♗d2 since 12...♗xc4 13 dxc4 ♕d4 14 ♕e2 makes his superior pawn structure significant (14...♘e5 15 b3! with a serious advantage).

White can afford 14...♘xh4 15 g3 ♘f5 16 0-0-0 because Carlsen's knight can't reach d4.

For example, 16...g6 17 ♘e4 ♕g7 18 c3! 0-0? 19 g4 hxg4 20 ♕xg4 and ♖h3/♖dh1.

12 ... ♗xc4!

Now 13 dxc4 ♘e5! 14 ♕e4 ♕d4 makes it even chances. But since Giri still believed he was much better he continued...

13 ♕xc6+ ♔f8

14 dxc4 ♘xh4

He was wrong. For example, 15 ♗f4 ♕e8! and 16 ♕e4 f5! 17 ♕b7 ♕c8 and an endgame would be no more than equal because he is the one with doubled pawns now.

15 0-0 ♘f5

16 ♘e2?

Giri was too concerned about ...♘d4. He would not be worse after 16 ♖d1 ♘d4 17 ♕e4 and 17...f5 18 ♕d3 followed by ♘e2.

16 ... ♖c8!

Now 17 ♕f3 g5 and 18...g4 is dangerous for White. Carlsen's ability to steadily expand on the kingside is the most surprising feature of this game.

17 ♕a4 ♖c7

Later Carlsen said he wasn't concerned about making the objectively best moves.

"I had confidence to play the man and not the position," he said.

Computers wanted 17...♕c7 and they showed how strong 18 ♗f4 ♕b7 19 ♖ad1 h4 and 20...h3 was.

18   ♗f4   ♖d7

By denying his opponent the most useful moves, such as ♖ad1, Carlsen forces Giri to consider the marginal ones.

To play 19 ♕c6 he would admit his 17th move was wrong and that he needs his queen on the long a8-g2 diagonal. But that would not solve his kingside problems after 19...h4 and 20...g5!.

19   c3?

Giri may have rejected 19 ♘g3 because of 19...♘d4, which threatens 20...h4 21 ♘e4 ♘e2+ and ...♘xf4.

But 20 ♖fe1 h4 21 ♘e4 and 22 c3 was safe enough.

Carlsen would probably have answered 19 ♘g3 with 19...♘xg3 20 ♗xg3 h4.

Then 21 ♗f4 h3 22 ♕c6! would defend the kingside.

Instead, Black has reasonable winning chances after 21...g5 22 ♗e5 f6 23 ♗c3 ♕c7 (to stop ♕c6!) 24 ♗a5 ♕d6 25 ♖ae1 e5.

19   ...   g5!

It seemed that 19 c3 would allow White to challenge the d-file with ♖ad1.

But that isn't enough now after 20 ♗h2 h4 21 ♖ad1 ♖xd1 22 ♖xd1 ♕a8! and ...h3.

Better is 22 ♕xd1 ♕a8 23 ♕d3 but 23...♕b7 24 b3 ♔g7 and ...♗f6/...♖d8 is close to a win.

20   ♖ad1?   ♖xd1

21   ♖xd1

This time 21 ♕xd1? ♕xd1 22 ♖xd1 gxf4 was not an option.

22   ...   ♕a8

22   ♗c7

A desperation trap is 22 ♗e5 so that 22...f6 23 ♖d7 gxf4 24 ♖xa7 ♕e4? 25 ♖a8+ ♔g7 26 ♖xh8 ♔xh8? 27 ♕e8+ ♔g7 28 ♘g3!

(28...♘xg3?? 29 ♕xe7+! and White is better).

But this is wishful thinking. Black can win with, for example, 22...♕e4! 23 ♗xh8 ♘h4!.

22   ...   h4!

There is no way for White to sufficiently control h3.

For example, 23 ♖d3 h3 and now 24 ♖xh3 ♖xh3 25 gxh3 ♘h4! and wins (26 ♔f1 ♕g2+ 27 ♔e1 ♘f3+ 28 ♔d1 ♕f1+).

Or 24 gxh3 ♘h4 25 ♖g3 g4! and 26 hxg4 ♕e4 27 ♕d1 ♘f3+ 28 ♔f1 ♖h1+. Also, 26 ♖xg4 ♘f3+ 27 ♔f1 ♖xh3.

23   f3   h3!

White resigns

Giri has nothing to play for after ...hxg2.

For example, 24 ♕b5 hxg2 25 ♔xg2 ♘h4+ or 25 ♔f2 g4! and ...♕xf3+ or ...♗h4+.

Even 24 ♗e5 hxg2 25 ♗xh8 ♕xf3 and ...♕e3+ is lost.

60
Prodigies – Past and Present

Alireza Firouzja was born in June 2003 and was one month old when Carlsen won this book's Game 1. By 2020 fans were fascinated by Firouzja's spectacular rise. He was the national (adult) champion of Iran at age 12 and became a grandmaster two years later. When 2019 began his rating was well below Carlsen's at the same age (15½) but by year's end he was well ahead of Magnus's pace.

There was some bad blood between the two after their game at the 2019 World Blitz Championship in Moscow. Firouzja outplayed Carlsen but lost on time due to a strict interpretation of the forfeiture rules. Three weeks later he was leading the Wijk aan Zee tournament, one and a half points ahead of Carlsen. They were paired one day later in the most closely watched game of the tournament.

Alireza Firouzja – Carlsen
Wijk aan Zee 2020
Ruy Lopez, Berlin Defense (C65)

1	e4	e5
2	♘f3	♘c6
3	♗b5	♘f6
4	d3	

One of the facts of Berlin Defense life is that Black has to be willing to defend a slightly inferior endgame after 4 0-0 ♘xe4 5 d4 ♘d6.

Carlsen said he was "happy" when Firouzja played 4 d3 and allowed a "position with a bunch of pieces on the board."

4	...	d6

5	c3	a6

This rare move transforms the opening into a Steinitz Defense Deferred (1 e4 e5 2 ♘f3 ♘c6 3 ♗b5 a6 4 ♗a4 d6) but in a quiet version with d2-d3.

6	♗a4	♗e7
7	0-0	0-0
8	♖e1	♖e8
9	♘bd2	

Both players had been moving quickly. Firouzja thought for ten minutes here, perhaps over 9 d4 and 9...b5 10 ♗b3 ♗g4.

9	...	♗f8
10	h3	b5

11 &c2

A more familiar pattern is 11 &b3 ♘a5 12 &c2 c5 13 ♘f1 ♘c6. That transposes into another Lopez variation, named after Herman Pilnik.

That usually begins 1 e4 e5 2 ♘f3 ♘c6 3 &b5 a6 4 &a4 ♘f6 5 0-0 &e7 6 ♖e1 b5 7 &b3 0-0 8 c3 d6 9 d3!? and has a reputation for unambitious stodginess.

11 ... &b7

12 d4 g6

In fact, this transposes into yet another Lopez variation, which can come about by the modern move order of 1 e4 e5 2 ♘f3 ♘c6 3 &b5 a6 4 &a4 ♘f6 5 0-0 &e7 6 ♖e1 b5 7 &b3 d6 8 c3 0-0 9 h3 &b7 10 d4 ♖e8 11 ♘bd2 &f8 12 &c2 g6.

It is a difficult position for either side to handle because of subtle possible changes in the pawn structure.

Some changes would give White a small – or larger plus – while others hand Black the advantage.

For example, 13 b3 &g7 14 d5! ♘b8 15 ♘f1 c6 16 c4! cxd5? 17 cxd5 ♘bd7 18 &e3 favors White's space edge.

But if Black keeps the pawn tension with 16...♕c7 17 &e3 ♘bd7 he approaches equality after 18 ♖c1 ♖fc8.

Moreover, 18 a4? is at least equal for Black after 18...bxc4 19 bxc4 a5! and ....&a6 – as we will see.

13 a3

Another comparison is very instructive. After 13 a4 &g7 14 d5 ♘b8? Black is not developed well enough to meet 15 &d3!.

Then 15...c6 16 dxc6 &xc6 17 axb5 drops a pawn and 15...bxa4 16 &c2 and 16 &xa4 is a significant positional advantage for White.

If 14...♘e7, instead of 14...♘b8, he can reinforce the pawn chain, 15 c4! c6 16 b3 and 16...bxc4 17 bxc4 a5 18 ♘f1 &a6 19 ♘e3 and &a3.

The difference between Black's knight being on e7 in this case and on d7 is more than trivial.

13 ... ♘b8

White's last move gave Magnus time to redevelop his knight. He is, in effect, playing the Lopez's

Breyer Variation, in which Black is willing to spend tempi to get his knight onto its best square, d7.

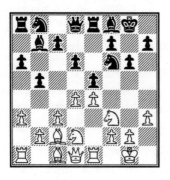

14   d5

White can justify 13 a3 with 14 b4! followed by ♗b2 and a3-a4 or c3-c4. That is a basic theme of the Breyer Variation.

For instance, 14 b4 ♗g7?! 15 d5 ♘bd7 16 ♘b3! followed by ♘a5 is excellent for White.

Better is 14...♘bd7 15 ♗b2 ♘b6 with a difficult struggle ahead (16 dxe5 dxe5 17 c4 c5).

14   ...   c6

Firouzja begins to realize that he has an unpromising pawn structure but shouldn't change it.

After 15 dxc6?! ♗xc6 16 ♘f1 ♘bd7 17 ♘g3 ♕c7 Black can prepare for an explosive ...d5 with ...♕b7 and ...♘c5. An exchange on d5 would reveal he is better developed than White.

15   c4   ♘bd7

16   a4

Once again in a Carlsen game it is difficult to identify a single move that sent his opponent's position downhill. But his 14th and 16th moves can share a single question mark.

After 16 b3 ♕c7 17 ♘f1 ♖ec8 we would get a position like the game.

But White's a-pawn would not be a weakling (18 ♘e3 bxc4 19 bxc4 ♗a6).

16   ...   ♕c7

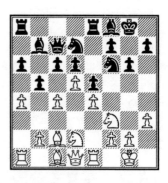

17   b3

Firouzja invested 23 minutes on this move and was soon more than half an hour behind Carlsen.

He must have considered 17 axb5 axb5 18 ♖xa8 ♖xa8 because it is consistent with his previous move.

But then 19 cxb5? exd5 is very bad because his pawn center is destroyed.

And 19 dxc6 ♗xc6 20 cxb5 ♗xb5 is merely bad (21 ♘b1 ♕b7 22 ♘c3 ♗c6 and eventually ...d5).

364

That leaves 19 b3 ♗a6 and ...bxc4, when Black can keep a mini-initiative for some time.

17 ... ♖ec8

Another bad version of the pawn poor structure is 18 dxc6 ♗xc6 19 a5 ♖ab8 and ...♘c5.

18 ♖a2

Carlsen threatened 18...cxd5 19 cxd5? ♕xc2.

If White had not lost a tempo earlier (13 a3/16 a4) he would have played ♘f1. That would allow him to defend the c2-bishop with ♘e3, rather than ♖a2.

Note that 18 ♗d3? cxd5 18 exd5 ♘xd5! 19 cxd5 ♕c3 is worse.

18 ... bxc4

19 bxc4

The Firouzja fans who followed the game on-line must have been puzzled. Chessbomb.com, for example, said he had played the best available moves since 15...♘bd7. But his numeric disadvantage had steadily grown.

19 ... a5!

Black should keep the c4-pawn as a target, rather than 19...cxd5? 20 cxd5 a5 21 ♘b3 ♗a6 22 ♗d2!, which is even.

20 ♘f1?

Ultimately, this is the losing move because Magnus never gives him a chance to recover.

Firouzja needed to play 20 ♘b1! and ♘a3 so that the c4-square is covered and there is a chance to blockade the queenside with dxc6/♘b5.

He would have reasonable chances of defending after 20 ♘b1! ♗a6 21 ♘a3 cxd5 22 cxd5 ♖ab8 23 ♗e3 or ♗d2.

Or after 21...♖cb8 22 dxc6 ♕xc6 23 ♘b5.

20 ... ♗a6

21 ♘e3 ♘c5

22 ♘d2

Now White has to be constantly on guard for ...♘d3. He should insert 22 dxc6 ♕xc6 23 ♘d5 before ♘d2.

22	...	cxd5
23	cxd5	♖ab8
24	♗a3	♕d8
25	♕f3	

25 ... h5!

A useful space-gaining move. White's problems are illustrated by 26 ♖b1 ♖xb1+ 27 ♗xb1 ♘xa4.

Or 27 ♘xb1 ♘d3 when Carlsen's pieces are swarming.

26	♖aa1	♗h6
27	♖ab1	♖xb1
28	♖xb1	♔g7

With an opponent in time trouble, Carlsen sticks to non-forcing moves. His king defends the f6-knight and frees his queen to move.

29	♘ef1	h4
30	♘e3	♗f4
31	♘ef1	♕c7

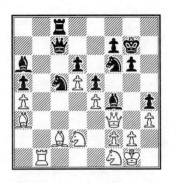

Firouzja spent eight of his remaining 12 minutes here to take in how bad things were.

He has some tactical resources, including traps such as 32 ♘e3 ♘b7 33 ♖b2 ♕c3 34 ♘df1 ♕xa3?? 35 ♘f5+!.

But 32...♘cd7! (or 32...♘d3) is better since 33 ♗b3 ♗d3 34 ♖d1 ♘c5 is getting close to a loss.

32	g3?	hxg3
33	fxg3	♗h6
34	h4	

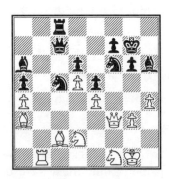

Carlsen took nearly half of his remaining 27 minutes here because he has a choice of winning the a-pawn, calculating

34...♘cd7 or inserting 34...♕a7 first. All are good.

34 ... ♕d7

Computers prefer the threat of discovered check, 34...♕a7, followed by 35 ♔h1 ♘cd7 36 ♗d1 ♕d4 37 ♗b2 ♕d3 38 ♕xd3 ♗xd3 39 ♖a1 ♘xe4.

35 ♔g2

Carlsen would have won on the c-file after 35 ♗xc5 ♖xc5 36 ♗d1 ♕c7 and ...♖c3, e.g. 37 ♖b3 ♖c1! 38 ♔g2 ♕c5.

35 ... ♘xa4

36 ♗xa4 ♕xa4

37 ♗xd6 ♕d4!

The threats include 38...♖c2.

On 38 ♔h1 Black wins with 38...♘e8! 39 ♗a3 ♗xd2 or 39 ♘b3 ♕d3!.

38 ♕f2 ♕xf2+

39 ♔xf2

Now 39...♘g4+ 40 ♔e1 ♗d3 41 ♖d1 ♖c2 is strangulation. And 40 ♔f3 ♖c3+ 41 ♔xg4? ♗c8 is mate.

39 ... ♗xf1

This wins a piece (40 ♘xf1 ♘xe4+) – yet Peter Svidler said this was the best position Firouza had in the last ten moves. He could have fought for a while with 40 ♔xf1 ♗xd2 41 ♗xe5. But:

White resigns.

Carlsen finished second in the tournament, behind Fabiano Caruana, but legal sports betting made him the solid favorite to successfully defend his world championship title in the next year.

When over-the-board competition shut down due to the Covid-19 pandemic, he helped organize the first on-line super-tournament, the Magnus Carlsen Invitational. He won it as well as the FIDE Steinitz Memorial tournament and looked forward to his next challenges.

Index of Opponents

(numbers refer to games)

Index of Openings
(numbers refer to games)

ECO Openings Index

(numbers refer to games)

Index of Middlegame Themes
(numbers refer to games)

Active defense – 6, 9, 12, 15, 21, 26, 33, 34, 36, 42, 54

Bishops of opposite color – 4, 6, 8, 12, 21, 31, 32, 35, 40, 48

Center pressure – 2, 5, 23, 34, 48

Deep calculation – 6, 7, 9, 18, 19, 20, 25, 26, 33,34, 36, 38, 42, 45, 54, 56, 58

Exchange sacrifice – 9, 12, 13(a), 18, 26, 39, 39(a), 39 (b), 48(a), 58

Good knight versus bad bishop – 32, 38, 47, 49, 50

King in center attack –7, 11, 17(a), 26, 45, 52

King prophylaxis – 25, 27, 42

Kingside attack – 1, 2, 4, 7, 8 (a) 10 (a), 13, 20, 22, 23, 25, 27, 30, 33, 35, 37, 42, 48, 52, 55, 56, 57, 58, 59, 60

Maneuvering – 2, 4, 8, 12,12 (a), 15, 21, 31, 32, 40, 60

Opposite wing castling – 7 (a), 11, 19, 23, 25, 27, 36, 38, 42, 48 (b), 54, 56

Pawn(s) sacrifice – 2, 4, 5, 6, 7, 7(a), 9, 10 (a), 11, 19, 21, 24, 26, 27, 30, 31, 32, 34, 38, 42, 45, 47, 48, 51, 56, 57

Piece sacrifice – 8(a), 17 (a), 22, 26, 27, 49(a), 54, 56

"Playability" decisions – 9, 11, 15, 21, 32, 34, 38, 39, 39 (a), 39 (b), 46, 47

Queen sacrifice – 1, 3, 4, 33, 42

Queenless middlegame – 10, 24, 53

Swindling bid – 6, 20, 21, 25, 34, 36, 44, 54, 56, 57, 58, 59

Two-bishop advantage – 15, 26, 53, 54

Two-front pressure – 2, 4, 13, 20, 32, 38, 43, 45, 47, 49, 56

Index of Endgames

(numbers refer to games)

Other chess books available from Batsford

BATSFORD

www.batsford.com

**BOBBY FISCHER
REDISCOVERED**
Andrew Soltis
9781849946063 | £16.99 | PB
312 pages

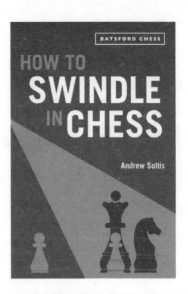

HOW TO SWINDLE IN CHESS
Andrew Soltis
9781849945639 | £16.99 | PB
240 pages

**300 MOST IMPORTANT
CHESS POSITIONS**
Thomas Engqvist
9781849945127 | £16.99 | PB
304 pages

**365 CHESS
MASTER LESSONS**
Andrew Soltis
9781849944342 | £16.99 | PB
384 pages

A TO Z CHESS TACTICS
George Huczek
9781849944465 | £17.99 | PB
352 pages

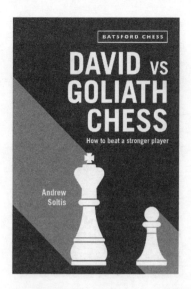

DAVID VS GOLIATH CHESS
Andrew Soltis
9781849943574 | £15.99 | PB
238 pages

WHAT IT TAKES TO BECOME A CHESS MASTER
Andrew Soltis
9781849940269 | £14.99 | PB
208 pages

PAWN STRUCTURE CHESS
Andrew Soltis
9781849940702 | £16.99 | PB
286 pages

100 CHESS MASTER TRADE SECRETS
Andrew Soltis
9781849941082 | £14.99 | PB
208 pages

YOUR KINGDOM FOR MY HORSE: WHEN TO EXCHANGE IN CHESS
Andrew Soltis
9781849942775 | £15.99 | PB
208 pages

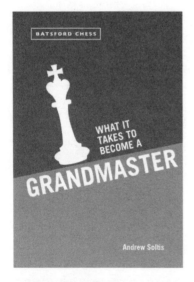

WHAT IT TAKES TO BECOME A GRANDMASTER
Andrew Soltis
9781849943390 | £15.99 | PB
320 pages

NEW ART OF DEFENCE IN CHESS
Andrew Soltis
9781849941600 | £15.99 | PB
288 pages

MY 60 MEMORABLE GAMES
Bobby Fischer
9781906388300 | £15.99 | PB
384 pages

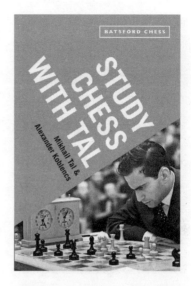

STUDY CHESS WITH TAL
Mikhail Tal, Alexander Koblencs
9781849941099 | £15.99 | PB
272 pages

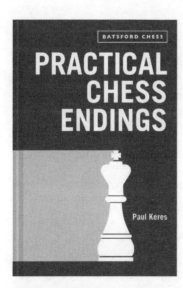

**PRACTICAL CHESS
ENDINGS**
Paul Keres
9781849944953 | £16.99 | PB
352 pages

**THE MOST INSTRUCTIVE
GAMES OF CHESS**
Irving Chernev
9781849941617 | £15.99 | PB
320 pages

THE ART OF CHECKMATE
Georges Renaud, Victor Kahn
9781849942706 | £15.99 | PB
224 pages

BATSFORD'S MODERN CHESS OPENINGS
Nick De Firmian
9781906388294 | £22.95 | PB
720 pages

THE WISEST THINGS EVER SAID ABOUT CHESS
Andrew Soltis
9781906388003 | £15.99 | PB
304 pages

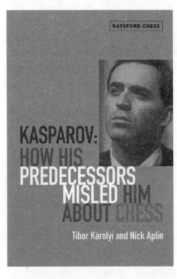

KASPAROV: HOW HIS PREDECESSORS MISLED HIM ABOUT CHESS
Tibor Karolyi, Nick Aplin
9781906388263 | £14.99 | PB
272 pages

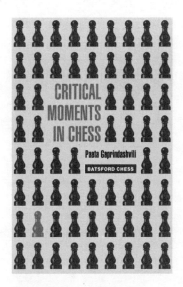

**CRITICAL MOMENTS
IN CHESS**
Paata Gaprindashvili
9781906388652 | £15.99 | PB
288 pages

**THE BATSFORD BOOK
OF CHESS**
Sean Marsh
9781849941648 | £14.99 | HB
208 pages

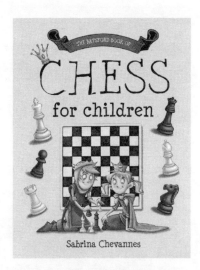

**THE BATSFORD BOOK OF
CHESS FOR CHILDREN**
Sabrina Chevannes
9781849940696 | £12.99 | HB
128 pages

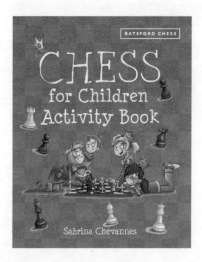

**CHESS FOR CHILDREN
ACTIVITY BOOK**
Sabrina Chevannes
9781849942843 | £9.99 | PB
120 pages